The
PRINTED MAPS OF
DEVON
COUNTY MAPS 1575-1837

The PRINTED MAPS OF DEVON

COUNTY MAPS 1575-1837

KIT BATTEN   FRANCIS BENNETT

DEVON BOOKS

First Published in Great Britain in 1996 by Devon Books

British Library Cataloguing in Publication Data

Data for this publication is available from the British Library

ISBN 0 86114 900 9

DEVON BOOKS
Official Publisher to Devon County Council

Halsgrove House
Lower Moor Way
Tiverton
Devon EX16 6SS
Tel: 01884 243242
Fax 01884 243325

Reprographics by Peninsular Repro Services, Exeter
Printed and bound in Great Britain by Ebenezer Baylis & Son Ltd

CONTENTS

ACKNOWLEDGEMENTS   vi

PREFACE   vii

LIST OF COLOUR PLATES   viii

INTRODUCTION   ix

EXPLANATION   xvi

REFERENCES   xviii

A LIST OF THE MAPS   xix

COLOUR PLATES   xxi

THE PRINTED MAPS OF DEVON   1

BIBLIOGRAPHY   238

INDEX   239

ACKNOWLEDGEMENTS

We would like to thank the following for their permission to use illustrations making it possible for this to be the first fully-illustrated county bibliography (numbers refer to maps, not page numbers):

British Library	2, 3, 26, 112, 117.
Clive Burden and Philip Burden	61, 75.
Eugene Burden	41.
Tony Burgess	95.
Albert Field	23.
Malcolm Woodward	11.1 (Plate 3.), 19, 58.
Exeter Westcountry Studies Library	47, 48, 76, 79, 83, 91, 93, 109, 110.

Our thanks to Herr Werner Kost and his wife, Siegried, for their patience in the photography of the majority of the illustrations.

PREFACE

Many roads lead to Rome and many paths lead to map-collecting.

Although we both come from different parts of the county and from different backgrounds and occupations the collecting of maps of Devonshire brought us both together. Working in isolation we had both begun to compile lists of county maps. As soon as we appreciated how much work the other had achieved, it was clear to both that co-operation was needed.

Neither of us had realised the difficulty in compiling a cartobibliography – and neither did we suspect how fascinating it would turn out. The stories behind the maps are often intriguing – the more one discovers the more one wants to know. Cartography, like all sciences, encourages investigation and each new item leads to another. Like an encyclopaedia the neighbouring pages are often more interesting and lead to ever more investigation. How much simpler it would be to see the world through the eyes of the crew of Lewis Carroll's 'Bellman' when...

> *he had brought a large map representing the sea*
> *without the least vestige of land*
> *and the crew were much pleased when they found it to be*
> *a map they could all understand.*

...but how much duller!

In some ways we could be accused of doing the same! We have decided to stop on the occasion of Queen Victoria's accession to the throne in 1837: a date which comes after the Reform Bill but before the advent of the railways and one that (nearly) avoids the multi-reproductions possible through lithography. In combining our efforts we have, however, identified 117 separate plates, listed over 300 states and referenced nearly 1200 sources of atlases and maps. If we had continued this work would have had to be twice the size and, although perhaps only about 50 map plates would be added to those listed here, another five years or more would be needed for research. Perhaps a future edition will one day include this.

We would like to take this opportunity to thank all those without whose help this cartobibliography could not have been completed; firstly those individuals who have so generously given us access to their personal collections or who have, so often, resolved difficult problems: Clive and Philip Burden, Eugene Burden, Tony Burgess, Donald Hodson, David Kingsley, David Webb and Malcolm Woodward; and secondly the librarians and curators who have helped us examine their collections or answered our queries and especially Geoffrey Armitage at the British Library, Francis Herbert of the Royal Geographical Society, and Ian Maxted of the Exeter West Country Studies Library.

As always with a work involving so much time it is the families who must suffer most and we would like to thank Joan for her support and editing and Karin, Katrina and Kim for their encouragement.

In the course of our researches we may have omitted something, overlooked a source or falsely interpreted our notes. We apologise for any errors and welcome correspondence from fellow enthusiasts and collectors.

April 1996

Kit Batten
Auerhahnweg 7
70499 Stuttgart
Germany

Francis Bennett
Menryn
Newton Ferrers
Devon PL8 1BW

LIST OF COLOUR PLATES

The Colour Plates are on pages xxi-xxviii.

Plate 1.   **1.2 Saxton**   An Atlas of England and Wales

Plate 2.   **4.2 van den Keere/(Speed)**   *Guilielmi Camdeni, Viri clarissimi Britannia*
             4.4 van den Keere/(Speed)   *England Wales Scotland and Ireland Described*

Plate 3.   **11.1 Jansson**   *Des Nieuwen Atlantis Aenhang*

Plate 4.   **12.1 Blaeu**   *Nuevo Atlas del Reyno de Ingalaterra*

Plate 5.   **37.7 Bowen**   *The Large English Atlas*

Plate 6.   **63.1 Smith/Jones/Smith**   *Smith's New English Atlas*

Plate 7.   **71.1 Cary**   *Cary's New English Atlas*

Plate 8.   **81.4 Rowe**   *New British Atlas*

INTRODUCTION

The history of the printed maps of Devon is very much a story of the development of the Atlas in Great Britain. Many of the maps were first printed for sale on single sheets. However, when a series was complete the sheets would be collected together to form atlases or topographical works of England, England and Wales, Great Britain or the United Kingdom. Over eighty of the maps illustrated here were considered as part of such an atlas: originally printed with the idea of covering the whole country in a comprehensive work to be bought first by the landed gentry and later by the affluent middle class. The remainder were either produced as cards, usually playing cards or some game, or to accompany a work specifically covering Devon, such as an agricultural review. A smaller number are parts of unfinished series.

Our aim has been to compile a definitive list of the printed maps up to 1837. Queen Victoria's accession is a convenient break point in the development of maps in Devon, just before the advent of the railways and the plethora of lithographic maps.

We hope this short introduction to the early mapping of the county will also help those who are not familiar with printed maps and explain some of the techniques, problems and terminology.

Printing

The first printed maps of the fifteenth century used the wood-cut, a relief process where the back is cut away leaving the design raised. This was ideally suited for the early books for it needed no greater pressure than the moveable type-face and was easily incorporated onto the printed page. The wood-cut was extensively used until the middle of the next century and maps of England or Britain by such cartographers as Martin Waldseemüller and Sebastian Münster are fairly common. Both the National Maritime Museum and the Royal Geographical Society have examples of woodcuts showing the entrance to Plymouth Sound but woodcuts were not employed for county maps even when the technique was revived in the 19th century for magazines and encyclopaedias. No true woodcut map of Devonshire is known. The only copy printed from a wood block is William Pinnock's fascinating map from *The Guide to Knowledge*. (**108**) This had the map engraved into the wood resulting in a 'reversal', showing white lines on a black background.

It was copper plate engraving that dominated the reproduction of maps for some three hundred years. The technique had long been developed in Italian art and it was ideally suited to reproduce the fine line of the draughtsman and surveyor. Here the design is cut into the metal, the plate is then inked and wiped clean, leaving the ink within the incised lines. Passing the plate through rollers under pressure 'lifts' the lines onto the paper. These inked lines stand proud of the surface, and can be felt on today's bank notes, where the method is still used. As this technique uses pressure the paper often bears evidence of the edges of the copper plate. It had many advantages over the wood-cut. The engraver could work much faster and could use many other techniques: dots, pecked lines, stipples and lettering of greater fluency – for example the Mercator-style flourishes used by Jan Jansson (**11**) to fill empty areas or sea. Changes too were that much easier; lines could be burred or hammered out and re-engraved. The Dutch mastered this technique early on and Christopher Saxton employed Flemish engravers for most of his maps, for example Remigius Hogenberg who engraved the map of Devon. He also employed a few local artisans who soon developed their own style and techniques including Augustine Ryther who signed his work *Anglus*.[1] In the seventeenth century other refugees engraved or published important maps, such as Pieter van den Kee (**4** and **13**), Herman Moll (**25**) and John Rocque. (**28**) Although some English engravers such as Emanuel Bowen and Thomas Kitchin became proficient and were highly admired, British supremacy in map-engraving really began in the late eighteenth century with John Cary standing out among the many. (**51, 54, 69, 71, 80**)

Copper engraving had the major disadvantage of eventually wearing down so that strengthening of incised lines was needed or even a new plate, as can be seen with some of John Cary's maps. Cary's *New and Correct English Atlas* (**51**) was re-engraved (**73**), and his *Traveller's Companion* (**55**) was re-engraved twice (**69** and **92**) although the second plate might have been lost in a fire. Sometimes it is possible to detect thickening of lines (**6.9**) or see cracks in the plate (see p.xii). Not until the 1800s was it possible to engrave on steel. This allowed a longer print run, hence maps engraved on steel are more common. James Pigot's series for his *Directories* from the mid 1820s were the first to employ this technique. (**98**)

Acid etching was introduced in the 1800s and, though giving the designer much greater flexibility, was not often used for maps. Here the design is cut through a wax coating applied to the plate; the plate is then immersed in acid which eats into the exposed copper, creating the etched image. Etched lines tend to end square or blunt, whereas the engraved line tapers to a point: Wenceslas Hollar's famous *Quartermaster's Map* is a good example.

Lithography was invented in 1798. It was found that in drawing with special greasy ink or crayon on a flat limestone slab the grease was absorbed; the image would then accept printer's ink which was repelled by the rest of the stone, provided the surface was kept moistened. The technique began to be used in 1820 and in the map trade in the late 1830s. Although at first sight similar, it can be distinguished from engraving by the absence of raised lines and especially the plate block mark. Its use developed rapidly and enabled changes to be easily and quickly made. A number of maps originally engraved were later reproduced as lithographs. Some of Cary's maps were republished by G F Cruchley (**73** and **92**), the Ebden (**95**) and Teesdale (**99**) series are also good examples; Pigot's series of small maps were also produced in this fashion. (**114**)

Paper

Until the nineteenth century paper was hand-made from finely chopped rags pulped in water. A wire mesh screen was dipped into the mix attracting a thin layer of the pulp. The water was drained off, the sheet partly dried then removed and hung until completely dry. The lines of the mesh, including any water-mark motif, are clearly visible when the sheet is held up to the light. In the second half of the 18th century the wires were replaced by woven brass cloth and the lines disappeared, although the paper-makers still used their wire watermarks. Copies of Saxton are known with a number of different watermarks (see p.3) and copies of Richard Blome's maps (**14**) have a jester watermark like the joker found on playing cards. This 'fools-cap' is said to have given rise to the name of the paper size.

The maximum sheet size of the paper was about 700 by 800 mm (24" by 28"), determined both by the practical size of the screen and the printing presses. This standard sheet produced the various book sizes. A once-folded sheet is *folio*, folded twice into four pages is *quarto* (4to), folded again is *octavo* (8vo), four-times folded is *duodecimo* (12mo), and *octavo* folded is *sextodecimo* (16mo) (75 by 87 mm or 3 inches by 4½ inches). But the sizes vary to suit plate and publisher. The largest single sheet maps of Devon are those of Emanuel Bowen (**37**) with sheets measuring to 580 x 745 mm and the Greenwoods (**97**) at 650 x 780 mm. Disregarding the playing cards and similar, a number of maps compete for the prize of the smallest Devon map: Matthew Simmons (**9**) with a map size of 40 x 35 mm, John Luffman of 60 mm diameter (**66**) and Aristide Perrot at 50 mm square (**94**) are among the smallest.

Colouring

Colouring was usually undertaken at the purchaser's request. For shields standard conventions were used, either letters or hatching or both. For example O stood for Gold or Yellow and the area was dotted. The Dutch, Jansson (**11**), Blaeu (**12**) and others, reversed the red and blue convention. For the map itself there were also standards: boundary lines were shown in different colours on each side, sometimes with areas colour-washed; woods and seats were green; rivers and the sea, or just the sea-coast blue; towns were red. All else was left to the colourist's imagination. It is difficult without experience to judge whether or not the colour was original, early or modern. Early greens can sometimes be an indication, with the penetration through the paper caused by the acidity of the verdigris mixture. However, good colour added later does not usually affect the price and collectors can choose for themselves whether to buy a map coloured or uncoloured.

Topography

A map is a topographical drawing and, while being drawn to an accurate horizontal scale, should still show those features which cannot be seen from the vertical viewpoint. The map-maker, from the first, introduced or copied conventional signs, pictures and symbols.

Saxton's map (**1**) illustrates many of these signs in their first form: rivers run from a single line to the double line of both banks; woods are shown by single trees; hills are shown by sugar-loaves shaded on the east side. These loaves vary to satisfy the engraver's taste: alpine mountains for Jansson (**11**), clefts for Blome (**14**) and joined-in lines by Thomas Kitchin (**34**). They were omitted by some, especially Benjamin Donn (**44**, **45**), and those who probably – and correctly – did not like the idea of the multi-molehills. But as a convention it remained until Cary abandoned it in the 1790s. In 1801 Charles Smith's atlas (**61**) introduced hachuring which was then used for larger-scale maps to become fully conventionalised and improved by the Ordnance Survey.

Saxton's towns were shown by a small group of buildings, with church and spire, villages by a church only, while Exeter has a cathedral spire and cross. The churches often contained a circle to show the actual town centre. Houses, the seats of the gentry, have a crenellated block or tower. It is interesting to note that Plymouth, though named, has its symbol on St. Nicholas (now Drake's) Island. William Kip (**5**) improved and enlarged the town symbols but still showed Plymouth in the Sound – a fault corrected by John Speed.

On small-scale maps town symbols became simpler and more conventional with smaller places shown only by a circle. But on larger scale maps, such as Bowen's map of 1754 (**37**), block plans of streets and buildings began to be used. In 1720 Bowen had also introduced the pegged asterisk to show the number of members returned to parliament. (**24**)

At first the sea was either stippled, plain or had the Flemish *shotsilk* technique, or zig-zag effect. Saxton and Kip employed the former and the latter first appeared on Keere's map (**4**), was added to John Speed's later issue of 1614 (**6.3**) and is finally found on John Bill's map of 1626 (**8**). This sea-infill was not used by either Jansson or Joan Blaeu. Form-lines, where the sea-coast shading is drawn parallel to the coast suggesting contours, appear first on Thomas Badeslade's map of 1741. (**27**) Patrons and the landed gentry were flattered not only by dedication or armorial shields, but by the pictorial insertion of a ring round their parks (dotted by Saxton, but a proper fence by Speed) and by the subscribers' name on Donn's survey.

Dating

Plates passed from hand to hand, publisher to publisher: dating a detached map can be extremely difficult. Once engraved an impression can be taken at any time. Some original plates still exist: a map plate by Cary was successfully reprinted only a few years ago; and a plate believed to come from an early version of Saxton's wall map has been found in printable condition[2].

One can establish that a print comes from an engraving partly by feel and partly by the recess formed by the plate, and one can also ascertain that the paper was hand-made. Together these establish authenticity but not a date. A watermark is a help and a guide, but only to the manufacturer's mould.

Most dating must be *terminus post quem* 'later than'. A date, the signature of surveyor or engraver, the imprint of the publisher all indicate, like the watermark, only the earliest possible date.

If we find the same map within a bound atlas it can be dated by the title page; but even this dating is unreliable. Atlases were often reprinted with previous title pages unchanged. Atlas bibliographers realise this and often note the issue date as distinct from the title date. This other date is often found from the publishers' advertisements, entries in the *Term catalogue*, or from other dates in prefaces, within the text or on other maps. Sometimes atlases were combined or bound together, and knowing the date of the second can also date the first. Speed's *Theatre* and *Prospect of the most famous parts of the World*, and the miniature Speed issues of Keere are good examples.

But all of this does not necessarily date the map. There are many instances of atlases using previously printed maps. Paper and printing costs were high and publishers would often bind in earlier sheets. There are many copies of *Cary's New and Correct English Atlas* of 1793 with maps from the 1787 issue. And many an atlas was a compilation or, to use that delightful word, a factice – sheets gathered together from various sources. The Overton Atlases of the early 18th century are good examples, often containing a mixture of Speed, Blaeu and Jansson maps.

Other more important dating guides are the alterations to the print, additions and erasures, corrections and embellishments, and also the text of the atlas or history when that is printed with or behind the map. A good example of a print change is Speed's Devon (**6**) where the imprint is added and later altered; the sea is at first plain, then shaded; an extra coat of arms is added and Roman and ancient British names introduced. The text on the reverse of these maps also changes. A better example of text changes can be seen with Keere's map of 1605, the reverse shown below, comes from the 1627 edition.

D E V O N - S H I R E.

CHAPTER IX.

DEVON-SHIRE, by the *Cornish Britaines* called *Deuinan*; and by contraction of the vulgar *Denshire*, is not deriued from the *Danes*, as some would haue it, but from the people *Danmonij*, the same we will speake of in *Cornwall*, and whom *Ptolemie* hath seated in these Westerne Borders.

(2) The West of this County is bounded altogether by the Riuer *Tamar*: the East is held in with the verge of *Somerset-shire*: and the North and South sides are washed wholy with the Brittish and Seuerne Seas: Betwixt whose shoares from *Cunshere* in the North, vnto *Salcombe Hauen* entering in at the South, are fiftie fiue miles: and from the *Hartland Point* West, to *Thorncombe* East, are fiftie-foure: the whole Circumference about two hundred and two miles.

(3) The Ayre is sharpe, healthfull and good: the Soile is hilly, wooddy and fruitfull, yet so as the hand of the Manurer must neuer be idle, nor the purse of the Farmer neuer fast shut, especially of them that are farre from the Sea, whence they fetch a sand with charge and much trauell, which being spread vpon the face of the earth, bettereth the leannesse thereof for graine, and giueth life to the Glebe with great efficacie.

(4) As *Cornwall*, so this hath the same commodities that arise from the Seas: and being more inlanded hath more commodious Hauens for Shippings entercourse, among whom *Tynes* is famous for *Brutes* first entrance, if *Geffry* say true, or if *Hamillan* the Poet tooke not a Poeticall libertie, when speaking of *Brute*, he wrote thus:

The Gods did guide his sayle and course: the winds were at command:
And Totnes was the happie shoare where first he came on land.

But

The later variations of the text help to identify the editions and the following table gives the clues to the date:

	1627	1627 (32)	1627 (46)	1665	1676
position of **vulgar**	vul – 1st line gar – 2nd line	1st line	1st line	vul – 1st line gar – 2nd line	2nd line
spelling of **Ptolemy**	**Ptolemie**	**Ptolomie**	**Ptolomy**	**Ptolomy**	**Ptolomy**

Paragraph numbers were not in brackets for the 1627 (46) edition. A final estimate of age can be made from the condition of the plate, its wear and tear. The quality of the print deteriorates with the number of impressions taken; later copies will be fainter.

Sometimes plates are touched up and lines strengthened as can be seen on the Speed copy of 1743. Sometimes the plate cracks, an irreparable state which will show on any subsequent printing. The Keere map (**4**) finally developed three cracks, all visible on the 1646 edition. Although the appearance of these cracks has been suggested as a means for dating editions, they can at best help to date individual maps. Whereas Skelton[3] identifies two cracks in Devon from 1646 and three from 1662 it has been noted that some later editions have less: there are none at all in a British Library copy of 1646, there are only two in the Whitaker copy of 1662, and only two in the Royal Geographical Society copy and a private copy of 1668 showing that atlases were made up from prints in various states.

Dating is the sum of all of these aspects but at the best can only be approximate and still a case of 'it cannot be earlier than'.

The First County Maps

The art of Geography advanced hand-in-hand with Technology. The first woodcut map of Britain appeared in Münster's edition of Ptolemy in 1540, and the first copperplate map was produced by George Lily, a Catholic exile in Rome, in 1546.

In England interest in geography spread quickly. People like John Rudd, Saxton's master and teacher, John Norden and Robert Adams were proposing surveyed maps of the whole country. The government was also realising the advantages of having detailed knowledge of the country and its coasts. Henry VIII's engineers had drawn up defence maps for the principal channel ports, including Plymouth and Dartmouth. William Cecil, Queen Elizabeth's Chief Minister, saw the need for an overall picture of the country. He formed a large collection of maps, and in 1570 he backed Thomas Seckford's sponsorship of Saxton. The true survey of the country and of the counties began.

Gerard Mercator's map of 1564 was supposedly based on information and surveys produced by Laurence Nowell but when Saxton mapped the counties in the 1570s he was surveying an almost unknown country. Apart from the inaccurate maps of the British Isles and some local estate surveys previous knowledge relied on written itineraries such as Leland, on hearsay and on local knowledge. Saxton's atlas, one of the first as such in Europe[4] must have been a revelation. It created a view of England that shaped the regional identity together with the interdependence of the part with the whole of the country – a dependence which was to become so important in the 17th century upheavals.

From the beginning of the Renaissance maps were also valued as pictures and decorations. John Dee (1527-1608), the mathematician and astronomer, noted in 1570 that the gentry acquired maps 'to beautify their halls, Parlers, Chambers, Galeries, Studis, or Libraries, liketh, loveth, getteth and useth Mappes, Charts and Geographical Globes'. As examples of the interest and the variety one need look no further than the county illustrations of Michael Drayton's *Poly-Olbion* (**7**) and the early sets of playing cards with their clumsy little maps of the, very convenient, 52 counties of England and Wales.

Accuracy and Scale

How accurate was Saxton's map? It is reasonable to assume that he surveyed the county using the known and established beacon points. A tally of these listed and mapped some 90 points[5]. A simple triangular grid based on these covers the whole county, apart from the coast line, and only twice does the gap or bearing exceed 12 miles. One can imagine Saxton climbing up to each point, reading off the angles to the heliographic signaller and sketching in the rivers and towns that he could see. One wonders how many helpers he had and one marvels at the distance he must have walked in the five years he took to survey the whole country. This is, of course, all conjecture but his map is testimony to the overall accuracy he achieved. Compared to the Ordnance Survey and allowing for his longer mile the north-south distance from Prawle Point to Foreland is short by but half a mile.

When looking at early maps one must remember that the standard statute mile of 1760 yards (1 degree = 69 miles) was not finalised until 1685. Saxton only showed degrees on his wall map which had three scales bars: Great, Middle and Small, measurable as 50, 55 and 60 miles to the degree.

The first map to show degrees, Bill in 1626[6], has one scale, and 1° = 54 miles. Robert Morden in 1695 produced the second map with degrees which also has three scales: 1° = 56, 59 or 63 miles (**21, 22**). If we take a distance as the crow flies – Plymouth to Exeter is 36 miles – and compare the three county maps, the respective lengths of a mile in yards are; Saxton 1995, Bill 2137, and Morden 1812 yards. Saxton used the middle mile, Morden the small mile and Bill the great mile. While this satisfies the first two it leaves Bill's map inaccurate, even to his own scale.

Apart from Bill all the Saxton derivatives, Speed, Keere, Jansson, Blaeu and Blome are drawn to the same middle mile. In all of these the distance from Plymouth to Exeter is more or less correct at approx 35 miles, allowing for the town centres and symbolism. But interestingly the distance from Plymouth to Barnstaple is only c.45 miles, some 4 miles short. Moll in 1724 made it 46½ miles and on Donn's survey in 1765 it is 47¼ miles (Donn is perhaps always short, for his Plymouth to Exeter distance is only 34¼ miles). Cary in 1787 copied Donn but corrected the distance to c.50 miles on his road map of 1789. One must be careful in considering distances and figures for, apart from the engravers inaccuracies and vagaries, the size of the print can vary and hand-made paper can shrink.

In 1675 John Ogilby's road survey was compiled using the statute mile and this first appeared on Moll's Devon map of 1724 (**25**), influenced no doubt by Moll's own road maps derived directly from Ogilby. From then on the statute mile was used by most surveyors and noted above the scale bar.[7]

Derivation and Deviation

To a great extent cartography relies on the draughtsman's ability to copy. Until the Ordnance Survey there were only three surveys of Devon of any importance: Saxton, Ogilby and Donn. Of these only the first and last cover the county. With one or two exceptions all the others are copies. Richard Gough, in 1780, summed it up perfectly: 'the several sets of county maps professing to be drawn from the latest observations they are almost invariably copies of those that preceded them'.

When Saxton's privilege or court monopoly expired the copying began, relying on both his wall map of the British Isles and his county maps. He had proved that maps had both practical and artistic values, and others were quick to seize on the public demand.

John Speed in 1610 created perhaps the most popular of all the county maps. He always admitted that 'he had put his sickle into other men's corne', but he must have visited Devon in order to include the hundreds. The boundaries of the hundreds – the administrative areas created in Saxon England and retained almost to the end of the l9th century – were known only to the local inhabitants. Rivers and streams formed the usual boundary line and when the line ran across country it was often marked by so called *turning stones*. However, there were some surveys and maps available: John Norden, cartographer and surveyor, like Saxton with government backing, had completed a manuscript survey of Cornwall in 1596 and also a survey of Crediton hundred in 1590[8]. But the lack of real knowledge is illustrated by Speed incorrectly showing large parts of eastern Dartmoor as part of Roborough and Plympton hundreds. Another example of copying error is shown when Speed, like Saxton, incorrectly places three villages south instead of east-by-south of Milton Abbot. Also, on learning that they lay in Lifton Hundred, he wrongly adjusted the boundary to suit not knowing they were in an 'island' surrounded by Tavistock Hundred. One should compare Donn's correct version of 1765. (**44**)

The popularity of Speed's map was increased by the insertion of a copy of John Hooker's map of Exeter and by the arms of the nobility, which gave more interest and decorative appeal. Like Saxton, Speed had government backing and monopoly and when this expired his map too was extensively copied.

Saxton's Tamar gently meanders southwards without any real definition. But Speed saw or was told of the noticeable westward bow in the river just north of Cargreen, although he placed it incorrectly further south by Saltash. This variation gives a key to the source of later copies: Saxton was copied by Bill and Morden while Speed was copied by Jansson, Blaeu, Blome and John Seller. Keere's map of 1648 was also a copy of Speed and not of his own earlier version of Saxton in 1605.

The line of the River Tamar also illustrates those few maps which contained original work. Norden's survey of Cornwall suggests Speed's river line. Joel Gascoyne's large scale map of Cornwall in 1699, the first to show a nearly correct line, was partly accepted by Moll in 1724 and more fully by Kitchin in 1750. (**34**)

Lundy was not shown on a Devon map until Jansson's revision of 1652. (**11.3**) Saxton's plates were printed throughout the seventeenth century and when Philip Lea produced his atlas of *All the Shires of England and Wales* in 1689 he arranged for Francis Lamb to redraw the Devon plate which had been lost, perhaps in the Fire of London. (**19**) Lamb chose to copy from Speed, including the shields, hundreds, roads, and the plan of Exeter; and for good measure he added Jansson's Lundy.

Roads

Up to 1695 no roads were clearly shown on any maps of Devon. In 1625 Norden produced his *Intended Guyde for Travailers*, which included for the first time the triangular distance tables that we still use today. This was reissued by Matthew Simmons in 1635 (**6**) together with small county maps copied from Saxton's wall map. Small and indicative only, with code letters for towns, the roads themselves were omitted. The armies in the civil war relied on these or on Thomas Jenner's reissue (**10**) with slightly larger maps. Jenner also reproduced the Saxton wall map, redrawn in sections by Hollar as the *Quartermaster's Map;* it still did not show roads until reissued in 1671.

By 1675 John Ogilby had surveyed on foot with his perambulator the 7500 miles of the principal roads of England and Wales, and published his *Britannia*. This showed the roads and their junctions, towns, hills and rivers, in a strip form, each with a compass rose to show direction.

In 1676 Robert Morden produced a set of playing cards, each with a small county map showing Ogilby's roads but often inaccurately: the road from Ashburton goes directly to Plymouth and not through Brent or Plympton, though both are shown. Finally in 1695 Morden introduced accurate roads on his series of county maps (to accompany a new translation of William Camden's *Britannia*. (**21**) From this time roads became a standard feature. A folio size map such as Ogilby's *Britannia* being impractical for travellers the map trade introduced, in the early 1700s, the reduced strip-map pocket-book including those of John Senex or Owen and Bowen. (**24**) Although strip-maps continued in use it was Cary in 1787 (**51**) who produced the first county map to show all the principal roads, followed in 1789 by his small but accurate *Traveller's Companion*.

Longitude and Latitude

John Bill in 1626 was the first to introduce border scales of longitude and latitude, but these were of little use to the local observer. Slightly more useful was Robert Morden's addition in 1695: he added a time scale showing the seconds and minutes after London in the top border; a pattern repeated by Kitchin and Jefferys in 1749. (**33**)

Before the seventeenth century it was usual for the prime meridian to be drawn through the Canaries or the Azores-islands 'West of all the Old World and East of America'. Although Bill used the Azores, by the end of the century British cartographers were using London as zero: Morden in 1695 (**21**); Moll in 1724. (**25**)

Though the Royal Observatory was established in 1675 and Edmund Halley, of comet fame, set up the first transit there in 1721, the county cartographers still used St Paul's, as Cary noted in 1787. Charles Smith's atlas map of 1801 was the first map of Devon to be labelled *West of Greenwich* (**63**) and Benjamin Baker's map of 1791 was so amended when reissued in 1806. (**57.2**)

Interestingly John Andrews' *Geographical Atlas* of 1798 measured from St Paul's and gave figures for various towns including Exeter at 3°28'. While Smith showed 3°40', Morden and Moll had shown 3°42' from London, and Kitchin, Cary and Baker 3°32' from Greenwich (St. Paul's is 5' west of Greenwich and the correct figure is 3°32'). The inaccuracies suggest that seldom did surveyors check earlier figures, even though John Harrison's famous chronometer was in use from 1765.

Latitudes also varied. Morden and Donn showed the county between 50°15' and 51°16' (**21**, **44**), and Moll 50°12' and 51°17' (**25**) yet Kitchin drew 50°77' and 51°14' (correct figs are 50°12' and 51°15').

Maps were seldom graticuled: the first Devon map was Schenk and Valk's variation of Jansson in 1714 (**11.4**). Although John Seller included grid lines on some of his county maps (not Devon) it was not until 1789 that James Haywood (**53**) used the latitude and longitude lines and so provided the first cross reference, the technique finally adopted by the Ordnance Survey.

Coastline

Although charts of the coast were readily available the early surveyors do not seem to have used them. In 1584 Lucas Wagenhaer's sea atlas was published (with maps of the Devon coast dated a year earlier). This was the first marine atlas with details of the English coast. An English translation, *Mariner's Mirror*, appeared in 1588. The detail followed the old portolan tradition 'Accuracy for the pilot'. The charts have two scales; a large one for usable harbours and a smaller one for the coastline.

An early land surveyor like Saxton can be excused an inaccurate coastline, and for him Wagenhaer came too late. But why did no one else notice and then correct? The south coast especially shows some of these early inaccuracies: the mouth of the River Yealm is usually depicted pointing due south instead of west; the River Dart appears east of Froward Point and not in Start Bay; Penlee Point is shown north-east of Rame not due east. Although Greenville Collins, in 1693, produced his *Coasting Pilot* with more accurate charts (still with an incorrect River Yealm), it was not until the next century that a county surveyor altered the old copied coastline. When Moll produced his atlas, in 1724, he not only changed the line of the Tamar but he also correctly extended Start Bay to include the entrance to the River Dart.

This new south coast shape was copied by later cartographers, though some, like Kitchin and Jefferys in 1749, still retained the earlier Saxton form. Kitchin and Bowen in the 1750s adopted Moll's coastline but placed Devon 5' further south: a mistake copied on all their own maps and later in maps published by Alexander Hogg in 1784 (**50**), and John Lodge in 1788 (**52**).

However, with Donn's survey in 1765 a nearly accurate county map was achieved – to see just how accurate compare his Tamar and coastline with that of the Ordnance Survey. Donn's work became the basic Devon to be copied by Cary in 1787 and in 1789, and by Smith in 1801, and changed only with the advent of new main roads, turnpikes and canals.

In 1809 the Ordnance Survey map of Devon was published (**74**), although we have to wait until 1820, when the Ordnance's 'Bellman' introduced on to a large blank sheet of 600 mm by 300 mm, the tiny 75 mm by 25 mm Lundy island. The Survey became the accepted basis for most, if not all, of the reduced scale county maps that followed.

The subsequent history of county mapping was, more or less, one of wholesale copying of the Ordnance Survey's work. With the single exception of the Greenwood brothers, who surveyed Devon in 1825 and 1826 and published their nine-sheet map in the following year (**96**), all other maps were copies of Ordnance Survey work. Even John Cary, who had surveyed large areas of England to produce his highly accurate maps, resorted to copying. His last county map of Devon in 1813 was advertised: 'reduced from a survey made by order of the Board of Ordnance'. (**80**)

Notes

1. J B Harley; Christopher Saxton and the First Atlas of England and Wales 1579-1979; in *The Map Collector*, September 1979 Issue 8; p.8.
2. Tony Campbell; A False Start on Christopher Saxton's Wall-map of 1583?; in *The Map Collector*, September 1979; Issue 8.
3. R A Skelton; *County Atlases of the British Isles*; Carta Press; 1970; see table on p.59.
4. The Hungarian Wolfgang Lazius mapped Austria in 1561; Johann Stumpf had mapped Switzerland 1548-1552.
5. Percy Russell; *Transactions of the Devonshire Asscociation*; 87; 1955.
6. Van den Keere's miniature atlas of 1605 (**4**) has degrees of latitude only on his maps of Ireland.
7. For a comparison of scales based on Somerset see K Needell; Mile Scale Error ...; *IMCoS JOURNAL*; Spring 1987.
8. See H Lawrence's article in *IMCoS JOURNAL*, Vol. 1.5 Sept. 1981.

EXPLANATION

Definition

For the purpose of this cartobibliography, a county map of Devon means a printed map published specifically to show the whole of Devonshire on one or more sheets. Devon has not been grouped with other counties in any atlases; however, one popular work (Drayton 1612), one almanac-style work (Ezekiel 1816) and one government map show Devon together with Cornwall (**7, 83, 117**) and one government map shows Devon together with Somerset. (**110**) Maps of the South-West, maps which show only part of the county, coastal charts and road books are excluded. It is hoped that a further volume will list these. It is also intended to publish the details separately with the illustrations on CD-Rom.

Order

The maps are listed in chronological order of first appearance. Subsequent issues are dealt with at the same time as the main entry.

Heading

In labelling the maps the chosen order of preference throughout is surveyor, draughtsman, engraver, author, publisher. The map is given the name of a surveyor, if known, where the map is believed to be the result of an original survey. Otherwise the name of the draughtsman, the engraver, the author of the original work, or the first publisher in that order is used to help in identification. Names joined by a slash, eg Cowley/Dodsley, indicate that both (or all) were connected with the original issue and both (or all) names are found in works of reference and/or dealer's catalogues in connection with this map. A slash is also used to identify separate works by the same draughtsman/engraver, eg Neele/Fraser and Neele/Vancouver. In some cases maps are commonly associated with another mapmaker, eg van den Keere (1605) with Speed or Overton's copy (**18**) with Jansson, or a later publisher, eg Rocque's publication of Read's maps: in these cases the alternative name is added in brackets, eg Overton (Jansson) or Read (Rocque).

Date

The date listed is the one that appears on the first edition of the map or, if it is undated, the date of the publication in which it first appeared. (See also Publications below.)

Biographical Note

Wherever possible a short biographical sketch is given of the surveyor and/or publisher, together with a brief history and description of the map or atlas. There is also a note covering those copies that appeared after 1837.

Size

This gives the dimensions in millimetres, vertically then horizontally, between the outer frame lines. In the absence of frame lines, the dimensions are those of the printed map. Where the map has a panel of information or a title extension this is noted, together with an indication of the size of the complete engraving and of the map panel or area. Because of variations in paper shrinkage small differences can be expected. Lithographs may differ widely in size, being reduced or enlarged by photographic or other means.

Scale

The wording on the map is shown in bold type. The figure in brackets refers to the scale bar. The reference **British Miles** (1+10=11 mm) **miles** means that the scale shows 1 mile to the left of zero and 10 miles to the right, the whole measuring 11 mm. **British Miles** is written above or at front of the scale bar and **miles** after or below.

Inscriptions and Place-Names

The title, imprint and names that appear on the map are given in bold print using the original spelling. Punctuation is omitted if unclear.

Editions

The main entry shows the title and features that appeared on the first edition of the map. Subsequent states, with a note of the variations, are listed below. Information is complete up to the year 1836. Later issues have been noted in the previous biographical sketch.

Position of Features on Maps

Following the popular method, the position of each feature on the map is given, where appropriate, in brackets by reference to the following grid:

Aa	Ba	Ca	Da	Ea
Ab	Bb	Cb	Db	Eb
Ac	Bc	Cc	Dc	Ec
Ad	Bd	Cd	Dd	Ed
Ae	Be	Ce	De	Ee

Where a large feature extends over more than one square of the grid the position of the centre is given, except when the feature is in a corner when the corner reference is given. When the feature is outside the inner border the reference is followed by 'OS'. Position information is given where this feature changes during the lifetime of the map. Some maps, due to their size, have only a part illustrated.

Publications

The first date is the date of issue of the atlas or the date printed on the map, whichever is the earlier, eg Saxton's map is dated 1575 not 1579 as it was printed before the atlas and the map is dated. Reissues with information on known changes follow. Facing each description is an illustration of one issue of the map.

After the description of an edition of each map there is a list of the titles of atlases, books or other publications in which the map appeared. The title (which may be shortened, omissions being shown by dots) is given in italics, using the original spelling but in lower case except for initial letters. This is followed by the place, the publisher and the year of publication. If the year is shown without brackets, eg 1742, this is the date given on the title page. If more than one date is shown, separated by commas, these are the dates of successive editions of the same publication. If the date is shown in the form 1742 (1745), this means that although 1742 is the date on the title page, there is other evidence to indicate a later (or earlier) publication. Dates in brackets alone indicate that there is no date on the title page and the date is conjectured. Where a map was produced as a folding map this is mentioned.

REFERENCES

Following the publication details of each map or atlas references have been included. The first in bold print identifies written reference materials.

Roman   Thomas Chubb; *The Printed Maps in the Atlases of Great Britain and Ireland 1579-1870*; London; W Dawson; 1977.
S   R A Skelton; *County Atlases of the British Isles; 1575-1701*; Carta Press; 1970.
H   Donald Hodson; *County Atlases of the British Isles*, Vol 1 & Vol 2; Bracken Press; 1984& 1989.
Jolly   David Jolly; *Maps in British Periodicals*; Jolly; 1990 & 1991.
KM   C Koeman; *Atlantes Neerlandici*; Amsterdam; Theatrum Orbis Terrarum; 1967.
M&K   Mann & Kingsley; Playing Cards; in Vol. 87 of *Map Collector's Circle*; 1972.

This is followed by references to the location of atlases and maps. Locations in brackets imply loose sheets: in square brackets those not inspected by the authors.

Adm.	Admiralty Library, London.
B*	Bodleian Library (includes the Allen collection), Oxford.
BCL	Birmingham Central Library.
BL*	British Library (and British Museum), London.
BRdB	Bibliothèque Royale de Belgique, Brussels, Belgium.
BvF	Provinciale Bibliotheek van Friesland, Leeuwarden, Netherlands.
C*	Cambridge University Library.
Cardiff	Cardiff Central Library.
CB	Collection of Clive Burden.
DEI	Devon and Exeter Institution, Exeter.
E*	Exeter Westcountry Studies Library.
EB	Collection of Eugene Burden.
FB	Collection of Francis Bennett.
Field	Collection of Albert Field.
Gard.	Gardner Collection.
GL	Guildhall Library, London.
KB	Collection of Kit Batten.
Haarlem	Haarlem Library, Haarlem, Netherlands.
Hunt.	Huntingdon Library.
Leeds	Leeds Library.
Leyden	University of Leyden Library, Leyden, Netherlands.
Lib. Cong.	Library of Congress.
LS	Landesbibliothek Stuttgart, Germany.
LUL	London University Library.
MCL	Manchester City Library.
NDL*	North Devon Library, Barnstaple.
NHL	Naval Historical Library, London.
NLS	National Library of Scotland, Edinburgh.
NLW	National Library of Wales, Cardiff.
NMM	National Maritime Museum, Greenwich.
NYPL	New York City Public Library.
MW	Collection of Malcolm Woodward.
P	Private collection.
Ply*	Plymouth Public Library.
Radcliffe	Radcliffe Camera, Oxford.
RGS*	Royal Geographical Society.
RRL	Reading Reference Library.
TB	Collection of Tony Burgess.
TQ	Torquay Museum.
W	Whitaker Collection, University of Leeds.
WM	Wisbech and Fenland Museum.

* A source list, with shelf-marks, of those atlases and maps identified has been compiled by the authors and lodged in these libraries.

A List of the Maps

The maps are numbered in chronological sequence of first publication. The date given is that which is known or surmised. The chosen order of preference throughout the catalogue is surveyor, draughtsman, engraver, author, publisher. Names joined by a slash indicate that both/all were connected with the original issue. A slash is also used to identify separate works by the same draughtsman/engraver. Where maps are commonly associated with another mapmaker or printer the alternative name is added in brackets. Works not in italics were issued without title page.

1.	1575	C Saxton	An Atlas of England & Wales
2.	1590	W Bowes	A Pack of Playing Cards
3.	1605	W Bowes	A Pack of Memory Cards
4.	1605	v d Keere/(Speed)	The Counties of England and Wales
5.	1607	Kip/(Saxton)	*Britannia*
6.	1610	J Speed	*The Theatre of the Empire of Great Britaine*
7	1612	M Drayton	*Poly-olbion*
8.	1626	J Bill	*The abridgement of Camden's Britania*
9.	1635	M Simmons	*A Direction for the English Traviller*
10.	1643	T Jenner	*A Direction for the English Traviller*
11.	1644	J Jansson	*Des Nieuwen Atlantis Aenhang*
12.	1645	J Blaeu	*Theatrum Orbis Terrarum*
13.	1648	P van den Keere	*Atlas minor*
14.	1673	R Blome	*Britannia*
15.	1676	R Morden	*The 52 Counties of England & Wales* – Playing Cards
16.	1676	W Redmayne	*Recreative pastimes* – Playing Cards
17.	1681	R Blome	*Speed's Maps Epitomiz'd*
18.	1685	Overton/(Jansson)	Overton Atlas III
19.	1689	Lamb/Lea/(Saxton)	*All the Shires of England & Wales*
20.	1694	J Seller	*Anglia Contracta*
21.	1695	R Morden	*Camden's Britannia*
22.	1701	R Morden	*The New Description and State of England*
23.	1717	J Lenthall	A Pack of Playing Cards
24.	1720	Bowen/Owen	*Britannia Depicta*
25.	1724	H Moll	*A New Description of England and Wales*
26.	1732	R W Seale	*Nine New & Accurate Maps*
27.	1741	Badeslade/Toms	*Chorographia Britanniae*
28.	1743	Read/(Rocque)	*The English traveller*
29.	1744	Simpson/Walker	*The Agreeable Historian*
30.	1744	Cowley/Dodsley	*The Geography Of England*
31.	1748	Hutchinson/Osborne	*Geographia Magnae Britanniae*
32.	1748	J Hinton	*The Universal Magazine*
33.	1749	Kitchin/Jefferys	*The Small English Atlas*
34.	1750	T Kitchin	*The London Magazine*
35.	1750	Exshaw/(Kitchin)	*The London Magazine And Monthly Chronologer*
36.	1750	G Bickham	*The British Monarchy*
37.	1754	E Bowen	*The Large English Atlas*
38.	1755	Bowen/Martin	*The General Magazine of Arts and Sciences*
39.	1757	P Meijer	*Algemeene Oefenschoole*
40.	1759	J Gibson	*New and Accurate Maps of the Counties*
41.	1761	R Bennett	The New English Atlas
42.	1763	E Bowen	*The Royal English Atlas*
43.	1764	T Kitchin	*England Illustrated*
44.	1765	B Donn	*A Map of the County of Devon*
45.	1765	Donn/Jefferys	*A Map of the County of Devon*
46.	1765	J Ellis	*The New English Atlas*
47.	1767	J Gibson	*The Universal Museum*
48.	1767	E Bowen	*Atlas Anglicanus*
49.	1769	T Kitchin	*Kitchin's Pocket Atlass*
50.	1784	Hatchett/Walpoole/Hogg	*The New British Traveller*
51.	1787	J Cary	*New and Correct English Atlas* I
52.	1788	J Lodge	*The Political Magazine*
53.	1789	Haywood/Harrison	*The History of England*
54.	1789	Noble/Cary	*Britannia*
55.	1789	J Cary	*Cary's Traveller's Companion* I
56.	1790	J Aikin	*England Delineated*
57.	1791	B Baker	*The Universal Magazine*

58.	1791	W Tunnicliff	*A Topographical Survey*
59.	1794	Neele/Fraser	*General View of the County*
60.	1796	Mutlow/Marshall	*The Rural Economy of the West of England*
61.	1798	Rowe/Fairburn	*The Game of English Geography*
62.	1799	Baker/Faden	*The County of Devon*
63.	1801	Smith/Jones/Smith	*Smith's New English Atlas*
64.	1803	J Wilkes	*Encyclopaedia Londinensis*
65.	1803	R Butters	*An Atlas of England*
66.	1803	J Luffman	*A New Pocket Atlas and Geography*
67.	1805	Cole/Roper	*The British Atlas*
68.	1805	C Cooke	*Topographical Survey of Devonshire*
69.	1806	J Cary	*Cary's Traveller's Companion* II
70.	1806	Neele/Vancouver	*General View of the Agriculture of ... Devon*
71.	1807	J Cary	*Cary's New English Atlas*
72.	1808	Cooper/Capper	*A Topographical Dictionary of the U. K.*
73.	1809	J Cary	*New and Correct English Atlas* II
74.	1809	Mudge/OS	*The Second Part of the General Survey*
75.	1811	Rowe/Allen	*A Geographical Game – Allen's English Atlas*
76.	1811	W Ebden	*Laurie & Whittle's New Map of Devonshire*
77.	1812	J Wallis	*Wallis's New Pocket Edition of the English Counties*
78.	1812	J Wallis	*Wallis's New British Atlas*
79.	1812	Neele/Cundee	*The New British Traveller*
80.	1813	Palmer/Cary	*A Topographical Map of Devonshire*
81.	1816	R Rowe	*The English Atlas*
82.	1816	Dix/Darton	*A Complete Atlas of the English Counties*
83.	1816	E A Ezekiel	*The Exeter Pocket Journal*
84.	1817	Langley/Belch	*Langley's New County Atlas*
85.	1819	Crabb/(Ramble)	A Set of Cards
86.	1819	Neele/Pinnock	*The History and Topography of Devonshire*
87.	1820	Hall/Leigh	*Leigh's New Pocket Atlas*
88.	1820	Wallis/Reid	*The Panorama: or Traveller's Instructive Guide*
89.	1822	Mutlow/Lysons	*Magna Britannia*
90.	1822	J Walker	*Crosby's Complete Pocket Gazetteer*
91.	1822	Gardner/Smith	*Smith's New English Atlas*
92.	1822	G & J Cary	*Cary's Traveller's Companion* III
93.	1822	Smith/Davies	*The Exeter Pocket Journal*
94.	1823	A M Perrot	*L'Angleterre*
95.	1825	Ebden/(Duncan)	*Ebden's New Map of the County of Devon*
96.	1827	C & J Greenwood	*Map of the County of Devon*
97.	1829	C & J Greenwood	*Greenwood and Compy's Atlas*
98.	1829	J Pigot	*Pigot & Co's British Atlas*
99.	1830	H Teesdale	*A New Travelling Atlas*
100.	1830	T L Murray	*An Atlas of the English Counties*
101.	1830	S Hall	*A Topographical Dictionary of Great Britain*
102.	1831	Walker/Fisher	*Devonshire Illustrated*
103.	1831	Creighton/Lewis	*A Topographical Dictionary of England*
104.	1832	Dawson/Netherclist	*Parliamentary Representation*
105.	1832	Dawson/Gardner	*Report from Commissioners*
106.	1832	W Cobbett	*A Geographical Dictionary*
107.	1833	Scott/Fullarton	*A New and Comprehensive Gazetteer*
108.	1833	Archer/Pinnock	*The Guide to Knowledge*
109.	1833	J Wyld	*Map of the County of Devon*
110.	1833	House of Commons	*Accounts and Papers*
111.	1834	Dower/Moule	*Moule's English Counties*
112.	1834	M M Rodwell	*The Geography of the British Isles*
113.	1835	Creighton/Lewis	*A Topographical Dictionary of England*
114.	1835	J Pigot	*Pigot & Co's Pocket Atlas*
115.	1836	W Schmollinger	*The History of Devonshire*
116.	1836	J & C Walker	*This British Atlas*
117.	1836	S Arrowsmith	*Third Report from HM Commissioners*

PLATE 1.   SAXTON 1575

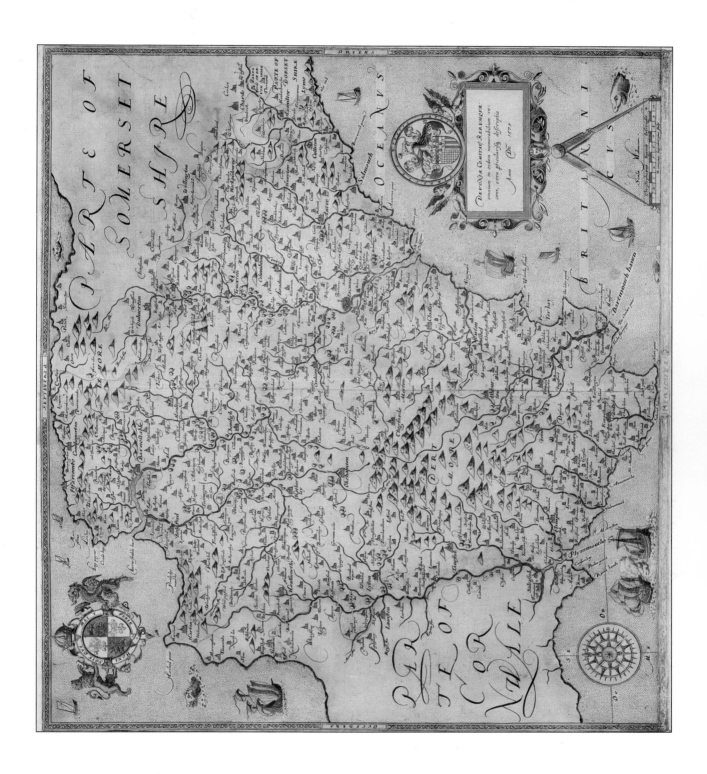

1.2 Saxton An Atlas of England and Wales

PLATE 2.   VAN DEN KEERE 1605

4.2 van den Keere / (Speed)   *Guilielmi Camdeni, Viri clarissimi Britannia* (above)
4.4 van den Keere / (Speed)   *England Wales Scotland and Ireland Described* (below)

PLATE 3.

JANSSON 1644

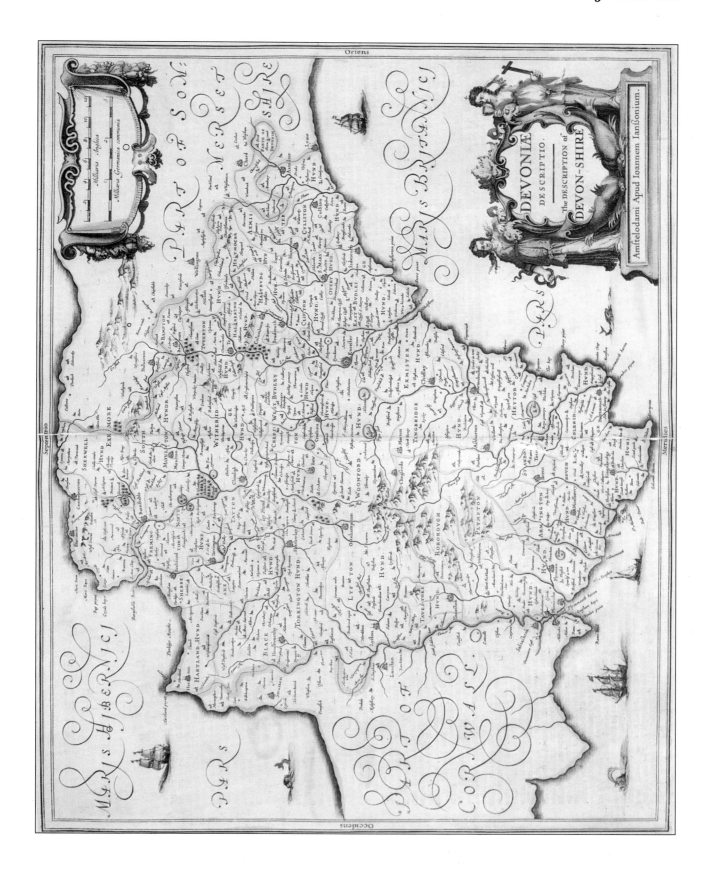

11.1 Jansson *Des Nieuwen Atlantis Aenhang*

PLATE 4.

BLAEU 1645

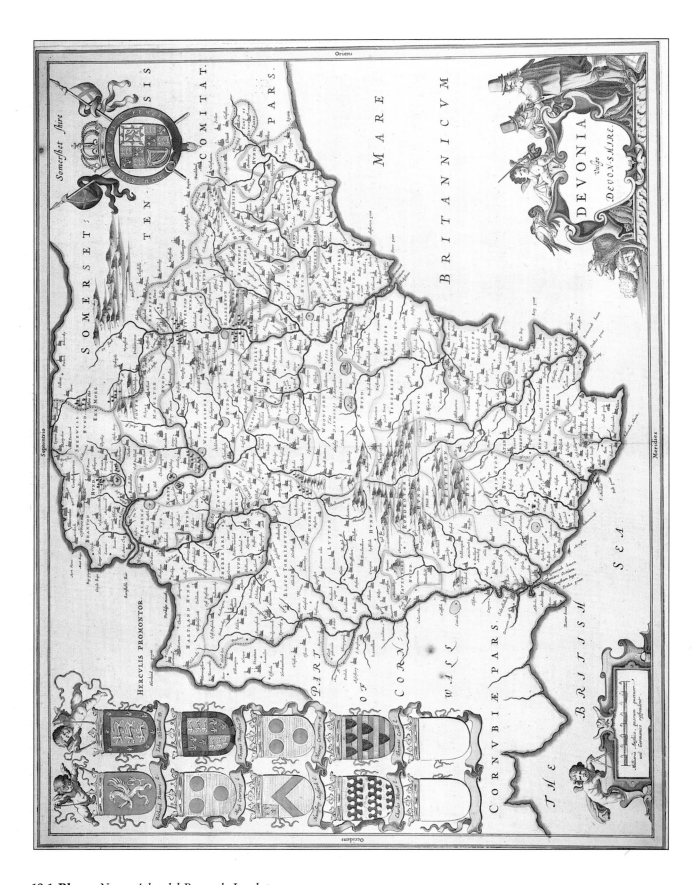

12.1 Blaeu *Nuevo Atlas del Reyno de Ingalaterra*

PLATE 5.

BOWEN 1754

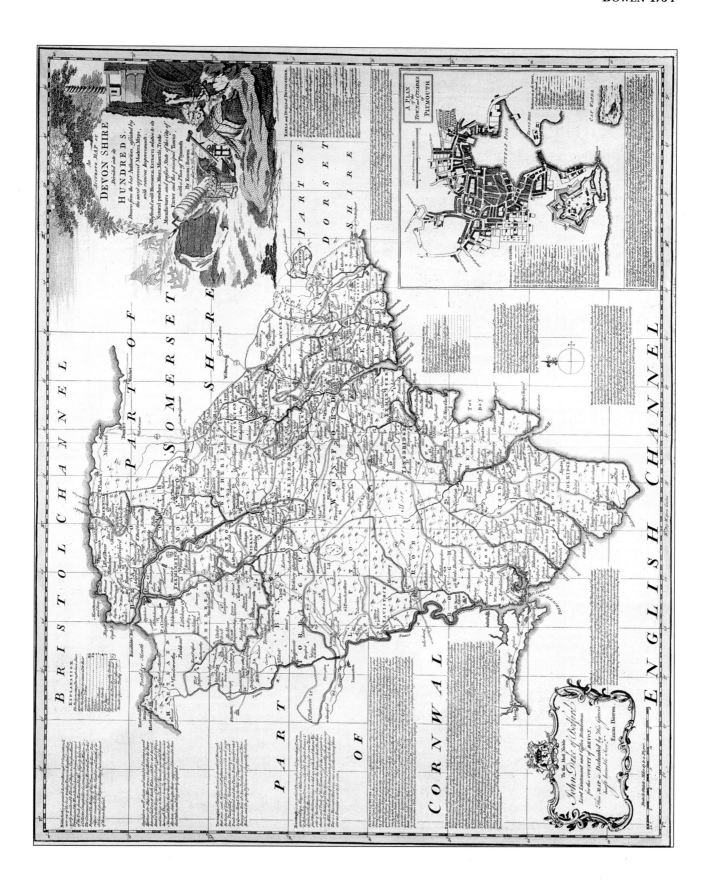

37.7 Bowen *The Large English Atlas*

PLATE 6.   SMITH/JONES/SMITH 1801

63.1 Smith / Jones / Smith *Smith's New English Atlas*

PLATE 7.

CARY 1807

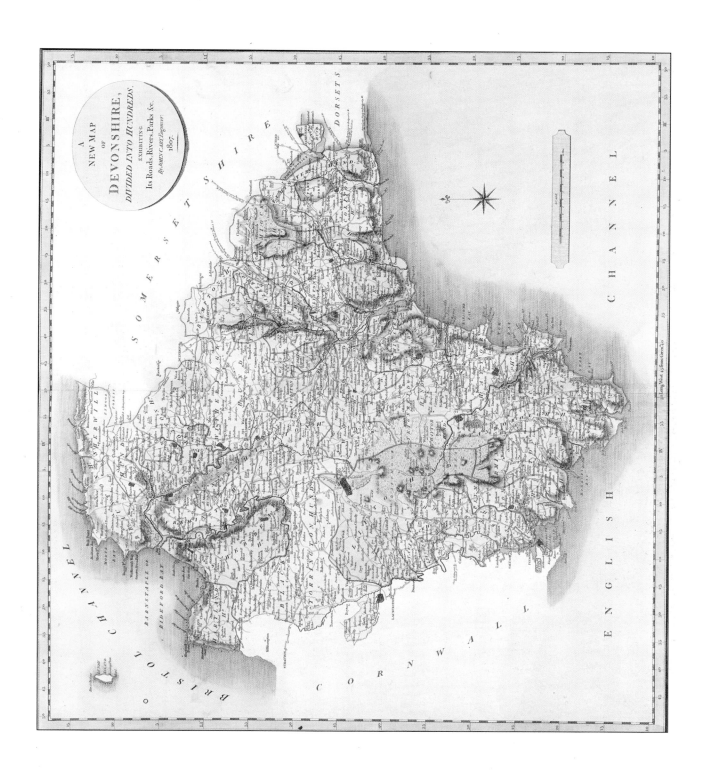

71.1 Cary *Cary's New English Atlas*

PLATE 8.

ROWE 1816

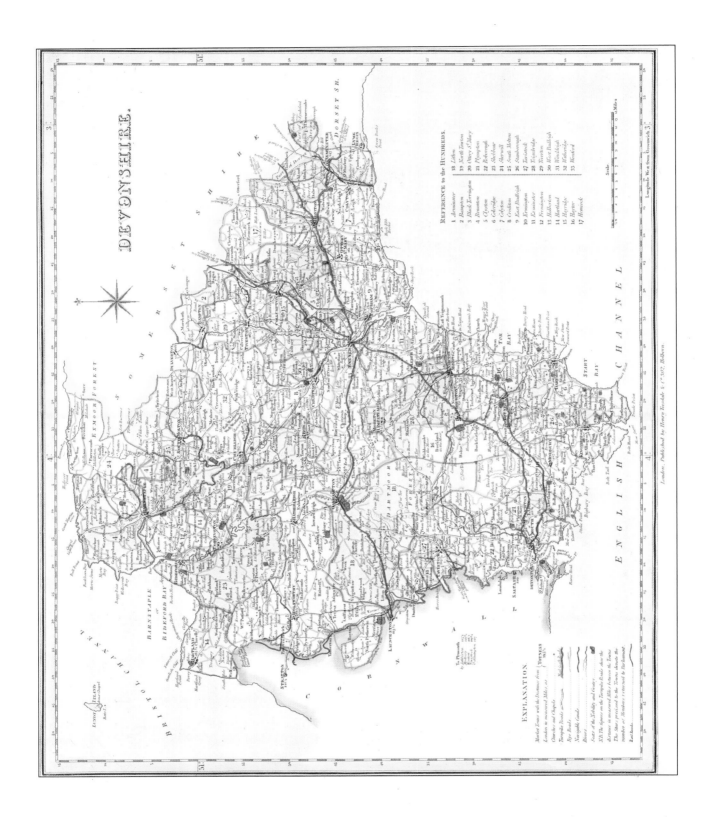

81.4 Rowe *New British Atlas*

The
PRINTED MAPS OF
DEVON
COUNTY MAPS 1575-1837

In meed of these great conquests by them gott,
Corineus had that province utmost west...
And Debon's shayre was that is Devonshyre.

SPENSER: Faerie Queene, II, x, 12.

CHRISTOPHER SAXTON
1575

A number of English cartographers were active during the sixteenth century. In 1546 George Lily's map was the first copper plate print of the British Isles. Laurence Nowell, completed a manuscript map in 1563 and this was followed by a map by Gerard Mercator in 1564. Abraham Ortelius printed maps based on the manuscript maps of Humphrey Lhuyd (1527-68) in 1573. But, it was not until 1583 that a large-scale map of the islands based on original work was produced by Christopher Saxton, the culmination of many years work which also saw the production of the first atlas of the English and Welsh counties, one of the first national atlases ever produced.

Christopher Saxton (1542-1610), the Father of English Cartography, was born near Dewsbury in Yorkshire. For most of his working life he was first and foremost a surveyor. He became, as a young man, an assistant to the vicar of Dewsbury, John Rudd[1], an enthusiastic and skilled cartographer himself. Rudd had declared his interest in mapmaking as early as 1534 and by 1560 it was known that he planned to carry out a countrywide survey as a preliminary to the production of a map of England. A receipt for money signed by Saxton shows that he travelled with Rudd. In the company of Rudd, Saxton would have met the Lord Treasurer, Lord Burghley, and possibly through him also Thomas Seckford, a lawyer and influential court official in his office of Master of Requests.

Working under the patronage of Seckford, Saxton began his own surveys in 1570 and the first maps were completed in 1574. He was granted a ten-year licence to make and market maps in 1577. There are no records of Saxton's methods of survey but he would also have relied on the Lily and Mercator maps, estate maps, local surveys and on the results of John Rudd's surveys.

It could not have been easy to find English engravers[2] skilled enough for copper engraving and many maps were prepared by Flemish Protestant refugees. Nine maps in the atlas are signed by Remigius Hogenberg including that of Devon, five by Leonard Terwoort and one each by Johannes Rutlinger and Cornelis de Hooghe. However, three English engravers did work for Saxton – Augustine Ryther (Anglus) a Yorkshireman like Saxton, Francis Scatter and Nicholas Reynolds. After each county survey the maps were printed and sold separately at a price of fourpence each.

Proof copies of the maps were sent to Lord Burghley as early as 1574 and the proof copy of Devon was found in Burghley's own set. Between 1579, when the atlas was entered in the Stationer's Hall records, and 1590, with the advent of the definitive version, some six editions are known with no changes to the Devon map (some changes to other maps were made) with differing contents' pages and map order and four typesettings. There were also two versions of the portrait of Queen Elizabeth I. There was no title page. The maps were reissued with amended date by William Web, probably in response to demand during the civil war. Although the majority of the maps were not reprinted until Philip Lea's edition, Skelton[3] speculates that an edition of 1665 was planned but not produced. By 1689 the original Saxton plate of Devon (and also that of Northumberland) had been destroyed or lost. Possibly victims of the Great Fire it does seem strange that only two plates were lost or damaged. However, Lea commissioned Francis Lamb to engrave a new copy of Devon for *All the Shires of England and Wales* (19). Saxton maps continued to be printed until about 1770.

The county maps are very attractive and considering the publication time and date very accurate, but sometimes not as detailed as one might expect. The boundaries of Devon's hundreds are not outlined (only five counties had hundreds shown), nor is there any indication of roads, although river bridges are shown. The maps were not all drawn to the same scale. Devon is the only map with a compass, possibly as it was tilted a few degrees to fit the page. The Royal Arms are shown together with those of Seckford with his motto: pre-1576 *Pestis Patriae Pigrities*, (later it became *Industria Naturam Ornat*). The various collections can be dated by the variations outlined above and by alterations made to other county maps. Interestingly the village of Ashbrittel is in Devon in all editions but on the Somerset map it is in Somerset in one state and in the neighbouring Devon on the second state. One atlas in the British Library is believed to have been owned by James I.

[1.] David Marcombe; John Rudd: a forgotten Tudor Mapmaker?; *The Map Collector*, No. 64, Autumn 1993.

[2.] See J B Harley; Christopher Saxton and the First Atlas of England; in *The Map Collector*, Issue 8 Sept. 1979; p.8.

[3.] Skelton entry 80, pp 121-3; based on the work of Lynam and Whitaker.

Size 400 x 445 mm.
Plate 1

Scala Miliarium (10=68 mm).
Scale 1M=6.8 mm.

DEVONIAE COMITAT, RERUMQUAE omnium in codem memorabilium recens, vera pticularisq descriptio. Anno Dn. 1575 in strapwork frame with the arms of Thomas Seckford **PESTIS PATRIAE PIGRITES** above. Royal Arms with initials **ER**. Signature: **Remigius hogenbergius sculp.**

1.	**1575**	Proof copy from Lord Burghley's own collection.	BL.

2. 1579   Imprint: **Christophorus Saxton descripsit** added above scale-bar.

An Atlas of England & Wales
Collections had no title page: Devon was map no. 24, 4 or 6, but unnumbered.
There is a full page engraving of Queen Elizabeth I followed by 3 pages; shields, catalogue and index together with a general map of England and Wales.
(London. C Saxton. 1579.)   **I-VI, S1**, BL, W, B, RGS, BCL.

3. 1642   Date in title altered to **1642**. Now map no. 3. Alteration of some map titles from Latin to English carried out but not to Devon.

The Maps of all the Shires in England and Wales. Exactly taken and truly described by Christopher Saxton. And graven at the Charges of a private Gentleman for the publicke good. Now newly Revised, Amended, and Reprinted.
London. William Web. 1645.   **VII, S27**, BL, B, C.

Although watermarks have been used to date maps this is liable to be inaccurate and at best can only show the earliest possible date. The approximate dates for watermarks are:

Bunch of Grapes with **A** left and **F** right	is *c.*1565
Bunch of Grapes with **B** left and **C** right	is *c.*1579
Bunch of Grapes with Fleur de Lys	is *c.*1579
Crossed Arrows	is *c.*1588
Kneeling Saint with Cross	is *c.*1600.

W Bowes
1590

Playing cards were common in Europe in the late fifteenth century. In times when there was little or no organized schooling they were fairly widely used for educational purposes with texts on a great variety of subjects. The earliest records of such cards in England date to 1463 when a prohibition on the importation of cards was published. The standard pack, first introduced from France, has remained constant since the sixteenth century: fifty-two cards made up of four suits, with thirteen cards in each. The spades, hearts, diamonds and clubs are of French origin, and might seem rather lacklustre compared to the colourful and complex German (acorns, leaves, bells and hearts) or Italian (cups, swords, coins and sticks) counterparts.

In 1590 the first geographic set of cards bearing county maps appeared in England, followed by a second in 1605 (**3**); evidence points to W Bowes being the author of both packs[1]. The 52 county maps in this first series are copied from the small general map of England and Wales in Christopher Saxton's atlas, and show only the county boundary, principal towns, rivers, hills and woods. The towns are indicated by initial letters, and their character is shown by symbols explained in a legend on a separate card. The 60 cards were engraved on four sheets. Devon was on the fourth sheet together with a reduced copy of Braun and Hogenberg's view of London. Devon as the largest county in its suit was the King (thirteenth card). There were no suit marks. Almost exact copies of these maps together with John Norden's road distance tables appeared in Matthew Simmons' *Direction for the English Traviller* (**9**).

No later edition of the playing cards is known; but a set in private ownership forms part of a bound volume of ten plates published as a collection, with a printed title-page listing the plates and the instruction card signed *W. B. inuent. 1590*. The second pack of cards has the imprint *W. Bowes Inventor*, hence the assumption that they are both by the same person.

There is strong evidence to suggest that the maps were engraved specifically for Bowes by Augustine Ryther, one of the engravers employed by Saxton. An important cartographic achievement of the pack was the fact that it represented the first publication of each English and Welsh county as a separate map; Saxton had grouped a number of counties together.

The small map is surrounded by a wide decorative frame (the example in the British Library being coloured green – the text panels are pink), and information about the county is given in eight lines of text from William Camden's *Britannia*, four lines above and below the map.

Size of card 94 x 57 mm.	Scale bar (10=6 mm).
Map panel 48 x 48 mm.	Scale 1M=0.6 mm.

The number **XIII** in Roman numerals in central panel. **DENSHIRE** in upper and lower panels which contain topographical information including distances (above) and general information (below).

1. 1590   Set of playing cards
         London. W B. 1590.   **S2, M&K1**, BL[2], RGS.

---

[1] See especially Mann and Kingsley; PLAYING CARDS; *The Map Collectors' Circle*, No. 87, 1972.
[2] Illustration courtesy of the British Library.

2.1 Bowes a playing card

3

W Bowes
1605

Prior to cards that we recognise as playing cards, various *memory* cards had been produced[1]. These rarely had suit marks as they were used mainly for instruction. But, in 1605 a pack of memory cards complete with thumbnail sketches of the counties appeared with suit marks. From the first introductory card it is clear that the cards were produced during the reign of James I and the imprint is *W. Bowes Inventor*. In 1590 a set of cards (**2**) was signed *W B inuent* so it is assumed both packs were by the same hand. The inscription Gillam A Cart on the Jack of Clubs led to the suggestion that the designer was *William* Bowes. However, in a recent article, Gillam A Cart has been identified as Guilleme Acart, a member of a Rouennais family of playing card makers.[2]

The pack produced in 1605, only known in a proof copy in the British Library, consists of 59 cards, 7 being introductory cards. The cards are divided into ten panels, in four rows. The suit marks and card values are contained in the upper and lower central panels: each card is so divided as to provide instruction on such subjects as philosophy and morals, religion, agriculture and geography and also a perpetual calendar. The map is very similar to the earlier 1590 map but at approximately half the scale – and measures 16 x 21 mm; and the topographical description below it is, as in the 1590 cards, from the text of William Camden's *Britannia*. The same towns are marked with initial letter as on the previous cards. A further map of Devon, 6 mm[2], is present on one of the introductory cards to the set. This contains a miniature reproduction of all the county maps in one suit as well as instructions.

Maps next appeared on playing cards in 1676 with the appearance of cards by Robert Morden and William Redmayne (**15**, **16**).

Size of card 90 x 52 mm.	Scale bar (10=3 mm).
Map panel 25 x 25 mm.	Scale 1M=0.3 mm.

DEVON S: in panel bottom right. King of spades; King in upper and lower middle sections, spade sign only in upper central panel. The card has been cut from a sheet and mounted on board.

1. 1605   Set of memory cards
                     London. W Bowes. 1605.   **M&K2**, BL[3].

---

[1]. Mann and Kingsley; PLAYING CARDS; *The Map Collectors' Circle*, No. 87, 1972.

[2]. David Kingsley in a letter to the *IMCoS Journal*, Autumn 1993.

[3]. Illustration courtesy of the British Library.

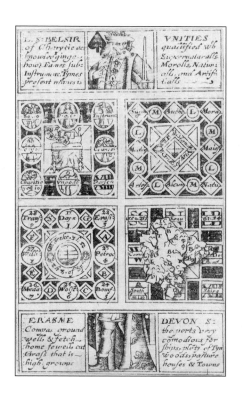

3.1 Bowes a memory card

4

Van Den Keere/(Speed)
1605

London in the late sixteenth century was a refuge for many from the Low Countries seeking to escape religious persecution. Pieter van den Keere (1571-*c*.1646) was one of these refugees. He moved to London in 1584 with his sister who married Jodocus Hondius. He returned to Amsterdam in 1593. He engraved a large number of maps for important cartographers, amongst these a map of London for John Norden's *Speculum Britanniae,* an *Atlas of the Netherlands* (1617-22) and one complete and one incomplete set of county maps of the British Isles.

Keere engraved plates for 44 maps of the counties, some dated 1599. The English maps were based on Saxton, the Scottish on Ortelius and the Irish on a map by Boazio which he had engraved. These maps were not published at once in book form. One source suggests that individual maps were on sale in Amsterdam between 1605 and 1610, but perhaps they only existed in proof form until 1617 when Willem Blaeu issued them with an abridged Latin edition of William Camden's *Britannia* by Regner Vittelius. In this issue, *Viri clarissimi Britannia*, the maps often contain printer's signatures, or collation reference letters and numbers in addition to page numbers. The map of Devon (on p.113) is the first page of an *H* series (p.115 is H2, p.117 is H3 etc.). The map is bound in sideways and east may be at the top or bottom of the page. The *H* appears inside the map border, either easily seen, in Somerset, or partly concealed within the shotsilk sea off the Cornish coast. Where the map is backed with the Latin text (*DAMNONII. C. Iterior* ...) and has the page number 113 left or right it will also have the printed H. This does not follow for all the maps but when collation occurs and the map is printed on the right hand page a signature letter will appear (eg Oxford has been seen with P, Hartford Q3, Norfolk T30, Lincoln Y2 etc).

While the original maps had no text on the reverse (or manuscript text) references in the later printed text suggest a date of 1605 or shortly after.[1] For the 1617 issue maps of the British Isles and Yorkshire were added, the latter derived from Saxton. The title page of this edition is signed *Guilielmus noster Janssonius,* the Latinized form of Blaeu's name he used up to 1619. Pieter van den Keere himself signed his maps *Petrus Kaerius.*

Sometime before 1619 George Humble, John Speed's publisher, came into possession of the plates (**6**). Knowing the popularity of Speed's *Theatre* and the liking for miniature atlases Humble reissued the Keere maps as a pocket edition *abridged from a far larger volume by J Speed.* In 1627, he added the abridged text and hence they mistakenly became known as *Miniature Speeds.* Of the 63 maps in the Atlas, 40 were reworked from the Keere plates, 16 copied from Speed and a further 7 maps were added. The pocket atlas was reissued as late as 1676.

A number of Devon towns do not appear on the map of Devon itself but do appear on the maps of neighbouring counties, correctly placed in Devon; Sauldon, Clauton, St Giles, Siddenham, St Budix and Redfort appear on the Cornwall map; Uplyme, Axmouth and Beare on the Dorset map; and Hight and Baunton on the Somerset map. Devon was the only map with a compass, perhaps to show that Devon had been tilted slightly to fit the frame.

These were not the only county maps to be engraved by Pieter van den Keere. About 1620 he started working with Jan Jansson and in 1648 the German edition of *Atlas Minor* contained maps of four Irish provinces and eight English counties including another map of Devon (**13**).

Size 85 x 120 mm.   **Scala Miliarium** (10=16.5 mm).
Plate 2   Scale 1M=1.65 mm.

DEVONIA. Signature: **P. Kaerius caelavit.**
Maps have no page number and no text on reverse (or have manuscript text).

1. 1605   Collection of Maps of the Counties of England and Wales   IX, S4, BL, RGS, (E).

---

[1] See H Wallis in *Atlas of the British Isles* (Facsimile); H Margary; Lympne Castle; 1972.

2. 1617 Page number **113** and an horizontal **H** type printed on map (see above). Latin text by Regner Vittelius on reverse.
(*Guilielmi Camdeni* was reprinted in 1639 with maps by Bertius.)

Guilielmi Camdeni, Viri clarissimi Britannia, sive florentissimorum
Regnorum Angliae, Scotiae, Hiberniae, & Insularum adjacentium ... descriptio.
Amsterdam. Guilielmi Ianssonij (W J Blaeu). 1617.   **X**, **S12**, BL, C, W, RGS.

3. 1619 Title is now **DEVONSHIRE**, the cartouche extending to the border. Plate number **7** (Be) added. No text on reverse. No page number or signature (ie no 113 or H).

England, Wales And Ireland: The severall Counties, Abridged from A farr larger vollume: By John Speed ...
to bee sold by George Humble in pops head alley
London. George Humble. (1619).   BL.

4. 1627 Number **7** erased and − **9** − added (Ed) above title. Reverse has English text taken from first Devon page of Speed. (See p.xi)

England Wales Scotland and Ireland Described and Abridged With ye Historie
Relation of things worthy memory
These were printed by John Dawson but the text was corrected for the later issue.
London. George Humble. 1627.   **XI**, **S17**, BL.
London. George Humble. 1627 (1632).   **XII**, **S19**, BL, W.

England Wales Scotland and Ireland Described
Issued bound with *A Prospect of the Most Famous parts of the World ... performed by John Speed,*
Printed by M.F. (Miles Fletcher) for William Humble dated 1646.
London. William Humble. 1627 (1646).   **XIII**, **S37**, BL, W.

Two cracks appear in Devon − at Bideford Bay and at letter **D** of title (see p.xi).
Sometimes bound with *Prospect.*   (E), (NDL).

England Wales Scotland and Ireland Described
London. Roger Rea the Elder and younger. 1662[1].   **XV**, **S69**, W, BCL.

England, Wales, Scotland and Ireland Described (No title-page.)
Text reset; bound with *Prospect* with a title page *Printed by M.S.* (Mary Simmons)
London. Roger Rea. 1665.   **S82**, [Gard.].

5. 1666 The plate has been touched up; **S** of **SHIRE** goes into lower border and half-circle by scale now completed through border. 3 cracks evident in Devon plate (see p.xi).

England Wales Scotland and Ireland Described
London. Roger Rea. 1666, (1668).   **XVI**, **S83**, [B]; **S86**, BL, RGS.

England Wales Scotland and Ireland Described
Text again reset dated 1676. Bound with *Prospect* dated 1676. Collective title page
An Epitome of Mr John Speed's Theatre ... And of His Prospect ... 1676.
London. Thomas Bassett and Richard Chiswell. 1676.   **XVII**, **S93**, BL, W.

---

[1]   Clive Burden has a copy with the 1627 title-page with a Roger Rea label pasted over it.

5

KIP/(Saxton)
1607

William Camden (1551-1623) eminent historian and antiquarian was headmaster of Westminster School, London in 1593 and appointed Clarenceaux King of Arms in 1597. He first published his *Britannia*, a description and history of Britain, in 1586. Written in Latin and with only a general map of the country it still proved very popular. He is known to have visited Devon in 1596[1], probably collecting information for one of the later editions. The sixth edition included the county maps with Latin text on the reverse. The maps, mostly engraved by William Kip and William Hole, were generally copied from Saxton (even to the name on the maps – but some spellings vary, eg Okehamton, Barnstable, Plymouth and Otterey), though six maps were derived from John Norden, and one from George Owen. The general map was copied from Gerard Mercator. Translations of Camden's text by Philemon Holland were published in English in 1610 but not on the reverse of the map. Among the printers were Felix Kingston, Richard Young and John Leggatt.

Britannia was widely popular and abridged versions were issued by W J Blaeu using Keere's maps in 1617 (**4**), by John Bill with his own maps in 1626 (**8**) and by Joan Blaeu in 1639 with Mercator's regional maps. Later still, fresh translations appeared with new maps well into the nineteenth century. Robert Morden (**21**) and John Cary (**54**) produced versions and Samuel Tymms used maps by J Walker in *Camden's Britannia Epitomized and Continued* as late as 1842 (see **90**).

The Atlas noted by Chubb (XXI) as by Christopher Browne in 1752 must be presumed only a collection. It contains variations and was not an entire set. Moreover, though Browne may have obtained the Kip and Hole plates this is the only set known and he had ceased trading by 1714.

Camden refused a knighthood and his last academic achievement was the founding of a chair at Oxford University in 1622, known as the Camden Professorship of Ancient History. In 1838 the Camden Society was founded in his honour and still survives today.

Size 290 x 332 mm

Scale bar (10=52 mm).
Scale 1M=5.2 mm.

DEVONIAE Comitatus Vulgo Den: Shyre quam olim DANMONII Populi Incoluerant in cartouche.
Signatures: **Christophorus Saxton descripsit.** and **William Kip Sculp:**.

1. 1607   Latin text on reverse: p.143 of Cornwall and 144 **DANMONII_DENSHIRE.**

Britannia, sive florentissimorum Regnorum Angliae, Scotiae, Hiberniae, et Insularum ...
Gulielmo Camdeno Authore.
London. George Bishop & John Norton. 1607.   **XVIII, S5**, BL, B, (E).

No text on reverse: 1st English edition.

Britain Or A Chorographical Description of the most flourishing Kingdomes,
England, Scotland, and Ireland, and the Ilands adioyning.
London. George Bishop and John Norton. 1610.   **XIX, S6**, BL, B, (E).

2. 1637   Plate number **3** (Ae) just above signature[2]. No text on reverse.

Britain	**XX, S23**, (E), (DEI), (NDL).
London. Andrew Heb. 1637.	BL.
London. William Aspley. 1637	B.
London. Andrew Crooke. 1637.	W.
London. Joyce Norton & Richard Whitaker . 1637.	[NLS].
London. George Latham. 1637.	[P].

[1.] Cited in *Catalogue II*, published by Lesley Aitchison; 1995.
[2.] Possibly added earlier: Leicester with plate number appeared 1622; this 2nd English edition was registered in 1625.

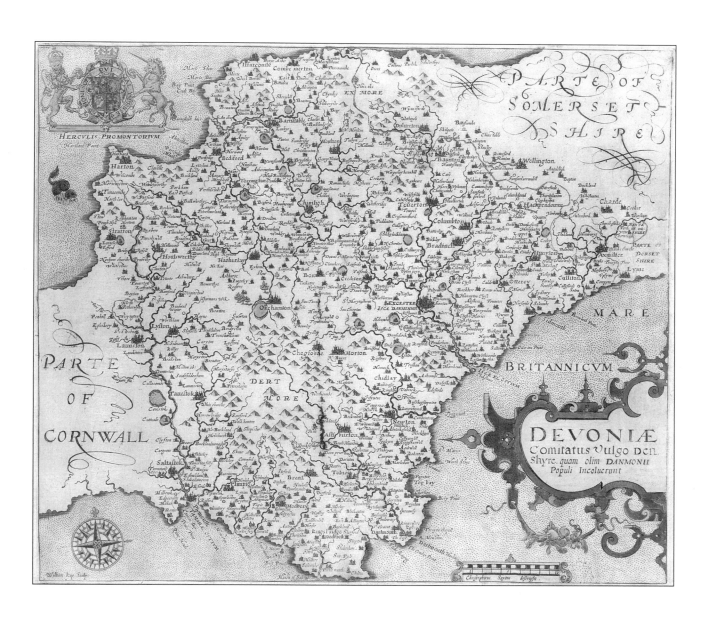

5.1 Kip *Britain*

6

JOHN SPEED
1610

John Speed (1552-1629) was born at Farndon in Cheshire and followed his father's trade as a tailor. By 1584 he had moved to London with his wife (Susanna who bore him twelve sons and six daughters) and been made a Freeman of the Merchant Tailors Company (1580). He was a keen amateur historian and map maker, producing maps for the Merchant Tailors in 1598. He became a member of the Society of Antiquaries where it is likely that he came into contact with the leading historians of the day such as Sir Robert Cotton, William Camden, whose text he had read, and perhaps even Christopher Saxton. His interests came to the notice of Sir Fulke Greville who made him an allowance so that he should be free to write an history of England and, by courtesy of Queen Elizabeth, he worked from a room in the Custom House.

A good historian he was a great gatherer of information: *I have put my sickle into other men's corne.* Most of his map material was copied from Saxton: however, John Norden (*c.*1548-1625) and William Smith (*c.*1550-1618) had produced maps of some counties and Gerard Mercator maps of the regions. Yet Speed must have travelled extensively, for his maps go well beyond those of his predecessors. By including the hundreds, the inset town plans and heraldic devices of his maps and modifying the Camden text in the atlas he assured its success and lasting appeal. The first maps engraved for the atlas were printed in 1605-06 (although most of the dated maps show 1610) and were on sale between then and 1610-11, when the *Theatre of the Empire of Great Britaine* and the *History*, which often accompanied it, was issued in full. Speed's drafts were taken to Amsterdam, engraved by Jodocus Hondius, then taken back to London for printing. The Devon map was copied directly from Saxton and the map of Exeter is taken from Braun and Hogenberg's engraving (1587) of a plan by John Hooker. The Cornish boundary has a minor error: Mount Edgcombe, shown in Devon on the Cornwall map, is situated in Cornwall on the Devon map; a mistake copied by both Jan Jansson and Joan Blaeu, and hence by all who derived their maps from these sources.

In 1627, just before he died, Speed published *A Prospect of the Most Famous Parts of the World* (title copied from Ortelius) which, combined with the 1627 edition of the *Theatre*, became the first World Atlas produced by an Englishman.

Speed's publishers, John Sudbury (*d.*1621) and his nephew George Humble (*d.*1640), received a 21-year privilege in 1608 and exploited it to the full issuing 12 editions of the work. George Humble also obtained the van den Keere plates (4) and published these miniature maps to coincide with issues of Speed's large atlas, hence the name *Miniature Speeds*. William Garrett bought the plates in 1659 and immediately sold them to Roger Rea. By 1675 Thomas Bassett (*fl.*1659-93) and Richard Chiswell (1639-1711) had bought the plates and obtained a 10-year privilege to print. They then sold the plates or single sheets to Christopher Browne (*fl.*1684-1712). Henry Overton acquired the plates *c.*1711 and used them in collections of maps. Overton's nephew sold them to Dicey & Co. in 1754. Single sheets were still being sold as late as 1770.

Size 375 x 510 mm.   THE SCALE OF MILES (10=65 mm).
                                                                        Scale 1M=6.5 mm.

DEVONSHIRE WITH EXCESTER DESCRIBED And the Armes of such Nobles as have borne the titles of them. Royal Arms. Boat in Bristol Channel (Ba). Inset plan of **EXCESTER** in frame together with city arms. Inset left, eight coats of arms.

1. (1610)   Proof copy without text, known only as a single sheet. Possibly pre-1610.   P.

2. (1610)   Proof corrected: boat removed from Bristol Channel (Ba); No text on reverse.
             Hundreds shown and titled; panel introduced for imprint (Be) which reads
             **Performed by Ihon Speede And are to be sold in popes-head Alleye
             by Iohn Sudburi & George humble. Cum privilegio.**   XXIII, BL, RGS.

continued ...

6.9 Speed a dissected map

2. 1610 cont. English text on reverse begins: **Book 1. DEVON-SHIRE Chap.10.**

The Theatre of the Empire of Great Britaine: Presenting An Exact Geography of the Kingdomes of England, Scotland, Ireland, and the Isles adioyning. With The Shires, Hundreds, Cities, and Shire-townes, within ye Kingdome of England, divided and described by Iohn Speed.
London. John Sudbury & George Humble. 1611 (1612).

XXIV, **S7**, BL, RGS, W, (E).

3. 1614 Shotsilk sea-shading added. Text reset: border of capital **D** given cable pattern (printed by Thomas Snodham).

The Theatre of the Empire of Great Britaine
London. Sudbury and Humble. 1614 (1616).   **XXIV**, **S10**, BL, (E).

Theatrum Imperii Magnae Britanniae: Exactam Regnorum Angliae, Scotiae, Hiberniae et Insularum adiactentium Geographia ... Latin text on reverse.
London. Sudbury & Humble. 1616.   **XXIVa/b**, **S11**, BL, RGS, W.

Reissued in Amsterdam by Jodocus Hondius 1621 and Jan Blaeu in 1646.

4. 1623 British tribes and Roman stations added, eg The **DANMONII** and **ISCA DANMONIOR** on road between Exeter and Okehampton, possibly by Renold Elstrack who signed Norfolk. Also issued without text in response to demand by armies in the Civil War.

The Theatre of the Empire of Great Britaine
London. Sudbury & Humble. 1614 (1623).   **S14**, W, BCL.

English text reset: capital **D** given plain double border. Was now sold
with first issue of *A Prospect of the Most Famous Parts of the World Printed by John Dawson for George Humble, and are to be sold at his shop in Popes head Palace, 1627.*

The Theatre of the Empire of Great Britaine
London. G Humble. 1627.   **XXV**, **S16**, BL, B[1], RGS, (E).

Text reset: **in** is now on the 2nd line – **Hundreds | in Devon-shire**..

The Theatre of the Empire of Great Britaine
London. G Humble. 1627 (1632).   **S18**, BL.

Text reset: the capital **D** has a lady and a knight on either side (not scribe).

The Theatre of the Empire of Great Britaine
London. W Humble. 1627 (1646).   **S36**, BL.
London. W Humble. 1650 (with *Prospect* still dated 1646, printed by
John Leggatt) and reissued in 1650 (1651), 1650 (1652), 1650 (1653), 1650 (1654) .

S48, W; **S50**; **S51**; **S55**; **S57**, Gard.

[1.] A copy in the Bodleian Library has been printed on a large sheet with two sets of lists pasted on the sides and the text pasted below in eight columns finishing with a colophon: Imprinted **London by T Snodham for John Sudbury and George Humble, and are to be sold in Popes-head Palace, 1615**. Text is 1614 (1616) version.

5. 1665   Imprint: **Performed by Ihon Speede And are to be sold by Roger Rea the Elder and younger at ye Golden Crosse in Cornhill against the Exchange.**

The Theatre of the Empire of Great Britaine
Issued with: *A Prospect of the most Famous parts of the World* dated 1662.
London. Roger Rea the Elder and Younger. 1650 (1665).   **XXVII, S81,** BL, W.

6. 1676   Arms of **Wil: Cavendish E. of Devon** (Ad) added (**Of** in Part of Cornwall removed). Imprint changed to: **Performed by Ihon Speede And are to be Sold by Tho: Bassett in Fleetstreet, and Ric: Chiswell in St Pauls Churchyard.**

The Theatre of the Empire of Great Britaine
London. Bassett & Chiswell*see* Bassett & Chiswell. 1676   **XXVII, S92,** BL, RGS, (E).

Atlas Anglicanus
As above without text in collection of maps possibly presented to Charles II in 1681.
London. John Seller. (1681).   **XXVIII,** BL.

7. 1695   Devon (& 4 other maps) had imprint of Browne: **Corrected and Sold by Chrystopher Browne at the Globe near the West End of St Pauls Church London.**

(DEI).

Atlas without title page or text.
London. Christopher Browne. 1695.   **S116,** NMM, CB.

England Fully Described – Speed (Overton) I & Speed (Overton) II
London. Henry Overton. (1713), (post-1716).
H135, [NLW]; **XXIXa, H136,** BL, NMM.

8. 1720   Imprint: **Performed by John Speed and Sold by Henry Overton at the White Horse without Newgate London.** Roads added. Also sold as a dissected map.

England Fully Described – Speed (Overton) III
London. Henry Overton. (1720).   **XXX, H137,** B.

9. 1743   Retouching of shading to hills, end of plumes of helmet more feathery and stonework to Exeter walls almost lost under angled shading. Also sold as a dissected map.

(E), (DEI).

England Fully Described – Speed (Overton) IV
London. H Overton. 1743.   **XXXI, H138,** BL.

Atlases with no title pages – Overton Atlas VII & VIII   **H143a,** CB; **H144,** BL.

10. 1756   Imprint altered to: **Performed by I Speede and are to be Sold by C Dicey & Co: in Aldermary Church-yard London.**

The English atlas (manuscript title in the Cambridge copy)
This was a mixed atlas of Speed and other maps. Sheets were also sold singly.
London. Dicey & Co. (1756-1770).   **XXXII, H145,** BL, C, (E).

7

MICHAEL DRAYTON
1612

Michael Drayton (1563-1631), an Elizabethan poet and friend of Edmund Spenser (1552-99), published the first part of his life's work, a book of songs containing 18 illustrative maps in 1612; reprinted a year later as *Poly-Olbion or A Chorographicall Description of Tracts, Rivers, Mountaines, Forests and other Parts of the Renowned Isle of Great Britaine*; and published with a second part in 1622, bringing the total number of maps to 30. The maps, usually of two counties, are allegorical in nature and few geographical features are precisely shown. Emphasis is on the rivers, which are each named and with its own nymph or goddess. Here and there a few towns are named. The maps are without county boundaries, scale, title or pagination. Each map illustrates a song from the lengthy verse-travelogue which contains some fifteen thousand lines. Although they are amongst the most curious maps of the counties ever issued and have little geographical value they are very decorative and charmingly illustrate the romantic side of the Elizabethan age. The book was reissued in facsimile by the Spenser Society in 1890.

The title page has the imprint: *Inrave by W. Hole* and it is believed he engraved the county maps. William Hole, together with William Kip, had already produced maps for William Camden's *Britannia* (**5**) to illustrate the prose descriptions of the country. The Drayton maps seem rather fantastic, but when one keeps in mind the sea monsters and other figures often seen in Saxton's maps or indeed in the maps engraved by Hole for Camden (Warwickshire has Neptune disporting with a naked female) then the maps lose a little of their strangeness but none of their attraction.

Devon is drawn together with Cornwall, but Lundy is shown on the map of Somerset and Gloucester which is the most attractive of all the maps. The Welsh and English choirs serenade each other across the Bristol Channel. The island's nymph has a bird on her head, probably a puffin (*Lundy* in Norse means *puffin island*).

Michael Drayton died in 1631 a respected man even though the *Poly-Olbion* never achieved the popularity he had hoped for. Nevertheless, he was buried in Westminster Abbey with a suitable monument.

Size 245 x 320 mm.

Devon and Cornwall were printed together as the first map in the anthology. The map is without title, the names of the shires being engraved on the map as: **CORNWAL** and **DEVON SHYRE**.

1. 1612	*Poly-olbion* London. M Lownes, I Browne, I Helme and I Busbie. (1612).		**XXXIII**, S8, BL.
2. 1613	The number of the relevant text page has been added to the plate: Number **I** added (EaOS) and also just within the map itself.		
	Poly-Olbion or A Chorographicall Description of Tracts, Rivers, Mountaines, Forests, *and other Parts of this Renowned Isle of Great Britaine* London. M Lownes, I Browne, I Helme and I Busbie. 1613.		**XXXIV**, S9, BL.
	Poly-Olbion or A Chorographicall Description (in two parts) Part two has title-page: *The Second Part, or A Continuance of Poly-Olbion ...* Reissued with 12 additional maps; printed by Augustine Mathewes. London. Iohn Marriott, Iohn Grismand and Thomas Dewe. 1622.		**XXXV**, S13, BL.

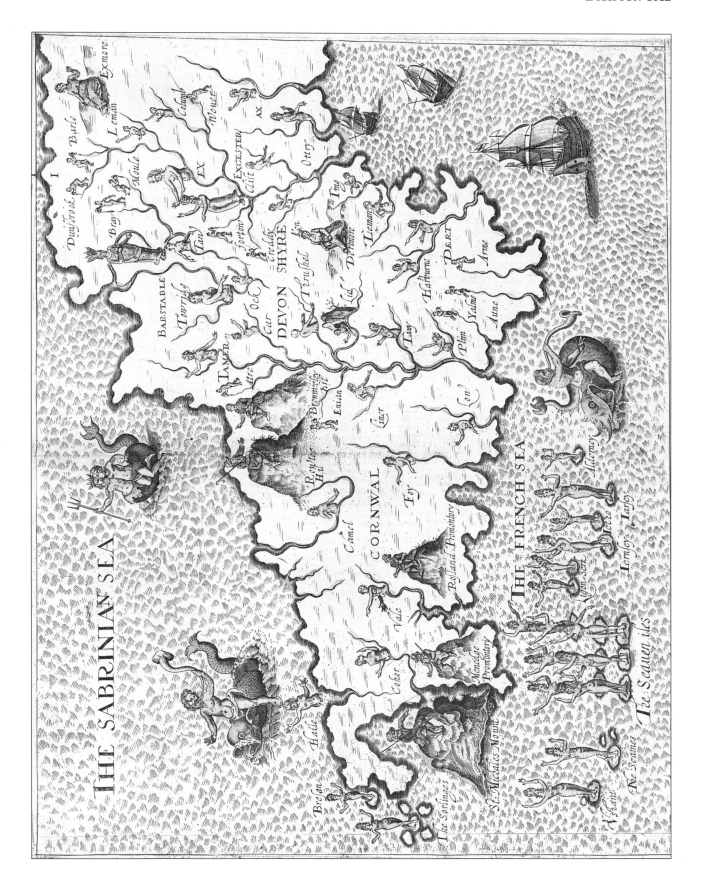

7.2 Drayton *Poly-Olbion*

8

JOHN BILL
1626

John Bill (*fl.*1591-1630), son of Walter Bill a husbandman of Wenlock in Shropshire, was a publisher and bookseller who worked in London from around 1590 until his death in 1630. He was apprenticed to John Norton (25th July 1592), three times Master of the Stationers Company, and admitted Freeman into the same company in 1601. Bill was a successful businessman and Latin scholar and was an acknowledged authority on stationery. He was commissioned by Sir Thomas Bodley to travel abroad and purchase books and he became a frequent visitor to the Frankfurt Book Fair. Thomas Bodley, founder of the Bodleian Library, Oxford, came from Devon. He was born in Exeter in 1544 and married Sarah Ball of Totnes on 19th July 1586.

Sometime before 1618 Robert Baker, the King's printer, sold his moiety of the business to Braham North and John Bill and this arrangement was confirmed by Royal Charter in 1627. Bill was succeeded by his son, also John Bill, when he died on 5th May 1630.

The only two publications with which he seems to have been associated, after establishing himself as a publisher in 1604, were the English text version of the Ortelius Atlas in 1606 (with John Norton) and *The Abridgement of Camden's Britania* in 1626. The county maps based indirectly on the surveys of Christopher Saxton, were the first English and Welsh county maps to show longitude based on Mercator's prime meridian (through the island of St. Michael's in the Azores). The map of Devon is clearly based on van den Keere's 1605 map (**4**); it is similar in size and simpler although a surprising number of places are named. Part of Cornwall and Part of Somersetshire are also named but no seas, which are the last to be drawn in the Flemish shotsilk technique. The northern coast is cut off near Ilfracombe where the map has been tilted to achieve north at the top. The engraver is not known.

On the reverse of each map is a description adapted from Camden of the county following. Each map faced its description and Devon has a text on Dorset on the reverse. Some pages of the book were printed more than once as there are typographic differences in a private collection to the text of other counties. In the copy held by the British Library Devon was printed upside-down.

Size 88 x 115 mm.   **A Scale of Miles** (10=17 mm).
                                                             Scale 1M=1.7 mm.

DEVON SHIRE. Latitude, longitude and compass directions just outside border.

1. 1626   *The abridgement of Camden's Britania With the Maps of the severall Shires of England and Wales*
                London. Iohn Bill. 1626.

                                             XLI, S15, BL, (E).

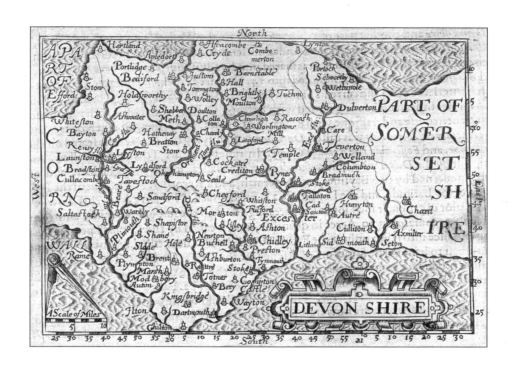

8.1 Bill *The abridgement of Camden's Britania*

MATTHEW SIMMONS
1635

A bookseller in 1635, Matthew Simmons (*fl.*1635-54) became a printer in 1641. He is notable as the publisher of John Milton's works and a popular news-sheet from 1649. His only cartographic work was *A Direction for the English Traviller*, the earliest English road book with maps. The book contained thumbnail maps copied from the set of playing cards issued in 1590 by Bowes (**2**) combined with triangular distance tables invented and published by John Norden in his *Intended Guyde for English Travailers* (1625). There are slight changes: some names are shortened, Ottery St Mary becomes Autre, one or two mileages are different and the compass direction is entered after the town name. The recorded distances use the Old English Mile of 2428 yards. Rivers form the main feature of the maps and towns were indicated only by initial letters. There were later editions on a larger scale from 1643 onwards by Thomas Jenner and John Garrett (**10**). Although he had sold the plates to Jenner by 1643, Simmons continued to print them. Later his wife, Mary Simmons, printed for Jenner and his son, Samuel, for Garrett.

An attractive roundel frontispiece map of Britain included in this work was signed by William Kip (and by H W as *Exc* - no doubt Hans Woutneel). This was probably engraved about 1602, the date of a companion roundel of the world used elsewhere. However, it is improbable that the map plates were engraved before 1625 when Norden's distance tables appeared. The maps are attributed to Jacob van Langeren, but the imprint of his name on the title page was worked over an earlier erasion. Jacob Florensz van Langeren must be the second of that name (grandson of the first). Although he came from a famous family of cartographers little is known of his life. He appears to have lived in Brussels. There is no record of him visiting Britain; but he is known to have been busy in 1636 – fighting against the French and Dutch![1] He produced other plates for Jenner between 1635 and 1640.

The map itself, measuring 40 x 35 mm, is an exact copy of the Bowes' map, although the letters are a little thicker, the rivers thinner, there are no hills and adjoining areas have been named. Some of the distance table spellings are interesting, eg Ockington for Okehampton is very unusual while Autre for Ottery is taken from Saxton.

Size 100 x 100 mm.	Scale bar (10=5.5 mm).
Map (triangle) area 75 x 75 mm.	Scale 1M=0.55 mm.

Deuonshire in triangular table of distances with Exeter to Chimley in top line and Axminster to Dartmouth on left hand side.

1.	1635	*A Direction for the English Traviller by Which he Shall be inabled to Coast about all England and Wales ... Are to be sold by Mathew Simons at the Golden Lion in Ducke laine, Ao.1635. Jacob van Langeren sculp.* London. Matthew Simmons. 1635.	**XLIV**, **S20**, BL.
2.	1636	Plate number added – **13** – badly engraved (CeOS). *A Direction for the English Traviller* London. Matthew Simmons. 1636.	**XLV**, **S21**, BL.
3.	1636	Mileages from London added. *A Direction for the English Traviller* London. Matthew Simmons. 1636.	**S22**, BL.

[1.] R A Skelton; *County Atlases of the British Isles*; Carta Press; 1970; p.64.

Deuonſhire.	Exeter.	Dartmouth	Kings-bridge	Plymouth	Taueſtoke	Heldeſworthy	Bydiforde	Barſtable	Moulton	Bampton	Collombton	Chegforde	Ockington	Hatherley	Chydley	Newtō Buſhell	Aſhburton	Totnes	Tyuerton	Bradninge	Autre	Hunyton	Ilfarcōbe	Culliton	Torrington	Chimley
AxminſterNW	20	40	43	50	44	46	42	38	30	20	14	31	35	36	24	28	33	36	18	15	11	7	42	5	39	30
ChimleyNW	16	35	35	33	23	17	12	10	8	15	16	15	10	8	20	23	24	29	13	16	21	24	17	28	9	159
TorringtōNW	24	40	40	43	23	10	5	8	11	22	25	20	14	8	27	30	29	33	21	25	30	32	14	36	159	
Cullitōn E	16	34	39	46	40	43	40	35	29	19	12	20	31	34	20	23	30	33	17	12	7	5	40	128		
IlfarcōbeNW	32	53	53	47	36	23	10	7	13	21	30	31	26	20	38	40	40	46	25	30	37	36	155			
HunytonNE	12	33	38	44	39	40	35	32	24	15	8	25	28	30	19	24	27	30	12	8	5	129				
Autre E	9	29	34	39	34	39	33	30	24	16	8	20	22	27	15	18	23	26	12	7	132					
BradningeNE	7	30	35	38	30	30	27	23	16	10	3	19	20	21	16	20	23	27	6	140						
Tyuerton N	11	35	38	40	31	39	23	19	12	6	5	20	20	20	20	24	26	30	139							
Totnes S	20	8	8	17	18	31	38	40	35	36	29	15	20	26	12	9	6	148								
AſhburtōSW	16	13	13	17	16	30	33	33	30	31	26	9	16	21	8	6	152									
NewtōBuſhelS	13	13	15	22	20	30	34	34	29	29	21	11	18	24	4	147										
Chidley S	8	16	20	15	21	29	31	30	26	25	17	10	16	20	142											
HatherleyNW	19	34	21	26	16	10	12	14	15	23	23	12	6	163												
OckingtōW	16	28	26	22	13	13	17	19	18	24	22	7	160													
ChegfordSW	12	21	21	20	14	20	24	24	21	21	20	157														
CollōbtonNE	9	33	37	40	34	33	27	23	16	9	134															
Bampton N	18	40	43	45	36	30	23	17	10	135																
MoultonNW	19	41	42	40	30	20	13	8	149																	
BarſtableNW	25	45	48	40	30	18	7	154																		
BydifordeNW	27	45	44	37	27	17	164																			
HeldeſworthyNW	29	39	36	27	17	174																				
TaueſtokeSW	25	15	20	10	128																					
PlymouthSW	32	22	15	179																						
Kings-bridgSW	28	8	167																							
DartmouthS	24	160																								

The ſeauere ſea. N.

Dorſetſhire Eaſt

Cornwall Weſt

ye Brittaiē ſea. S.

9.3 Simmons *A Direction for the English Traviller*

THOMAS JENNER
1643

Thomas Jenner (*fl.*1618-73) a print seller, publisher, puritan and parliamentarian is best known for two cartographic works; the reissue of Matthew Simmons' *A Direction for the English Traviller*, and a map of England and Wales known as the *Quartermaster's Map*. The first he issued in 1643, having reworked the plates used by Simmons (**9**) in 1635-36, the maps being redrawn at twice the original scale with place names shown in full; John Norden's distance table remains although the border and London mileage line were partly erased. The order in which the maps were revised makes it seem likely that these maps were issued to meet the demands of the armies in the Civil War. *A Direction for the English Traviller* is without text; loose maps of *A Book of the Names* can only be distinguished by the text listing the hundreds and parishes below the map and on the reverse.

Size 100 x 100 mm.	Scale bar (10=11 mm).
Map (triangle) area 75 x 75 mm.	Scale 1M=1.1 mm.

Deuonshire in triangular table of distances as Simmons (**9**). Border and London mileage line partly erased. Plate number (**13**) still just visible.

1. 1643   *A Direction for the English Traviller*
London. Thomas Jenner. 1643.   **XLVI, S25**, BL, RGS, B, W, (E).

A *Booke of the Names of all the Hundreds contained in the Shires of the Kingdom of England ...*
Usefull for Quartermasters, Brief-Gatherers ...
Only one copy known. List of Hundreds precedes the map.
London. Thomas Jenner. 164(4).   **S26**, CB.

2. 1657   **Devon-shire.** (CaOS) and the page number **37** (EaOS) are printed above the map. List of towns below and on reverse. Spellings **Bag-point** and **S Annes Chappel, Bra.**

A Book of the Names of all Parishes
London. Thomas Jenner. 1657.   **XLIX, S62**, BL, RGS, B.

Minor map reworking. Text reset: spellings **Bap-point** and **S Annes Chappel, Bra.**

A Book of the Names of all Parishes
London. Thomas Jenner. 1662.   **L, S70**, BL, RGS.

3. 1668   Title is wrongly reproduced **Devonstire** on both pages 37 and 39.
Text spellings **Bag-point** and **S Annes Chappel, brant.**

A Book of the Names of all Parishes
London. Thomas Jenner. 1668, 1668.   **S87**, W; **LI, S88**, BL.

A Book of the Names of all Parishes
London. John Garrett. 1677.   **LII, S98**, BL, RGS.

Text lists deleted.

A Direction for the English Traviller
London. John Garrett. (1677).   **XLVII, S99**, B.

A Direction for the English Traviller
London. John Garrett. (1680).   **XLVIII, S101**, BL.

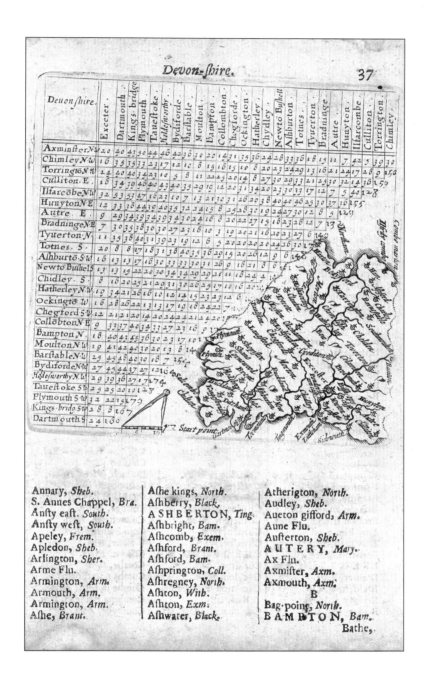

Annary, *Sheb.*
S. Annes Chappel, *Bra.*
Ansty east. *South.*
Ansty west, *South.*
Apeley, *Frem.*
Apledon, *Sheb.*
Arlington, *Sher.*
Arme Flu.
Armington, *Arm.*
Armouth, *Arm.*
Armington, *Arm.*
Ashe, *Brant.*

Ashe kings, *North.*
Ashberry, *Black.*
ASHBERTON, *Ting.*
Ashbright, *Bam.*
Ashcomb, *Exem.*
Ashford, *Brant.*
Ashford, *Bam.*
Ashprington, *Coll.*
Ashregney, *North.*
Ashton, *With.*
Ashton, *Exm.*
Ashwater, *Black.*

Atherigton, *North.*
Audley, *Sheb.*
Aueton gifford, *Arm.*
Aune Flu.
Austerton, *Sheb.*
AUTERY, *Mary.*
Ax Flu.
Axmister, *Axm.*
Axmouth, *Axm.*
B
Bag-poing, *North.*
BAMPTON, *Bam.*
Bathe,

10.2 Jenner *A Book of the Names of all Parishes*

11

JAN JANSSON
1644

Jan Jansson the Elder was a publisher in Arnhem who produced the new *Atlas Minor* in 1607 in conjunction with Jodocus Hondius. This association introduced the Janssons to the Mercator/Hondius family and the younger Jan married Hondius' daughter in 1612. Gerard Mercator (1512-94) was the leading Dutch cartographer in the latter half of the century. He formulated his own map projection and was the first to use the term *Atlas* for a collection of maps.

Jodocus Hondius (1563-1611), a master engraver, acquired the Mercator business in 1606 and produced the second edition of the Mercator Atlas in 1607. His sons, Henry (1587-1638) and Jodocus (1594-1629) were also first-class engravers and continued updating and reissuing the atlas. Jodocus, like Mercator, had once been a religious refugee in London and there he most likely met John Speed for whom he engraved a series of county maps (**6**).

Jan Jansson (1588-1664) joined the firm in 1633. The first English edition of the Hondius/Mercator *Atlas* came out in 1636 and in the German edition of the same year the first British county maps appeared. In the Dutch Appendix of 1644 further county maps were introduced including Devon. The fourth volume of the *Novus Atlas*, containing the full set of the British maps, appeared in 1646.

Jansson was now the sole owner and, like his great rival Blaeu (**12**), determined to produce a full atlas of the world. The *Atlas* continued to expand and was finally completed in a 9- or 11-volume edition. The two great Dutch atlases appeared almost simultaneously and have much in common, especially their derivation from Speed; it is sometimes suggested that Jansson copied Blaeu. Apart from the imprint difference, Jansson used flamboyant lettering, as did Mercator, and had two scales.

After Jansson's death his son-in-law, Johannes van Waesberghe, carried on the business. When he died the plates were sold at auction. Peter Schenk and Gerard Valk acquired the British plates and sold individual maps. They then sold the plates or, more likely, quantities of maps to Henry Overton, Carol Allard and John Seller who included the maps in their collections.

Size 380 x 490 mm.   **Milliaria Anglica** (12=78 mm) and
Plate 3   **Milliaria Germanica communia** (3=78 mm).
                                                          Scale 1M=6.5 mm.

DEVONIAE DESCRIPTIO. The DESCRIPTION of DEVON-SHIRE with imprint: **Amstelodami Apud Ioannem Ianßonium**. Dutch text on reverse: **HET GRAEF SCHAP DEVONIA OF DEVONSHIRE.** No shields covering area of Cornwall.

1. **1644**   *Des Nieuwen Atlantis Aenhang*
             Amsterdam. Jan Jansson. 1644.   **KM Me75a**, [Haarlem], (FB), (MW[1]).

2. **1646**   Eight coats of arms added in the area of Cornwall (Aa-Ad).

             Novus Atlas Sive Theatrum Orbis Terrarum- Vol. IV Great Britain
             Latin text I of Camden's *Britannia* on reverse ends with word **quinde**.
             Amsterdam. Jan Jansson. 1646.   **LXX**, **S34**, BL, C, (DEI), (NDL).

             Le Nouvel Atlas ou Theatre du Monde (French text)   (E).
             Amsterdam. Jan Jansson. 1646, 1647, 1656.

                                                  S35; **LXXII**, **S39**, BL, W; **S61**, BCL.

             Novus Atlas Oder Welt-Beschreibung (German text)
             Amsterdam. Jan Jansson. 1647, 1649, 1652, 1647 (1658).
                        S40, [Hunt.]; **LXXIV**, **S46**, BL; **LXXIII**, **S53**, BL, NMM; **S63**.

[1.] Illustration courtesy of Malcolm Woodward.

2. cont.   *Nieuwen Atlas, ofte Werelt-Beschrijvinghe* (Dutch text)
Amsterdam. Jan Jansson. 1647, 1649, 1652, 1653, 1659.
S41 [BvF]; **S47** [Hunt.]; **LXXVI, S54**, Adm.; **S56** [BRdB]; **S67** [Lib. Cong.].

Novus Atlas Absolutissimus. Das ist Generale Welt-Beschreibung
German text. Page 175, Sign Fff.
Amsterdam. Jan Jansson. 1647 (1659).
S68, NMM.

3. 1652   **Lunday** added (Ab). Hartland Hundred and Launston corrected. No text.

Novus Atlas Sive Theatrum Orbis Terrarum Tomus quartus
Amsterdam. Jan Jansson. 1652.
LXXV, S52, C^1, (E^2).

Novus Atlas Sive Theatrum Orbis Terrarum Tomus quartus
Latin text II. Last word on page 134 is **quin**.
Amsterdam. Jan Jansson. 1659.
LXXVII, S66, BL, B, RGS, (E), (DEI).

Guilielmi Cambdeni Brittannia Magna Illustrata
Latin text II. One copy known.
Amsterdam. Jan Jansson. (1659).
CB.

Overton Atlas II[3]
London. John Overton. (1675).
S91, CB.

Atlas Major
Amsterdam. Carol Allard. (1705).
LXXX, H130, BL.

4. 1714   Imprint now **Amstelodami Apud P. SCHENK et G. VALK.** Exeter as street plan.
Graticule added with latitude and longitude noted. Plate number **3** (Ee). No text.

Nieuwe Atlas
Amsterdam. Johannes Covens & Cornelius Mortier. (1707-41).
KM C&M10.

Atlas Anglois Ou Description Generale De L'Angleterre
London. D Mortier. 1714, 1715.
H131, W; **H132** [P[4]].

Nova Totius Geographica Telluris Projecto
Amsterdam. Gerard Valk. (1717).
[Sold at Sotheby's 13.4.1989.].

Composite atlas with no title page.
CB.

5. 1715   Map is not numbered.

Atlas Anglois part of *Nouveau theatre de la Grande-Bretagne*
The atlas contains a Supplement published by J Groenewegen & N Prevost dated 1728.
London. D Mortier. 1715 (1728).
KM Val2, H133, [Lib. Cong.].
London. Joseph Smith. 1724 (1728).
LXXXI, H134, BL.

[1.] Skelton descibes a 1652 atlas (**S52**) with no text: the date could be a misprint for 1656 but Part II is dated 1662.
[2.] Exeter copy above may be from Allard, *c.*1705.
[3.] Overton Atlas I had Bleau's map (**12**), later Overton atlases used the copy (**18**).
[4.] Atlas formerly belonging to Dr. Eric Gardner, present whereabouts unknown.

12

JOAN BLAEU
1645

The Blaeu family were probably the finest of all the Dutch cartographical publishers and their *Atlas Major* is still regarded as the finest of the age. Willem Blaeu (1571-1638) was a globe and instrument maker and founded the business in Amsterdam in 1599. He was trained in astronomy and the sciences by Tycho Brahe, the celebrated Danish astronomer. At first he published single maps and his 20-sheet world map is highly acclaimed. Until 1617 he often signed his works Guilielmus Janssonius or Willems Jans Zoon, his patronymic name, but after that time he seems to have decided on Guilielmus or G. Blaeu. By 1628 he had produced maps and works covering the whole field, hydrographical, topographical and celestial.

In 1630 he acquired 37 plates of the Mercator Atlas from Jodocus Hondius II to add to his own collection and with the publication of his *Appendix* Blaeu began his lifetime's work: a major atlas intended to include the most up-to-date maps of the whole of the known world. Five years later the first two volumes of the *Atlas Novus* or *Theatrum Orbis Terrarum* were published. He was very interested in quality and production and introduced the new press with a sliding bed, enabling the printer to see more easily what he was doing. Highly successful and well appreciated in Holland he was appointed Hydrographer to the East India Company in 1633. When he died his two sons succeeded to the business. However, Cornelis died in 1642 and it was Joan (or Jan, but signed himself Iohannem) Blaeu who produced the fourth volume, containing the British county maps, in 1645.

The *Atlas Novus* was finally completed in 1655 with the sixth and final volume. No sooner was it published than Joan commenced his masterpiece, the *Atlas Major*, and in 1662 all eleven volumes were finally complete containing some 600 maps and 3000 pages of text.

In February 1672 a disastrous fire destroyed Blaeu's printing house in the Gravenstraat and the Devon plate with many others was lost. A year afterwards Joan Blaeu died. The firm's surviving stocks of plates and maps were gradually dispersed, some of the plates being bought by Frederic de Wit and Schenk and Valk before final closure in about 1695. Large stocks of printed maps enabled collections to be put together, eg John Overton's Overton Atlas I of 1670 and an atlas of the Royal Geographical Society both contain Blaeu's Devon.

The map of Devon is based on Speed with many of the tribal names added in 1623. Like Jan Jansson (compare **11**) the maps do not show roads, nor the inset of Exeter but the coats of arms are present. Both Devon maps are very similar as far as detail is concerned. However, Blaeu's map is neater and more delicately engraved. The sea areas are often illustrated by Jansson (Devon has boats and fish) but not by Blaeu. Jansson, who is often accused of copying from Blaeu, is more flamboyant in his lettering (compare for example surrounding county names and sea areas). On the reverse of each map (except the Overton) is a text taken from William Camden's *Britannia.*

Size 390 x 490 mm.
Plate 4

Milliaria Anglica ... (8=50 mm).
Scale 1M=6.4 mm.

DEVONIA vulgo DEVON-SHIRE.

1. 1645   *Guil. et Ioannis Blaeu Theatrum Orbis Terrarum, sive Atlas Novus* - Part IV
         Latin text: Page 116, Sign Gg.
         Amsterdam. Joan Blaeu. 1645, 1646.   **LIX, S28, BL; S30.**

1. cont.

Le Theatre du Monde ou Nouvel Atlas
French text: Page 105, Sign Dd.
Amsterdam. Joan Blaeu. 1645, 1646, 1648. **S29**, LS, B; **S31**, [LUL]; **S43**, BL.

Novus Atlas, Das ist Welt-beschreibung
German text: Page 113, Sign Gg.
Amsterdam. Joan Blaeu. 1645 (1646), 1646, 1648. **S32**; **S33**; **S44**, W.

Toonneel des Aerdrycks, oft Nieuwe Atlas
Dutch text. Page 105, Gg (last page of Cornwall, first of Devon).
Amsterdam. Joan Blaeu. 1646 (1647). **KM B142A**, **S38**, CB.

Theatrum Orbis Terrarum sive Atlas Novus
Second Latin text: Page 95, Sign Dd.
Amsterdam. Joan Blaeu. 1648. **LXII**, **S42**, BL, B, ¢, W.

Vierde Stuck der Aerdrycks-beschryving ... Engelandt (E).
Dutch text reset: Page 91, Sign Cc.
Amsterdam. Joan Blaeu. 1648, 1648 (1664).

LXI, **S45**, BL; **LXV**, **S77**, BL, ¢.

Nuevo Atlas del Reyno de Ingalaterra (E).
Spanish text: Page 105, Sign (page 104) Cg. Most of the second edition (1662 – *Inglaterra*) had a
French text with Spanish text pasted over.
Amsterdam. Joan Blaeu. 1659, 1662. **S64**, W; **LXVII**, **S73**, BL, ¢.

Geographiae Blavianae, Volumen Quintum, quo Anglia (typographic title-page)
Latin text and engraved title-page *Anglia, quae est Europae liber XL.*
Amsterdam. Joan Blaeu. 1662.

LXIII, **S71**, BL, C, NMM, (DEI).

Cinquiéme Volume de la Geographie Blavianae, Contenant l'Angleterre (E).
French text: Page 81, Sign Z. Latin verses translated into poetry.
Engraved second title page *Angleterre, qui est le XI. livre de L'Europe.*
Amsterdam. Joan Blaeu. 1662, 1663.

LXIV, **S72** B, ¢; **S75**, BL, NMM.

Cinquiéme Volume de la Geographie Blavianae, Contenant l'Angleterre
Engraved title page *Angleterre, qui est le xl. livre de L'Europe* dated 1662.
Amsterdam. Joan Blaeu. 1667. **LXVI**, **S84**, BL, BCL.

Overton Atlas I – Collection of maps
London. J Overton. (1670). **S89**, Adm.

13

PIETER VAN DEN KEERE
1648

In 1628 Jan Jansson had a series of new miniature plates engraved – some by Abraham Goos, others by Pieter van den Keere – for his *Atlas Minor*. These new plates with 17 British regional maps, otherwise similar to those of Jodocus Hondius, were then printed in subsequent editions of Jansson's *Atlas Minor* from 1628 to 1651. In the German edition of 1648[1] eight maps of English counties were added. These maps, all copying John Speed (pre-1623), were from plates by van den Keere who had already produced one series of miniature county maps (**4**). Pieter van den Keere died *c.*1646 so the maps must have been engraved some time before publication.

Pieter van der Aa (1659-1733) acquired the plates and printed from these for his *Nouveau Petit Atlas* published in Leyden in 1712. Judging by the obvious erasures from the plate another elaborate title must have been engraved, on an as yet unidentified state, sometime between 1651 and 1712. One can also see some of the old cursive script (the *OF* of Part of Somerset).

A Dutchman from Leyden, van der Aa produced a number of world atlases, some in several volumes, in the first half of the eighteenth century. The maps relating to the British counties were published in the fourth section of the *Petit Atlas*. The twenty-six maps in this section, which is devoted to Great Britain and Ireland, also include maps of the Irish counties, northern and southern Scotland, each country on its own as well as one map of the whole British Isles. Maps printed from these plates were being sold as late as 1738 by Covens and Mortier and later by another Amsterdam publisher Gerrit Tielenberg although a map of Devon has not been found.

Size 155 x 202 mm.   **Milliaria Anglica** (12=32 mm).
                                                        Scale 1M=2.6 mm.

DEVONIAE DESCRIPTIO.   Signature: **Petrus Kaerius Caelavit.**

1. 1648   **VON ENGELANDT** above the top border centrally 600 mm in length and page number **35** (EaOS). Reverse, page 36, has German text from Camden.

Atlas minor Gerardi Mercatoris
Amsterdam. J Jansson. 1648.   **KM Me203**, [NYPL].

2. 1651   Length of title **VON ENGELANDT** increased to 800 mm.

Atlas minor Gerardi Mercatoris
Amsterdam. J Jansson. 1651.   **KM Me204**, BL.

3. 1712   Title is erased and replaced by **Comté de Devon** in elaborated half-panel (Ee). Scale is altered to **Lieues d'Angleterre** in small panel (Ea). The border has the inner line graduated, longitude reading from West – 26°30 to 29°20. The names of the adjoining areas are now in Roman script and in French.

L'Atlas Soulagé de son gros et pesant fardeau Part IV
Leyden. P van der Aa. 1712.   **KM Aa5**, [Leyden], (DEI).

4. 1729   The map has an engraved frame around with imprint **A Leide, Chez Pierre vander Aa Avec Privilege.** Total size 230 x 395 mm.

La Galérie Agréable Du Monde Vol.10, No.17
Map is unnumbered in BL copy but number 30, numbered 17 by Koeman.
Leyden. P van der Aa. 1729.   **KM Aa9**, BL.

---

[1] The authors are grateful to Raymond Frostick for information relating to these maps.

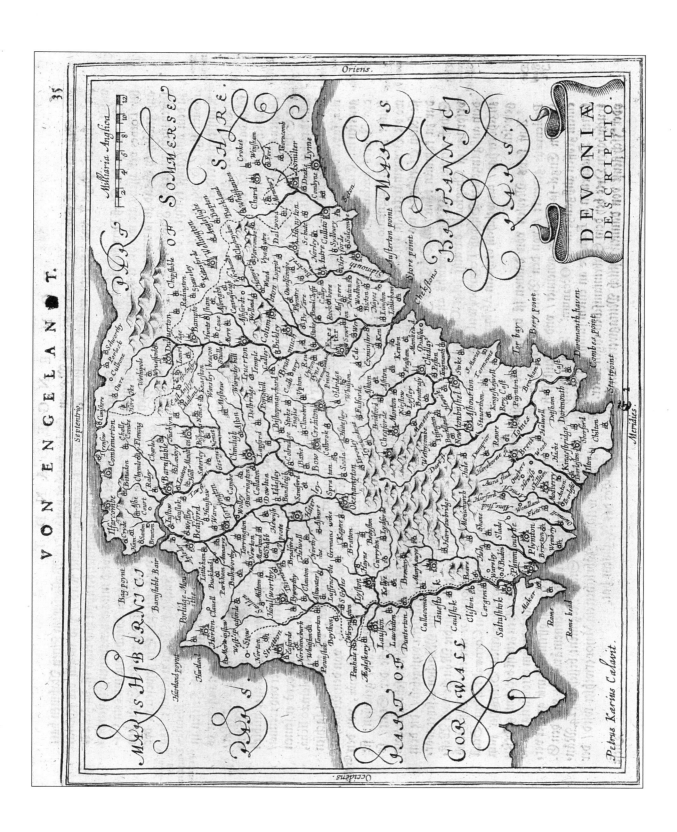

13.2 v. den Keere *Atlas minor Gerardi Mercatoris*

14

RICHARD BLOME
1673

Heraldic writer and cartographer, often financing his publications by subscriptions, Richard Blome (1641-1705) flourished in the latter half of the seventeenth century. He was a prolific, but not an original worker and was frequently accused of plagiarism. Bishop Nicholson in 1696 complained *A most entire piece of theft out of Camden and Speed*; a rather unfair criticism as all contemporary map publishers had made use of one or the other. Quality is another matter and the maps are considerably poorer than the maps of Blaeu and Jansson. Although, according to one modern writer *His maps were attractive and quaintly designed and they still retain their charm*[1] this is not a view shared by all. *The maps were of indifferent quality and their popularity with present-day collectors is hard to understand. ... poor in execution with crude lettering and ornamentation*[2].

The *Britannia* was originally intended to be one in a series of four volumes, the first two being a translation of Bernhard Varenius' *Geographia Generalis* with 100 maps, and *A Geographical Description of the Four Parts of the World*. The third volume was the English Atlas. A fourth volume of sea charts was probably shelved with the announcement of John Seller's forthcoming work on the same lines.[3]

The maps of the *Britannia*, arranged in alphabetical order, are closely copied from Speed (in later states) reduced to roughly two-thirds the scale but reproducing virtually all names and symbols. The titles, in elaborate cartouches, are followed by Blome's name, generally with the addition *by His Matys Especiall Command* as in Devon. Each has, also within a florid cartouche, the coat-of-arms of the person to whom it is dedicated. Devon was dedicated to John Greville, Earl of Bath, the Lord Lieutenant of Devon and Cornwall.

The maps were printed by Thomas Roycroft but only six maps were signed, including two (Scotland and Ireland) by Richard Palmer, who engraved the later map of Devonshire (**17**). Other maps were engraved by Wenceslas Hollar and Francis Lamb. This first series of county maps (folio, 50 maps) was not a success; it was followed by an issue of smaller maps entitled *Speed's Maps Epitomiz'd* (**17**). These are embellished, like those in *Britannia,* with dedications to county dignitaries, often the same person, which were amended or sometimes erased in later editions.

Skelton[4] lists one atlas in a private collection printed for John Wright in 1677, but as he points out this was probably made up of remainder sheets and only a very limited number of copies would have been issued.

Size 255 x 310 mm.

A Scale of 10 Miles (10=43 mm).
Scale 1M=4.3 mm.

A MAPP of DEVON SHIRE With its Hundreds. Imprint: **by Ric: Blome by His Ma^tys Especiall Command**. Dedication: **To the Rt Honble Iohn Earle of Bath**.

1. 1673   *Britannia: or, A Geographical Description of the Kingdoms of England, Scotland and Ireland*
London. Richard Blome. 1673.

XCIX, S90, BL, B, (E), (DEI).

[1]. Moreland and Bannister, *Antique Maps*, Phaidon: 1986 (89).

[2]. A G Hodgkiss; *Discovering Antique Maps*, Shire Publications; 1977 (88).

[3]. R A Skelton; *County Atlases of the British Isles*, Carta Press; 1970; p.140.

[4]. R A Skelton; *ibid*; p.156-**S100**.

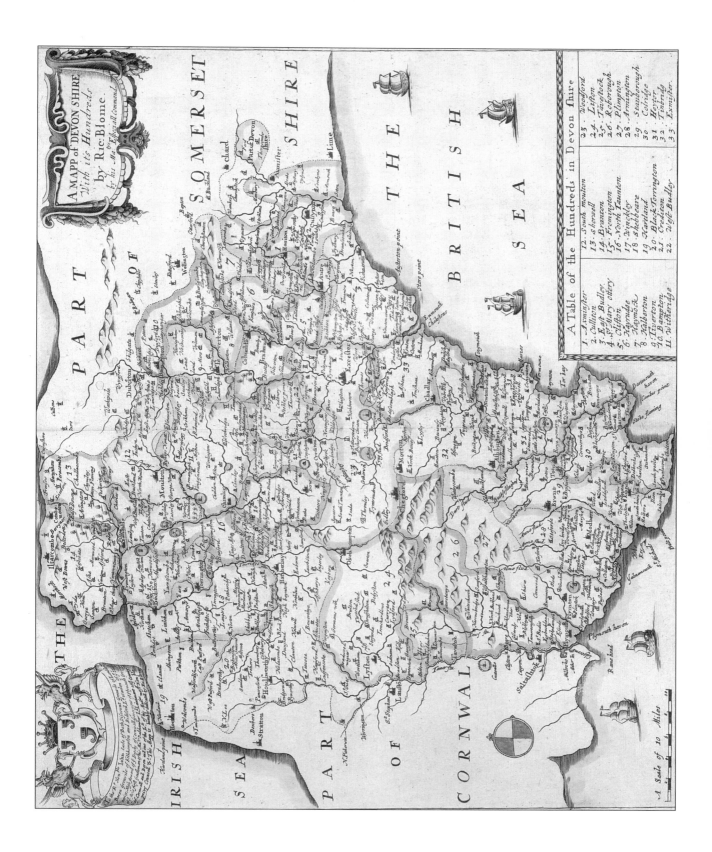

14.1 Blome *Britannia*

15

ROBERT MORDEN
1676

Some 80 years after the first appearance of maps on playing cards (see Bowes **2, 3**) both Robert Morden and William Redmayne (**16**) produced packs of cards of English and Welsh counties with Morden's being advertised in the Easter Term Catalogue of 1676 as *The 52 Countries of England and Wales* (sic).

There were 54 cards in Morden's set with the description and title on the first and a general map on the second. The Northern counties are represented by Clubs, Eastern counties by Hearts, Southern counties by Diamonds and the Welsh counties by Spades. All the Kings were portraits of King Charles II in a circle and each Queen was a head of Catherine of Braganza. The suit marks, when desired, were stencilled on by hand. This was the first Devon map to give an indication of the roads, ostensibly taken from John Ogilby's strip road maps of 1675; however, the main road from Exeter to Plymouth bypasses Chudleigh and the road Exeter-Torrington is not in Ogilby. As spellings vary considerably several engravers may have been employed.

The maps are either found as playing card sets or bound with the cards mounted in a pocket atlas duodecimo, preceded by a title page bearing the title from type. The last known 17th-century edition of Morden's cards appeared in 1680, only four years after their first appearance. Copies of these cards by John Lenthall appeared in 1711 (**23**). The original maps reappeared post-1772 without suitmarks but with a page of accompanying text giving county history, topography and other relevant information, printed for H Turpin, 104 St John's Street, West Smithfield. Homan Turpin was in business at this address 1764-87; the publication is not listed in his catalogues of 1770 and 1772. The first state was issued in facsimile edition by Harry Margary of Lympne Castle in 1972. Morden also produced two atlases of county maps (**21, 22**).

Size of card 90 x 55 mm.	**Miles** (10 =10 mm).
Map panel 58 x 55 mm.	Scale 1M=1 mm.

Devon Sh: and **IX** and a red diamond stencilled in top panel. Arabic **9** is added left, obscured by stencil. Neighbouring counties not named. Towns shown by circles.

1.	1676	*The 52 Counties of England and Wales* London. Robert Morden, Will Berry, Robert Green and George Minikin. 1676.	S94, M&K3, BL, W, GL.
		Mounted and bound as an atlas without suit marks.	S94a, M&K3, W.
2.	1676	**Pt. of Cornwall** and **Pt. of Som** added.	
		The 52 Counties of England and Wales Second Edition London. Morden, Berry, Green and Minikin. 1676.	S95, M&K3, BL.
3.	1680	Additions, eg **Sheepwash, Dodbrook** and **Topsham**. Horton altered to **Hartland**. Towns are shown with church-like signs.	
		The 52 Counties of England and Wales Third Edition With stencilled suitmarks bound in volume. London. Morden, Berry, Green and Minikin. (1680).	S102, M&K3, [Gard.].
		A Pocket Book of all the Counties of England and Wales Without suitmarks in book form – (8vo) maps mounted two to a page London. Robert Morden and Joseph Pask. (1680).	CVIII, S103, M&K3, BL.
		A Brief Description of England and Wales London. H Turpin. (1773).	CIX, M&K3, BL, W.

15.2 Morden a playing card (left)
15.3 Morden *A Brief Description of England and Wales* (right)

16

WILLIAM REDMAYNE
1676

In the same year as Robert Morden (**15**) produced his pack of playing cards William Redmayne advertised a pack of cards in the Trinity Term catalogue. Although presumably in competition with Morden the cards do not bear comparison with either Morden's, or even with W Bowes' cards from the turn of the century (**2, 3**).

The maps in this set are very small and distorted, and have neither compass indicator nor scale. They have an indifferent text above and below the crudely engraved map. On the face of each map the suit mark is engraved in outline and was then filled in by hand; the value is engraved on the right. The arrangement of suits is different to that of Morden and court cards have a regal figure beside the map. The cards were reprinted in 1677 when red was represented by engraved vertical bars and black by cross-hatching. The names of the editions below come from the Term Catalogue (states 1 and 2) and magazine advertising (state 3).

John Lenthall specialised in playing cards and from 1711 to 1734 regularly advertised his collections. These included in January 1716/17 the modified Redmayne set and this date has been adopted here. He also offered another set of county map cards, copied from the Morden cards of 1676, for sale (**23**).

According to Mann and Kingsley[1] there were three different stamps used on cards during the period 1711-1717 including two 6d tax stamps. On the evidence of these and the corresponding stamp on the King of Spades they suggest the third state might have appeared as early as 1711.

Size of card 91 x 55 mm.   Scale 1M=1 mm.
Map panel 30 x 55 mm.

DEVON - SHIRE at top of card. **VII** with suit mark, Clubs, superimposed on map.

1. 1676	*Recreative pastime by Card play* London. W Redmayne, H Mortlock, R Turner, H Cox, and B Billingsley. 1676.	
		S96, M&K4, BL[2], W, CB.

2. 1677	The suit mark is engraved with cross-hatching. Cards are known with and without stencilling over the suitmark.	
	Geographical, Chronological and Historiographical Cards of England and Wales The suit mark (clubs) is engraved with cross-hatching. London. W Redmayne. (1677).	**S97, M&K4**, CB.

3. 1717	A narrow foliated border has been engraved in place of the previous border.	
	Historiographical Cards London. J Lenthall. (1717).	**M&K4, H146**, [GL].

---

[1] Mann and Kingsley, PLAYING CARDS: *The `Map Collectors's Circle*, No.87. 1972; pp.18-19.
[2] Illustration courtesy of the British Library.

DEVON – SHIRE.

Is bounded on the W.st with the River
Tamar, on the S.th the Ocean, on the E.st
Dorsetshire, and Somerset shire, and
on the N.th the Bay of Severn,

Excetter

VII

It's Rich in Mines, pleasant medows,
divers woods, Excetter is the chief
Citty,
Sr Francis Drake was borne in this shire,
the most excelent for Navigtion of his
time, In it are 394. Parishes and
many Rivers,

16.1 Redmayne a playing card

17

RICHARD BLOME
1681

Richard Blome's first series of county maps (**14**) was followed in 1681 by an issue of smaller maps, *Speed's Maps Epitomiz'd*, engraved by Wenceslas Hollar and Richard Palmer, who signed six of the maps including the map of Devon. Most of these maps were engraved at about the same time as the maps for *Britannia* and many have imprints with earlier dates (eleven maps are dated either 1667 or 1671). Devon may have been available as a single sheet as early as 1668. Evidence of an earlier version shows in the poor erasions of a first dedication. As in *Britannia* each map was dedicated to a county dignitary, this often being amended or erased in later editions. Obviously Blome had erased the dedication before the first printing; but a map of Devon in an earlier form is not known.

William Oldys[1] wrote a translation of *Britannia* in 1735, printed and published by R Penny. This appeared in four volumes and was unfinished. Only the first and fourth volumes have a title page: Volume I is undated but Volume IV is dated 1735. Cornwall and Devon are the first two counties in the work and are the only ones to have the map.

Size 187 x 235 mm. **Acale of 10 Miles** (32 mm).
Scale 1M=3.2 mm.

A MAPP of DEVON SHIRE With its Hundreds. Signature: **R:P. Sculp**. Signs of badly erased shields and cropped names, eg (Bag p)**eynt** and (Cre)**die Baye** (Aa).

1. (**1681**)	Loose sheet, probably a proof. Paper size 210 x 340 mm – map unfolded.		(KB).
2. 1681	Dedication **To ... Sr William Courtenay** (Aa).		
			(E).
	Speed's Maps Epitomiz'd London. R Blome. 1681.		**CX, S104**, BL.
	Speed's Maps Epitomiz'd London. Sam Lownes. 1685.		**S105**, W.
3. 1693	Dedication removed, **St Georges Channel** and **Hartland Poynt** added where dedication was and cropped names now written in full.		
	Cosmography and Geography (3rd impression) London. Richard Blome. 1693.		**S114**, W, C, (E), (TQ).
4. 1715	Plate number, **11**, above title (Ea). An issue folded three times *to fit the pocket*.		
	England Exactly Described ... Printed Coloured and Sold by Tho: Taylor London. Thomas Taylor. 1715.		**CXXXVI, H139**, BL, RGS, W, C, B.
5. 1717	Roads added. Distances between towns added in circles.		
			(DEI).
	England Exactly Described ... London. Thomas Taylor. 1717.		**CXXXVIa, H140**, BL, W, RGS, BCL.
	England Exactly Described ... Printed Coloured and Sold by Tho: Bakewell London. Thomas Bakewell. 1731.		**CXXXVIb/c, H141**, BL, W, C.
	Britannia ... by William Cambden ... translated into English by W. O. Esq. London. R Penny. (1735).		**H141**, B.

[1.] Donald Hodson; *County Atlases of the British Isles Vol I*, Bracken Press; p.55.

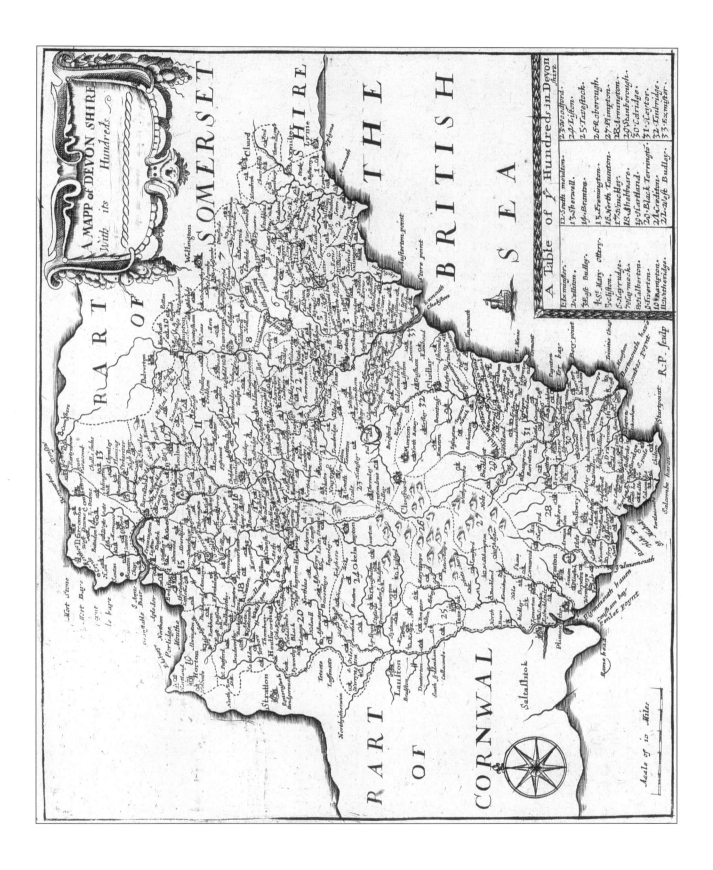

17.1 Blome proof state

18

OVERTON/ (Jansson)
1685

John Overton (1640-1713) and his son, Henry, produced a number of atlases and maps from 1665 to *c.*1755. They never possessed a complete set of county map plates and made up their atlases in the early Dutch tradition by using the prints of other publishers, notably the maps of Blaeu and Jansson. Only when these were not available did they arrange for a plate of their own to be produced.

Overton's Atlas I (*c.*1670) included Blaeu's *Devoniae* and Atlas II (*c.*1675) Jansson's *Devon-Shire*. Both collections were largely made up from sheets bought from Peter Stent's estate in late 1665 after he died in the plague. Probably because there were too few copies of some counties, John Overton had new plates of five counties engraved between 1666 and 1685: Berkshire, Somerset and Sussex were all copied from Speed while Devon and Wiltshire were from Jansson. Devon was a very close copy of Jansson 1652 edition (**11.3**) complete with coats of arms, including Lunday (sic), and even to the extent of reproducing the Jansson imprint. The Overton copy may be identified by the absence of the hyphen in the title 'DEVON-SHIRE' which appears in the Jansson original. The other obvious changes are the misspelling HEYTON for HEYTOR, TORRTNGTON for TORRINGTON and Part of Dersetshire (sic) added in Dorset.

In 1707 John Overton sold his stock to his son, Henry, who revised only the map of Devon for the 1713 issue, replacing the Jansson imprint with his own. This version appeared in Overton VI.

The engraver is unknown but the revised imprint is believed to be the work of Sutton Nicholls. He was employed by Overton in 1711-12 and engraved at least five maps for him. He was later employed by Robert Morden engraving maps for Camden's *Britannia* and one map for the *New Description* (**22**).

John Overton acquired the Speed plates from Christopher Browne before 1700 and after 1716 the Overtons produced Speed collections as well.

On Overton's death in 1751 he left the stock to his nephew, also Henry. But in 1754 W and C Dicey had purchased the Overton plates and although they inserted their own imprint on the Speed map (**6.10**) there was no further change to the Overton Devon, if it was ever reprinted.

Size 380 x 490 mm.

Milliaria Anglica (12=78 mm) and
Milliaria Germanica communia (3=78 mm).
Scale 1M=6.5 mm.

DEVONIAE DESCRIPTIO. The DESCRIPTION of DEVON SHIRE with imprint: **Amstelodami Apud Ioannem Iaßonium**.

1.	**1685**	Overton Atlas III London. John Overton. (1685).	S107, [Adm.].
		Overton Atlas IV London. John Overton. (1690).	**S111**, BL.
		Overton Atlas V London. John Overton. (1700).	**S121**, CB.
2.	**1713**	Roads added. Imprint changed to: **Printed and Sold by Henry Overton at the white Horse without Newgate LONDON: 1713.**	
		England Fully Described (title on Whitaker atlas) – Overton Atlas VI London. Henry Overton. 1713 (post-1716).	**H142**, BL, RGS, W.
		Atlas with no title page London. Henry Overton. (1716).	CB.

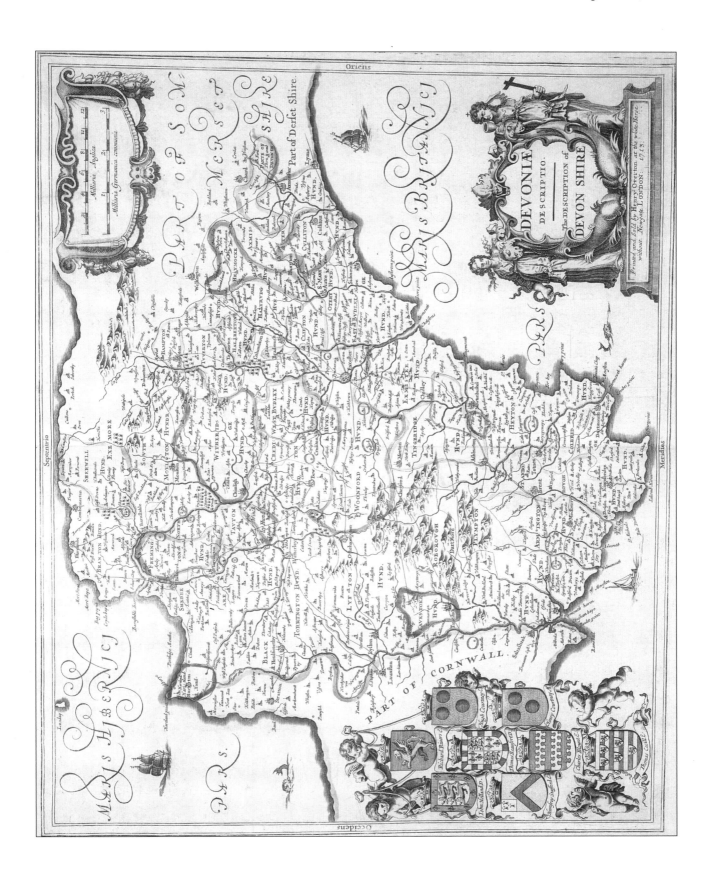

18.2 Overton *England Fully Described* (Overton Atlas VI)

19

LAMB/LEA/(Saxton)
1689

Philip Lea (*d*.1700), publisher and instrument maker, worked with many leading cartographers including Morden and Moll. He acquired Christopher Saxton's plates some time after 1665 (later than the Web issue, **1.3**) and republished the famous Wall Map in 1687. Although Lea obtained most of the Saxton county plates, Devonshire and Northumberland were missing. Possibly casualties of the Great Fire it seems strange that only two plates were lost or damaged. Whatever the reason, Lea had these two plates replaced by new ones. Devon was signed by Francis Lamb and was a copy of Saxton but with much additional information included from other sources, such as the coats of arms including that of William Cavendish, hundreds, markets and Exeter inset which matched the changes that Lea had carried out to his other Saxton maps. Other changes were the erasure of the Royal and Seckford Arms; erasure of decorative details; and reengraving of titles and scales.
Lamb (*fl.*1670-1700) engraved maps for Petty's *Geographical Description* for Seller and charts for Greenville Collins. He engraved a number of Richard Blome's maps and at least two maps (*Kent* and *Essex*) intended for an uncompleted atlas by John Ogilby as well as some of the famous road maps.

Size 390 x 440 mm.   **A Scale of Miles** (10=66 mm).
                                                            Scale 1M=6.6 mm.

DEVON=SHIRE Described by C: Saxon (sic). **Corrected Amended and many Additions by P: Lea**. Signature: **Francis Lamb Sculp** (AeOS). Inset plan of **EXCESTER**.[1]

1.	1689	*All the Shires of England and Wales* London. Philip Lea. (1689).	S110, BL, RGS, (E).
2.	1694	**Saxton** corrected. Roads, crosses and Exeter's mitre added. Latin names from Speed, eg **ISCA DANMONIOR**. Note **Brixham key ye Princ of Orang Land.**	
		The Shires of England and Wales London. Philip Lea. (1694).	VIII, S112, BL, W.
		Atlas Anglois London. Philip Lea. (1694).	S113, CB.
3.	1732[2]	Imprint; **Sold by Geo: Willdey at ye Great Toy, Spectacle, China ware, and Print Shop, the Corner of Ludgate Street near St Pauls London** (Ae) below shields.	
		The Shires of England and Wales London. George Willdey. (1732).	H183, BL, W, (B).
4.	1749	George Willdey's imprint removed.	
		The Shires Of England and Wales ... Sold by Thomas Jefferys. London. Thomas Jefferys. (1749).	H184, BL[3].
		Atlas without title-page. (Cluer Dicey and Co. also sold loose sheets.) (London. Dicey & Co. 1772.)	H185, W.

[1.] Illustration courtesy of Malcolm Woodward.

[2.] In *Devon & Cornwall Notes & Queries XX (I)* 1938 Daphne Drake refers to two issues: 1720-46 with Thomas & John Bowles imprint; and 1763 with imprint of Robert Sayer. Sir H G Fordham in his 1914 Hertfordshire supplement lists a 1733 Thomas Bowles edition.

[3.] An atlas without title page but the copy in the Walker Collection (W3, **H183**) has a title-page with reference to Jeffrys bound in later by Harold Whitaker and presumed to come from this later edition.

Whitaker

19.2 Lamb/Lea *The Shires of England and Wales*

20

JOHN SELLER
1694

John Seller (1632-97) is thought to have been one of six men found guilty of treason at the Old Bailey of whom four were subsequently hanged. Pardoned and released he later received official favour becoming Hydrographer to Charles II in 1671, later to James II and Queen Anne.

Although also known as a maker of mathematical instruments and globes he was primarily a publisher of marine and terrestrial atlases and his output was considerable and wide-ranging. His principal work was the *English Pilot* based on Dutch charts, but he only completed the first volume. As a draughtsman he worked with Philip Lea on his revised Saxton Atlas of 1689 and it was to Lea that he sold his few folio county maps when he abandoned his *Atlas Anglicanus* (see Speed 6).

In 1694, Seller published his small county atlas, the *Anglia Contracta*. The engraver is unknown but the maps were simple, reduced copies of Speed. Many maps had Seller's name, ornate cartouche title frame and graticule of miles but not Devon. Included in the original *Anglia Contracta* was a panoramic view of *The Prince of Orange Landing at Tor Bay ... 1668*.

After a break of sixty years Francis Grose (c.1731-91) reissued the maps in his *Antiquities* including a short text and a list of the most important sites, added below the map, headed *DEVONSHIRE*. The reverse has a list *ANTIQUITIES in this COUNTY worthy notice*. There are at least six text versions of the Grose issues: the front side ends with *Topsham*, and has either *Loman*, or *Loman.* on the reverse; the front side ends with *Axminster* or *Axminster*, with *VOL.II* bottom left, the fourth line on the reverse ending *It is di-* (ie *di-/vided* on two lines); alternatively, the text on the first side is without *VOL.II* bottom left and the fourth line of the reverse ends *It is divided* and with two variations of text – this has either the modern *s* or the antiquated *f* for s.

Size 120 x 145 mm.

English Miles (12=22.5 mm).
Scale 1M=1.9mm.

DEVON SHIRE in square frame. Scale bar in plain rectangular frame. **Excester** shown.

(E), (NDL).

1. 1694	*Anglia Contracta ... By John Seller* London. J Seller. (1694).		**CXVIII, S115**, BL, B, W.
	The History of England ... By John Seller London. John Gwillim. 1696.		**S119**, BL.
	The History of England ... By John Seller London. H Newman. 1697.		**S120**, CB.
	Camden's Britannia Abridg'd Vol 1 London. Joseph Wild. 1701.		**CXX, S122**, BL, RGS, W.
	The History of England ... The Third Edition by John Seller London. J Marshall. 1703.		**CXXI, S124**, BL, RGS.
	Camden's Britannia Abridg'd Vol 1 London. Isaac Cleave. 1711.		CB.

2. 1773   **DEVONSHIRE** in oval frame. No frame to scale bar. Additions, eg **Dawlish**, **Teignmouth**, **Eddystone Light House** (Be). **EXETER**.

(E), (DEI).

The Antiquities of England and Wales ... by Francis Grose
London. S Hooper. 1773 (1787).   **CXXII**, BL; **CCXLVII**, W.

The Antiquities of England and Wales ... by Francis Grose ... New Edition.
London. Hooper and Wigstead. (1815).   BRL BL.

20.1 Seller *Camden's Britannia Abridg'd* (1701)

21

ROBERT MORDEN
1695

Robert Morden (*fl.* 1668-1703) occupied premises in New Cheapside and Cornhill where he carried on business under the sign of *The Atlas* as a map and book seller and maker of instruments and globes. He produced playing cards (**15**), maps of various parts of the world and a series of county maps for an issue of *Camden's Britannia* ; a new translation by Doctor Edmund Gibson in 1695. Gibson, only 26 at the time, subsequently became Bishop of London. Morden may have first engraved another series of maps for this work which were rejected as being too small (see **22**).

The maps are elegantly engraved with no decoration except the shell-type cartouches containing the title and Morden's name: five are signed by Sutton Nicholls, and two by John Sturt, as engraver. Most maps bear the imprint of the three booksellers who published the *Britannia* implying that they owned the plates. Devon (based on Saxton, but with an error to the Dorset border) shows latitude and longitude (from the prime meridian of St. Paul's Cathedral, London) along the foot marked at 5' minutes and along the top in minutes of time from London: this is the second set of county maps to have latitude and longitude (see Bill **8**), and the earliest to have longitude from London and to indicate local time.

Watermarks (horse, spread-eagle and running hare) have been suggested as a method of dating individual maps but these only show the earliest possible date of the paper[1].

The British Library has a copy of *The History of Devonshire* by Rev. Richard Polwhele, published by Cadell, Johnson and Dilly (1797), which contains Morden's map in state 3. A map is not called for in the table of contents and other copies seen either have no map or contain maps by Cary[2].

Size 355 x 420 mm.   **A Scale of Miles** (60, 56 and 52 mm).
                                    Scale 1M=6 mm.

DEVONSHIRE By Rob^{rt}. Morden. Imprint: **Sold by Abel Swale Awnsham and Iohn Churchil.**

1. 1695   *Camden's Britannia, Newly Translated into English ... Publish'd by Edmund Gibson*
         A few copies were printed on large thick paper 370 x 430 mm.
         London. A Swale and A & J Churchill. 1695.   **CXIII, S117,** BL,W, (E), (DEI), (NDL).

2. 1722   Changes in Okehampton area; **Sawford=Courtney** for Samford and **Hunichurch** for Hunichurchligh, Sele becomes **Zeal Monachorum**, Swarton becomes **Soreton**; **Chagford** spelling corrected; Clifton Hundred erroneously changed to **CLISTON**.

         Britannia: Or A Chorographical Description Of Great Britain. The Second Edition ...
         printed by Mary Matthews ... and sold by William Taylor
         London. Awnsham Churchill. 1722   **CXV, H169,** BL.

         Britannia ... The Second Edition
         London. James and John Knapton and 10 others. (1730).   **H170,** B, BCL.

3. 1753   Main roads are now shown with double lines.
                                                         (TQ).
         Britannia ... The Third Edition
         London. R Ware and 14 others. 1753.   **CXVI, H171,** BL, W.

         Britannia ... This Fourth Edition
         London. W Bowyer and others. 1772.   **CXVII, H172,** BL.

[1]   Eugene Burden; *County Maps of Berkshire;* (1988) 1991; p.27.
[2]   The British Library has 2 copies with Cary's Map from *New and Correct English Atlas* (**51.6**). William Upcott in his bibliography of works on *English Topography* (1878) lists Cary's *New English Map* (**71.3**) of 1811 as being present.

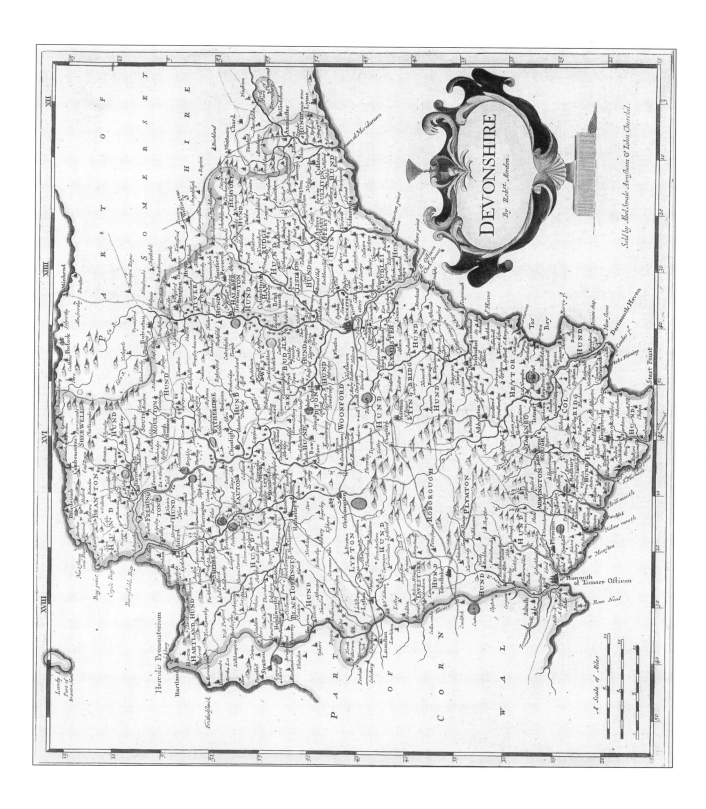

21.3 Morden *Britannia*

22

ROBERT MORDEN
1701

Morden possibly engraved this series of maps in 1693 for inclusion in the *Britannia* (**21**) but rejected them as too small. The greater inaccuracy when compared with his larger map is one reason for assuming that this map was produced earlier: Bishops and Kings Staunton not Steighnton; and Saltashtok not the more modern Saltash. The 1708 edition was intended as a road book (with *A table of the Roads*) with maps revised by Herman Moll (**25**) including upside-down directions.

Also in 1708 John Nicholson started to compile *a new compleat system of geography*, the *Atlas Geographicus* but decided with John Morphew to publish Britain separately as *Magna Britannia et Hibernia*. Published in 92 parts starting in 1714, Devon was issued in Sept/Nov 1716 in Nos 11 and 12. Thomas Cox, publisher, acquired the publication in 1724 and completed the work in 1731. From advertisements in newspapers it seems that Rev. Anthony Hall (1679-1723) of Queen's College, Oxford, was the compiler, basing the text on Camden but supplementing it with local information.

Counties were also sold separately, possibly to clear stocks, but each with a new title page: eg *A Compleat History of Devonshire ... Printed by E & R Nutt and sold by T Cox Cornhill MDCCXXX*.

Cox sold the entire work to Caesar Ward and Richard Chandler. They corrected the title, omitting the reference to Ireland. Variants were issued by Ward and Chandler (eg BL and E copies below) with differing title pages as late as 1745. Individual counties were sold with the old title page with a pasted slip over the Cox imprint. Chandler died in 1744 and Ward became bankrupt in 1745. Counties were still being sold off at the end of the century with dubious title pages, eg *A Topo-graphical Ecclesiastical And Natural History of* [blank] ... *by Thomas Cox. In the Savoy: sold by M Nutt* ... with text: copies of Devon are known with and without the final mileages sheet.

Size 175 x 215 mm.   **A Scale of 10 Miles – Great**, **Midle** and **Smal** (30, 28 & 27 mm).

Scale 1M=3 mm.

DEVON SHIRE by Robt Morden. No compass.

1.	**1701**	*The New Description and State of England* London. Robert Morden, Thos Cockerill and Ralph Smith. 1701. **CXXIV, S123**, BL, RGS, B, (E); CB[1].	
		The New Description and State of England. The Second Edition London. S and J Sprint, J Nicholson, and S Burroughs; A Bell and R Smith. 1704. **CXXV, H125**, BL, C; **H126**, B, CB (4to).	
2.	**1708**	Main roads double-lined and new roads added (eg Dartmouth-Newton Bushel). Compass (Dd). Directions added outside the county (**to London** at Ford), also upside-down in Cornwall. Towns added, eg **Beare Alston** and **Dodbrook**.	
		Fifty Six New and Accurate Maps ... Begun by Mr Morden: Perfected ... by Mr Moll London. John Nicholson, John Sprint, Andrew Bell and Ralph Smith. 1708. **CXXVI, H127**, BL, RGS, B.	
		Magna Britannia et Hibernia Antiqua et Nova ... Mr Cambden (in parts) London. John Morphew. 1716. **H128**, BCL.	
		Magna Britannia et Hibernia Vol. 1 London. M Nutt and J Morphew. 1720. **CXXVII, H128**, B, RGS.	
		Magna Britannia Antiqua et Nova London. Caesar Ward and R Chandler. 1738 (1739). **CXXVIII, H129**, BL, CB, E.	

[1.] Also reissued by same publishers in 4to format with unfolded maps (previously unrecorded edition).

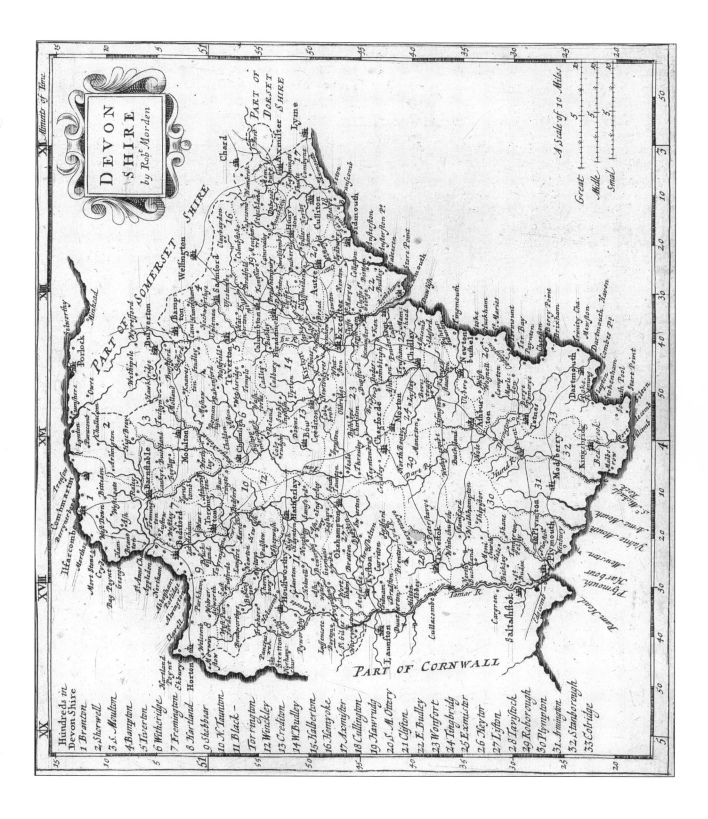

22.1 Morden *The New Description and State of England*

23

JOHN LENTHALL
1717

The stationer William Warter and his apprentice (1699-1706), son-in-law (1706) and successor (1711) John Lenthall specialised in the publication of playing cards. The first two packs were created by Warter in 1698 (Proverb cards) and 1707 (Arithmetical cards). Three further packs were published jointly by the partners in 1709 and during the next fourteen years John Lenthall steadily added to his stock of cards, frequently by purchasing existing plates which had been engraved many years before.

Some time before 1716/17 William Redmayne's cards (16) came into his possession and these were reprinted and sold as *Country cards* and later as *Historiographical cards*. Lenthall produced a second set of map playing cards in 1717. These cards were copies of those produced by Robert Morden in 1676 (15) but with some changes and new suits; Devon was now the nine of Spades, not Diamonds as before. Each suit was printed on a single sheet which was then cut up. Whilst this set of cards is usually dated 1717, Mann and Kingsley[1] suggest that it could be dated 1711 or earlier based on tax stamp evidence. However, the first advertisement for these cards appeared in the *Evening Post* of 22 Oct. 1717 ... *this day are published 20 entertaining Packs of cards curiously engraven on Copper Plates, Sold by John Lenthall, Stationer.* No. 5 in the list was: *Map-Cards, describing the 52 counties of England and Wales, each Card being a distinct Map.* The date of this advertisement has been adopted here. The cards were advertised up to April 1752.

Differences to Morden include spelling of *Breadth* in lower panel (*Bredth* in Morden), the adjacent counties are included similar to later Morden issues. A group of 17 cards of the Lenthall set has been found in a book which once belonged to the engraver John Sturt (or Stuart), together with a complete set of the Morden cards. This has led to the supposition that Sturt was the engraver and because the Morden set had no suit marks he misplaced the counties in the four suits. The existence of a Devon card in the first state is assumed on the evidence of the second state and the number of other counties in the first state; no card of the Spade suit has as yet been found in this state.

The costs of the packs varied considerably: 1722 – 2s; 1733 – 5s; 1741 – 4s; 1750 – 2s6d as compared to Redmayne's cards on sale in 1677 at 6d a pack.

Size of card 95 x 60 mm.
Map panel 60 x 60 mm.

Miles (10=10 mm).
Scale of 1M=1 mm.

Devon Shire in upper panel with Roman **IX** and stencilled suit. A plain double line border.

1. 1717	Pack of playing cards (this state is supposed – see text) London. J Lenthall. 1717.		**H147a, M&K5.**
2. 1717	Card is now printed with decorated border.		
	Pack of playing cards London. J Lenthall. (1717).		**H147b, M&K5**, Field[2]

[1.] See Mann and Kingsley; PLAYING CARDS: *The Map Collectors' Circle*, No. 87, 1972; p.20.

[2.] Illustration courtesy of Albert Field.

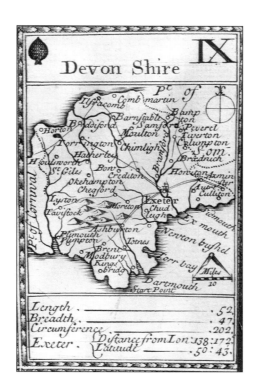

23.2 Lenthall a playing card

24

BOWEN/OWEN
1720

Thomas Bowles issued a pocket book of roads in 1720 complete with county maps and topographical information. The maps were engraved by Emanuel Bowen. The space between county boundary and frame is taken up with descriptive details, compiled by John Owen, lawyer and antiquarian, who was admitted to the Middle Temple in 1718. These notes relate to the geography and history of the county, a practice carried to great lengths in Bowen's later and larger atlases (**37, 42, 48**). *Britannia Depicta or Ogilby Improv'd* contained the small county maps and strip road maps based on the road maps of Ogilby, the whole amounting to two hundred and seventy-three plates: *the Whole for its Compendious Variety and Exactness, preferable to all other Books of Roads hitherto Published or Proposed; and calculated not only for the use of the Traveller but the general use of the Gentleman and Tradesman.* Despite their small dimensions, the county maps contained much information such as hundreds, rivers, hills, towns (with parliamentary representation indicated by asterisks), churches, roads and the arms of William Cavendish.

For the 1764 edition the mileages on page 176 (the page of text on Exeter) were altered and Bediford changed to Biddeford[1].

Size 180 x 110 mm.   **English Miles** (15=24 mm).
Map panel 112 x 112 mm.   Scale 1M=1.6 mm.

DEVON SHIRE. Reverse (p.147) is a road map of Chester to Whitchurch.

1. 1720   *Britannia Depicta Or Ogilby Improv'd*
                  (Two variations are known; with and without rapes on p.8.)
                  London. T Bowles & E Bowen. 1720.   **CXLVII, H149**, BL, W, BCL.

2. 1720   A short extension line is found at end of map after the amount paid by the county. Similar lines on reverse after note in border on Wem and K George on very last line.

                  Britannia Depicta ...
                  London. T Bowles & E Bowen. 1720 (3 issues), 1720 (1722), 1720 (1723).
                  H150, [NLW]; **H151**, BL; **CXLVIII, H152**, BL; **CXLIX, H153**, BL; **H154**, BL.

                  Britannia Depicta ... Ye 4th Edition
                  London. T Bowles & I Bowles. 1724.   **CL, H155**, BL, W.

                  Britannia Depicta ... The fourth Edition
                  London. T Bowles. 1730, 1731[2], 1736[3], 1749, 1751, 1753.
                  CLI, H156, [NLS, B]; **CLII, H157**, BL; **CLIII, H159**, W; **CLIIIa, H160**, [MCL]; **CLIV, H161**, [BL]; **CLIVa, H162**, [BL].

                  Page 147 (the reverse) has a cross added to Chester and a margin note added under Church Stretton relating to the distance between Chester and Bristol.

                  Britannia Depicta ...
                  London. T Bowles. 1759.   **CLV, H163**, BL.

                  Britannia Depicta ...
                  London. Carington Bowles. 1764, (post 1764). **CLVI, H164**, BL; **H165**, BL.

[1.] The authors are grateful to David Webb for the notes concerning changes to map and reverse page.

[2.] Reprinted in facsimile by Britannia Publications; 1979.

[3.] Donald Hodson refers to a 1734 atlas (**H158**) but no copy has been found. Clive Burden has a 1731 edition with a 1736 type-setting and suggests that this might be the missing edition referred to.

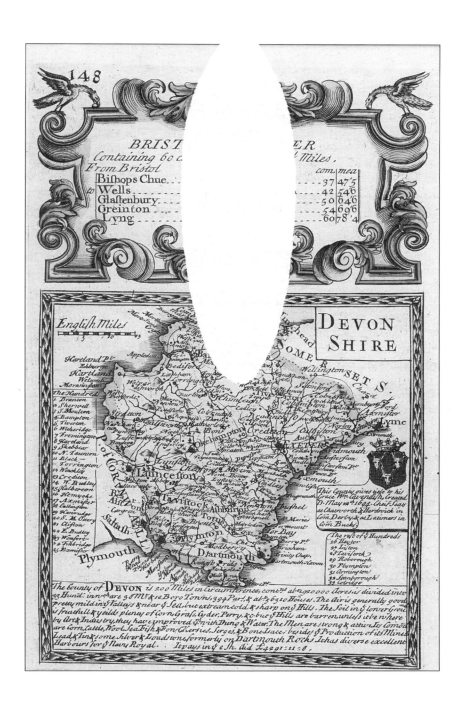

148

BRIST... ...ER
Containing 60 c... ...t Miles.
From Bristol   com mea
Bishops Chue. 37 47.5
to Wells 42 54.6
Glastenbury 50 64.6
Greinton 54 69.6
Lyng 60 78.4

DEVON SHIRE

24.1 Bowen/Owen *Britannia Depicta Or Ogilby Improv'd*

51

25

HERMAN MOLL
1724

Herman Moll (*fl.*1688-1732), a Dutch engraver, came to England about 1680 and by the end of the century had become a leading geographer and publisher. He produced many maps of all parts of the world, ranging from roads to continents and was associated with Greenville Collins and John Seller. His set of county maps are similar to Robert Morden's smaller maps (**22**), which he had revised. They are, however, distinctive for the antiquities engraved in the margins. The Devon map has illustrations of a Saxon coin struck at Exeter and an Andromache, right, and engravings of the Eddystone lighthouses of Winstanley and Rudyerd, left. Moll has upside-down directions in Cornwall and also a list of five mines; these features were included in a number of later maps as much of Moll's work was copied by others (see especially **26**, **28** and **29**).
The Bodleian Library has a unique example of *The Compleat Geographer, fourth edition* published in London by John Knapton and 22 others dated 1723. However the maps may well have been added later which would explain the anomaly in the dating.[1] Whitaker recorded an edition of *A New Description* dated 1733: London. J Wilford, T Bowles, C Rivington & J Bowles; this has been lost.[2]

Size 185 x 310 mm.   **English Miles** (20=52 mm).
Map area 185 x 255 mm.   Scale 1M=2.6 mm.

DEVON SHIRE By H. Moll Geographer. Engravings left and right of map.

1. 1724	*A New Description of England and Wales*		**CLX**, **H173**, BL, W, BCL, (E), (DEI).
	London. H Moll, T Bowles, C Rivington and J Bowles. 1724.		
2. 1724	Plate number **4** added (AaOS).		(TQ).
	A New Description of England and Wales		
	London. H Moll, T Bowles, C Rivington and J Bowles. 1724.		**H173**, C.
	A Set of Fifty New and Correct Maps		
	London. H Moll, Tho. Bowles and J Bowles. 1724.[3]		**CLXI**, **H174**, BL, W, RGS, C.
	A Set of Fifty New and Correct Maps		
	London. T Bowles and J Bowles. 1739.		**CLXII**, **H176**, BL, C.
3. 1747	Plate number changed to **12** (AaOS).		
	The Geography of England and Wales		
	London. T Bowles and J Bowles. 1747.		**H177**, C.
4. 1753	Drawings have been cut from plate.		
	H Moll's British Atlas; Or, Pocket Maps of all the Counties		
	London. Tho. Bowles and J Bowles & Son. 1753.		**CLXIII**, **H178**, NHL, CB.
5. 1775	Second plate number added (EaOS). Roads added with directions outside county.		
	The Traveller's Companion: Or, A Complete Set Of ... All The Counties ...		
	London. John Bowles. (1775).		P[4].

[1.] Donald Hodson; *County Atlases of the British Isles Vol. I*; Tewin Press; 1989; pp 118.
[2.] Donald Hodson; *ibid*; pp.119-122.
[3.] Reprinted in facsimile by Old Hall Press; (1994).
[4.] The authors are grateful to Donald Hodson for this information.

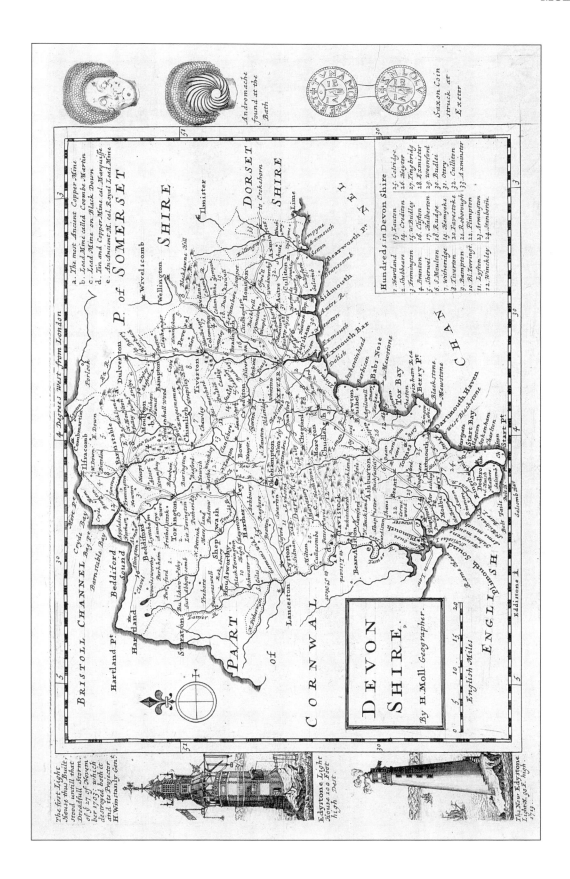

25.1 Moll *A New Description of England and Wales*

26

RICHARD WILLIAM SEALE
1732

About 1732, Henry Overton together with John Hoole, published a set of nine counties including a map of Devon copied directly from that of Herman Moll (**25**). The nine maps were engraved by Richard William Seale on two copper-plates and the prints were joined side by side to produce a large single sheet[1].

The maps were intended to be sold as a wall screen and not as individual counties. The full title (with its descriptive note *With the Roads & Distances of Places all done from the Newest Surveys, Adorned with the ARMS of all the Corporations and Borrough Towns in each COUNTY*) is engraved across the full width of the double sheet and Seale's signature appears outside the bottom border. The whole sheet is 578 x 946 mm.

The maps are arranged on the sheet in the same order as the title, reading from top left to bottom right arranged in three rows of three. Devon was therefore in two halves. The Devon map can be clearly differentiated from Moll's. Seale prefers the "long s"; there are occasional spelling differences eg Crokehorn and Straton (Moll) appear now as Crookhorn and Stratton; Moll has upside-down directions to roads in Cornwall and each map has coats of arms outside the borders instead of Moll's engravings. Both maps have a key denoting some of the important mines.

Overton and Hoole are known to have been in partnership from about 1724 to 1734; the earliest known date for Seale is 1732. No other set of counties in the same series is known. According to Hodson the maps are listed in an Overton and Hoole catalogue dated 1734 and the plates must have remained in Overton's stock until his death in 1751. The plates then came into the hands of Robert Sayer and the sheet appeared in catalogues issued by Sayer in 1766, by Sayer and John Bennett in 1775 and by Sayer's successors, Robert Laurie and James Whittle in 1795. After this the map is no longer recorded.

The British Library has two examples. One is a complete wall sheet and the other has the maps cut, joined and bound into book form with the general title discarded.

Richard Seale produced one county map for *The Large English Atlas*; a map of Middlesex which is striking for the large number of shields which surround it. He also produced maps for the *Universal Magazine* and maps for Rapin's *History of England.*

Size 185 x 315 mm.	**English Miles** (20=52 mm).
Map area 185 x 255 mm.	Scale 1M=2.6 mm.

DEVON SHIRE. Outside frame are two columns of five coats of arms, left and right of map.

1. 1732	*Nine New & Accurate Maps Of The Southern Counties Of England*		
	Viz; Cornwal, Devon, Somerset, Wilts, Dorset, Hants, Surrey, Sussex & Wight-Isle.		
	Imprint of wall sheet: **Printed and Sold by Henry Overton & I: Hoole at ye White Horse Without Newgate LONDON**.		
	London. H Overton & J Hoole. (1732).		BL.
	As book containing county maps as above. All imprints cut from sheet.		BL[2], CB.

---

[1]. Donald Hodson; *County Atlases of the British Isles Vol. I*; Tewin Press; 1989; pp 182-3.

[2]. Illustration courtesy of the British Library.

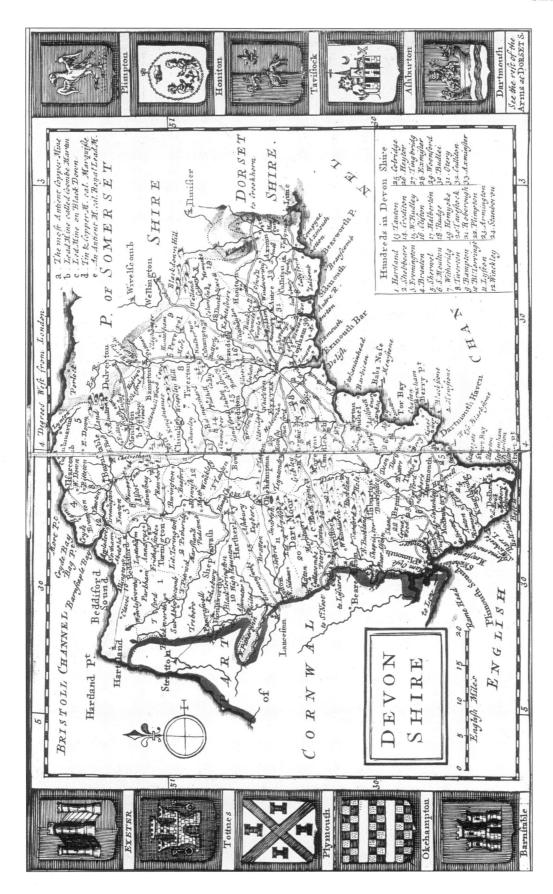

26.1 Seale *Nine New and Accurate Maps*

27

BADESLADE/TOMS
1741

Thomas Badeslade (*fl.*1719-45) was a noted surveyor and engineer concerned with waterway improvements especially of the reclamation of the Fens. He also prepared the maps for *Chorographia Britanniae*, a series of small county maps reputedly produced for George II for an intended royal tour of England and Wales. Each map, engraved by William Henry Toms, has a column of historical and topical notes of local interest. The atlas appeared in 1742 but many of the maps, including Devonshire, are dated 1741. There were possibly three or more printings of this edition including one quarto edition. Though some counties show Herman Moll's influence this is not apparent for Devon. The coasts are more detailed and the South Wales coast is also shown. The large number of surviving examples of the atlas shows that it was a considerable success. It was advertised regularly and was soon being retailed by twenty-six booksellers. It was the first eighteenth century county atlas to be pocket size (with sheets folded and bound it measured 165 x 105 mm) and, like its roadbook equivalent *Britannia Depicta*, it immediately found a ready market.

Size 145 x 145 mm.   **English Miles** (20=29 mm).
Map panel 145 x 100 mm.   Scale 1M=1.45 mm.

A Map of DEVON SHIRE. West from London (CaOS). Page No. **13** (EaOS). Imprint: **Publish'd by the Proprieters T Badeslade W H Toms Septr. 29th. 1741.** (CeOS). Signatures: **T. Badeslade delin** (AeOS) and **W. H Toms Sculpt** (EeOS).

1. 1741 *Chorographia Britanniae. Or a Set of Maps of all the Counties*
London. W H Toms. 1742.   **CLXX, H188**, BL, W, B, RGS, (E).

2. 1742 Numerous place names are added or revised. North Devon coast has **Cryde B, Mort Pt** and **Lynton** added. South Devon coast has **Armemouth, Barr I, Chilton, Start B, Stokentinhead, Dolish, Exmouth** and **Autre R**. Many roads are now added eg Exeter to Axminster, Bampton, Barnstaple and Hatherley.

Chorographia Britanniae
London. W H Toms. 1742.   **CLXXI, H189**, BL, RGS.

3. 1742 Imprint now: **Publish'd by the Proprieter   W H Toms Sept. 29. 1742.** Note on fair at Plymouth Dock added under Plymouth in text.
                                                                  (DEI).

Chorographia Britanniae
London. W H Toms. 1742.   **H190**, [NHL].

Chorographia Britanniae ... The Second Edition
London. C Hitch and W H Toms. 1745.
                                  CLXXII, CLXXV/VI, H191, BL, B, C, W.

Chorographia Britanniae
London. J Clark, C Hitch and W H Toms. (1746).   **CLXXIII, H192**, BL, W.

Chorographia Britanniae
London. C Hitch, W Johnston and W H Toms. (1749).   **CLXXIV, H193**, BL, W.

A Map of DEVON SHIRE. West from London   13

27.3 Badeslade/Toms *Chorographia Britanniae*

28

READ/(Rocque)
1743

The English traveller was a part-work advertised late in 1743 to appear weekly complete with a map. Thomas Read, the advertiser, had produced 38 county maps by mid-1744 with accompanying texts rewritten from Thomas Cox's *Magna Britannia* (**22**). The maps were issued before the text. The Devon map appeared in January 1743/4 and the text over six weeks, March-April 1744. Title pages, preliminaries and indexes were printed in 1746 to allow subscribers to bind the collected parts into three 8vo volumes which included 32 or 33 maps (editions vary). The maps are very similar to those used by Robert Walker (**29**) and both include engravings of the old and new Eddystone lighthouses copied from Herman Moll (**25**) on which the map is based, including his upside-down directions. Devon is one of the few counties with such embellishments. There may well have been some cooperation between Read and Walker.

In 1753, the maps without the texts appeared in *The Small British Atlas* under the imprint of John Rocque. Of Huguenot extraction, Rocque began his career in 1734: his French extraction is reflected in the sub-title to his *Small British Atlas*, which was *Le Petit Atlas Britannique*. Surveyor, engraver and publisher, Rocque earned a considerable reputation as a skilled large-scale surveyor, especially for his town plans which included a very large scale plan of London on 24 sheets, and a large-scale map of Exeter. By 1753 he had become Topographer to the Prince of Wales. A fire in 1750 destroyed a large amount of Rocque's stock and this might have encouraged him to acquire the Read plates. His *Small British Atlas* contained the maps that had already appeared (separately and bound) in *The English traveller* plus 19 modified Read maps of the outstanding counties. On his death (*c.*1762) his wife, Mary A Rocque, carried on the business. There is an unusual composite atlas in the Bodleian Library (Gough – Cornwall 17) that includes the Read maps of Devon and Dorset together with both John Norden's and Pieter van den Keere's maps of Cornwall.

Size 150 x 190 mm.

English Miles (20=50 mm).
Scale 1M=2.5 mm.

DEVON SHIRE. (CaOS). Compass (Aa).

1. 1743	*The English traveller* – Part 9 published 28. Jan. 1743/4 London. T Read. 1743.		**H197**.
	The English traveller Vol 1 London. T Read. 1746.		**CLXXXV**, **H197**, BL, (E).
2. 1753	Plate number has been added and erased, traces can still be seen (Ea).		
	The Small British Atlas (One copy in private hands, probably a proof, has evidence that the plate number was added and badly erased showing damage to the paper itself, *c.*1753.) London. John Rocque. 1753.		**H198**, [P]. **H199**, C.
	The Small British Atlas London. John Rocque and Robert Sayer. 1753.		**CCVII**, **H200**, BL, RGS, W.
3. 1762	Plate number **9** added (EaOS).		
			(NDL).
	The Small British Atlas London. John Rocque. 1762, 1764.		**CCVIII**, **H201**, B, C; **CCIX**, **H202**, W, C.
4. 1764	Page number erased and other changes, eg *Hart on* erased at Hartland Point.		(FB).

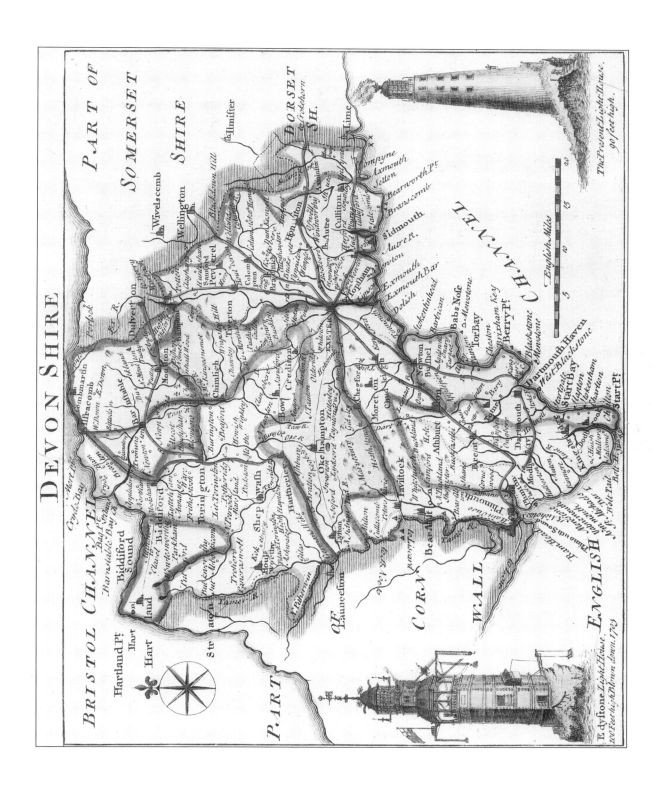

28.2 Read *The Small British Atlas*

29

SIMPSON/WALKER
1744

A part work that appeared almost simultaneously with Thomas Read's *English traveller* (**28**) was a topographical work published by Robert Walker entitled *Agreeable Historian or Compleat English Traveller* and compiled by Samuel Simpson. Both works included maps based on Moll's (**25**); the text of both works was largely copied from Thomas Cox's *Magna Britannia* (**22**). Beginning in December 1743 and appearing weekly the 109 printed parts of *Agreeable Historian* would have been completed towards the end of 1745, and by inference Devon would have appeared early in 1744. The work is found bound in three volumes (8vo) with a title page dated 1746. Forty-two county maps were published in the three volumes and without any imprint; most have the arms of the county identifying them from the Read maps.

On inspection it can be seen that, although very similar to Read's maps, the lettering is often slightly different or at an angle. The Devon maps in both cases have the insets of the old and new Eddystone lighthouses, copied from Herman Moll, and include his upside-down directions in Cornwall. The Walker, however, has the arms of Devonshire and the compass is on the right (not left).

As Walker's atlas appeared almost simultaneously with Read's *English traveller* one must surmise that both works were produced in competition, but the similarities are intriguing. The texts are so alike and the dates of publication coincide to such an extent that Hodson has concluded that the text compiler must have been shared and some cooperation took place[1].

There is reference to a copy of the map with a page number (*20*); but this has not been substantiated.

While Walker is known as the publisher of a number of part-works and of the *London and County Journal*, nothing is known of Samuel Simpson.

The copy in the British Library does not contain Devon.

Size 150 x 195 mm.

English Miles (20=50 mm).
Scale 1M=2.5 mm.

DEVON SHIRE (CaOS). Compass (Eb). **The Arms of Devon Shire** (De).

·**1. 1744**   *The Agreeable Historian, Or the Compleat English Traveller*
London. R Walker. (1744).   **H204**.

The Agreeable Historian, Or the Compleat English Traveller
London. R Walker. 1746.   **CLXXXIV, H204**, B.

---

[1] Donald Hodson; *County Atlases of the British Isles Vol. II*; Tewin Press; 1989; pp.42ff.

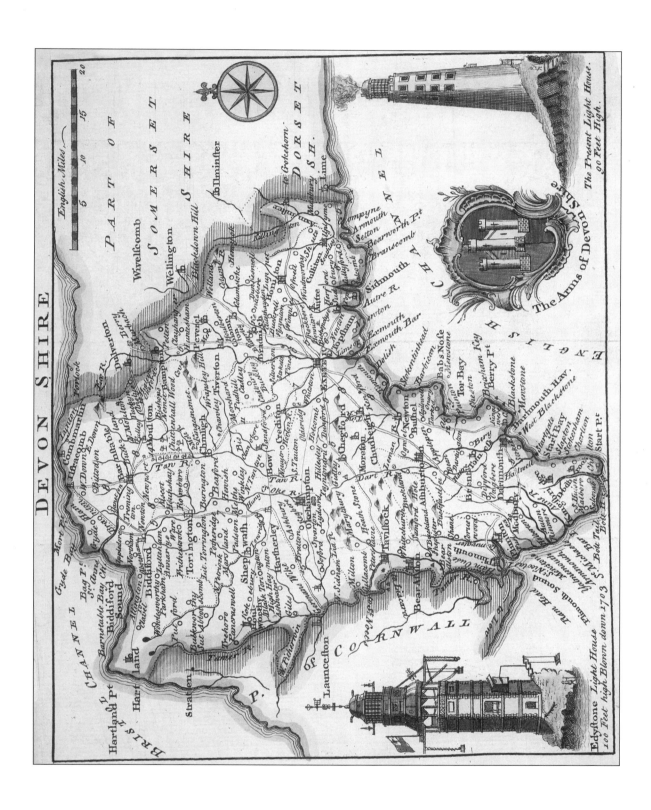

29.1 Simpson/Walker *The Agreeable Historian, Or the Compleat English Traveller*

30

COWLEY/DODSLEY
1744

Robert Dodsley (1703-64) of Nottinghamshire was a successful publisher, writer, poet and dramatist who also founded the *Annual Register* in 1758. He had premises at Tully's Head in Pall Mall, London from 1735, in partnership with his brother James from 1755. Among his publications were *Roads of England and Wales*, 1756, and *England Illustrated* in 1764 with maps by Thomas Kitchin (**43**). He was friendly with leading figures of his age such as Dr Johnson, Alexander Pope and Oliver Goldsmith. Dodsley was highly regarded and deserved the praise *that admirable patron and encourager of learning.*

John Cowley (*fl.*1733-44), Geographer to His Majesty and engineer, co-operated with Dodsley on their atlas *Geography Of England.* Although dated 1744 the atlas appeared in 1743, being advertised in *The General Evening Post* 24-26 November, 1743.[1] Such post-dating was common when an atlas appeared towards the end of the year. In January 1740 Dodsley began to publish *The Publick Register: or Weekly Magazine* and in March he introduced short topographical descriptions of the counties together with maps. Six, ending with Cornwall, were issued, after which the magazine was discontinued largely due, he implied, to the costs of the Stamp Act. Determined to succeed, Dodsley went on to produce the *Geography Of England.* The texts and maps were revised and new maps were engraved by another hand. Devon was a crude copy of Morden (**22**) even to the misdrawn Dorset border. The map is poor with many incorrect roads.

The maps, without the accompanying topographical texts, were also published in 1745 under R Dodsley and Mary Cooper's imprint as a *New Sett of Pocket Mapps.* There were two issues of this with different title pages; with and without the folding plan of London and Westminster that appeared in the original volume. When *Geography of England* appeared again in 1765 under the imprint of James Dodsley, Robert's brother, the text had been reset and the county maps were omitted.

Mary Cooper, together with her husband Thomas before his death, was an important distributor of published material and both were well-known in the London publishing trade. They acted as agents for the distribution of many of Dodsley's books and periodicals.

Size 134 x 180 mm.

Scale of Engl. Miles (10=21 mm).
Scale 1M=2.1 mm.

An Improved MAP of DEVON-SHIRE, containing the Borough and Market Towns, with those adjoyning; also its Principal Roads and Rivers by I Cowley Geographer to his Majesty.

(NDL), (E).

1. 1744	*The Geography Of England* Also available as separate sheets. London. R Dodsley. 1744 (1743).		**CLXXXI, H194**, BL, RGS, W.
	A New Sett of Pocket Mapps …Shewing The Situation of all the Cities… London, R. Dodsley and M. Cooper. 1745.		**CLXXXIII, H195**, C.
	A New Sett of Pocket Mapps … In which particular regard has been had to the river and the roads… London, R. Dodsley and M. Cooper. 1745.		**H196**, [GL].

---

[1] Donald Hodson; *County Atlases of the British Isles Vol. II*; Tewin Press; 1989; p.6.

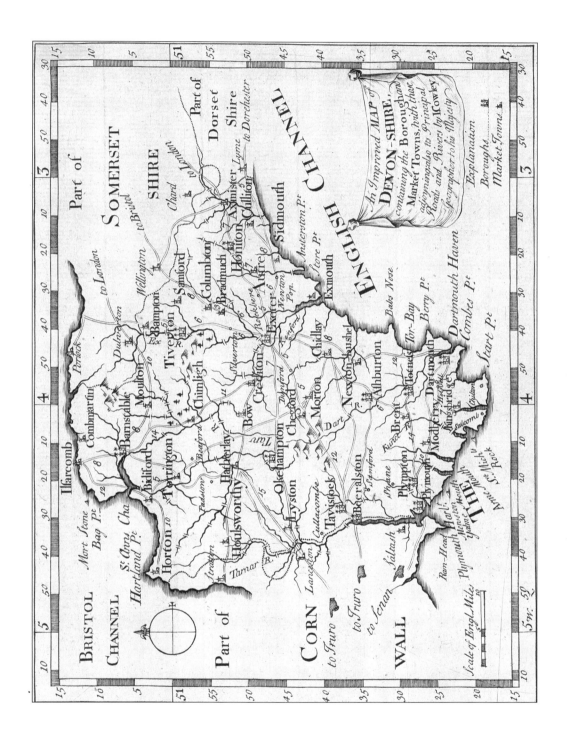

30.1 Cowley/Dodsley *The Geography Of England*

31

HUTCHINSON/OSBORNE
1748

John and Thomas Osborne published a number of cartographic works. Thomas Osborne produced an *Ancient Geography* in 1741, based on Hondius; they also cooperated in the production of Salmon's *Modern History* 1744-6; and in 1748 they produced an attractive set of county maps, *Geographia Magnae Britanniae*.

It is probable that Thomas Hutchinson engraved the map of Devon for *Geographia Magnae Britanniae* as his name appears on the map of Gloucestershire, which is in a similar style, and also on the map of England and Wales. The maps were based on those in Robert Morden's *Britannia* (**21**): most major roads are shown although few towns are included. Two editions were issued, both dated 1748, but with a change to the list of publishers: Samuel Birt, one of the original publishers, died in 1755 and his name was omitted from the second edition. There were no changes to the map plates for this second issue, even some basic errors were left unchanged (eg Ottery, or Autre as Saxton spelt it, is misspelt Aubry).

The publishers also owned the copyright to Daniel Defoe's *A Tour Through the Whole Island of Great Britain*. Subsequently the atlas was sometimes advertised *as a suitable companion and proper supplement* to the Defoe book and also contained adverts for the Defoe book in the preliminary pages[1].

One of the publishers was Andrew Millar (spelt Miller in the second edition). He announced plans for a Scottish atlas in 1745 together with Mary Cooper as bookseller. This does not seem to have been very successful and only a map of Lothian has been found. However, at the same time as the *Geographia Magnae Britanniae* appeared, he and the same co-publishers brought out a companion volume *Geographia Scotiae*. All but five of the maps for the Scottish atlas were signed by Kitchin.[2] Cambridge University Library has a copy of both bound together.

Size 145 x 170 mm.

Miles (15=34 mm).
Scale 1M=2.27 mm.

A Correct MAP of DEVON SHIRE. Plate number – 9 – (EaOS).

1. 1748 *Geographia Magnae Britanniae*
(London). S Birt, T Osborne, D Browne, I Hodges, I Osborne,
A Millar and I Robinson. 1748. **CXC, H205**, W, RGS, C, BCL.

Geographia Magnae Britanniae
(London). T Osborne, D Browne, J Hodges, A Miller, J Robinson,
W Johnston, P Davey and B Law. 1748 (1756). **CLXXXIX, H206**, BL, C.

[1.] Donald Hodson; *County Atlases of the British Isles Vol. II*; Tewin Press; 1989; p.47.

[2.] Donald Hodson; *ibid*; Appendix I.1.

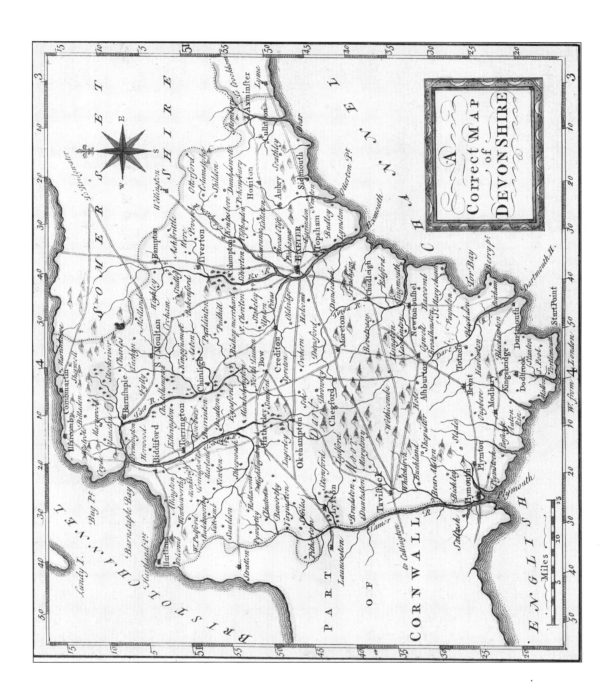

31.1 Hutchinson/Osborne *Geographia Magnae Britanniae*

32

JOHN HINTON
1748

John Hinton (*fl.*1745 *d.*1781) was a bookseller and publisher of renown, especially for his publication of atlases and maps by Emanuel Bowen and Thomas Kitchin and *The Universal Museum and Complete Magazine of Knowledge and Pleasure* (1747-1803). This later became *The Universal Magazine* (1804-1814) and *The New Universal Magazine* (1814-1815).

Hinton's contribution, which appeared in the magazine between 1765 and 1773, consisted of 39 plates of road maps and counties. The road maps were based on John Ogilby's *Britannia* of 1675, and were much larger than the many contemporary pocket-size editions of road books that had become fashionable.

The Universal Magazine was published monthly, two volumes per year, with Volume I for June-December 1747. The county maps were among the best executed and most attractive of the magazine maps, many having decorative cartouches. Presumably Hinton planned to produce maps of all the counties leading to an *English Atlas* but only a few were printed. In January 1749 the map of Devonshire appeared opposite p.38. It was very much in the style of Emanuel Bowen. Other maps were engraved by Kitchin and Richard Seale. The magazine was well-produced and well managed but suffered greatly on John Hinton's death. An arguably inferior second series of county maps by Benjamin Baker (**57**) was published in the same magazine beginning in 1791. Whereas the Hinton map has a baroque title frame and Arms of Exeter the later maps were more detailed though not as decorative.

Size 170 x 195 mm.

English Miles (15 =27 mm).
Scale 1M=1.8 mm.

A MAP of DEVON-SHIRE Drawn from the best Authorities. Imprints: **Engraved for the Universal Magazine**. (CaOS) and **Printed for J. Hinton at the Kings Arms in St Pauls Church Yard London 1748.** (CeOS). With **The Arms of Exeter**.

1. 1748   *The Universal Magazine of Knowledge and Pleasure ...Vol. 15 Published Monthly according to Act of Parliament, for John Hinton, at the Kings-Arms in St Paul's Church-Yard.*
London. J Hinton. 1749.

CLXXXVIII, Jolly UNI5, (E), (DEI).

An untitled atlas with *Maps of the English Counties from the Universal Magazine,*
Vols 1-40. (1747-67).   C.

An untitled atlas with various county maps.   BL.

32.1 Hinton *The Universal Magazine of Knowledge and Pleasure*

33

KITCHIN/JEFFERYS
1749

In November 1748 a group of London publishers, M Payne and 8 others, issued the first number of a new part-work *The Small English Atlas*. Whether Payne and his co-publishers finally completed the series is not known, but during the following year Thomas Kitchin and Thomas Jefferys had acquired the publication and produced the first bound editions. According to an advertisement Devon appeared in December 1748 in Part III. Two well-known booksellers were involved in its distribution: Mary Cooper and M Payne.

Both Kitchin and Jefferys had been apprenticed to Emanuel Bowen and both were destined to become Geographer to the King, the title Bowen held before them. Kitchin finished his apprenticeship in 1739 and established his own business two years later (see also **34**, **35**, **43**, and **49**).

Jefferys produced a great many maps including Donn's important map of Devon (**44**, **45**).

The maps for *The Small English Atlas* were printed four to a plate and Devon would have been printed with Leicester, Somerset and Durham, but no copy of a full plate has been found. Laurie and Whittle were offering the atlas until the early 1820s, probably using sheets acquired when they took over Robert Sayer's business. Later issues can only be told apart by the wear to the plate.

Size 180 x 135 mm.   **English Miles** (15 =25 mm).
Map area 110 x 132 mm.   Scale 1M=1.6 mm.

A Map of DEVONSHIRE (CaOS) and text below map begins **DEVONSHIRE Is bounded ...**

(E).

1. 1749	*The Small English Atlas* London. Kitchin & Jefferys. 1749.		**CXCII, H209, BL, RGS, B, W.**
	The Small English Atlas London. Kitchin & Jefferys. 1751.		**CXCIII, H210, RGS, C.**
2. 1751	Plate number – **13** – added (EaOS).		
	The Small English Atlas London. Kitchin & Jefferys. 1751.		**H210, W.**

3. 1775 Text below map begins: **This COUNTY contains 1 City, 11 Boroughs and 26 Market Towns.** The list of towns following is in alphabetical order. The detached part of east Devon, just in Dorset, is coded (a) and a note is found just above the compass. Hundreds are shown by dotted lines.

The Small English Atlas   **H211, RGS, W, B.**
London. Robert Sayer, John Bennett, John Bowles, Carington Bowles. (1775).

An English Atlas Or A Concise View of England And Wales
London. Robert Sayer and John Bennett. 1776.   **H212, CB.**

An English Atlas Or A Concise View of England And Wales
London. Robert Sayer. 1787.[1]   **CCLIX, H214, C.**

An English Atlas Or A Concise View of England And Wales
Reissued 1794 with a table with Laurie and Whittle imprint; and in 1796 with a dated Laurie and Whittle imprint on a general map.
London. Robert Sayer. (1794), (1796).   **H215, W; H216, [P].**

---

[1] Hodson (**H213**) and Chubb (**CXCIV**) record an issue of *The Small English Atlas* (London. Robert Sayer. *c.*1785) once belonging to Sir H G Fordham. An untitled atlas in the Whitaker collection (W60) is believed to be this edition.

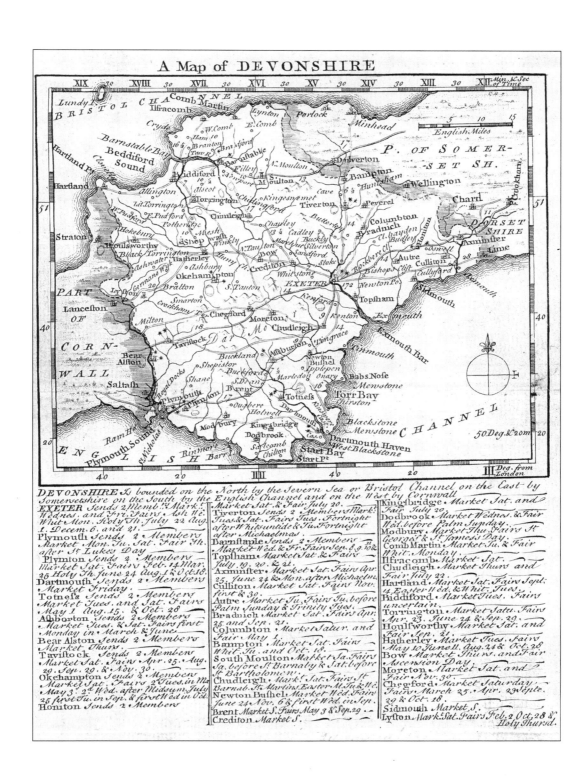

33.1 Kitchin/Jefferys *The Small English Atlas*

34

THOMAS KITCHIN
1750

The London Magazine: Or, Gentleman's Monthly Intelligencer appeared from 1st May 1732 until 1st July 1783 printed for Robert Baldwin. At its peak, in 1739, the magazine sold some 8000 copies. Although each magazine had a title page these were often lost or discarded when the magazines were bound. A set of English and Welsh county maps, engraved by Thomas Kitchin, was issued between 1747 and 1763 but at irregular intervals. The map of Devon, was based on Robert Morden's map for *Britannia* (**21**), although the Cornish border was based on Joel Gascoyne's important large-scale survey of Cornwall of 1699. Devon appeared in August 1750, in Vol. 19. opposite p.342. Each county map illustrated an account of the county, largely taken from Cox's popular *Magna Britannia* (**21**). From May 1741 a Dublin edition of the magazine appeared with extremely close copies of the maps (**35**).

In 1769 Devon, and nine other maps by Kitchin from *The London Magazine,* appeared in *England Displayed. Being a New, Complete, and Accurate Survey and Description Of The Kingdom of England, And Principality of Wales.* The information relating to England was *revised, corrected, and improved, By P Russell, Esq;* and that of Wales, *By Owen Price.* The printers were Adlard and Browne of Fleet Street. Thirty-three of the other maps were by Thomas Read as used by John Rocque in *The Small British Atlas,* four by George Rollos and one by Thomas Bowen. The maps were reissued with minor changes in historical and topographical works by Alexander Hogg.

Size 205 x 180 mm.   **British Statute Miles 69 to a Degree** (20=49 mm).
                                                                    Scale 1M=2.5 mm.

DEVONSHIRE Drawn from the best Surveys, Maps, Charts, &c and Regulated by ASTRON[L]. OBSERVAT[NS]. By T. Kitchin Geog[r]. Imprints: **For the London Magazine.** (CaOS) and **Printed for R. Baldwin Jun[r] at the Rose in Pater Noster Row** (CeOS). **The Arms of Exeter.**

1. 1750   *The London Magazine*
                     London. R Baldwin junr. 1750.   **CLXXXVII, H229,** BL, RGS, C, B, (E).

2. 1769   Imprints removed. Published in weekly parts, bound in two volumes; first 7 parts
                     contained the Kitchin maps. White paper, slightly shorter than that of above editions.

                     England Displayed ...
                     London. S Bladon, T Evans, J Coote, W Domville and F Blythe. 1769.
                                                              CCXXXVI, H203, BL, W, BCL, (E), (NDL), (DEI).

3. 1786   Somerset coast extended into title panel. The Boswell *Antiquities* were printed on pale-blue
                     coloured paper.   (DEI).

                     Historical Descriptions of New and Elegant Views of the Antiquities of England and Wales ...
                     by Henry Boswell assisted by Robert Hamilton.
                     London. Alexander Hogg. (1786).   **CCLVII,** BL, W.

                     Complete Historical Descriptions ... by Henry Boswell
                     London. Alexander Hogg. (1790).   CB.

                     The Antiquities of England and Wales ... by Henry Boswell
                     London. Alexander Hogg. 1795.   B.

                     A New and Complete Abridgement ... by Francis Grose
                     London. H D Symonds and Alexander Hogg. 1798.   W.

For the London Magazine.

BRISTOL CHANNEL

DEVONSHIRE
Drawn from the
best Surveys,
Maps, Charts, &c.
and Regulated by
Astron: Observat.ns
By T. Kitchin Geog.r

The Arms of Exeter

Explanation
Borough Towns with the N.o of Memb.rs they send to Parliam.t by Stars.
Market Towns
Parishes or Villages
Great or Direct Post Roads
Principal Cross Roads
Cross Roads
B. Part of Devon Sh.

British Statute Miles 69 to a Degree.
2 4 6 8 10 12 14 16 18 20

Longitude W. from London

Printed for R. Baldwin Jun.r at the Rose in Pater Noster Row.

34.1 Kitchin *The London Magazine*

35

EXSHAW/(Kitchin)
1750

A series of county maps engraved by Thomas Kitchin had appeared in Robert Baldwin's *The London Magazine* between 1747 and 1763 (**34**). Almost simultaneously close copies of these maps were published in Dublin by Sarah and John Exshaw. They appeared in *The London Magazine And Monthly Chronologer*, also known as *Exshaw's Magazine*.

This magazine appeared from May 1741 to December 1794[1] and was initially published by Edward Exshaw. He was later joined by John Exshaw in 1745 and after Edward's death in 1748 Sarah became the joint publisher. After 1755 the quantity of material from other sources increased as the Dublin magazine established itself, which is reflected in the change of name in 1755 to *Gentleman's and London Magazine and Monthly Chronologer*.

As with the London issues, the maps illustrated articles describing the counties, yet the first Dublin map did not appear until 1749, coinciding with the tenth in the London series (Oxfordshire). The county maps were issued until 1752 but only 28 were published. The two very similar maps of Devon appeared in August 1750 in both issues implying a large amount of cooperation.

The Devon map is different in a number of features to the map in the London edition. Apart from the obvious imprint differences, the Exshaw map omits the dashes filling the lines after the explanation of symbols; the town symbols for Kellington in Cornwall and Prickworthy near Barnstaple are missing; Kegbere by Okehampton is now Kegiere and Honiton misspelt as Hointon, Ilfracombe as Ifracomd; Taw River and Holberton near Tiverton are not named; also the S of Sh(ire) in the last line of the explanation, the hill chain on the Somerset border and the siting of trees are different. While the map of Devon from *The London Magazine* was reissued, the Dublin version does not appear to have been reprinted.

Size 205 x 180 mm.

British Statute Miles 69 to a Degree (20=49 mm).
Scale 1M=2.5 mm.

DEVONSHIRE Drawn from the best Surveys Maps, Charts, &c and Regulated by ASTRON[L]. **OBSERVAT**[NS]. **By T. Kitchin Geog**[r]. Imprint: **For the London Magazine.** (CaOS) with date **Aug**[st]. **1750.** and number **P. 402.** (both EaOS). Second imprint: ***Printed for S. & I. Exshaw* Dublin.** (CeOS). **The Arms of Exeter.**

1. **1750**	*The London Magazine And Monthly Chronologer* Dublin. Sarah and John Exshaw. 1750.		**Jolly GAL27**, B.

[1.] Donald Hodson; *County Atlases of the British Isles Vol. II*; Tewin Press; 1989; Appendix I.2.

Aug. 1750. P. 402.

DEVONSHIRE
Drawn from the
best Surveys
Maps, Charts &c.
and Regulated by
Astron. Observat.
By T. Kitchin Geogr.

BRISTOL CHANNEL

The Arms of Exeter.

Explanation.
Borough Towns with the
N. of Memb.^{rs} they send
to Parliam.^t by Stars.
Market Towns.
Parishes or Villages.
Great or Direct Post Roads.
Principal Cross Roads.
Cross Roads.
B. Part of Devon Sh.

British Statute Miles 69 to a Degree.

Longitude W. from London.

Printed for S. & I. Exshaw Dublin.

35.1 Exshaw *The London Magazine And Monthly Chronologer*

73

36

GEORGE BICKHAM
1750

In October 1743 George Bickham advertised *The British Monarchy*, a topographical work that would later include some forty-eight maps and 180 copperplate illustrations (including Edystone Lighthouse in the text on Devon). Very few complete copies have survived: two early copies are known with the added title-page *Description of the several Counties of South Britain.*

George Bickham (Senior) was a famous engraver and the descriptive text of the volume is written in his elegant calligraphy. He was an expert in this field writing various books on the subject including *The Universal Penman*, one of the finest English books on calligraphy. His son, also George, was equally a master engraver and was responsible for most of the birds-eye views. A third Bickham, John, was also an engraver and publisher. *The British Monarchy* was published in monthly parts from 1743, probably completed in 1749. This was a very beautifully produced volume consisting of descriptive text and historical notes illustrated originally with five rather sketchy maps probably by Bickham senior (The King of Great Britain's Dominions in Europe, Africa and America; British Isles; Ireland; Scotland; and a Chart of the Sea Coasts).

Towards the end of 1749 the Bickhams reissued the work in two-weekly parts, this time including the county maps. The work was in two volumes, with the first advertised, bound (ie complete) in January 1751/2. Volume Two followed, completed probably in 1755. Three title pages are known with dates 1743, 1748 and 1749. The atlases vary in content, none contains every plate of the 42 views of the counties, North and South Wales and sea coast. This was reproduced in facsimile by Frank Graham (Newcastle-upon-Tyne) in 1967.

George Bickham died in 1771 and his stock was sold. A Laurie and Whittle reprint followed in 1796; they possibly acquired the plates when they bought Robert Sayer's stock in 1794. A limited number of maps in an interim state are known: this was possibly a proof printing by Robert Sayer or Laurie & Whittle.

Size 222 x 138 mm.   Scale is irrelevant.

A Map of DEVONSHIRE West from London Inscrib'd to the Earl of Orford – Lord Lieutenant &c. of yᵉ County (CaOS) together with instruction to binder **after page 43** (EaOS). Below map two lines of attractive calligraphy with mileages beginning with **From Crookhorn to Axminster 13.2.** The third line contains imprint: **by G. Bickham according to Act 1750**

1. 1750	*The British Monarchy ... With Maps of each County in a New Taste, ...* *Publish'd according to Act of Parliament, Decembr. 2d. 1749, ...* London. G Bickham junr. 1749.	
	CLXXVIII; CLXXIX, H217, BL, W, B, BCL.	
2. (1775)	The title line has been erased. The plate was reduced (*c.*22 mm) removing the list below the map.	(FB).
3. 1796	Title added **DEVONSHIRE** (CaOS) and added plate number **9** (EaOS). *A Curious Antique Collection of Birds-Eye Views Of The Several Counties in England & Wales* London. Robert Laurie and James Whittle. 1796.	
	CLXXX, H218, BL, W, C, (E).	

36.3 Bickham *A Curious Antique Collection of Birds-Eye Views*

37

EMANUEL BOWEN
1754

John Hinton initially published the maps in the *Large English Atlas* as a series beginning in 1749 and intended to be issued monthly. The only large format county maps available were reprints of Saxton or Speed, Blaeu or Jansson (Morden's *Britannia* maps were neither sold singly nor as an atlas).

Hinton engaged Emanuel Bowen and Thomas Kitchin to engrave a set of large scale county maps with up-to-date details. The map of Sussex appeared in May 1749 and the first five maps appeared monthly as planned. After that progress was haphazard. In 1752, after 25 maps had been completed, Hinton pulled out and handed over to John Tinney (*fl.*1721-61), a prominent map and print seller who was in business in 1734 and selling maps as early as 1737.

In April 1754 the first five of Tinney's commissioned maps appeared including Devon. Three more maps appeared in 1755. After this time Tinney, probably for financial reasons, went into partnership with members of the Bowles family and Robert Sayer, all successful print sellers. Eight further maps followed, the last in 1760, with the last three by a different engraver. The first advertisement for the Atlas by name appeared in May 1760. The ownership continually changed hands as the various shares were sold or exchanged. Carington Bowles (*qv* p.100) left his father, John, in 1764 and took over his uncle's business. In 1767 both he and Robert Sayer produced atlases with their own title pages. Robert Wilkinson acquired John's interest in 1779. These changes are reflected in the imprints and title pages. However, it is apparent that old stocks of maps and title pages were used to make up atlases and to add to the confusion the maps were sold singly, and by others. Thomas Jefferys sold copies in a slipcase but cut so tightly that page numbers and imprints were lost. Robert Sayer took over Jefferys' stock on his bankruptcy. Sayer died in 1794 and was succeeded by Laurie and Whittle. Bowles and Carver took over the business of Carington Bowles when he died in 1793 and they later sold out to Robert Wilkinson.

Devon was engraved by Emanuel Bowen, map and print seller, who worked in London from about 1714 onwards producing some of the best and most attractive maps of the century (see especially **38**). A recurring feature of Bowen's work, evident even on the early road maps (**24**), was his habit of filling every corner and space of the map with jottings and footnotes, both historical and topographical which is repeated here and in his later atlases (**42, 48**). Devon was dedicated to John, Duke of Bedford who was Lord Lieutenant of the county. It also had an inset map of Plymouth which was reputedly copied by French spies[1]. Devon was based largely on Morden's map (**20**) but was graticuled and the Cornish border was copied from Joel Gascoyne's large-scale survey of Cornwall. Most maps were also available as a dissected map in slipcase from 1767 onwards. Laurie and Whittle continued to offer the atlas into the early 1800s.

Size 520 x 670 mm.
Plate 5

British Statute Miles (18=104 mm).
Scale 1M=5.7 mm.

An ACCURATE MAP OF DEVON SHIRE Divided into its HUNDREDS. Drawn from the best Authorities assisted by the most approved Modern Maps, with various Improvements. Illustrated with HISTORICAL EXTRACTS relative to its Natural produce, Mines, Minerals, Trade, Manufactures and present State of the City of Exeter and the principal Towns, with a Plan of Plymouth By Eman: Bowen Geog^r to His Maiesty. Inset map of Plymouth. Imprint: **Sold by I. Tinney at the Golden Lion in Fleet Street London.** (CeOS).

1. 1754	Rivers not named. One collection exists and some loose maps.		
	London. John Tinney. (1754).		C, (KB).
2. 1754	Rivers named, **Starcross** added, **Upottery** replaces Upautre.		
	London. John Tinney. (1754).		**CXCV**, BL, (E).

[1.] Entries 105-107 in E Stuart; *Lost Landscapes of Plymouth*; Alan Sutton and Map Collector Publications; 1991.

3. 1760   New imprint: **Printed for T Bowles in St Pauls Church Yard, John Bowles & Son in Cornhil, John Tinney & Robert Sayer, in Fleet Street**.

The Large English Atlas
London. T Bowles, J Bowles & Son, John Tinney and Robert Sayer. (1760).
       H221, W; **CXCVI**, **H221**, BL[1].

4. 1763   Tinney's name removed from imprint leaving gap. Plate **9** (EaOS and EeOS).

The Large English Atlas
London. T Bowles, John Bowles and Robert Sayer. (1763).   **H223**, RGS.
London. John Bowles, Carington Bowles and Robert Sayer. (1764).   **H224**, BL.

5. 1764   New imprint: **Printed for Carington Bowles in St Pauls Church Yard, John Bowles in Cornhil _____ & Robert Sayer in Fleet Street.**
Plate numbers now **11** (EaOS) and **9** (EeOS).

The Large English Atlas
London. T Bowles, John Bowles and Robert Sayer. (1764).   **H223**, C, (E), (DEI), (TQ).

6. 1767   New imprint: **Printed for Carington Bowles in St Pauls Church Yard, & Robert Sayer in Fleet Street.**

The Large English Atlas
London. T Bowles, John Bowles and Robert Sayer. (1767).   **H223**, CB.
London. John Bowles, Carington Bowles and Robert Sayer. (1767).   **CXCVII**, **H224**, B.
London. Carington Bowles. 1767, 1767 (1771), 1767 (1784).   -; [NMM]; **H225**, W.

The Large English Atlas with second title page *Le Grand Atlas Anglois*
London. Robert Sayer. (1767).   **H226**, BCL.

7. 1780   New imprint: **Printed for Carington Bowles in St Pauls Church Yard, & Robert Sayer in Fleetstreet & Robt Wilkinson. No. 58, in Cornhill.**
       (E).

The Large English Atlas ... R Wilkinson Successor to Mr John Bowles, deceased
London. Robert Wilkinson. (1780).
       CXCIX, **H227**, BL.

The Large English Atlas
London. Robert Sayer. 1787.   **CC**, **H228**, BL.

8. 1794   New imprint: **London. Printed for Bowles & Carver, 69 St Pauls Church Yard, R Wilkinson, 58 Cornhill and Laurie & Whittle 53, Fleet St.**[2]

The Large English Atlas ... Carington Bowles Map and Print Seller
London. Carington Bowles. 1767 (post 1794).   **H225**, BL.

The Large English Atlas ... Robert Sayer, Map, Chart And Printseller
London. Robert Sayer. 1787 (post 1794).   **H228**, RGS.

[1.] First standard atlas of 45 maps.

[2.] These later atlases are factices, using old title pages, and including dissected and mounted maps.

38

BOWEN/MARTIN
1755

Emanuel Bowen (*fl.*1714-67), a Welshman, was the son of Owen Bowen of Carmarthenshire. He was apprenticed to another Welshman, the mapmaker Charles Price, in 1709. Price had served his own apprenticeship with John Seller and at the date of Bowen's indenture was in partnership with Senex, both of them important mapmakers. Athough still an apprentice until 1716, signed work by Bowen is known dated as early as 1714[1]. He produced a great number of important maps (see also **24** and **37**) and was geographer to both George II and Louis XV of France.

He was still at work over fifty years later and his influence continued in the careers of his son, Thomas, his son-in-law, Thomas Kitchin, and others of his apprentices, most notably Thomas Jefferys, his successor as Geographer to the King. Sadly neither of the Bowens were fortunate or successful. When Emanuel died he was almost blind and Thomas, who carried on the business, died in a Clerkenwell workhouse in 1790.

Benjamin Martin (1704-82), mathematician, instrument maker and compiler began life as a ploughboy in Surrey. He worked as a teacher in Guildford and spent his spare time studying. By 1737 he was a boarding school owner at Chichester and publisher of his *Bibliotheca Technologica*. He moved to London in 1740 and as inventor and maker of optical instruments opened a shop in Fleet Street. In 1782 he was made bankrupt and committed suicide.

In 1754 he announced his plans for a complete library of the arts and sciences; in January 1755 his new magazine came onto the market, issued monthly. From the beginning the *General Magazine of Arts and Sciences* contained county maps, many engraved by Emanuel Bowen. The magazine was unusual in that it was supposed to be collected, then separated into six individual volumes:

Volume I	– *The Young Gentleman's and Lady's Philosophy*
Volume II	– *The Natural History of England*
Volume III	– *A New and Comprehensive System of Philology*
Volume IV	– *A New and Comprehensive System of Mathematical Institutions*
Volume V	– *Bibliographica Philosophica*
Volume VI	– *Miscellaneous Correspondence*

Very few of the original bindings were kept and many volumes have the final title of the complete work. In 1759, the first part of the atlas being complete, a title page was printed for those subscribers wishing to bind the collected papers together. Volume Two with a further 27 county maps was completed in 1763. The series of maps was copied by Pieter Meijer (**39**).

The map of Devon, to be bound opposite p.22, is rather crude and is unusual as the hundreds are given letters and not numbers explained in a key; post stages are shown and distances between towns are inserted; directions in Cornwall are upside-down as they were in Herman Moll's map.

Size 175 x 195 mm. **British Statute Miles** (15=28 mm). Scale 1M=1.9 mm.

DEVONSHIRE Divided into its HUNDREDS, containing the City, Burough & Market Towns, with the Roads & Distances. By Eman: Bowen Geog[r]**. to His Majesty.** Imprint: **Engraved for the General Magazine of Arts and Sciences; for W. Owen at Temple Bar.** (CaOS).

1. 1755	*The General Magazine Of Arts and Sciences* London. B Martin. 1755.		**H230, BL, E.**
2. 1759	Imprint removed.		
	The Natural History of England Volume 1 London. W Owen. 1759.		**CCXV, H230**, B, W, RGS, C, E, (NDL).

---

[1] Laurence Worms; *Some British Mapmakers*; *Ash Rare Books Catalogue & Price List*, 1992.

38.2 Bowen/Martin *The Natural History of England*

39

PIETER MEIJER
1757

The first part of Pieter Meijer's *Algemeene Oefenschoole* appeared in 1763 although many maps are dated earlier, including the map of Devon which is dated 1757. The book was published in three parts with Devon appearing in part one. There were nearly thirty pages of text describing the topographical and historical background to the county (pages 28-56). The map of Devon was opposite page 29. Two attractive engravings in this volume showed the river Lid and Lidford (Gorge). Volumes two and three followed in 1770 and 1782 respectively with maps dated to 1770.

The map of Devon was a close copy of Emanuel Bowen's map (**38**) from *A Natural History of England* of 1759, first published in 1755 in *The General Magazine of Arts and Sciences*. The signatures on the Devon map are those of L Schenk and J Soon: although Berkshire is signed *L Schenk, Jansz: sculpsit, 1762*. Only maps in volume one have both signatures.

The cartouche was changed to accommodate the new Dutch title and the spaces after the Hundreds names were no longer filled with dotted lines. Apart from the obvious Dutch headings (Explanation, Hundreds) and Dutch names for the surrounding counties and seas the map is a faithful copy of Bowen's original with the upside-down directions in Cornwall. A second scale-bar has been added.

Size 170 x 190 mm.   **Engelsche Mylen** (15=28 mm) and **Duitsche Mylen** (3=26 mm).
                                                                        Scale 1M=1.9 mm.

DEVONSHIRE verdeeld in zyn Honderden of Rechtsgebieden, berattende alle de Steden, Burg-en Marktvlekken, met de Wegen, Afstanden, enz. Opgesteld door Eman Bowen, Landbeschryver van zyn Britt. Majesteit Te Amsteldam, by Pieter Meijer Uitgegeren. Signature: **L Schenk J Soon 1757**. (AeOS).

1. 1757   *Algemeene Oefenschoole van Konsten en Weetenschappen*
            Tweede Afdeeling; Eerste Deel (Part one of 3).
            Amsterdam. Pieter Meijer. 1763.   BL.

39.1 Meijer *Algemeene Oefenschoole*

JOHN GIBSON
1759

John Gibson (*fl.*1750-92) was a well-known geographer, engraver and draughtsman at No 18 George's Court Clerkenwell. He worked with Thomas Kitchin, Thomas Jefferys and with Emanuel Bowen (*Atlas Minimus* 1758) and produced maps for the *Gentleman's Magazine* 1758-63. Gibson also produced a number of maps between 1762 and 1770 for *The Universal Museum and Complete Magazine* which contained 10 county maps including Devon (**47**).

In 1759 (the date is taken from an advertisement) his miniature maps for John Newbery's atlas of 53 British county maps appeared in *New and Accurate Maps of the Counties of England and Wales* (12mo). This is a delightful series; each map has a delicate rococo title cartouche, compass, scale-bar, main roads, rivers and a number of place names. Below the map is an engraved topographical note giving the number of houses, inhabitants, parishes, members of parliament, and the main products and commodities within the county. Fine lines above some of the maps indicate that they were probably engraved and printed two or more to each plate.

John Newbery is well known to those interested in juvenile literature: he seems to have specialised quite early on in the publishing of books for children. He moved to London in 1744 producing *A Little Pretty Pocket Book* the same year and proceeded to publish all sorts of books for children. Most of his books sold for 6d. or a shilling; when the atlas appeared it was appreciably more expensive at 4 shillings. It was included in an advertisement with 11 other *useful and pretty books* and could well have been aimed at a younger audience. Newbery's son took over the business forming a partnership with Thomas Carnan. This dissolved about 1779. There was a further issue of the atlas in or after 1779 after the partnership broke up.

Size 112 x 65 mm.

English Miles (20=16 mm).
Scale 1M=0.8 mm.

Devon Shire. Plate number **10** (EaOS).

(E).

1. **1759**   *New and Accurate Maps of the Counties of England & Wales Drawn from the latest Surveys by J Gibson.* London. J Newbery. (1759).

    CCXIII, H219, BL, C, B.

    New and Accurate Maps of the Counties of England & Wales London. T Carnan. (1779).

    CCXIV, H220, B, W.

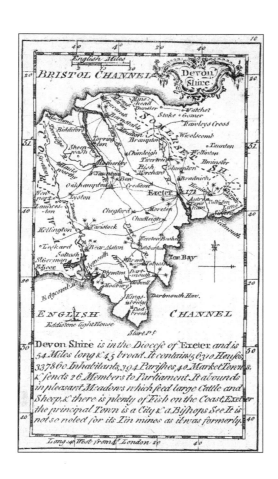

40.1 Gibson *New and Accurate Maps of the Counties of England & Wales*

41

RICHARD BENNETT
1761

During the eighteenth and nineteenth centuries there were a number of county topographical projects that started but were never completed. Often the project was abandoned before Devon was included: George Rollos completed five maps and Eugene Burden[1] has written about a series of Neele maps based on Cary's *Traveller's Companion* that included Bedfordshire to Derbyshire, but neither included Devon. However, some incomplete series did include Devonshire; the *Universal Museum* series (32) and a series by Richard Bennett.

Donald Hodson[2] recorded the finding of a collection of eleven county maps which had been discovered by David Smith in a copy of Owen's *New Book of Roads* (published by Goadby & Son). They were not printed in the original volume but had been bound in some time after publication with other maps from magazines. The maps were Bedfordshire to Essex omitting Devon.

Since then another set of these maps has been found[3]. These maps were bound into a copy of *A New Present State of England Vol I* printed for Henry Woodgate at the Golden Ball in Paternoster Row which it is assumed was published about 1760. This second set contains fourteen county maps: the eleven already recorded together with maps of Devonshire, Herefordshire and Rutland. Although Devon was bound in opposite page 76, the page on which the text of Devonshire begins, they were not intended for inclusion in this publication: the reference letters on the maps do not relate to the text. Roads are shown with distances between main towns in small circles, for larger towns such as Exeter and Barnstaple, the distance from London is given in a square frame. There are other symbols, e.g. R and V (rectories, vicarages), but no key. A note to Exminster Hundred (identified with an A) is in the Bristol Channel (Aa).

Hodson postulated that the maps were originally intended for inclusion in *The New English Atlas*. This was a project planned by Richard Bennett which never materialised. An advertisement in *The Public Advertiser* of 30 June 1761 announced the issue of *The New English Atlas* to be issued in parts. The atlas was to be printed for the proprietors and sold by Richard Bennett, Engraver, C G Seyffert, J Flyn, Engraver, S Hooper, C Corbett and J Pottinger.

The map of Devonshire obviously fills a gap in the first set. However, the other two maps present a puzzle: were they printed out of sequence or are there other counties still waiting to be discovered? Whatever the facts of the matter it seems certain that the Atlas was never completed and that collectors of the first maps bound them into other publications.

Size 163 x 132 mm.

English Miles (20=34 mm).
Scale 1M=1.7 mm.

DEVON SHIRE (CaOS).

1. 1761	Found in *A New Present State of England*		
	Imprint of *A New Present State of England* is London. Henry Woodgate. 1760.		EB[4].

[1] Eugene Burden; A minor mystery solved; in *The Map Collector 59*, Summer 1992.
[2] Donald Hodson; *County Atlases of the British Isles Vol. II*; Tewin Press; 1989; pp179-181.
[3] See *The Map Collector* 61, Winter 1992, p.54.
[4] Illustration courtesy of Eugene Burden.

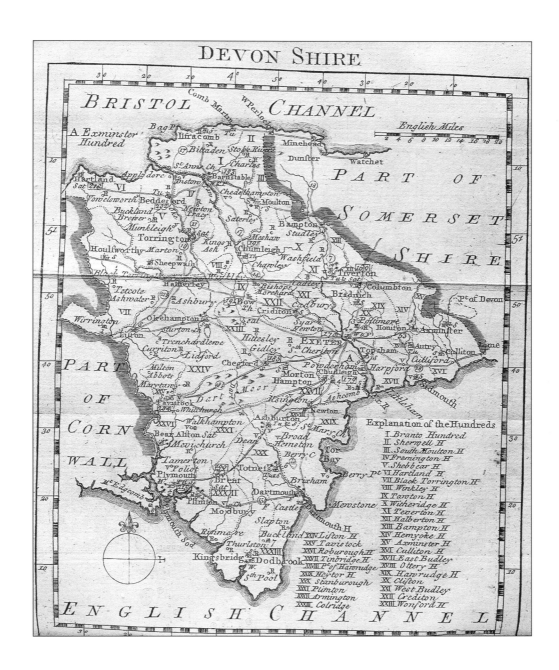

41.1 Bennett The Map as found in *A New Present State of England*

85

42

EMANUEL BOWEN
1763

The *Large English Atlas* with maps engraved by Emanuel Bowen and Thomas Kitchin had appeared in 1760 (**37**). Not long after, Bowen produced a similar set of maps for *The Royal English Atlas* which was to a great extent a copy of the former work somewhat reduced in size (folio, 44 maps). The title is in a new frame − actually a vignette scene of country life. The vast majority of the historical and geographical material, a hallmark of Bowen's work, is retained although sometimes shortened. A text on South Molton replaces that of Tiverton and some of the others lose a line or two; only the text on Totnes is appreciably shorter than before. An attractive vignette of Exeter Cathedral replaces the inset map of Plymouth. The title vignette with scenes of cider making is a reflection of Devon's importance in this respect. In 1750, possibly ten million gallons were made in the county: some was even made into still liquor and wassailing was still carried on at Christmas time.[1] In 1763 a Cyder Tax was imposed causing widespread unrest in the county and it was repealed in 1766.[2]

By 1746 Thomas (see **17.5**) and Elizabeth Bakewell had moved to Cornhill. Elizabeth took over the business on Thomas' death and was involved in selling Kitchin's *England Illustrated.* She also published jointly with John Tinney.

A third set of maps, smaller again, appeared in the *Atlas Anglicanus* (**48**) which also incorporated most of the text; Bowen and Owen had introduced text in the *Britannia Depicta* maps (**24**).

Size 405 x 490 mm.   **British Statute Miles** (15=71 mm).
                                                                    Scale 1M=4.7 mm.

An ACCURATE MAP of DEVONSHIRE Divided into its HUNDREDS, Drawn from the best Authorities & Illustrated with Historical Extracts relative to the Natural produce, Trade & Manufactures of the County. City and principal Towns: Describing also the Church Livings, Charity Schools &c. with other Improvements By Eman Bowen Geogr to His Majesty on a stone tablet in vignette of cider making and a boy fishing. Imprint: **Printed for John Bowles & Son at the Black Horse, and Mess: Bakewell & Parker in Cornhill, T Bowles in St Pauls Church Yard, H Overton without Newgate, T Kitchin on Holborn Hill, R Sayer and I Ryall in Fleet Street,** (CeOS). Plate number **No.10** (AeOS). Graticuled at 10` intervals.

1. 1763	*The Royal English Atlas*		
	London. Thomas Kitchin, Robert Sayer, Carington Bowles,		
	Henry Overton, Henry Parker, John Bowles and John Ryall. (1763).		**CCXVIII**, BL, W, B, C.
2. 1778	New imprint: **London. Printed for John Bowles. N^O. 13. Cornhill. Carington Bowles. N^O. 69. S^t. Pauls Church Yard. Robt. Sayer & John Bennett. N^O. 53. Fleet Street. as the Act directs. 1st. of Jany. 1778.** (CeOS).		
			(E).
	The Royal English Atlas		
	London. Carington Bowles. (1778).		**CCXIX**, BL.
	The Royal English Atlas		
	London. R Wilkinson. (1779).		C.
	The Royal English Atlas		
	London. R Sayer and J Bennett. (1779).		**CCXIXa**, B.
	The English Atlas		
	London. R Martin. (1828).[3]		**CCXCIX**, BL, RGS.

[1.] R Stanes; *A History of Devon*; Phillimore; 1986; p.80.

[2.] Cited in *Ambra Books Catalogue 114*, entry 97, 1995; issued by Ivor Cornish.

[3.] Reproduced in facsimile by David and Charles; Newton Abbot; 1971.

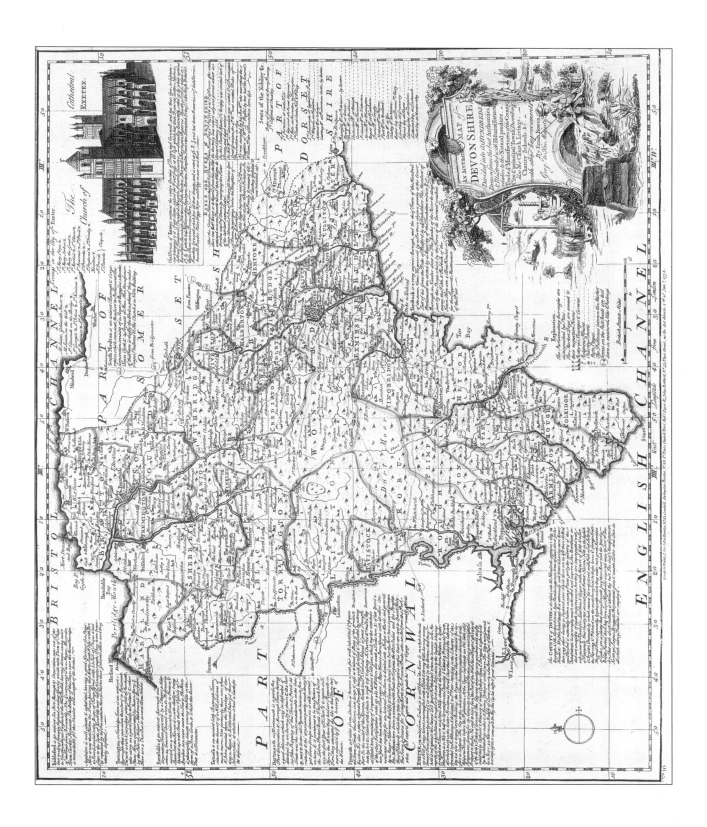

42.2 Bowen *The Royal English Atlas*

43

THOMAS KITCHIN
1764

Thomas Kitchin, Hydrographer to King George III, engraver and cartographer, was born in London in August 1719. He appears to have been the eldest of several children of Thomas Kitchin, a hat-dyer, and his wife Mary Birr[1]. Kitchin was apprenticed to the map-engraver Emanuel Bowen in December 1732. No premium was paid to Bowen, so it is thought that Kitchin was what was called an *apprentice for labour* – one to be trained as a journeyman assistant rather than as a future master. However, Kitchin married Bowen's daughter, Sarah, on Christmas Day 1739, just three weeks after his apprenticeship ended. Sarah died young and Kitchin remarried in 1762. His second wife was Jane Burroughs, daughter of Joseph Burroughs, a learned and respected preacher. Kitchin moved to St Alban's in the 1760s, where he died in June 1784. He is buried in that Abbey, but the inscription has not survived.

Kitchin did not become a partner and by at least 1741 was operating on his own account. Nevertheless, Kitchin and Bowen often worked together in their later careers, most notably on the *Large English Atlas* (37). They both became prominent members of the well-known Barbican (Paul's Alley) Chapel and very actively involved in the affairs of the Baptist community.

Working at premises in London's Holborn as an engraver and publisher, Kitchin produced a wide range of books on many subjects as well as topographical works. He also worked with Thomas Jefferys (33) and, apart from the atlases he published with him, he produced maps of every sort for magazines and books on history and the antiquities including county maps for *The London Magazine* (34).

In 1764 he engraved a map of Devon for R and J Dodsley's *England Illustrated, or, a Compendium of the Natural History, Geography, Topography, and Antiquities Ecclesiastical and Civil, of England and Wales* (4to, 54 maps). The same maps were re-used by the publishers in 1765 to produce *Kitchen's* [sic] *English Atlas: or, a Compleat Set of Maps of all the Counties of England and Wales.* An 18th century reviewer commended the maps as being *executed with a good share of elegance and neatness.* Although the graticuled maps are not very scarce in themselves, they are not often found in 18th century colour. The map was copied by Ellis, Hatchett and Lodge including the locations of Moll's mines, St. George's Channel and Seaton in the *Explanation* table (46, 50, 52).

Size 192 x 245 mm.

British Statute miles 69 to a Degree (24=50 mm).
Scale 1M=2.1 mm.

A New MAP of DEVON SHIRE, Drawn from the best Authorities: By Tho^S. Kitchin Geog^r. Engraver to H.R.H. the Duke of York.

(E), (NDL), (DEI).

1. 1764   *England Illustrated, Or, A Compendium Of The Natural History, Geography, Topography, And Antiquities Ecclesiastical and Civil, Of England and Wales. Vol I*
Also reissued in parts 1764-65 as advertised in the *Public Advertiser* 1 Feb. 1764.
London. R & J Dodsley. 1764 (First published December 1763).

CCXIV, H231, BL, W, B,

Kitchen's English Atlas: Or, A Compleat Set of Maps Of All The Counties of England and Wales ...
The Whole engraved ... By Thomas Kitchen, Geographer to His Royal Highness the Duke of York.
London. J Dodsley. (1765).

CCXXXVIII, H232, BL, B.

[1] See Laurence Worms' article in *The Map Collector*, Issues 62 and 63; Spring and Summer 1993.

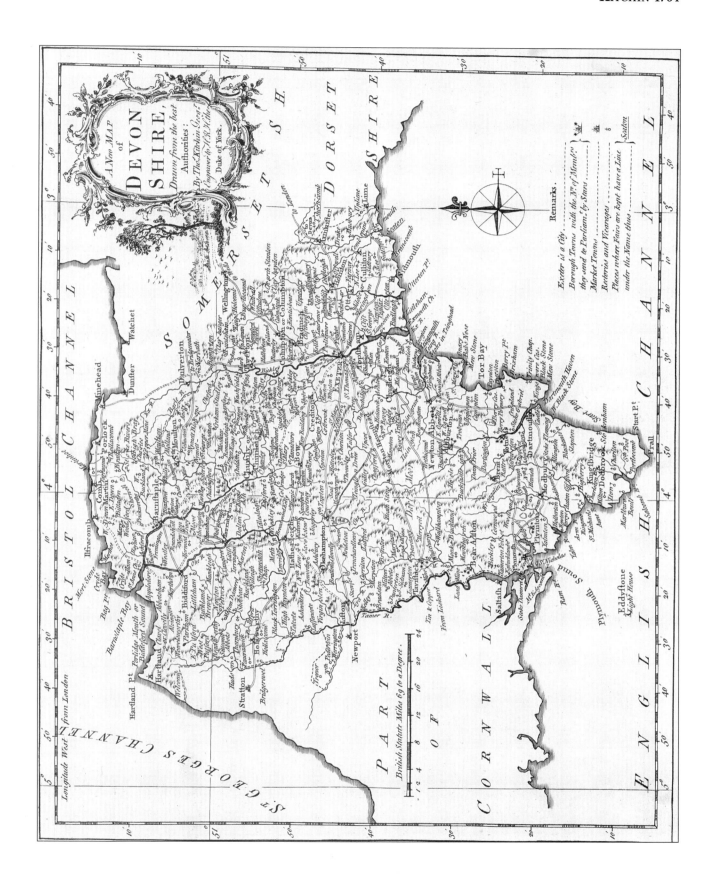

43.1 Kitchin *England Illustrated*

44

BENJAMIN DONN
1765

An important map for anyone interested in Devon maps must be the large-scale map produced by Benjamin Donn. In 1759 the Royal Society of Arts, then known as the Society for the Encouragement of Arts, Manufactures and Commerce, offered an annual award of £100 for the best original 1 inch to 1 mile county survey. Donn and Isaac Taylors (Dorset) submitted entries but Benjamin Donn was the first successful applicant with a twelve sheet map of Devonshire, engraved by Thomas Jefferys and published in 1765. A Devonian, Donn was a well-known mathematician as well as a surveyor and teacher of mathematics in Bideford before moving to Bristol. Also interested in tidal flows he published sets of figures for the S W of England.

Professor Ravenhill has written a very complete account of the events leading up to Donn's success.[1] Although Donn completed the first large-scale map of Devon, Joel Gascoyne from Hull who completed a map of Cornwall in 1699 planned to survey Devon shortly after this date but a lack of subscribers put paid to his plans. Surprisingly, only forty years later a Cornishman, Thomas Martyn, resurveyed Cornwall and published his map in 1748. He too planned to survey and map Devon and presented proposals in 1750. Professor Ravenhill recounts that he very probably began the survey but unfortunately died at Ashburton on Christmas Day, 1751. It was Donn's acquaintanceship with another Cornishman, William Borlase, a founder member of the RSA that led to the latter's acceptance of Donn's proposal to map Devonshire when it was submitted to the society in 1759. In 1787 Richard Cowl planned an up-dated map of Devon but died when he was thrown from his horse and his map was never completed. Cowl surveyed Plymouth in 1778, his map being published by William Faden in 1780.

Donn's map is graticuled, has a vignette title, inset plans of Exeter, Plymouth, Stoke Town and Plymouth Dock, and an inset map of Lundy. The map is dedicated to John Baring of Mount-Radford, an emigré who made his fortune through the Exeter cloth industry (and whose son founded the Baring Bank), and Mathew Lee of Ebford near Exeter. Donn is the first to identify the island in Bigbury Bay by the names *Bur Island or Borough Island*. Since Saxton most larger maps had referred to it as St Michaels or St Michaels Rock in reference to the chapel.[2] Accompanying the bound book of the twelve-sheet map was a general index map of the county (**45**). Some copies were printed on vellum and some of these hand-coloured.[3]

In 1799 William Faden issued a reduced copy of Donn's map engraved by Benjamin Baker on one sheet (**62**). In 1965, to celebrate the bicentenary of Donn's map, a facsimile was produced by the Devon and Cornwall Record Society together with the University of Exeter. This has a foreword by Professor Ravenhill.

Total dimensions 1800 x 1860 mm.

Statute Miles 69½ nearly to a Degree (8=202 mm).
and **Geographical or Sea Miles 60 to a Degree** (1=203 mm).
Scale 1M=25 mm (1").

A MAP of the COUNTY of DEVON, with the CITY and COUNTY of EXETER, Delineated from an Actual Survey by BENJAMIN DONN. Engraved by Thoˢ Jefferys, Geographer to His MAJESTY. Imprint: **Entered in the Hall Book of the Company of Stationers and Published according to Act of Parliament February 1ˢᵗ. 1765.** (CeOS – sheet 10).

1. 1765   *A Map of the County of Devon ... with the indexes of the Parishes, Seats &c. for the readier finding them on the Large Map. London Printed for the Author and Sold by the Booksellers of Devon, by Mr Johnston, in Ludgate Street; Mr Baldwin in Paternoster Row; and the Print-sellers of London. MDCCLXV.* London. B Donn. 1765.

BL, B, C, BCL, (E).

[1] W Ravenhill; The South West in the Eighteenth-Century Re-mapping of England; in *Maps and History in South-West England;* Ed. Barker, K and Kain, R; University Exeter Press; 1991.

[2] Kit Batten; The St. Michael's Mount of Devon shire; in *IMCoS JOURNAL* Issue 62; Autumn 1995.

[3] A full set on vellum was sold at Bonham's, Knightsbridge on 23rd May 1995 for £2990.

The following text appears within the map:

Whereas the Latitudes and Longitudes in this Map, differ considerably from those in the Survey of an adjoining County, as well as from common Charts, Books, &c. which also differ from each other. The Author thinks himself obliged to assure the Publick that these are taken with such Instruments and Care, as to leave no doubt of their Accuracy; and that the Latitudes of the Points, Headlands, Harbours &c. on the South Coast agree very nearly with the Chart of the late Excellent Astronomer D.r Halley, the difference seldom amounting to a Minute, and only in one single Case, viz.t the Start Point to 4 Minutes, which for the greater safety of Sailors, the Doctor seems to have designedly laid down a few Minutes more South.

A MAP
of the COUNTY of
DEVON,
with the CITY & COUNTY of
Exeter.
Delineated from an actual Survey, by
BENJAMIN DONN.
Engraved by Tho.s Jefferys,
Geographer to His
MAJESTY.

The Eddistone
Light House

44.1 Donn *A Map of the County of Devon* sheet IX with title vignette

45

DONN/JEFFERYS
1765

Thomas Jefferys (1719-1771) was one of the most important engravers of the eighteenth century. His considerable output covered the entire field of printing from maps to satires and portraits. Learning his trade as an apprentice with Emanuel Bowen he started on his own in 1745 as both engraver and publisher. He joined with Kitchin to produce *The Small English Atlas* in 1749 (**33**). He was appointed Geographer to Frederick Prince of Wales in 1748 and later to George III. In 1749 he acquired and published the Lea/Saxton plates from Willdey (**19**).

Jefferys devoted much of his time to large-scale maps of the English counties. The prize-winning map of Devonshire, surveyed by Benjamin Donn (**44**) was followed by others on a scale of one inch to the mile including Bedfordshire, Huntingdonshire and Oxfordshire and culminating in that of Yorkshire in 1771.

The expenses he incurred in the preparation of these maps were probably the cause of his bankruptcy in 1765. Robert Sayer came to his aid but only on condition that he became a partner and associate in some of his works. They must have got on fairly well as in 1768 they went to Paris together on a selling expedition. Faden joined forces with Jefferys in 1769, assisting him in his financial recovery, and took over a portion of the business after Jefferys' death in 1771. When Jefferys' American maps were later published the *West Indian Atlas* was published by Sayer (1775) and the *American Atlas* by Faden (1776).

Included with the 12-sheet Donn map is *a General View of the County, on One Sheet,* when it was published in bound form in a book. Each square on the general map corresponds to a sheet and is numbered I – XII. The hundreds are shown in capitals and there are points at sea with *Variation* followed by Roman numerals; one at Start Point; the other off Morte Point in the Bristol Channel. Lundy is shown, *Said to be part of the Hundred of Branton*; although a part of Hartland Hundred in the thirteenth century, by the nineteenth Lundy was part of Braunton Hundred.

In 1799 William Faden also issued a reduced copy of Donn's map engraved by Benjamin Baker on one sheet (**62**).

Size 485 x 535 mm.   **A Scale of Statute Miles** (10=61 mm).
                                        Scale 1M=6.1 mm.

A MAP of the COUNTY of DEVON abridged from the 12-Sheet SURVEY By Benjamin Donn. Engraved by Tho⁵ Jefferys Geographer to His MAJESTY.   Imprint: **Entered in the Hall Book of the Company of Stationers and Published according to Act of Parliament February 1ˢᵗ. 1765.** (CeOS).

1.	1765	*A Map of the County of Devon …*	
		Published in the bound volume of Benjamin Donn's 12-sheet map of Devon.	
		London. B Donn. 1765.	BL, B, C, BCL, (E).
		Example printed on vellum.	(TQ¹), (KB).

---

¹· Torquay Museum also has an incomplete set of the twelve-sheet map on vellum; sheets 1, 5, 6 and 10 are missing.

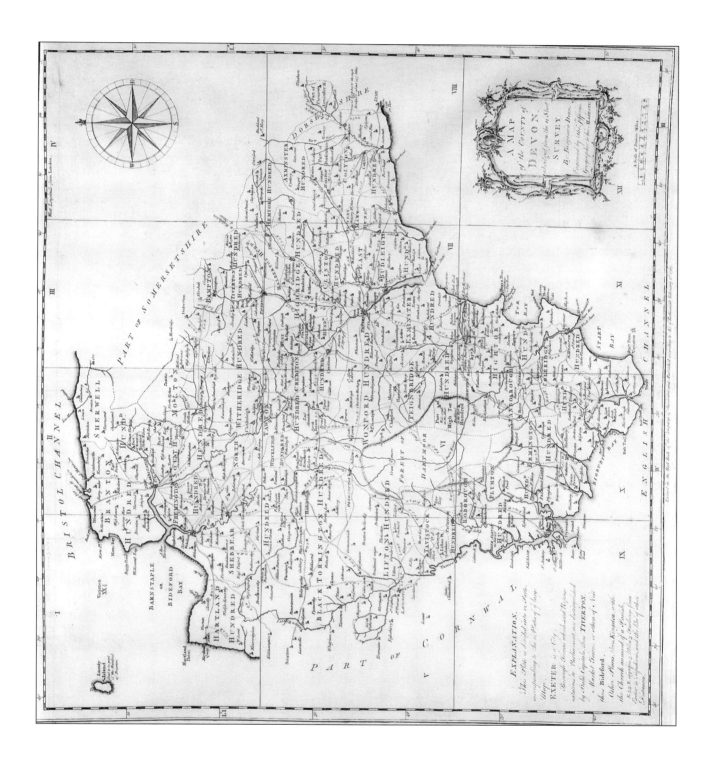

45.1 Donn/Jefferys *A Map of the County of Devon* printed on vellum

46

JOSEPH ELLIS
1765

Joseph Ellis (*fl.*1750-*d.*1796) of Clerkenwell, London, was a prolific English engraver in the late eighteenth century. In 1776 he engraved the maps of the *Hibernian Atlas* together with William Palmer, with whom he also produced a set of English county maps for *The New English Atlas*. The Devon map in this atlas is a very close copy of Kitchin's map in *England Illustrated* (**43**, and see also **50** and **52**). The engravers were Ellis and Palmer, Louis de la Rochette and W Fowler.

Many copies of Devon have Dorset on the reverse (denoted *). Devon has no Ellis signature but Dorset on the reverse does. In the 1765 edition Devon was incorrectly indexed 13. The 1766 issue had 48 maps (50 in list but Nos 3 and 4 were not issued) and Devon was correctly indexed. The 1773 maps are folded. The map is graticuled at full degrees.

Size 190 x 242 mm.

British Statute Miles 69 to a Degree (24=50 mm).
Scale 1M=2.1 mm.

A Modern MAP of DEVON SHIRE, Drawn from the latest Surveys; Corrected & Improved by the best Authorities. Imprint: **Printed for Rob**^t. **Sayer in Fleet Street, & Carington Bowles in S**^t. **Pauls Churchyard** (CeOS). Plate number **15** (EeOS).

(E), (NDL).

1. 1765	*The New English Atlas* London. R Sayer and Carington Bowles. 1765.		BL.
	Ellis's English Atlas in Fifty Maps London. R Sayer and Carington Bowles. 1766.		**CCXXVII**, BL, RGS; CB[1].
	Ellis's English Atlas in Fifty-four Maps London. Carington Bowles and R Sayer. 1766.		**CCXXVIIa**, BL*, B*, W*, CB.
	Atlas Britannique[2] London. R Sayer. 1766.		BL.
	Ellis's English Atlas in Fifty-four Maps London. Carington Bowles. 1768, (1789).		CB*, W; BL*.
	Ellis's English Atlas in Fifty Maps London. R Sayer, T Jefferys and A Dury. 1768.		[P*]; **CCXXVIII**, BL.
	Ellis's English Atlas in Fifty Maps. London. R Sayer. 1773.		**CCXXIX**, BL, BCL.
	Ellis's English Atlas in Fifty Maps. London. R Sayer and J Bennett. 1777.		**CCXXX**, BL, W, RGS.
	Ellis's English Atlas in Fifty Maps. London. Carington Bowles. (1785).		RGS.
2. 1796	Page number erased and new number **12** higher than before. Bedford on reverse.		
	Ellis's English Atlas in Fifty Maps London. Robert Sayer (actually Laurie & Whittle). 1796.		BL, RGS[3].

[1.] With publishers' names reversed on the title page.

[2.] For a collation of this atlas see R V Tooley's article in *The Map Collector*, Issue 8 September 1979; p.55.

[3.] A pencil note assumes it to be Laurie & Whittle, 1796, but a Saxon Heptarchy sheet has paper watermarked 18--

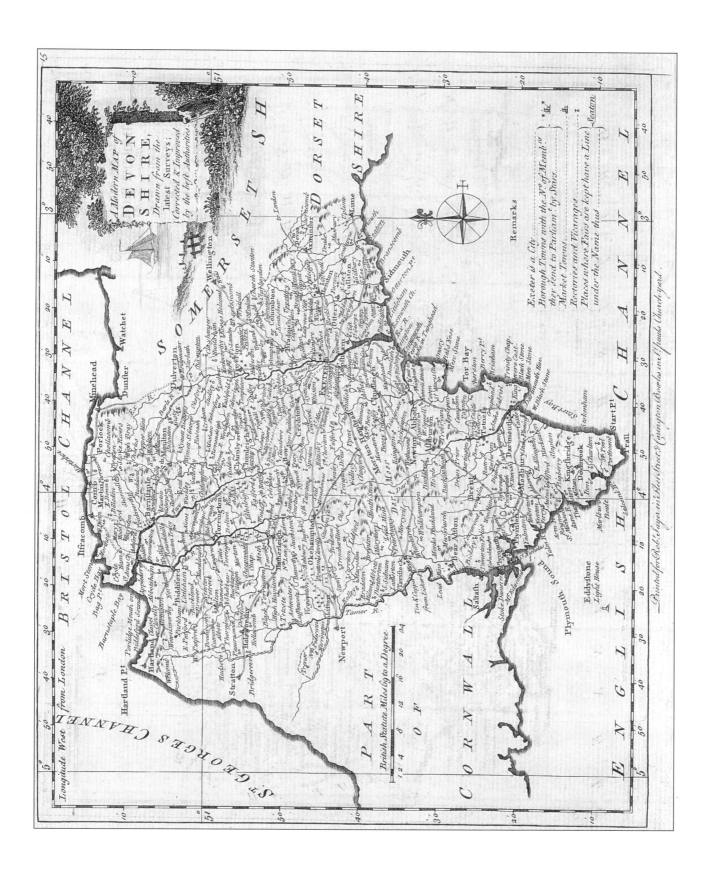

46.1 Ellis *Ellis's English Atlas*

47

JOHN GIBSON
1767

One of the more successful of the eighteenth century magazines was *The Universal Museum or Gentleman's and Ladies Polite Magazine of History, Politicks and Literature.* It was issued monthly between January 1762 and December 1764. It then continued as *The Universal Museum and Complete Magazine of Knowledge and Pleasure* and was again issued monthly, from January 1765 until December 1770, with a variety of maps including 10 county maps. Devon was included in this series (Vol.3, opp.p.358. July 1767). Most of the maps were probably engraved by John Gibson, although one by Thomas Kitchin (*Roads of England & Wales*) and another by W. Fowler (*Oxfordshire*) were included in the series.

The connection with Kitchin is clearly seen. Devon was a copy of Kitchin's map for the *London Magazine* of 1750 (**34**), but with the imprints to identify it and the cow and cowherd reversed. Market days have been added but the arms of Exeter omitted.

Although the British Library has a copy of the *Universal Magazine* the map of Devon is missing.

John Gibson had previously produced a charming set of miniature maps in John Newbery's *New and Accurate Maps* of 1759 (**40**).

Size 204 x 182 mm.

British Statute Miles (20=49 mm).
Scale 1M=2.5 mm.

An Accurate MAP of DEVONSHIRE from the Best Authorities by J. Gibson. Imprints: **Engrav'd for the Universal Museum and Complete Magazine.** (CaOS) and **Printed for J. Payne at No. 54 Paternoster Row.** (CeOS).

1. 1767   *The Universal Museum and Complete Magazine of Knowledge and Pleasure*
London. Publish'd Monthly by J Payne, at No 54 Pater Noster Row. 1767.
CCXXI, Jolly UMUS24, (E¹).

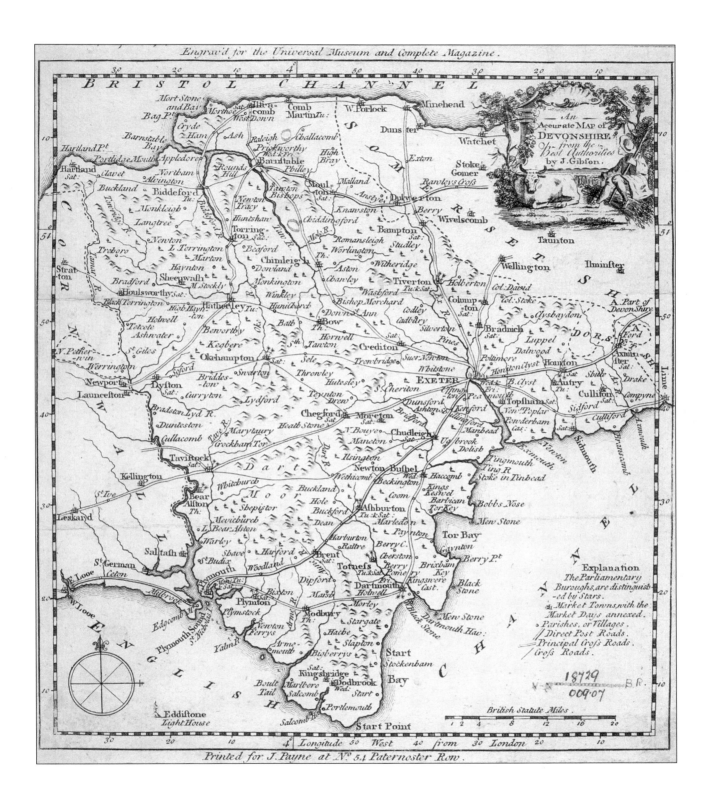

47.1 Gibson *The Universal Museum and Complete Magazine*

48

EMANUEL BOWEN
1767

In 1767 Emanuel Bowen and his son Thomas (*fl.*1749-1790) produced the *Atlas Anglicanus*. Although the maps are graticuled, the map of Devon is distorted and the scale inaccurate. The correct figures at latitude 51° for 1 degree latitude is 69.5 miles and for longitude is 43.4 miles. This would give scales of 1M=3.6 mm East-West and 1M=2.5 mm North-South. Consequently the map accentuates the East-West dimension. The topographical information had appeared in the *Large* and *Royal* atlases (**37, 42**) but the vignettes, insets and references to seats of nobility etc. were removed.

The maps were issued in 15 parts, each part containing three maps; Devon appeared together with Cornwall and Somerset.

Size 225 x 330 mm.   **British Statute Miles** (12=63 mm).
Scale 1M=5.2 mm.

DEVON SHIRE, Divided into HUNDREDS. Containing the City, Burough and Market Towns &c, with concise Historical Extracts, relative to its Natural Produce Trade and Manufactures. Describing also the Church Livings, with other Improvements not inserted in any other Half Sheet County Maps Extant. By Eman: Bowen Geogr**. to His late Maj**y**.** Page number **N**o**. 4.** (EaOS). Distances between towns are given.

1. 1767	*Atlas Anglicanus* London. T Kitchin. (1767).		BCL[1], B, W, C.

2. 1770   Imprint added: **Printed for T. Kitchin No 59 Holborn Hill.** (CeOS). Page number deleted. (E[2]), (DEI).

Atlas Anglicanus
London. T Kitchin. (1770).   **CCXXXII**, BL, RGS.

Atlas Anglicanus
London. T Kitchin and A Dury. 1777.   **CCXXXIII**, BL, B.

3. 1785   Title altered: **BOWLES's NEW MEDIUM MAP OF DEVONSHIRE, Divided into its HUNDREDS. Exhibiting the Roads, Towns & Villages: with their Distance from London. Church Livings, Seats of the Nobility and Historical Remarks.** in oval frame together with imprint: **LONDON: Printed for the Proprietor Carington Bowles, No 69 in S**t **Pauls Church Yard.** Plate no. 10 (EaOS). Imprint **Published as the Act directs. 3 Jan. 1785.** (CeOS).
Distances between towns erased, distances from London added.

(NDL).

Bowles's New Medium English Atlas
London. Carington Bowles. 1785.   **CCLV**, BL, W, B, C.

Bowles's New Medium English Atlas
London. Bowles and Carver. (1795).[3]   CB.

[1.] The Birmingham Central Library atlas dated by hand 1797, but this is undoubtedly an error. The mileages are those between towns, ie pre-1785.

[2.] Illustration courtesy of the Exeter Westcountry Studies Library.

[3.] This atlas has 36 maps in this state. Other maps have a revised imprint: **LONDON: Printed for the Proprietors Bowles & Carver, No 69 in St Paul's Church Yard**. It was advertised in a magazine in 1795. Devon may exist with this imprint.

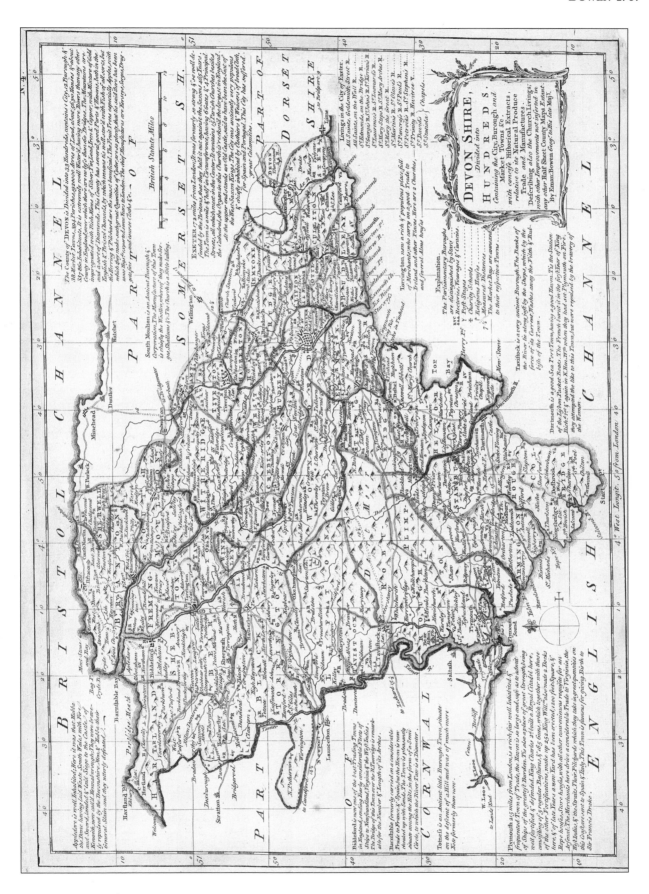

48.2 Bowen *Atlas Anglicanus*

49

THOMAS KITCHIN
1769

Although he collaborated with his former master and father-in-law, Emanuel Bowen, on many atlases Thomas Kitchin is known for a much wider variety of engraved work than Bowen. The most striking feature of his cartographic output is the sheer quantity of it. He was involved in the preparation and publication of more than a dozen different sets (and part sets) of county maps, including this set for *Kitchin's Pocket Atlas* which appeared in 1769 (oblong 8vo, 47 maps). He also engraved some of the most important individual maps of the 18th century and furnished illustrative maps for countless travel-books, geographies and gazetteers.

The maps published by Kitchin and J Gapper were said to be *the first set of counties, ever published on this plan*, ie to a uniform scale. This was not strictly true as Matthew Simmons' atlas of 1636 (**9**) had the same intention, though at a much smaller scale. The next atlas to be drawn to a uniform scale was that of the Greenwoods in 1834.

When the maps reappeared some 13 years later they were published by Carington Bowles. This was one of only two atlases to have the name Bowles in the title (the other was also a Bowen and Kitchin production – **48**). Carington was a member of a family of map sellers and publishers which, through four generations, contributed a great deal to English cartography.

Thomas Bowles, in all probability working from St Paul's Churchyard in London, was the father of John and Thomas Bowles. The latter as well as continuing his father's business became an established engraver of maps and prints including some notable engravings of plans and views of London, much of his work being sold through his brother, who using his patrimony started his own firm in 1723 and was involved in publishing for some sixty years. He published numerous maps and atlases and both their names are found as publishers of the maps of Hermann Moll (**25**).

Carington Bowles joined the family business in 1754 and the firm traded under the name John Bowles and Son. In 1764 Carington took over his uncle's business, his father continuing trading as John Bowles. Carington died in 1793 and his business was continued by his son and W Carver who traded for only two years as Bowles and Carver.

Although the atlas was listed in a Bowles and Carver catalogue in 1782 Chubb dated it 1785.

The map of Devon was larger than most and was folded and pasted in at the bottom left hand corner. Many maps were torn when they were removed from the atlas.

Size 308 x 280 mm.

British Statute Miles (18=63 mm).
Scale 1M=3.5 mm.

No title but **DEVON SHIRE** is written across the county, and it was graticuled at 4° West and 51° North.

1.	1769	*Kitchin's Pocket Atlass* London. T Kitchin and J Gapper. 1769.	**CCXXXV**, BL, C, W.
2.	1782	Title added: **BOWLES'S REDUCED MAP OF DEVONSHIRE**. (CaOS). Page number – **16** – added (EaOS).	
		Bowles's Pocket Atlas London. Carington Bowles. (1782).	**CCLVI**, BL, C.

49.1 Kitchin *Kitchin's Pocket Atlass*

50

HATCHETT/WALPOOLE/HOGG
1784

George Augustus Walpoole (or Walpole) was a British topographer responsible for only one notable cartographic work, *The New British Traveller*, which appeared in 1784. This was a five-part work and Walpoole was assisted in its preparation by *A Society of Gentlemen*. The folio atlas contains 23 plates most showing 2, though some 4, maps of the English counties with very decorative scrolls top and bottom. Devon was printed under Cornwall, consequently a loose copy of Devon will lack the upper scroll and sometimes the map is trimmed to the borders removing the bottom scroll and imprint. It was inserted opposite the first text page to Cornwall (p.388).

Although most of the maps were engraved by Thomas Conder, the signature of Hatchett is found under the map of Devon. Rather strangely, it appears only after changes were made for the second edition which although dated 1784 was issued *c*.1790. Many names are added to the second edition, eg Conder's name is added to the map of Northumberland and John Lodge's to a view of Dulwich College. Hatchett's name does not appear in the list of engravers on the title page.

The map of Devon has the coat of arms of Exeter; however a variation has been seen (only as a photocopy) with no coat of arms, implying an earlier issue but as it has finely trimmed borders the actual dating is uncertain.[1]

Devon is a close copy of the map in Thomas Kitchin's *England Illustrated* (**43**) and the Joseph Ellis map of 1765 (**46**) and of Lodge's Devonshire (**52**), although the Lodge is much larger. All four maps show the same mines, name St George's Channel and all use Seaton as the example of a town holding a regular fair in the Explanation table.

The British Library copy has an incomplete date and other copies inspected have also had part of the date deleted. In 1794 the maps reappeared, the atlas now entitled *The New and Complete English Traveller*, again prepared by *A Society of Gentlemen* but revised, corrected and improved by William Hugh Dalton.

Size 155 x 200 mm.

British Statute Miles 69 to a Degree (24=39 mm).
Scale 1M=1.62 mm.

A Modern MAP of DEVON SHIRE, Drawn from the latest Surveys; Corrected & Improved by the best Authorities. Imprints: **Engrav'd for WALPOOLE's New and Complete BRITISH TRAVELLER.** above map of Cornwall (CaOS) and imprint: **Published by ALEX^r HOGG at the King's Arms N°. 16 PATERNOSTER ROW** (CeOS). Scroll borders above and below.

1.	**1784**	*The New British Traveller... Published by George Augustus Walpoole* London. Alexander Hogg. 1784.	CCLI, BL, (E), (DEI).
2.	**1790**	Cartouche and coat of arms retouched. Signature added: **Hatchett Sculp^t** (EeOS). Imprint above 'Cornwall' erased together with all scroll work.	
			(E), (NDL), (DEI).
		The New British Traveller... London. Alexander Hogg. 1784 (1790).	W, BCL, E.
		The New and Complete English Traveller ... Revised, corrected and improved by William Hugh Dalton. London. Alexander Hogg. 1794.	CCLII, BL.

[1.] Kit Batten in a letter to the Editor; Wayward Walpoole; in *The Map Collector*, Winter 1995 Issue 71.

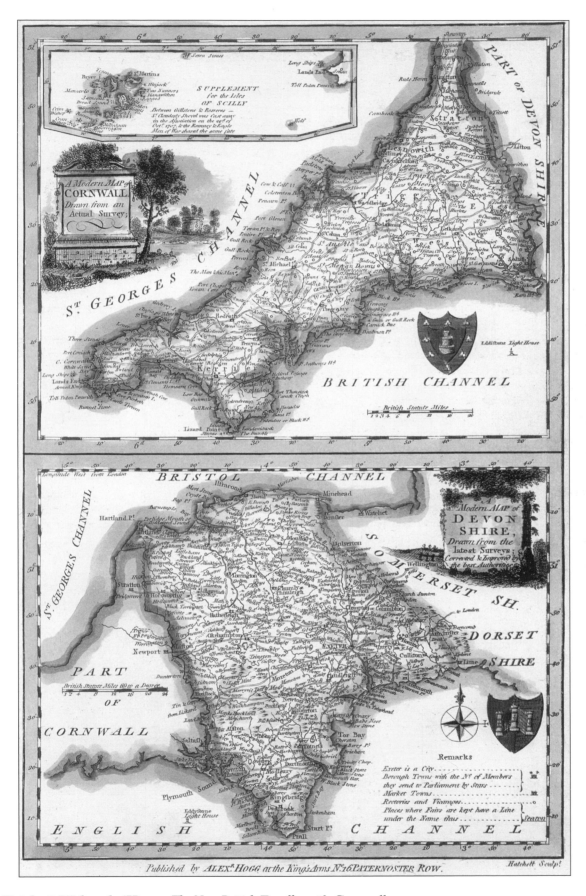

50.2 Hatchett/Walpoole/Hogg *The New British Traveller* with Cornwall

51

JOHN CARY
1787

John Cary's (see **54**, **55**) first county atlas, *New and Correct Atlas*, appeared in parts from 1787 to 1789. Originally the plan was to publish one part a month, each to include 4 counties, and Devon appeared in issue seven with Somerset, Shrops and Northants on February 26th 1788 (the first title page imprint was dated 1787). Later progress was slow and the final maps appeared in Spring 1789. Atlases were made up of whatever sheets were available. Devon was re-engraved before 1809 (**73**).

The British Library has two copies of *The History of Devonshire* by Rev. Richard Polwhele published by Cadell, Johnson and Dilly (1797) with Cary's map in state 6. The map is not called for in the contents: other copies seen contain this map, Cary's later map (**71**) or Morden's map (see **21**).

Size 210 x 265 mm.

Statute Miles 69½ to a Degree (10=29.5 mm).
Scale 1M=2.95 mm.

DEVONSHIRE with signature **By JOHN CARY Engraver**. Imprint: **London: Published as the Act directs, 1st. Sepr. 1787. by J. Cary Engraver Map & Printseller the corner of Arundel Street Strand.** (CeOS).

(E), (DEI), (Ply).

1.	**1787**	*Cary's New and Correct English Atlas* London. John Cary. 1787[1], 1787[2].	**CCLX**, BL, C; BCL.
2.	**1787**	**Berry** and **Abbey** added at Hartland.	
		Cary's New and Correct English Atlas London. John Cary. 1787[1], 1787[2].	P; BL, B, W, RGS.
		Cary's New and Correct English Atlas London. John Cary. 1793.	**CCLXI**, BL, W[3].
3.	**1793**	Directions added, eg **from Liskeard** and **to Dunster**. **Chard**, in Somerset, added.	
		Cary's New and Correct English Atlas London. John Cary. 1793.	P.
4.	**1793**	Imprint: **London: Published Jany. 1st. 1793. by J. Cary, Engraver & Mapseller, Strand.** The dates after 1793 are based on imprint of Dorset (1795) and watermarks.	(E).
		Cary's New and Correct English Atlas London. John Cary. 1793, 1793 (1795), 1793 (1802), 1793 (1804), 1793 (1808). **CCLXII**, B; **CCLXIII**, RGS, W, C; B, C; BL, RGS, ¢; BCL.	
5.	**1793**	**St Anns Chap** added on Lundy.	
		Cary's New and Correct English Atlas London. John Cary. 1793.	BCL.
6.	**1793**	Imprint removed.	
		Cary's New and Correct English Atlas London. John Cary. 1793.	BL, C, (E), (DEI).

[1.] Title page of atlas **Published as the Act directs Jan 1st, 1987.**

[2.] Title page of atlas **Published as the Act directs Sept 1, 1987.**

[3.] The description of the county was usually interleaved with variations of text layout; this copy has text on reverse.

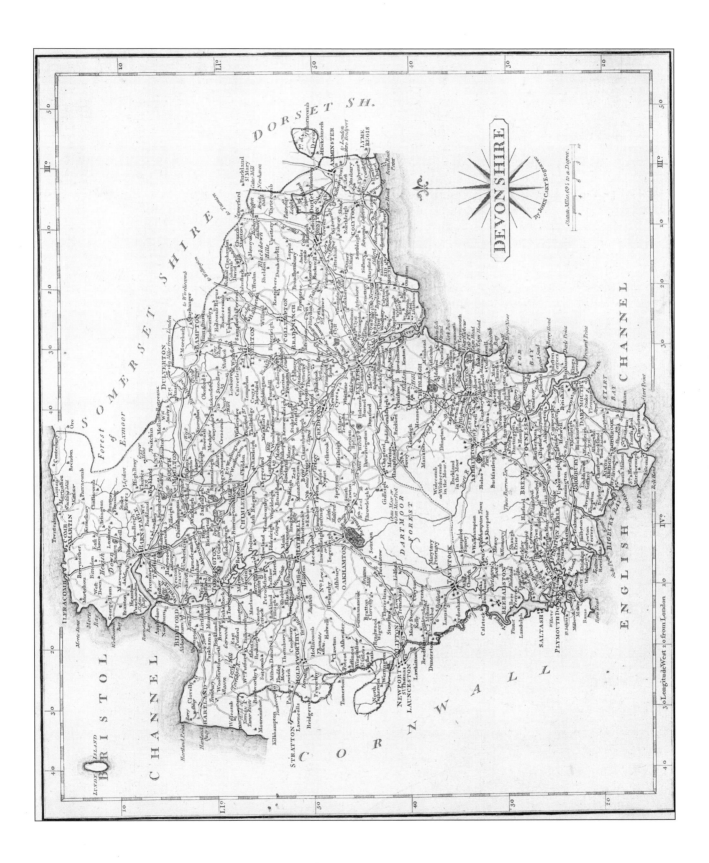

51.2 Cary *New and Correct English Atlas* the first engraving

52

JOHN LODGE
1788

John Lodge (*fl.*1754-96) a geographer and engraver at 45 Shoe Lane, London, produced many maps of the Americas and maps of canals for *The Gentleman's Magazine* and also engraved a series of county maps for *The Political Magazine and Parliamentary, Naval, Military, and Literary Journal* between the years 1782 and 1790. This magazine was issued monthly with occasional supplements, Volume I being published in 1780 with a Preliminary Number. From 1783 each volume included 6 months, and Devon appeared on Vol. 14, April 1788. The county maps appeared in atlas form five years later. Devon is very similar to Thomas Kitchin's map for *England Illustrated* (**43**) which was probably also the source of Joseph Ellis's map (**46**) and of Hatchett's map for Walpoole (**50**). The compass, scale, remarks, longitude and latitude are the same in each of the four maps but the lettering of towns is different, with slightly different alignment etc. The maps are different sizes with Lodge's map approximately twice as large as the other versions.

All four maps distinctively include tin, lead and copper mines; the same five mines as listed by Herman Moll in his map of 1724 (**25**). Moll had listed the mines partly because of their antiquarian importance, but by 1788 most mines were in decline. However, the Great Consols mine near Tavistock was producing large quantities of copper well into the nineteenth century: indeed Devon and Cornwall produced half the world's copper in the mid-nineteenth century. The three towns Ashburton, Tavistock and Chagford had owed their early growth to the fact that they were Stannary towns but by this time tin-mining was on a very small scale.

Full degrees of latitude and longitude are drawn on the map.

The early maps are all easily identified by the imprint. When the maps appeared in the atlas (8vo, 54 maps) in 1795 these were removed – the atlas has no title page but some copies have a title on the cover. One map has a watermark of 1795, others have a medallion with Britannia.

Size 260 x 320 mm. **British Statute Miles 69 to a degree** (24=68 mm).
Scale 1M=2.8 mm.

A NEW MAP OF DEVONSHIRE FROM THE LATEST AUTHORITIES. Imprints: **Political Mag. April 1788** (CaOS) and **London. Published as the Act directs. April 30. 1788. by J. Murray, N°. 32 Fleet Street.** (CeOS). Signature: **J Lodge Sculp.** (EeOS).

1. **1788**	*The Political Magazine*		
	London. J. Murray. 1788.		**CCXLIX, Jolly POL121, BL, BCL, (E).**
2. **1795**	Imprints and signature are erased.		
	Atlas of Great Britain and Ireland		
	London. J. Murray (1795).		**CCL, BL, W, B, C, (E).**

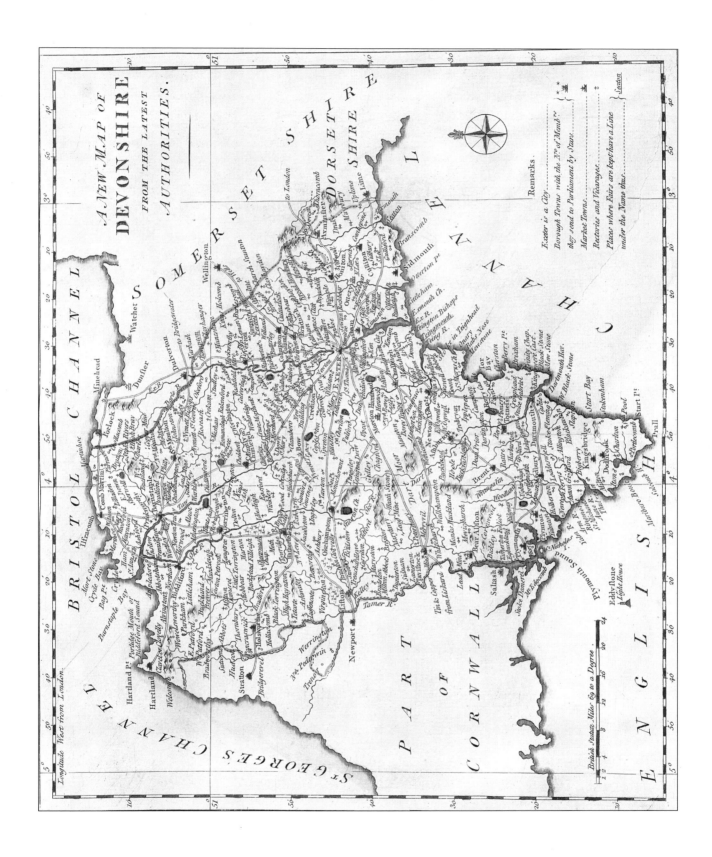

52.2 Lodge Atlas of Great Britain and Ireland

53

HAYWOOD/HARRISON
1789

John Harrison (*fl.*1784-1815) a printer and publisher at 115 Newgate Street London, produced the *Atlas* to accompany Nicholas Tindal's translation of *The History of England* from *c.*1784 until 1789 (a work originally by Paul Rapin de Thoyras and published *c.*1730-50). This included maps subsequently reissued in *Maps and Plans of Tindal's Continuation of Rapin's History of England*. Harrison employed several draughtsmen and engravers for the *History* including James Haywood and E Sudlow whose signatures are found on the Devon map. Other works by Harrison included a map of *Africa* (1787) and in 1791 a *School Atlas*.

In 1791 he published his atlas, *Maps of the English Counties* (folio, 38 maps), reusing the maps produced for *The History of England* including Devonshire. For the atlas a description of each county on two pages was interleaved. The map of Devon shows very little of the surrounding counties, labels Somerset as DEVONSHIRE and is graticuled. Other counties were amended or had information added when reissued in 1791, such as town names, rivers and market days etc but these have not been noted on Devon.

An edition in which the imprint is amended has also been recorded: the date or the last two digits of the date have been erased on some maps in an atlas now broken up (*General and County Atlas*: London. J Harrison. (1815))[1]. In addition Burden states one atlas has added plate number typed.

The Morning Herald of 2nd May, 1787, carried an advertisement for specimen county maps by John Harrison printed in crimson ink on white satin. It is possible that the Devon map was issued in this state. Some maps produced on silk in this way were designed as embroidery exercises for young women.

Size 330 x 445 mm.

English Statute Miles 69½ to a Degree (20=74 mm).
Scale 1M=3.7 mm.

A MAP of DEVONSHIRE ENGRAVED FROM AN ACTUAL SURVEY with Improvements. Imprint: **London, Engraved for J. Harrison, 115, Newgate Street, as the Act directs, 2d. July, 1789.** (CeOS). Signatures: **Haywood Del** (AeOS) and **Sudlow Sculp** (EeOS).

(E), (NDL).

1. 1789   *The History of England ... by Rapin de Thoyras ... translated into English ... by N Tindal ... embellished with Portraits of Kings, Queens ... and a Complete Set of Maps of all the Kingdoms and countries of the World and the Counties of England and Wales.* 4 Volumes.
London. John Harrison. 1785-1789.   CB.

Maps of the English Counties
London. John Harrison. 1791, 1792.   **CCXCI**, BL, C, CB; **CCXCII**, RGS.

[1.] Eugene Burden; *County Maps of Berkshire*; (1988) 1991; p.61.

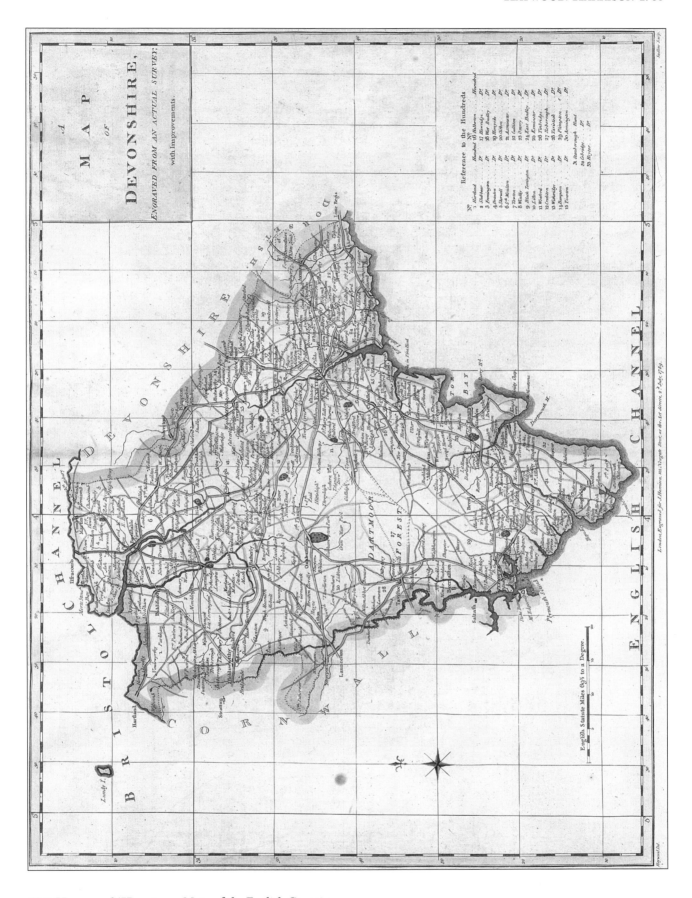

A
MAP
OF
DEVONSHIRE,
ENGRAVED FROM AN ACTUAL SURVEY;
with improvements

Reference to the Hundreds

Nº		Hundred	Nº		Hundred
1	Hartland		16	Halberton	Hundred
2	Shebbear		17	Hemiock	Dº
3	Fremington		18	Wer Budley	Dº
4	Braunton		19	Hayridge	Dº
5	Sherwill		20	Silferton	Dº
6	Sth Molton		21	Axminster	Dº
7	Tiverton		22	Colliton	Dº
8	Witsley		23	Ottery	Dº
9	Black Torrington		24	East Budley	Dº
10	Lifton		25	Exminster	Dº
11	Winkford		26	Teinbridge	Dº
12	Crediton		27	Roborough	Dº
13	Wonherdge		28	Tavistock	Dº
14	Hampton		29	Plimpton	Dº
15	Tiverton		30	Ærmington	Dº
			31	Stanborough	Hund
			32	Coleridge	Dº
			33	Heytor	Dº

English Statute Miles 69¼ to a Degree.

London, Engraved for J. Harrison, nᵒ 18 Wigate Street, as the Act directs, 2 July 1789.

53.1 **Haywood/Harrison** *Maps of the English Counties*

54

NOBLE/CARY
1789

John Cary (*d.*1835) was one of the finest English cartographers. Besides county maps (see **54**, **55**) his work covered world atlases, road maps, sea charts, town and canal plans. He became Surveyor of Roads to the General Post Office, commissioned to survey the roads of England in 1794.

John Cary came originally from Wiltshire, the son of a maltster. He was born in February 1755, the second son of George and Mary Cary. He had three brothers, Francis (1756-1836) also an engraver, William (1759-1825) a map publisher and globe maker with whom he collaborated, and George the elder (*d.*1830) who was a partner at 86 St James Street, London (1820). His two sons, George the younger (*d.*1859) and John, joined the firm in 1820. The business passed to G.F. Cruchley *c.*1844, and later to Gall & Inglis.

Cary's first county atlas was the *New and Correct* published in 1787 (**51**). In 1789 he produced maps for an edition of Camden's *Britannia* translated by Richard Gough (folio, in 3 Vols with 60 maps). This does not seem to have been very successful, although it was issued a second time in 1806. Meanwhile, however, the maps from this work were used by John Stockdale in his *New British Atlas* published in 1805. The map of Devon was drawn by E Noble.

John Stockdale (1749-1814), once both blacksmith and personal valet, became an important London publisher and edited and published the works of Dr Samuel Johnson in 1787. As well as producing the *New British Atlas* which employed Cary's *Britannia* maps, he also issued the second edition of *Britannia* in 1806.

Size 430 x 475 mm.   **Statute Miles 69$^{1}/_{2}$ to a Degree of Latitude** (1+10=64 mm).
Scale 1M=5.8 mm.

A MAP of DEVONSHIRE from the best AUTHORITIES with imprint: **Engraved by J Cary**. Signature: **E Noble delint et curavit** (EeOS).

1. 1789   Proof copy with the bottom border lower, only the coast shading breaking the inner line. The sheet height is 441 mm. **Longitude West from London** is engraved to the left of Bolt Head.

B.

2. 1789   As illustrated: Lundy and Prawle Point extend into border. **Longitude West from London** between inner, graduated and outer borders (Ce).

Britannia ... by William Camden ... Translated by Richard Gough ...
London. T Payne and Son, and G G J & J Robinson. 1789.
CCLXXI, BL, W, (NDL), (Ply).

3. 1805   Imprint: **Published by John Stockdale Picadilly 26th, March 1805.** added below title but above Cary's imprint. Road alterations and inclusion of waterways: Tamar Navigation, Tavistock Canal and intended Grand Western Canal.

(NDL).

New British Atlas
London. John Stockdale. 1805, (1809).   **CCCXIX**, B; BL, RGS, C, B, W.

Britannia   2nd Edition.
London. John Stockdale. 1806.   **CCLXXII**, BL, B, E.

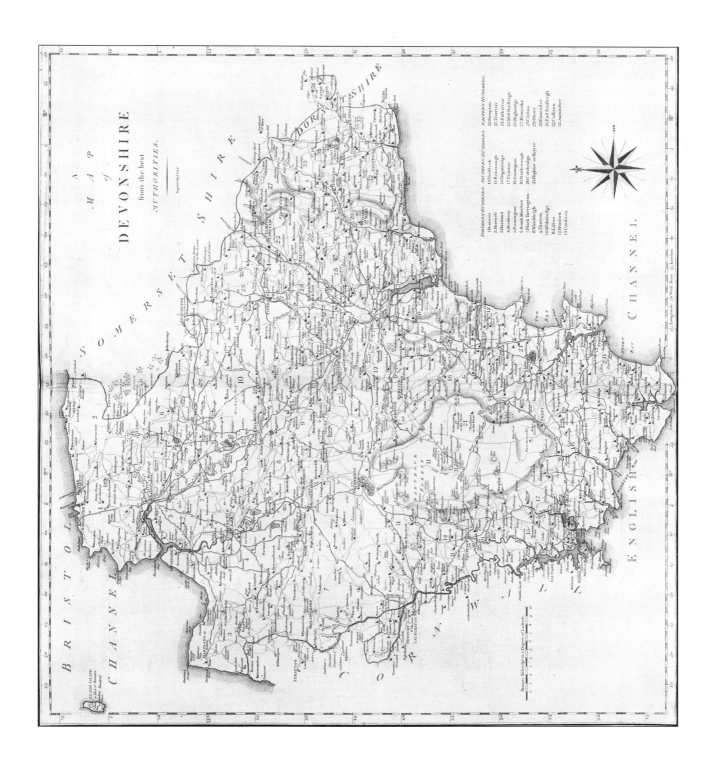

54.2 Noble/Cary *Britannia*

55

JOHN CARY
1789

John Cary has long been one of the most written about and admired of all the British mapmakers (see **54**). To Fordham[1] he was the founder of the modern school, *the most prominent and successful exponent of his time*, the cartographer who *first combined care and beauty of design, with something really approximate to geographical accuracy.*

The maps in each edition of *Traveller's Companion* are perfect examples of his craft. They combine simplicity of design with maximum accuracy. After the elaborate designs of the seventeenth century and the first half of the eighteenth they may even strike one as too plain (compared with Moll and Read from the early 1700s for example).

Cary's Traveller's Companion appeared for the first time in 1790 (small 8vo, 43 maps) although many maps, including Devon, were dated 1789. A number of maps have been found on card and many, including Devon, are the first states of the respective counties. The *Companion* was extremely successful and was reprinted many times. Most counties had substantial revisions and, like Devon, were completely re-engraved for the 1806 issue (**69**). The Devon plate was re-engraved a second time (**92**). Atlases in states 2 and 5 were printed in two variations, with or without maps on reverse; Devon has Dorsetshire on reverse.

Loose maps of Bedfordshire, Cheshire and Cumberland based on Cary's map have been seen and come from an unidentified journal with text headed *Outlines of British Geography*[2]. No copy of Devon is known.

Size 132 x 93 mm including title.

Statute Miles (10=13 mm).
Scale 1M=1.3 mm.

DEVONSHIRE. Signature: **By J. Cary** (AaOS) and **Engraver** (EaOS). Imprint: **London Published Sep[r]. 1. 1789 by J. Cary Engraver N[O]. 188 Strand.** (CeOS). Devonport identified only by **Dock**. Ottery St Mary is missing from last line of panel.

1. 1789	One of a number of maps mounted on card.		TB.
2. 1789	**Ottery St Mary** is added to last line of panel with mileage 160.		
	Cary's Traveller's Companion London. John Cary. 1790.	**CCLXXIII**, BL, B, W, RGS, C.	
3. 1790	Minor changes including addition of **Plymouth** to **Dock** and **Plymouth Sound**.		(P).
4. 1790	The Honiton to Taunton(e) turnpike moved west of the River Otter. Upottery and High Luxmore erased. The Turnpike from Launceston to Hatherley added.		
	Loose copy. Imprint has been cut off.		(FB).
5. 1792	New imprint: **London Published Sep[r]. 1. 1792 by J. Cary Engraver N[O]. 181 Strand.** Some changes, eg *ck* of Plymouth Dock erased and St Nicholas Island lost. The Honiton to Taunton(e) turnpike has been re-engraved. Comb Martin road upgraded.		
	Cary's Traveller's Companion London. John Cary. 1791.	**CCLXXIV/V**, BL, B, W, RGS, BCL.	

[1.] Sir H G Fordham; *John Cary, Engraver and Map Seller*, Cambridge; 1910.
[2.] Eugene Burden; *County Maps of Berkshire*; (1988) 1991.

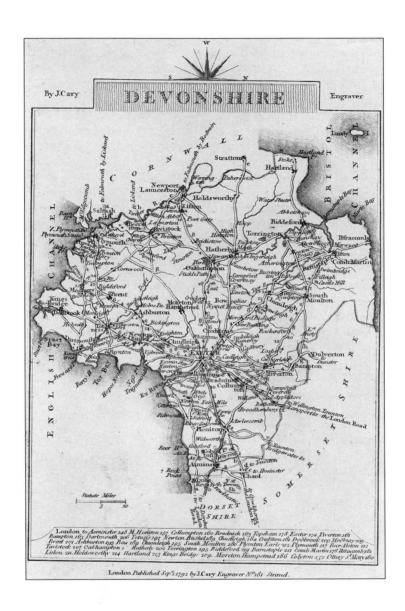

55.5 Cary *Traveller's Companion* the first of three engravings

56

JOHN AIKIN
1790

Dr John Aikin (1747-1822, sometimes spelt Aiken) studied medicine in Edinburgh and practised in Great Yarmouth. He retired after a stroke in 1792. A friend of Joseph Priestley (a theologian and scientist famous for making chemistry a modern science), and Charles Darwin (a visitor to Stoke Newington) Aikin devoted much of his time to writing. He wrote a number of pamphlets for dissenters and it was because of the hostile reception to his work that he moved to London in 1792. Aikin's other cartographic work *The History of the Environs of London* was published by John Stockdale in 1811.

Aikin first published his *England Delineated* in 1788 without maps.[1] The second (1790), and all subsequent editions except the last, contained 43 simplistic maps probably intended for schoolchildren. Considering the amount of information on a Cary or similar map from this time Aikin's map is very plain and austere. The map has no border. Maps of other counties later had lettering strengthened and/or modified but this is not apparent on the Devon map.

The map of Devon was bound in opposite page 340 on which the account of Devon begins. There is an interesting report of the goods sold in Exeter at this time. The page number on the map was engraved approximately 102 mm above and 20 mm to the right of the full stop after the map title. Consequently, it was very close to the edge of the page when this was printed and on narrow pages the number was sometimes cut or even excised completely. In addition page sizes vary by up to 5 mm in each direction affecting the chances of the number being removed during cutting and binding.

At least two separate manuscript maps of Devon exist which are close copies of the Aikin map. The paper of the second copy is watermarked Whatman 1834[2] and the map came from a manuscript atlas signed by Ebernezer Homann.

Joseph Johnson, the publisher, came from Liverpool and specialised in medical works. He was well-respected in the book trade but was imprisoned briefly for selling a pamphlet by Gilbert Wakefield.

Size of map area 105 x 130 mm.   Scale 1M=1.5 mm.
Size including page number 120 x 165 mm.

DEVONSHIRE. Plate number **39** (Ea).

1. 1790   *England Delineated or a geographical description of every county in England and Wales. ... by John Aikin* ... 2nd Edition.
London. J Johnson. 1790.   **CCLXXXVI**, BL, C, BCL.

England Delineated 3rd Edition.
London. J Johnson. 1795.   **CCLXXXVII**, BL, W.

England Delineated 4th Edition.
London. J Johnson. 1800.   **CCLXXXVIII**, BL, C.

England Delineated 5th Edition.
London. J Johnson. 1803.   BL, RGS.

England Delineated 6th Edition (last with maps).
London. J Johnson. (1809).   **CCLXXXIX**, BL, RGS.

[1.] Raymond Carroll in *The Printed Maps of Lincolnshire* (Society for Lincolnshire History and Archaeology, 1996) confirms that a copy of the first edition in the Cambridge University Library (CUL Atlas 7.78.24) has maps. These maps do not look as though they were bound in later which indicates either that it is a later copy, produced just before the second edition appeared, or that it was sold at the time that the second edition was on sale but with an old title page.

[2.] The authors are grateful to Malcolm Woodward for drawing these maps to their attention.

AIKIN 1790

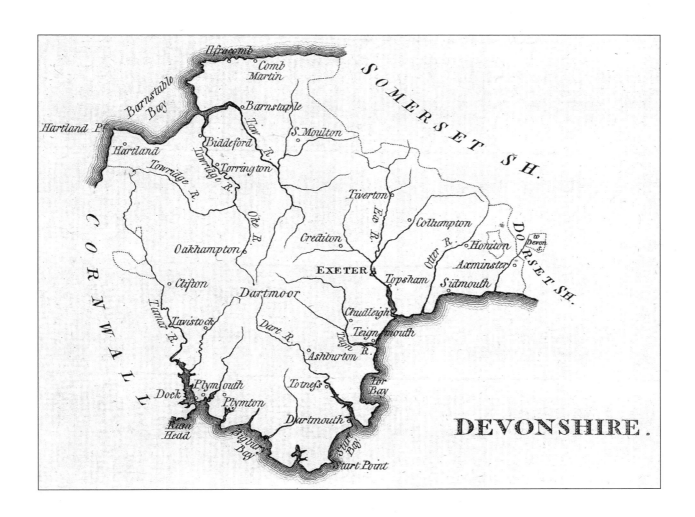

56.1 Aikin *England Delineated*

115

57

BENJAMIN BAKER
1791

Benjamin Baker (1766-1824) was born in London into a family of instrument-makers. At the age of fifteen or sixteen Baker was briefly apprenticed to a local watchmaker, but after two months transferred to the workshop of the map and lettering engraver William Palmer (1732-1812), a close neighbour of the Bakers, in New Street Square. Palmer's reputation was considerable. From his workshop came a number of engravers who were to make a name for themselves in the field of mapmaking – John Cary, John Russell, Robert Rowe, John Lodge, and Benjamin Baker.[1]

After his apprenticeship, Baker worked for fifteen years from premises in Islington. In 1804 he was appointed principal engraver to the Ordnance Survey. For the remainder of his career he led the team of engravers assembled, initially at the Tower of London, to work on the original series of the famous one-inch maps.

John Hinton produced the *The Universal Magazine of Knowledge and Pleasure* with the first, and arguably more attractive, series of maps between 1747 and 1766 (**32**). This was followed from 1791 by a second series of English and Welsh county maps. Benjamin Baker engraved most of this series of maps for the *Universal Magazine* before they were published in atlases. Devon first appeared in Volume 89 in November 1791 (Plate 9).

Laurie and Whittle acquired the plates some time between 1804 and 1806 and reprinted the maps with two pages of text giving a description of the county, antiquities, seats and a list of fairs and markets.

Later issues: There was one more issue of *A New and Improved English Atlas* in 1846. Devon has the imprint: *Published by R H LAURIE, No 53, Fleet Street, London.*

Size 180 x 227 mm.   **Scale of Miles** (15=34 mm).
Scale 1M=2.3 mm.

DEVONSHIRE with signature **Engrav'd By B. Baker. Islington.** In border **Longitude West from London**. (BeOS).

(E), (DEI).

1. 1791   *The Universal Magazine of Knowledge and Pleasure By William Bent, at the Kings Arms, Pater noster row* London. W Bent. 1791.

CCXCIII, Jolly UN15, C.

Maps of the Several Counties and Shires in England
London. Darton and Harvey. 1804.   C.

Atlas with no title-page   B.

2. 1806   **Longitude West from Greenwich** (Exeter is now 3°31 not 3°33.). Compass star around title oval, signature just legible. Plymouth Dock and the intended lines of the Grand Western canal and Tamer Navigation added. Imprint added: **Published 12**[th]**. October, 1806, by LAURIE & WHITTLE, N**[o] **53, Fleet Street, London.** (CeOS).

Laurie & Whittle's New and Improved English Atlas
London. Robert Laurie and James Whittle. 1807.   **CCXCIV**, BL, RGS, C, B, W.

A New and Improved English Atlas
London. James Whittle & Robert Holmes Laurie. 1816.   B.

---

[1]. Laurence Worms; Some British Mapmakers in *Ash Rare Books Catalogue and Price List*, 1992.

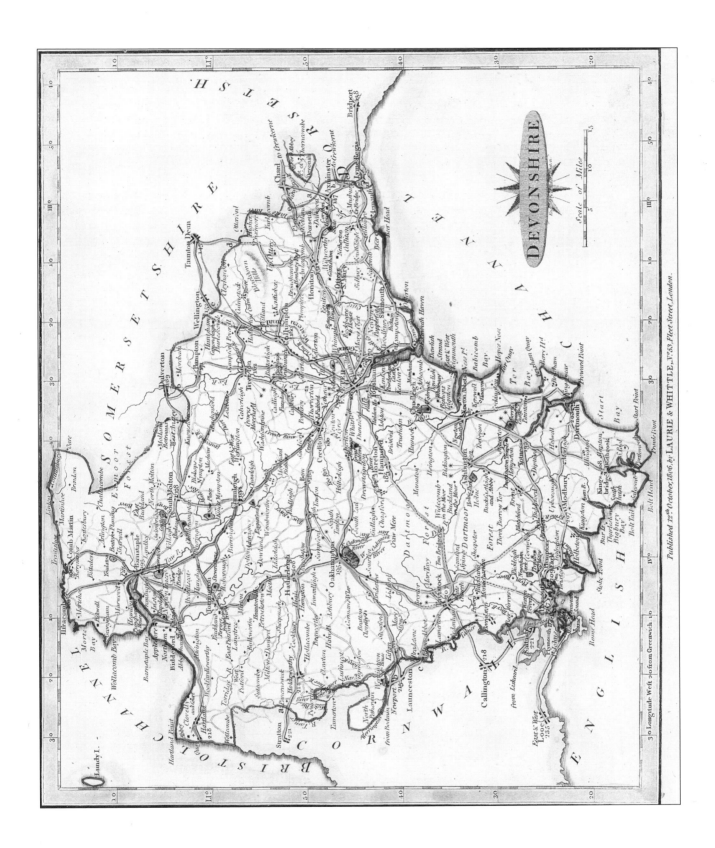

57.2 Baker *Laurie & Whittle's New and Improved English Atlas*

WILLIAM TUNNICLIFF
1791

William Tunnicliff, land surveyor, produced a set of maps which are little known and rarely appear on the collectors' market. However, as David Smith[1] writes, they deserve consideration as examples of the maps produced by the non-specialist map-maker to accompany roadbooks, commercial directories and so on.

In 1789 Tunnicliff published maps of six southern counties, three of these being earlier maps first available in 1787. This was followed in 1791 by six western counties including Devon – *Printed for the Author, by B C Collins, and sold by him; also by S Crowder, Paternoster Row, London; Messrs Trueman and Son, Exeter, and all other Booksellers.*

The maps, especially the later maps, have few topographical features and have scales from 3 to 6 miles to the inch. The conventional signs were standardised for the 1791 series to show market towns, villages, gentlemen's seats, turnpike roads, parks and county and hundred boundaries. Devon has a few short unnamed river estuaries but no rivers are detailed – only the Axe is shown in any length – otherwise few features are shown. Cranmere Pool and Three Barrow Tor are prominent on Dartmoor and Exeter is shown as the County of Exeter. Although Tunnicliff seems to have paid close attention to the development of canals, updating information for other counties, the Topsham to Exeter canal is not shown.

The lettering is generally attractively engraved with the names of the hundreds, which were generally hand-coloured, and printed in bold letters. There is no signature of engraver. The map extends into the border to east and west.

Size 596 x 564 mm.

Scale of Miles (10=72 mm).
Scale 1M=7.2 mm.

A New Map of DEVONSHIRE, by Willm Tunnicliff Land Surveyor 1791.

1. **1791**   *A Topographical Survey of the Counties of Hants, Wilts, Dorset, Somerset, Devon, and Cornwall, commonly called the Western Circuit*
One map of each of the six counties[2].
Salisbury. B C Collins; London. S Crowder; Exeter. Trueman & Son. 1791.

BL, B, RGS, BCL.

---

[1]   David Smith: The Maps of William Tunnicliffe; in *The IMCoS JOURNAL*; Issue No. 39; Winter 1989.
[2]   Illustration courtesy of Malcolm Woodward.

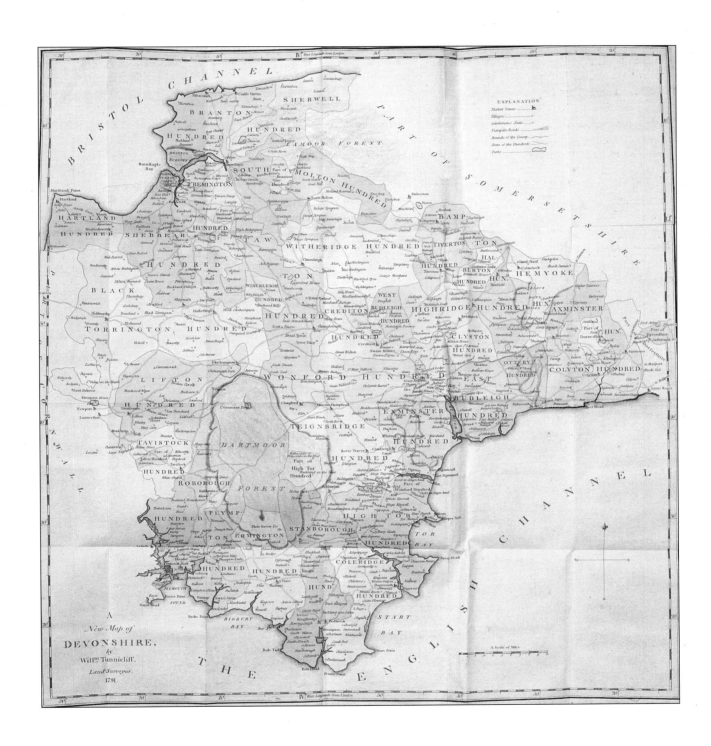

58.1 Tunnicliff *A Topographical Survey ...*

59

NEELE/FRASER
1794

In the late eighteenth century The Board of Agriculture was established by the Government to further a general improvement in land and farming use of the country. A series of county reports was produced including that of Sussex in 1793 by the Reverend Arthur Young, Secretary to the Board and Robert Fraser's paper on Devon of 1794. As Fraser makes clear in the introduction he planned his as a preliminary report to be expanded and completed later.

Each county report was written by a different author and although some maps are similar few have the name of the artist or the engraver. The map was probably engraved by Samuel John Neele who was to become a well-known engraver of county maps in the nineteenth century. Among those maps in the reports that are signed are Durham, with the signature – *Neele, sculpt. 362 Strand*, Berkshire *Neele sc,* and Sussex, *Neele sc Strand.*

The map of Devon included in Fraser's work was a geological view of the county and depicts the various soils of the county, depicted by shading and an explanation key. It shows major towns with small rectangles, small towns or villages with a cross. There are no roads. It is precisely drawn with outlined coast but no Lundy. Only Crockern Tor on Dartmoor is shown; whether this was because the tor was the ancient meeting place of the miners can only be conjectured.

Some of the information in this map was later used by Charles Vancouver in his work on Devon and the map found in his publication, *General View of the Agriculture of the County of Devon*, was engraved by Neele (**70**).

Robert Fraser was obviously impressed by what he saw: *The mild dispositions, affability, and kindness of its inhabitants, conspire with the temperature of the air, the fertility of the soil, and with the great beauty and variety of scenery, to render many districts of this county, particularly the southern, the most interesting and pleasing of any in the kingdom.* He was very concerned with reclaiming the waste lands of Dartmoor and this is explained at great length. Mention is also made in the introduction to a forthcoming map by Mr Charles Tozer, a surveyor at Broadhempston.[1] No such map has been found.

Fraser prepared a large number of reports for the government including agricultural reviews of Cornwall (1794) and County Wicklow (1801). He carried out a report on the coasts of Scotland in 1803 and one of his last reports was on the fisheries of Ireland completed in 1822.

The report on Somersetshire was written by John Billingsley and was first published with Cary's map of the county from his *New and Correct English Atlas* coloured to show the agriculture of the county. This was replaced in 1795 by a new map drawn by William White[2].

Size 237 x 215 mm.   Scale 1M=3.3 mm.

MAP of the SOIL of DEVONSHIRE.

1. 1794   *General View of the County of Devon with observations on the means of its improvement by Robert Fraser, M.A. Drawn up for the consideration of the Board of Agriculture and Internal Improvement. London, Printed by C MacRae MDCCXCIV.*
London. R Fraser. 1794.   BL.

[1.] *General View of the County of Devon;* reprinted in facsimile by Porcupines; Barnstaple; 1970; p.45.
[2.] Keith Needell: *The Printed Maps of Somersetshire;* July 1994.

59.1 Neele/Fraser *General View of the County of Devon*

60

MUTLOW/MARSHALL
1796

There was a great interest in agriculture, geology and economics in the late eighteenth and early nineteenth centuries as attested by the work of Fraser (**59**) and contemporaries who wrote similar tracts on the agriculture of the counties. In 1808 Charles Vancouver's *General View of the Agriculture of the County of Devon* was published complete with a map of Devon by Neele (**70**) and in 1820 William Smith would use the larger Cary maps to produce some fine geological maps (**71**).

Between 1791 and 1794 William Marshall traversed most of the greater Devon area and produced a two-volume work on the rural economies of the western counties. From the introduction it is clear that Devon was the focal point of his research but, as in agriculture county boundaries are meaningless, outlying districts were included. Consequently, Mutlow's map includes the whole of Devonshire, with parts of Somerset, Dorset and Cornwall; from the River Parret as far west as Padstow. The map is very simple with rivers shown but smaller rivers not named. Only larger towns are given and there are no roads. There are some antiquated spellings such as Dartmore and Tamer which one might not expect at this time. Other names are also somewhat unusual, eg Quantoc Hills and The Cornish Mountains.

Marshall was an early proposer (1790), and then perforce a competitor, of the Board of Agriculture which was established about 1792. Marshall's comprehensive work on the west country, based on his earlier experiences in the Midlands, looked at every aspect of farming and agriculture. He seems to have been very impressed with the sheepdogs in the east of the area. Another custom that interested him was Devonshiring, or Denshiring; this was the local method of 'burning the beat', or sodburning after harvest. The work was also published in Dublin by P Wogan, P Byrne, J Rice and J Moore. The only copy seen had no map.

Mutlow was an engraver in Russell Court, London who produced a number of maps related to the west country in this period. He engraved the map printed by Caddell in 1822 for Lyson's *Magna Britannia* (**89**) and executed a town plan of Exeter. He also produced two maps of Sussex in July 1798 for *The Rural Economy of the Southern Counties* again by William Marshall and the same publishers.[1]

Size 184 x 214 mm. Scale 1M=2.1 mm.

PART of THE WEST OF ENGLAND. Signature **H. Mutlow, sc. Russel Co**t**. London 1796** (EeOS).

1. 1796   *The Rural Economy of the West of England Including Devonshire and Parts of Somersetshire, Dorsetshire and Cornwall ... By Mr Marshall in Two Volumes.*
LONDON: Printed for G Nicol ... G G and J Robinson ... and J Debrett ... MDCCXCVI.
London. G Nicol, GG & J Robinson and J Debrett. 1796.   BL.

2. 1796   Date erased from imprint. Two notes added: **Published as the Act Directs** (AeOS) and **To be put in with a Guard before the Title Page** (CeOS).

The Rural Economy of the West of England Including Devonshire...
London. G Nicol, GG & J Robinson and J Debrett. 1796.   E, KB.

---

[1]   D Kingsley: *The Printed Maps of Sussex*, Sussex Record Society; 1982.

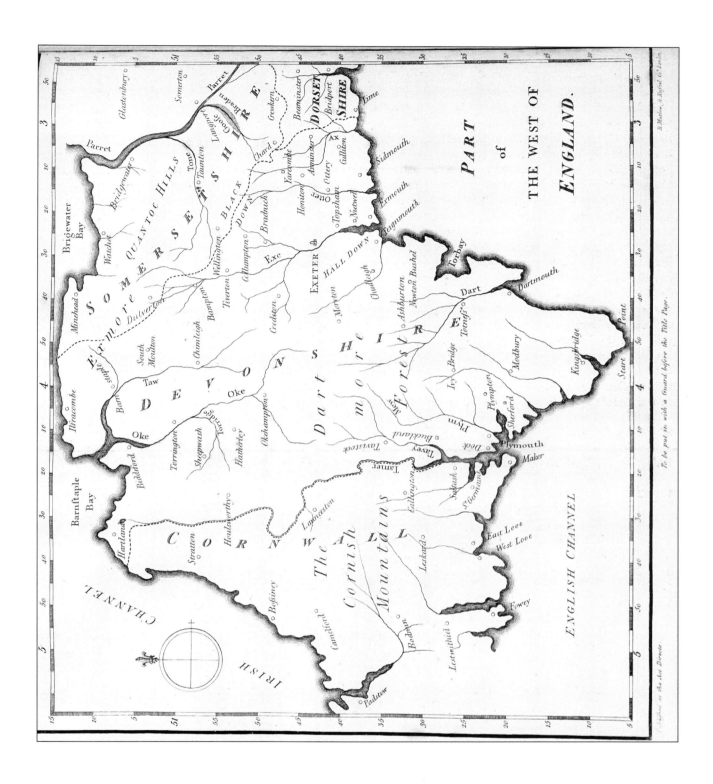

60.2 Mutlow/Marshall *The Rural Economy of the West of England*

ROWE/FAIRBURN
1798

In 1798 John Fairburn produced a game with a set of county maps engraved by Robert Rowe: ... *with the principal Town in each County and the Distance from London. Intended to render Fairburn's Game of English Geography clearly understood.* The date is taken from the Rules Sheet.

Each county is on a separate playing card with an extra card for Anglesey. The county town is in Roman capitals and its distance from London noted. The object was by question and answer to capture an opponent's card and match it with an adjoining county in the player's own hand, producing a flush in a similar way to that in the card game Rummy.

The set of rules included a general map of England and Wales and an introduction: *The Game of English Geography being a set of county maps on cards, with rules for playing. Engraved by Robert Rowe. The design of these cards is to unite instruction with amusement: they are intended to display the geographical division of England and Wales, the positions of the principal towns, with their distances from the metropolis, an accurate delineation of the turnpike roads, the courses of the several rivers and navigable canals, together with every information the size could possibly admit.*

Robert Rowe was responsible for a number of county maps over a period of eighteen years between 1798 and 1816. Two of his county maps of Devon were playing cards: the card described here; and a further card produced for Joseph Allen in 1811 (**75**). The later set is very similar but better executed and probably based on the set of cards produced for Fairburn. A third, larger, county map appeared in 1816 in his *English Atlas* (**81**).

This set of cards was possibly printed three times: Essex is known in an interim state, ie with the numbers added for the surrounding counties but no addition of new roads. It is possible that Devon also exists in this state.

Size 90 x 62 mm.   **Scale of Miles** (10=7 mm).
                                                                  Scale 1M=0.7 mm.

DEVONSHIRE. The Rules Sheet has the imprint: **Published Jany. 1st. 1798, by John Fairburn, 146, Minories, London**.

1. 1798	*The Game of English Geography Being a Sett of County Maps on cards, with rules for playing. Engraved by Robert Rowe. The Junction of the Counties in England and Wales with the principal Town in each County & the Distance from London. Intended to render Fairburn's Game of English Geography clearly understood.* London. John Fairburn. 1798.	CB[1].
2. 1798	Maps now have numbers to identify surrounding counties. Inner border has line added. Some roads added, eg Crediton to South Molton. *The Game of English Geography* London. John Fairburn. 1798.	CB.

[1.] Illustration courtesy of Clive Burden and Philip Burden.

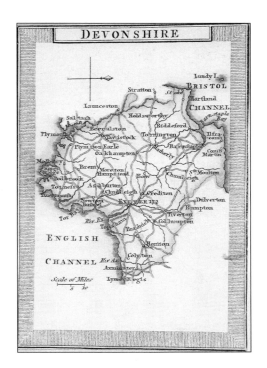

61.1 Rowe/Fairburn *Junction of the Counties in England and Wales*

62

BAKER/FADEN
1799

In 1759 the Royal Society of Arts had offered an annual award of £100 for the best original one inch to one mile county survey. Benjamin Donn was the first winner with his map of Devonshire, engraved by Thomas Jefferys, published in 1765 (**44, 45**). In 1799 William Faden (1749-1836) issued a one sheet variant of this map.

Faden was the son of a London printer. He served an apprenticeship with a local engraver and probably came to the map trade through engraving decorative cartouches. By 1773 he was in partnership with the family of Thomas Jefferys (*d.*1771), later succeeding Jefferys as Geographer to the King and eventually taking over Jefferys' business. Faden was a leading cartographer of his day and was often involved in engineering projects and published both maps and plans. Before the Ordnance Survey, he was publishing large-scale, detailed maps and the first Ordnance-style map (Kent 1801) was produced by him, privately engraved and published. Some of his plates were likewise adopted as official Admiralty Charts. Hence it is not surprising that he admired Donn's prize-winning map of Devonshire and on taking over Jefferys' stock issued a reduced version. This was engraved by Benjamin Baker (**57**).

The map illustrated has been trimmed close to the edge losing the signature and has uncommon additions which may have been added by a later owner for some official purpose.

Later issues: James Wyld the elder (1790-1836), took over the business of Faden and during the 1850s his son, James the younger (1812-87), published a copy of Faden's map with the imprint: *Published by JAs WYLD Geographer to HER MAJESTY Charing Cross East 185* (sic). This was available as a folding map with total dimensions 430 x 455 mm. The Wyld map still has the signature of Baker. The additions noted above are not present. Both of the Wyld's were Geographer Royal and as the imprint only mentions Her Majesty it is possible that the map was issued shortly after Prince Albert's death in 1861. The railway is now shown and extends to Paignton, which was reached in 1859.

James Wyld produced a further large-scale map of Devon, reduced from the Ordnance Survey of 1809, which appeared in 1833 (**109**).

Size 598 x 615 mm.

Scale of Statute Miles 69$\frac{1}{2}$ to a Degree.
(8 Furlongs and 14=124 mm).
Scale 1M=8.3 mm.

THE COUNTY OF DEVON, REDUCED FROM THE LARGE MAP BY BENJAMIN DONN; WITH ADDITIONS AND CORRECTIONS. LONDON. Published by W. FADEN, Geographer to HIS MAJESTY and to H.R.H. the PRINCE of WALES, Charing Cross. July 31st. 1799. Compass with Prince of Wales' motto **ICH DIEN** at north. Inset map of **The ISLAND of LUNDY**. Signature: **B Baker sculp** (EeOS).

1. 1799   *The County of Devon reduced from ... by Benjamin Donn*
London. William Faden. 1799.   (E).

The map has been trimmed close to the edge losing the signature. Two lines have been drawn horizontally just below Tavistock and through Tiverton. The numbers 1, 2 and 3 have been neatly added by hand at roughly (Ca), (Cc) and (Ce).

(KB).

62.1 Baker/Faden *The County of Devon, reduced from ... Donn* (see text)

63

SMITH/JONES/SMITH
1801

Charles Smith (*fl.*1800-52) established a London firm of engravers, stationers and mapsellers trading as Charles Smith & Son (1827-1852). His first county atlas *Smith's New English Atlas* was issued in 15 parts with an index and title page. Maps in parts 1 to 14 are dated 1801, the maps in part 15 and title page are dated 1804. The engravers Smith and Jones also engraved Sussex and Berks; Smith was probably no relation to Charles Smith.

The map has latitude and longitude in one degree intervals but this is the first map of Devon with *Longitude West from Greenwich* (between borders). The intended line of the Grand Western Canal is shown as well as the proposed Tamar Navigation between New Bridge and Tamerton.

Later issues: The *New English Atlas* in its folio format went into several editions with the date being amended for each edition in the title, (not all maps were redated at the same time, consequently some atlases have maps with other dates). The atlas was issued again *c.*1839 with the date *corrected to 1838* (Bristol Public Library) and *c.*1841 with the date altered *corrected to 1840.* Counties were also available on separate sheets, sometimes dissected or as folding maps *c.*1848. Later lithograph copies were available as folding maps in *Smith's New Series of County Maps* (*c.*1864), with mail roads deleted and R for railways replacing it. Dissected maps in slip cases are known for some counties with James Wyld's name on the cover.

The Smiths published a second county atlas in 1822 (**91**).

Size 445 x 492 mm.   **Scale** (8 Furlongs + 13 miles =84 mm) **Miles**.
Plate 6   Scale 1M=6 mm.

A NEW MAP of the COUNTY OF DEVON Divided into Hundreds with imprint: **LONDON Printed for C. SMITH N⁰ 172 Strand. January 6ᵗʰ. 1801**. Signature: **Smith & Jones sc. Pentonville** below compass point.

1. 1801   Issued in parts from 1801 to 1804 to complete the atlas.

     Smith's New English Atlas
     London. C Smith. (1801).   **CCCXI**, BL, B, C, W, BCL, (E).

2. 1804   New date under title: **January 6ᵗʰ. 1804**.

     Smith's New English Atlas
     London. C Smith. 1804.   W, B, (E).

3. 1804   Minor road changes, eg Tawton-Hatherleigh-Holsworthy-Stratton is no longer a turnpike and Molesmead Bridge above Oare in Somerset added.

     Smith's New English Atlas
     London. C Smith. 1804.   RGS, B, (C), (E).

4. 1808   New note below date **2nd Edition Corrected to 1808.** Symbol for turnpikes used for mail roads; turnpikes gets new symbol. G W Canal removed. Hatherleigh-Holsworthy again a turnpike but no mileage added.

     Smith's New English Atlas 2nd Edition
     London. C Smith. 1808.   **CCCXII**, BL, W, C.

     Also available dissected and mounted on linen.   (C), (E), (NDL).

5. 1818   **3rd Edition. Corrected to 1818.** G W Canal branch shown to Tiverton. Key for Turnpike Roads changed to **Great Roads**. Many other changes.

Smith's New English Atlas 3rd Edition
London. C Smith. 1818, 1820.   C; **CCCXIII**, BL.

6. 1821   **Corrected to 1821.** Plymouth Breakwater is shown. Also as boxed set of folding maps.

Smith's New English Atlas
London. C Smith. 1821.   **CCCXIV**, C, B, (NDL).

7. 1827   **Corrected to 1829.**

Smith's New English Atlas
London. C Smith. 1827 (1830), 1828 (post-1830).   **CCCXV**, TB; B.

8. 1832   **Corrected to 1832.** Parliamentary Divisions noted after hundreds. Explanation expanded to left of Hundred reference:
NORTH & SOUTH DIVISIONS: with symbols, stars, Maltese Crosses etc. for Parliamentary Representation. Tavistock Canal is shown.

Smith's New English Atlas
London. C Smith. 1832.   C.

Also issued as a dissected map in slip case.   (C).

9. 1834   **Corrected to 1835.** Signature is replaced by **Printed for C. Smith, Mapseller extraordinary to His Majesty. No 172 Strand, 1834.**

Smith's New English Atlas
London. C Smith. 1834 (1835).   **CCCXVI**, RGS.

64

JOHN WILKES
1803

John Wilkes was active between 1790 and 1828 (but was not connected with the Wilkes who wrote the well-known *North Briton*). He moved to London from Winchester in 1784 and in 1790, together with Peter Barfort, published the *Universal British Directory* and a year later a plan of London. Several additional maps of the counties were published by Wilkes and he also produced a map *British Colonies of North America* in 1797.

His county atlas, *Encyclopaedia Londinensis*, was published in parts from 1801. As some parts are missing the final total of maps is not known; eg Cambridgeshire was 'lost' for many years. Each of the maps is dated between 1801 and 1828. Devon is dated 1803 and appeared together with maps of Cornwall and Derbyshire (dated 1802) in Volume V which was published in 1810. However, many maps are found in collections which must have been bound together post-1828 when the series was finished. J Wilkes' name and that of Neele or J Pass, the engravers, appear on each map in the series. Wilkes was fined for piracy over the *Encyclopaedia* but nevertheless was able to protect his copyrights with Royal Patents.

The orientation is unusual for a map of this size. Although many miniature maps do not have north at the top most larger maps conform to convention. This map of Devon has north to the left of the page.

A loose copy of Devon in private hands has been reported with the plate apparently cut directly below the title omitting the publisher's imprint, but this has not been verified. However, Devon is known in two states. One loose copy of the second state below was taken from an oddly bound general atlas: *The book contained only a few of the counties up to Essex ... , the rest of the maps were of countries and continents and there did not appear to be any missing or lacking. The dates of the general maps were from 1796-1804. There was no title page and no indication of exact date.* It is believed that the book was bound possibly for educational purposes from what remained of the stock at the time[1].

Size 232 x 188 mm.

Scale of Miles (10=26 mm).
Scale 1M=2.6 mm.

DEVONSHIRE (CeOS) with imprint: **London Published as the Act directs. Feb. 14. 1803. by J. Wilkes.** Signature: **Neele Sculp. Strand.** (EeOS).

1. 1803	Probably available as published in parts.		(DEI), (NDL).

Encyclopaedia Londinensis; or, universal dictionary of arts, sciences, and literature ...Compiled ... by John Wilkes assisted by eminent scholars. Vol. V.
London. The Proprietors. 1810. BL.

Collections of maps with no title-page (*c.*1828) CB, B.

2. (1830) As above with the addition of bays, eg **Barnstaple** and **Bigbury**; towns, eg **Luppit** and **Higher Luxmore** near Honiton; river names, eg **Otter**, **Taw**, **Erne** and **Teign**; DORSETSHIRE has last 3 letters added; and mileage figure added at Dulverton. (KB), (MW).

[1.] The authors are grateful to Stephen Luck of Tooley Adams & Co. Ltd for providing this information.

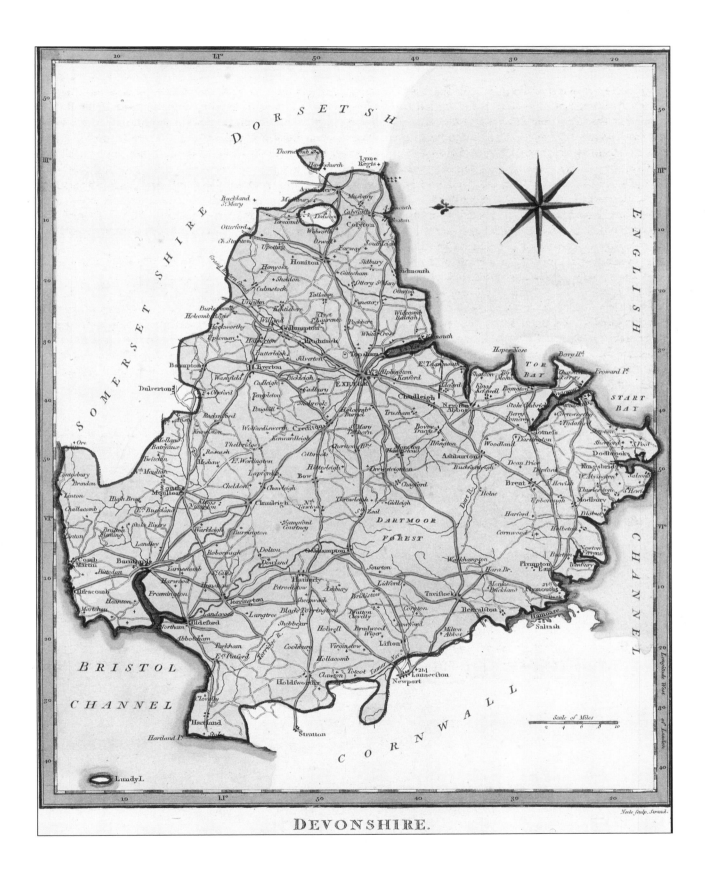

64.1 Wilkes *Encyclopaedia Londinensis*

65

R BUTTERS
1803

Butters (*fl.*1782-1803) was a publisher and bookseller first at 79 Fleet Street and later in Fetter Lane, London. He took over the *Political Magazine* in October 1789, his imprint replacing that of Murray. Most of the county maps produced for this publication between 1787 and 1790 were engraved by John Lodge (**52**).

Besides these maps, Butters was also responsible for a series of smaller maps that appeared in his *An Atlas of England*, (8vo, 40 maps) printed and published in 1803. An interesting feature of many of the maps is that they are drawn with north at the foot of the map, including the map of England. The map of Devon is also unusual in that the map is oriented with east to the top with lettering to be read holding the map this way up. Although very similar to other miniature maps of the time they may be identified from the fact that all, except Norfolk and Northamptonshire, have the title below the map. Only about forty place names are given and few roads shown. The map is very inaccurate: on the north coast only Hartland is shown and Barnstaple, Bideford and Ilfracombe are all missing. Combe Martin is shown near Swimbridge, and was probably in error for South Molton. Many other towns are misplaced or named in error, eg Bampton is written inside Somerset in place of Dulverton. It is almost as though Butters deliberately turned Cary upside down but then proceeded to confuse the names and positions of various towns.

There is no trace of the engraver of the maps. A compass was added to most counties for the second edition in 1805 but not to Devon. In 1803[1] and 1804 the maps were also used by William Green to illustrate his *Picture of England*.

Size 120 x 85 mm.   **Scale** (15=19 mm).
                                                                                    Scale 1M=1.3 mm.

DEVONSHIRE (CeOS).

1. 1803   *An Atlas of England Printed & Sold by R Butters, N⁰ 22 Fetter Lane, Fleet Street.*
         London. R Butters. (1803).   **CCCX**, C.

         The Picture of England illustrated with correct colour'd Maps of the Several Counties. In two volumes. By William Green. Vol. 1 London: Printed for Hatchard Book-seller to his Majesty, Picadilly.
         London. J Hatchard. 1804.
                                                CCCXVIII, BL, W, RGS.

         An Atlas of England
         London. R Butters. (1805).   BL.

---

[1] The only copy known has been broken up. The title-page read: *The Picture of England ... By the Author of the Spirit of English History.* London. J Hatchard. 1803.

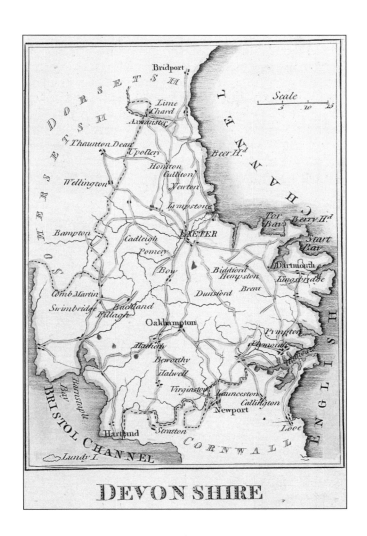

65.1 Butters *An Atlas of England*

66

JOHN LUFFMAN
1803

London engraver, publisher and professional goldsmith, John Luffman (*fl*.1776-1820) worked from various premises: 98 Newgate Street 1776, 85 London Wall 1780, Finsbury Square 1789, Inner Sweeting Alley, Royal Exchange 1799, Little Bell Alley, Coleman Street 1800, and finally 377 Strand from 1807. He was an author in his own right and an accomplished geographer.

His first works were engravings of the road maps in Taylor and Skinner's *Survey and Maps of the Roads of North Britain*, 1776, followed by some city plans and a number of county maps, including Rutland and Essex.

In 1803, Luffman engraved, printed and published the work for which he is best known, *A New Pocket Atlas*. The unusual circular maps with detailed descriptive text below are very popular. Each map was engraved with a text of topographical information below the map. In Devon, we are told, kerseys, serges, druggets, shalloons, narrow cloths, and bone lace are manufactured. This is an indication of the importance of the cloth industry in Devon. By the thirteenth century Devon was exporting wool from its six own native breeds of sheep and by 1500 was producing approximately ten per cent of Britain's cloth. In 1730, Tiverton alone had 56 tucking mills and Exeter was the third or fourth most important city based on the wealth of its cloth trade. Although the cloth industry as a whole continued into the nineteenth century, Exeter's share declined and by 1800 was minimal; beaten by competition from Lancashire, Yorkshire and Ireland[1].

Chubb (CCCXX) suggests that *An Atlas of the Counties of England* was published in 1805 based on the evidence of the *Map of Essex* (195 x 250 mm) which had the imprint *Published June 1. 1805 by J Luffman, Little Bull Alley, Coleman St. London. Plate No. 2.* This suggests an atlas or a work on Essex with two or more plates which is now lost.

Size 60 mm in diameter.	**Scale of 25 Miles**. Scale 1M=0.75 mm.

DEVONSHIRE. Imprint: **Sold by J. Luffman 28, Little Bell Alley, Coleman Street, London**. Plate number – 9 – 8 mm above top border (CaOS – sometimes only just visible).

1.	**1803**	*A New Pocket Atlas and Geography of England and Wales* London. J Luffman. 1803.	**CCCVIII**, BL, (E).
2.	**1803**	Plate number **9** immediately above top border.	
		A New Pocket Atlas and Geography of England and Wales London. J Luffman. 1803.	**CCCIX**, RGS.
		A New Pocket Atlas and Geography of England and Wales London. Lackington, Allen & Co. 1806.	BL.
3.	**1806**	Without plate number.	
		A New Pocket Atlas and Geography of England and Wales London. Lackington, Allen & Co. 1806.	B, W.

[1.] R R Sellam; *Aspects of Devon History*; Devon Books; (1962) 1985.

DEVONSHIRE is 70 miles in length from north to south, and 66 in breadth from east to west. It is divided into 33 hundreds, which contain 1 city, 38 market towns, 394 parishes, and 61,190 houses. The population amounts to 343,001.

The air is mild and healthy, and the soil remarkably fertile in corn and pasture. Apples abound, from which great quantities of rough cyder are made. The manufactures of this county consist of kerseys, serges, druggets, shalloons, narrow cloths, and bone-lace. Its pricipal rivers are the Tamar, the Tave, the Ex, and the Dart.

66.2 Luffman *A New Pocket Atlas and Geography*

COLE/ROPER
1805

The British Atlas, a joint work of George Cole (artist and cartographer) and John Roper (engraver) was composed of the maps and town plans drawn by Cole and others and engraved by Roper to accompany J Britton and E W Brayley's *The Beauties of England and Wales*. This was a topographic work published in parts with the maps usually separate, ie not included. Devon was dated, and probably available from, 1805.

Joseph Nightingale (*fl.*1806-20), in his *English Topography*, and Thomas Dugdale, in his *Curiosities of Great Britain* or *England and Wales Delineated*, republished the maps.

Later issues: Lucinda Tallis took over her husband's business when he died and reprinted the *Curiosities* (1842); their son, John Tallis, published this work with a new imprint *Drawn and Engraved for Dugdales England and Wales Delineated* (*c.*1843). Cole and Roper's maps were then progressively replaced with maps in a similar style by Joshua Archer. However, H G Collins used lithographs of Cole and Roper's maps in an untitled atlas with *Collins England* on the spine and in two atlases titled *Collins' Railway and Pedestrian Atlas of England* with two different title pages; *Darton & Co. and Collins brothers*; and *Darton & Co.* (all *c.*1858).

Size 175 x 230 mm.   **SCALE** (20=45 mm) **Miles.**
                                                              Scale 1M=2.25 mm.

DEVONSHIRE. Four imprints: **London; Published for the Proprietors by Vernor & Hood, Poultry; June 1st. 1805.** (CeOS); **Engraved by J. Roper, from a Drawing by G. Cole.** (AeOS); **to accompany the Beauties of England and Wales** (EeOS); and **Drawn and Engraved under the direction of J. Britton** just below **W. of Greenwich** in border (Ce).

1. 1805	With no title page; published in parts.		BL, C, (E), (NDL), (DEI).
	The British Atlas		
	London. Vernor, Hood and Sharp, and nine others. 1810.		B.
	London. Baldwin, Cradock & Joy. 1816.		**CCCXXXIX**, BL, W, B, BCL.
	English Topography ... by the Rev. J Nightingale		
	London. Baldwin & Joy. 1816.		**CCCLIII**, BL, B, W.
2. 1816	With imprint and signatures erased. Plate number **11** (EaOS) added.		
	English Topography ... by the Rev. J Nightingale		
	London. James Goodwin and Thomas McLean. 1816, 1816 (1827).		**CCCLIV**, BL: RGS.
3. 1835	A note **to Minehead** added in Somerset.		
			(DEI).
	Curiosities of Great Britain. England and Wales Delineated		
	London. Tallis & Co. 1835.		C, TB[1].

[1.] This edition has a second title page: *An Alphabetical Chronology of Remarkable Events by Leonard Townsend.*

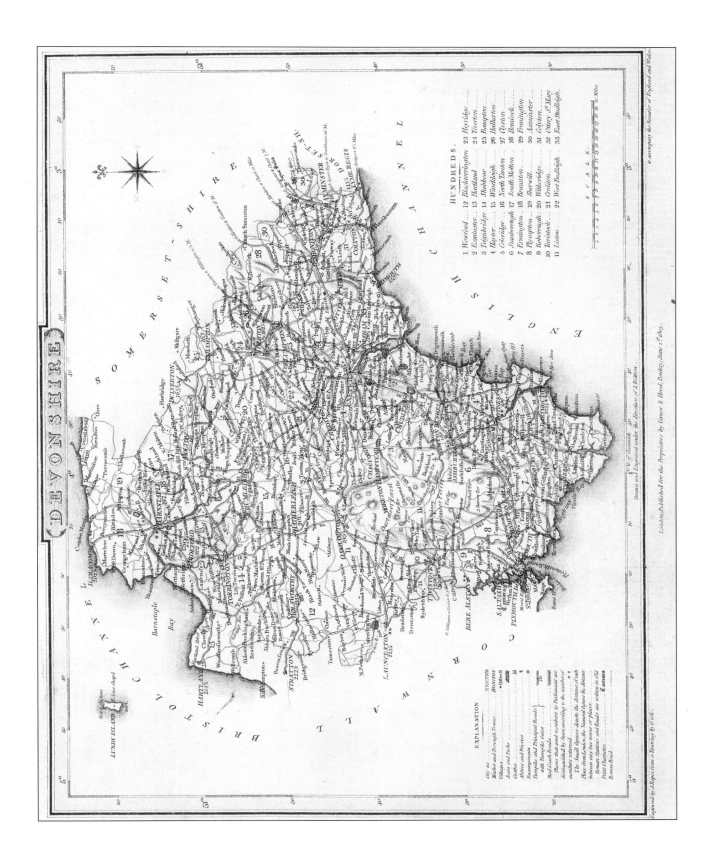

67.1 Cole/Roper *The British Atlas*

68

CHARLES COOKE
1805

Cooke's Modern British Traveller was written by George Alexander Cooke and published by Charles Cooke in forty-seven volumes, (12mo). These were without dates but are attributable to a period between 1802 and 1810; Devon's date is taken as 1805 on the evidence of an inscription in a copy in a private collection.

The counties were sold as *Topographical ... Description* or *Topographical Survey of the County* and contain a distance table and itineraries of main routes, besides descriptive text, index, etc. They were published and bound separately, or together with other counties (eg Devon with Cornwall and Dorset). After 1822 a complete *British Atlas* was published in 26 volumes. A Devon map with the last part of the imprint (see state 2 – *which distinctions are peculiar to the Superior Edition*) deleted is known[1]. From *c*.1817 these were *Printed, by Assignment from the Executors of the late C Cooke* with changes to the text and the inclusion of later statistical information, eg population figures. Later reprints, usually undated but sold as *Second Edition*, have been reported or seen with the map missing and published by Sherwood, Gilbert and Piper; Sherwood, Neely and Jones; or Sherwood and Co.

Charles Cooke and George Alexander Cooke were not related. Charles (1750-1816) inherited his publishing business from his father, John, in 1810.

Size 125 x 108 mm.

Statute Miles (10=13 mm).
Scale 1M=1.3 mm.

DEVONSHIRE. Compass and scale (Ae). Note: **Roads which in the Superior Edition are coloured Blue shew the route of the Mail Coaches.** (CeOS).

1. 1805	*Topographical Survey of the County of Devon* London. C Cooke. (1805).		FB.
	The Modern British Traveller ... or Tourist's Pocket Directory London. C Cooke. (1810).		**CCCV**, BL, B.
	Topography of Great Britain ... by George Alexander Cooke Vol 2. London. C Cooke. (1810).		B.
2. 1810	Hundreds added (Ae). Compass (Aa) and scale bar (Ee). New note: **The Cities and County Towns are denoted by red, and the respective Hundreds of the County by different Colours, which distinctions are peculiar to the Superior Edition.** (CeOS).		
			(E).
	Topographical Survey of the County of Devon London. C Cooke. (1810).		FB, KB.
	Topographical and Statistical Description of the County of Devon London. Sherwood, Neely & Jones. (1817).		P, E.
	Topography of Great Britain or British Traveller's Directory ... by G A Cooke London. Sherwood, Neely and Jones. (1817).		**CCCVI**, W.
3. 1824	Page number **45** added (EaOS). Additions, eg **Dawlish**.		
	Gray's New Book of Roads by George Carrington Gray London. Sherwood, Jones & Co. 1824.		**CCCXCII**, BL, W, B, (E).

---

[1] Eugene Burden; *County Maps of Berkshire.* The map was seen at a Map Fair; present whereabouts unknown.

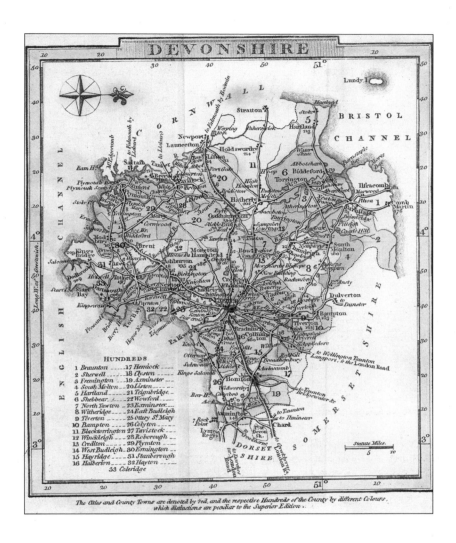

68.2 Cooke *Topographical Survey of the County of Devon*

69

JOHN CARY
1806

John Cary's *Traveller's Companion* appeared in 1789 (**55**) but most of the maps, including Devon, were re-engraved twice: in 1806 and in 1822 (**92**). Although this 1806 version of Devon looks very similar to the earlier engraving mileages between Honiton and Collumpton are new, Oakhampton and other towns are not horizontal, and the road SW of Samford Spiney is moved north across the river. The 1822 edition is entirely new both in format and engraving.

Size 130 x 94 mm including title.

Statute Miles (10=12.5 mm).
Scale 1M=1.25 mm.

DEVONSHIRE in extension to map at top which now has thin line under. **By J. Cary** (AaOS) and **Engraver** (EaOS). Imprint: **London Published July. 1 1806 by J Cary Engraver N⁰. 181 Strand**. (CeOS).

1. 1806 *Cary's Traveller's Companion*
London. John Cary. 1806. **CCLXXVI**, BL, RGS, C.

2. 1810 **London Published May 1810 by J Cary Engraver N⁰. 181 Strand.**

Cary's Traveller's Companion
London. John Cary. 1810 **CCLXXVII**, BL, RGS, B, W.

3. 1812 **London Published May 1812 by J Cary Engraver N⁰. 181 Strand.**

Cary's Traveller's Companion
London. John Cary. 1812. **CCLXXVIII**, RGS, W, C.

4. 1814 **London Published May 1814 by J Cary Engraver N⁰. 181 Strand.**

Cary's Traveller's Companion
London. John Cary. 1814. **CCLXXIX**, BL, RGS, C, (E).

5. 1817 **London Published Jan. 1. 1817 by J Cary Engraver N⁰. 181 Strand.**

Cary's Traveller's Companion
London. John Cary. 1817. C.

6. 1817 Grand Western Canal now shown from Somerset boundary to Butterleigh, near Tiverton. Roads added, eg Launceston-Holsworthy.

Cary's Traveller's Companion
London. John Cary. 1817. **CCLXXX**, BL, RGS, B, (E).

7. 1819 **London Published Jan. 1. 1819 by J Cary Engraver N⁰. 181 Strand.**

Cary's Traveller's Companion
London. John Cary. 1819. **CCLXXXI**, RGS, C.

8. 1821 **London Published Jan. 1. 1821 by J Cary Engraver N⁰. 181 Strand.**

Cary's Traveller's Companion
London. John Cary. 1821. **CCLXXXII**, BL, RGS, B, C.

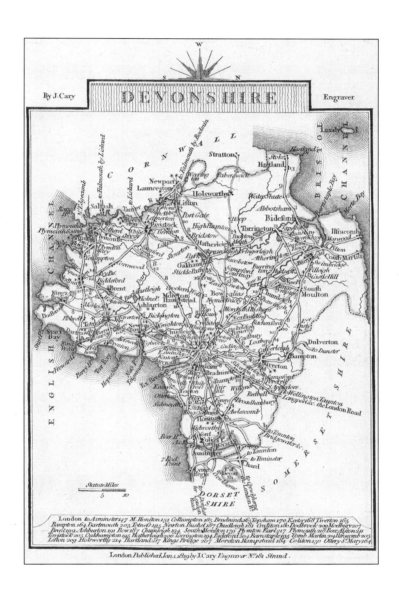

69.7 Cary *Traveller's Companion* the second engraving

70

NEELE/VANCOUVER
1806

Early in the 1800s the newly founded Board of Agriculture decided to expand the 18th century Agricultural Surveys and asked one of their leading surveyors, Charles Vancouver, to rewrite the report on the agricultural condition of Devon. Vancouver had previously written the reports for Cambridgeshire (1794) and Essex (1795). He also completed a report on Hampshire in 1813. He was able to base some of his report on the earlier preliminary report by Robert Fraser, *General View Of The County Of Devon* (**59**) and, no doubt, on Marshall's *Rural Economy* of 1796 (**60**).

Accompanying Vancouver's report was a map of Devon. The map is dated 1806 and the engraver was Neele, probably S J Neele, who produced a large number of maps for different publishers and who had probably produced the earlier map for Fraser. There is far more detail on this map regarding towns, roads and other features and considerable detail with regard to the geology and agriculture. Vancouver obviously made some use of Fraser's map as the notes in the explanation *Veins of Limestone described by Mr Vancouver* followed by *D⁰· by Mr Fraser* testify.

Other maps and plans that were included in this comprehensive work were of Sir Lawrence Palk's farm buildings at Haldon and a plan of his recently constructed quay in Torquay. These and all the animal, plant and machine engravings were executed by Neele. The Devon booksellers mentioned on the title page included E Upham, G Dyer, P Hedgeland and S Woolmer in Exeter as well as Cobley and Co. and Rees and Co. in Plymouth.

Richard Phillips (1767-1840), who also used the pseudonym Rev. J Goldsmith, led an interesting life, beginning as a schoolmaster and later working as a hosier. He was imprisoned for publishing Thomas Paine's *Rights of Man,* was Sheriff of the City of London and was knighted in 1808. He started the *Monthly Magazine* in 1796 – the editor was Dr John Aikin (see **56**).[1] He also published Capper's *Topographical Dictionary* (**72**).

Size 243 x 294 mm.

British Miles (10=33 mm).
Scale 1M=3.3 mm.

MAP Exhibiting the POLITICAL DIVISIONS with the Soil & Substrata of the COUNTY of DEVON Engraved for Mr Vancouver's Agricultural Report 1806. Imprint: **Neele, Sculp, Strand.** (EeOS).

1. 1806   *General View of the Agriculture of the County of Devon ... By Charles Vancouver. London; Printed for Richard Phillips, Bridge Street ... By B McMillan, ... Covent Garden.*
London. R Phillips. 1808.   BL, KB.

[1.] D Kingsley; *Printed Maps of Sussex*; Sussex Record Society; 1982.

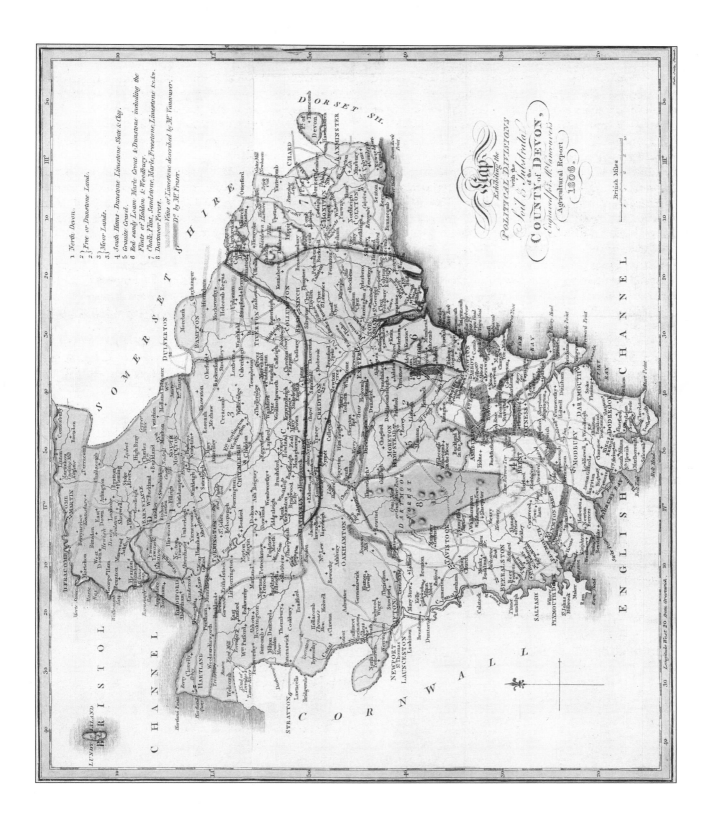

70.1 Neele/Vancouver *General View of the Agriculture ... of Devon*

143

71

JOHN CARY
1807

John Cary produced a series of large scale maps which were collected into a folio atlas in 1809 as *Cary's New English Atlas*. The Devon map is very detailed and shows most of the canals, both existing and proposed, with, for the Grand Western Intended Canal, a note: *no part of this line is yet executed 1807.*

William Smith (1769-1835), geologist and engineer, produced the first geological map of England and Wales. This famous work, based on another Cary map, was published on 15 sheets (5M=25 mm) in 1815: *The Delineation of the Strata of England and Wales.* Cary's county maps were also adapted by Smith to convey the data for his unfinished *New Geological Atlas* published 1819-24 – *calculated to elucidate the Agriculture of each County & to show the situation of the best Materials for Building, Making of Roads, the Construction of Canals, & pointing out those places where Coal & other valuable Minerals are likely to be found.*

Later issues: The Cary atlas was reissued in 1842 and 1843. In *c.*1844 Cary's plates passed to G F Cruchley who issued the maps as lithographs, and later to Gall and Inglis who continued to reproduce the maps, even keeping Cruchley's name on them. Until *c.*1895 the updated maps were reissued as folding maps in covers or as mounted maps with various titles: *Cruchley's Railway Map of ...*; *Cruchley's Railway and Station map of ...*; *Cruchley's County Map of ...*; *Cruchley's Railway and Station map of the County of ...*; and as maps for cyclists, tourists etc.

Size 482 x 537 mm.
Plate 7

SCALE (12 =69 mm).
Scale 1M=5.75 mm.

A NEW MAP OF DEVONSHIRE, DIVIDED INTO HUNDREDS EXHIBITING Its Roads, Rivers, Parks &c. By JOHN CARY, Engraver. 1807. Imprint: London: Published by J.Cary. Engraver & Mapseller, N^O. 181 Strand, Octr. 26. 1807. (CeOS).

1. 1807   *Cary's New English Atlas*
London. J Cary. 1809.   **CCCXXXIII**, BL, RGS, W, BCL.

    Also sold as a loose sheet or dissected, mounted, folded and cased.   (C), (E^1).

2. 1811   Date in imprint **Apr. 28. 1811.**

    Cary's New English Atlas
London. J Cary. 1811.   **CCCXXXIV**, RGS.

3. 1811   Date below signature now **1811.** (BL copy is untitled.)

    Cary's New English Atlas
London. J Cary. 1811^2.   BL, B, C.

4. 1818   Date below signature now **1818**, in imprint **Jany. 1st. 1818.**

    Cary's New English Atlas
London. J Cary. 1818.   **CCCXXXV**, RGS, C.

    Also as a cased sheet: **Sold at RATTLE & BRINE'S library** *see* Rattle & Brine's library **34 Brook-Street, BATH. Fancy Stationery, Prints &c.**   (E).

[1.]   Case title: A NEW MAP OF DEVONSHIRE, Divided into Hundreds; EXHIBITING THE WHOLE OF THE Turnpike and Cross Roads ... Sold by G Cruchley, Map-Seller and Publisher (From Arrowsmith's) No 338 Ludgate Street, St Paul's, London.

[2.]   William Upcott in his bibliography of works on *English Topography* (1878) lists the state as being present in a copy of the Rev. Polwhele's *History of Devonshire* (qv p.52).

5. 1820   Title and imprint dates changed to **1819**. New title added below the bottom imprint: **GEOLOGICAL MAP OF DEVON. by W SMITH. Mineral Surveyor.** together with **Note. The numbers attached to the description of each stratum refer to the Geological Table of British Organised Fossils which may be had of the Publisher Price 1s. 6d.**

A New Geological Atlas of England & Wales ... By William Smith
London. J Cary. 1820.   [Radcliffe].

6. 1821   As **71.4** above but title date now **1821**, and imprint date **Jany. 1st. 1821**.

Cary's New English Atlas
London. J Cary. 1821.   RGS.

7. 1824   Title date now **1824**. Imprint: **London: Published by G. & J. Cary. N°. 86, St James's Street, March 1st. 1824.**

Single sheets cut, folded and cased.   (C), (E).

8. 1824   Date in imprint now **1825**.

Cary's New English Atlas
London. J Cary. 1824 (1825).   RGS.

9. 1826   Date below signature and in imprint **1826**.

Single sheets cut, folded and cased.   (C), (E).

10. 1828   Title date and in imprint **1828**.

Cary's New English Atlas
London. J Cary. 1828.   **CCCXXXVI**, BL.

11. 1831   Title date and in imprint **1831**. Plymouth Dock now **Devonport**.
Brixton to Plymouth road added. Grand Western and Intended Tamar Navigation as far as New Bridge.

Single sheet, cut and folded.   (RGS).

12. 1831   **EXPLANATION** is added (Ae) with a key to Election Places (Maltese Cross).

Single sheet cut, folded and cased with Cruchley imprint.   (E).

13. 1834   Title date and in imprint **1834**.

Cary's New English Atlas
London. J Cary. 1834.   **CCCXXXVII**, BL.

COOPER/CAPPER
1808

Benjamin Pitts Capper produced one cartographic publication which was very popular. His *Topographical Dictionary* published by Richard Phillips contained 44 maps of the English counties and maps of England, Wales, Scotland and Ireland, all drawn and engraved by H Cooper.

Phillips also published Charles Vancouver's agricultural report on Devon (**70**) advertising Capper's *Topographical and Statistical Dictionary* by William (sic) Capper in Vancouver's work. The *Dictionary* was to be available with maps for £1.4s or the *Maps may be had done up in a separate Atlas, price 9s. half bound, or beautifully coloured, price 12s. half bound.*

Interestingly, the map of Devon was slightly tilted, the first time since van den Keere (1605); and the Welsh coast is shown for the first time since Badeslade and Toms (1741).

George Byrom Whittaker was a school-master prior to publishing and was also Sheriff of the City of London.[1] Originally G & W B Whittaker, the company became George Byrom Whittaker in 1826, Treacher & Arnott or Whittaker, Treacher & Co. in 1830 and finally Whittaker & Co. from 1836. About 1820 he acquired William Pinnock's *History and Topography* (**86**).

Later issues: The *Topographical Dictionary* was republished twice in 1839: once by Sir Richard Phillips & Co.; and once by Whittaker & Co. but with no further changes to the maps.

Size 100 x 175 mm.	**British Miles** (10=16 mm).
Map panel 100 x 130 mm.	Scale 1M=1.6 mm.

DEVONSHIRE. Imprint: **Published Janu^y 1, 1808, by R. Phillips. Bridge Street Blackfriars London** (CeOS). **Plate IX** (EaOS). Signature: **Cooper del^t et sculp^t.** (EeOS).

(NDL).

1. 1808   *A Topographical Dictionary of the United Kingdom by Benjamin Pitts Capper*
London. Richard Phillips. 1808.   **CCCXXVII**, BL, B, W.

An Atlas of the British Islands
London. Richard Phillips. 1808.   C.

A Topographical Dictionary of the United Kingdom
London. Longman, Hurst, Rees, Orme and Brown. 1813.   BL.

2. 1808   Cooper signature deleted.

A Topographical Dictionary of the United Kingdom
London. Richard Phillips. 1808.   W.

A Topographical Dictionary of the United Kingdom
London. Longman, Hurst, Rees, Orme and Brown. 1813.   **CCCXXVIII**, W.

3. 1824   New imprint: **Published by G & W B Whittaker. 13 Ave Maria Lane, 1824.** Revised statistics: houses (**71,486** was 57,955) and population (**439,040** was 343,004). Towns added, eg **Paignton, Littleham** and **Devonport**.

(E).

A Topographical Dictionary
London. Geo. B Whittaker. 1825, 1826.   **CCCXXIX**, BL; **CCCXXX**, BL.

A Topographical Dictionary.
London. Sir Richard Phillips and Co. 1829 (1834).   **CCCXXXI**, BL.

[1.] D Kingsley; *Printed Maps of Sussex*; Sussex Record Society; 1982.

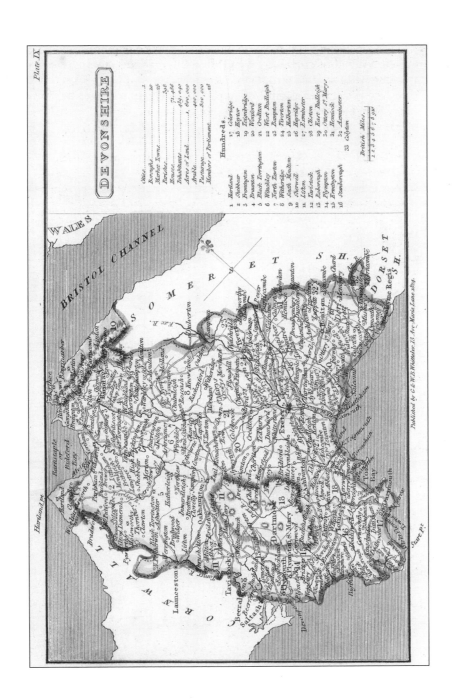

72.3 Cooper/Capper *A Topographical Dictionary*

JOHN CARY
1809

John Cary's *New and Correct English Atlas* first appeared in 1787 (**51**) but by 1809 the plates had been amended so often that new plates needed to be engraved. To identify this later version *Oakhampton* is spelt with *p* and there are three direction indicators, *The London Road*, outside the county eastwards.

Chubb lists *Cary's New and Correct ... corrected to 1827* (CCLXIX); no copy has been found.

Later issues: The atlas was reissued in 1840 and 1843 (however, both known copies have been lost). In *c.*1844 G F Cruchley acquired the plates and published lithographs in his atlas, *Cruchley's County Atlas of England & Wales*, in six issues from 1863 until 1875. The maps had new titles such as *RAILWAY & STATION MAP OF DEVONSHIRE WITH THE NAMES OF THE STATIONS* and imprints, eg *LONDON. PUBLISHED BY G F CRUCHLEY, MAPSELLER & GLOBE MAKER 81, FLEET STREET.* In *c.*1863 *Cruchley's Travelling County Atlas of England & Wales* was issued and *c.*1872 *Cruchley's New Pocket Companion South-West Division* appeared. There was constant updating of railway information.

Size 210 x 260 mm.   **Statute Miles 69¹/₂ to a Degree** (10=29 mm). Scale 1M=2.9 mm.

DEVONSHIRE with signature: **By JOHN CARY, Engraver.** Imprint: **London: Published July 1. 1809 by J. Cary Engraver & Mapseller Strand.** (CeOS).

1. 1809 *Cary's New and Correct English Atlas*
London. John Cary. 1809. **CCLXIV**, B, W, RGS, (E), (DEI).

2. 1812 Imprint now dated: **July 1. 1812.**

Cary's New and Correct English Atlas
London. John Cary. 1812. **CCLXV**, W, C.

3. 1812 Imprint now has no date. Grand Western Canal shown. (KB¹), (E).

Cary's New and Correct English Atlas ... corrected to 1818
London. John Cary. 1818. **CCLXVI**, RGS, C, W.

Cary's New and Correct English Atlas ... corrected to 1821
London. John Cary. 1821. **CCLXVII**, Cardiff, Ply.

Cary's New and Correct English Atlas ... corrected to 1823
London. John Cary. 1823, 1825, 1826. **CCLXVIII**, BL, RGS; W; [Leeds].

Cary's New and Correct English Atlas ... corrected to 1829
London. John Cary. 1829. BL, C, W.

4. 1831 New road from Brixton to Plymouth. Plymouth Dock changed to **Devonport.**

Cary's New and Correct English Atlas ... corrected to 1831
London. John Cary. 1831. BL, C, (E).

¹· From an atlas in the possession of P J Morris dated 1812 but now broken.

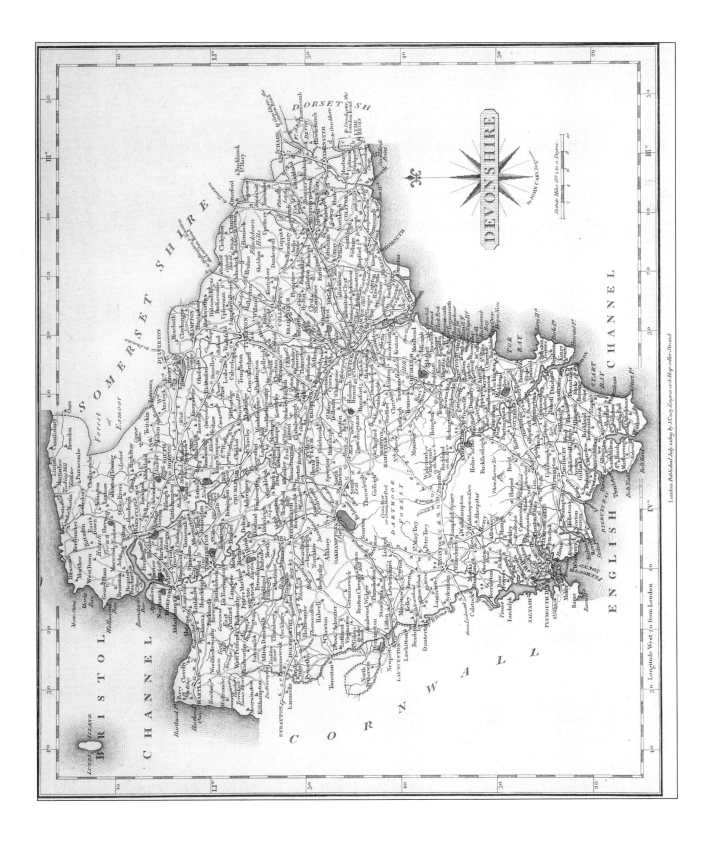

73.1 Cary *New and Correct English Atlas* the second engraving

74

MUDGE/ORDNANCE SURVEY
1809

The Ordnance Survey was officially constituted in 1791 under William Roy. William Mudge (1762-1820) was the Official Superintendent 1798-1820. Among those principally responsible for the survey, three were Devonians: Mudge was born in Plymouth; Simon Woolcot (1760-1819), mathematician and surveyor, was born in South Molton; and Robert Dawson (1771-1860), artist and draughtsman and inventor of hillscape drawing, was born in Plymouth and died at Woodleigh. (He was the father of R K Dawson, see **104, 105**). The engraving was arranged by James Gardner and executed by Benjamin Baker (**57**). The survey was continued after Mudge's death by Thomas Colby (1784-1852), who was Superintendent 1810-46.

Devon was the second Ordnance Survey county to be published after Essex: William Faden's large scale map of Kent in 1801, based on the Survey's results, was privately engraved and published. Devon consists of eight sections to make one map complete with piano key border, 2372 x 1815 mm, with title sheet, 340 x 422 mm, laid over on the sea area. The map excludes part of Hartland Point and a small part of the detached portion in Dorset. It was usually presented as a bound collection and supplied with a titled paper cover[1] or with the sheets cut up, mounted, folded and inserted into a book-bound box with the title sheet.

Later issues: Although originally on sale as a complete (county) set, it was not long before individual sheets were being sold. Only the two states which were published as a complete county map are listed below. Five main stages in subsequent sheet alterations can be identified although individual sheets had up to ten states[2]: scale bars were added to each sheet at an early stage but were so far beneath the neat lines that these were trimmed for the boxed sets; in 1824 James Gardner became agent for the sale of Ordnance Survey maps and added a piano-key border to each map, probably to encourage sale of single sheets, and his imprint *Sold by Ja*[s]. *Gardner, Agent for the Sale of the Ordnance Maps, 163, Regent Street, London;* then Ramshaw added his printer's imprint and prices; the prices being too high, most were soon reduced; finally, post-1835, geological information by Henry de la Beche was added.

Transfers *Printed from an Electrotype* were taken and single sheets, double sheets and boxed sets were produced (including the detached parts previously missing) until *c.*1880.

Sheet sizes: 602 or 585 x 905 mm.   **Scale One Inch to a Mile.**
                                                                          (1M=25 mm).

THE SECOND PART OF THE General Survey of England and Wales Containing the whole of DEVON And a portion of the adjoining counties DONE BY THE Surveyors of His Majesty's Ordnance, under the Direction of L[t]. **COL**[l]. **MUDGE, OF The Royal Artillery, F.R.S.** Each sheet has number **N**[o]___ (EaOS), and imprints: **Published 11**[th] **Oct**[r]. **1809 by L**[t] **Col**[l]. **Mudge, Tower** (AeOS or CaOS) and **Engraved at the Drawing Room in the Tower by Benj**[m]. **Baker & Assistants ... The Writing by Eben**[r]. **Bourne** (EeOS or CaOS). Sheets XXIV (DeOS) and XXVII (AdOS) have **Meridian of Butterton Hill Longitude 3**[o]**52'47".** **West**; Sheet XXIV has **Scale One** (EeOS).

1. 1809   As described.   BL, C (full sheet).

2. (1815)   All sheets have a scale-bar added (CeOS – see above). Six sheets have minor changes, eg XXII – XXIV – ENGLISH CHANNEL removed, South Wales coast added to XX and XXIII had **Inch to a Mile** added (EeOS).   BL.

[1.] Ordnance Survey of Great Britain PART the II[D] CONTAINING NEARLY THE WHOLE OF DEVONSHIRE. Part of Somersetshire, Part of Dorsetshire, Part of Glamorganshire, and in the Eastern Part of Cornwall COMPRISED IN Plates No. 20, 21, 22, 23, 24, 25, 26, 27.

[2.] It is not possible here to detail every change. This information is condensed from the facsimile of the West Country OS mapping produced by Harry Margary with an excellent introduction by J B Harley and Yolande O'Donoghue in; *The Old Series Ordnance Survey Maps of England and Wales – Vol II*, Lympne Castle; 1977.

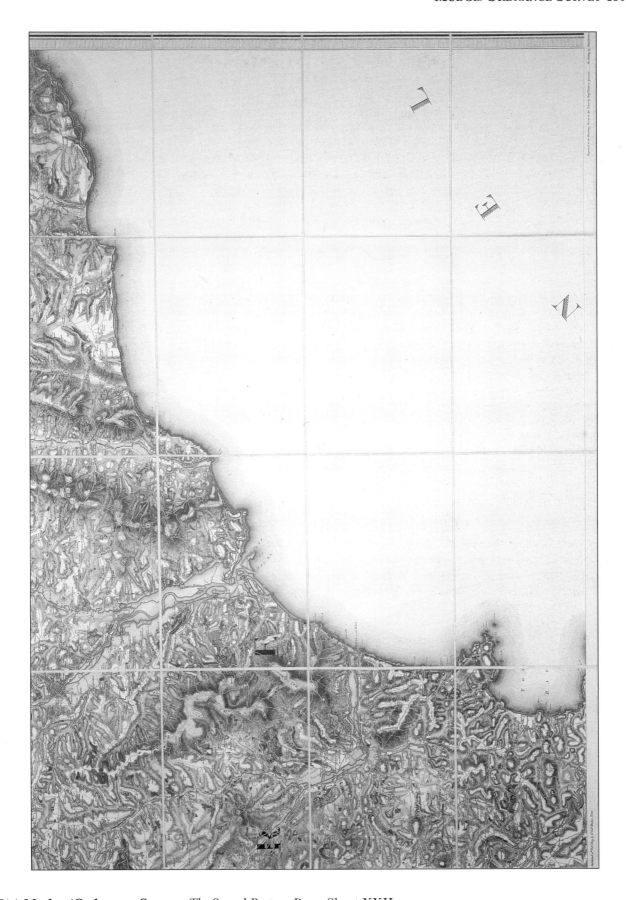

74.1 Mudge/Ordnance Survey *The Second Part ... Devon* Sheet XXII

75

ROWE/ALLEN
1811

Joseph Allen published a pack of playing cards which are described by Beresiner[1]. The original maps were printed as a pack of 43 cards (forty county maps, a map each of North and South Wales and England & Wales). Each card bears the imprint *Pub by J ALLEN, 3 Hampden Str. Sommers Town. 1811.* While most of the cards have a second imprint *Also by R. ROWE, No 19 Bedford Str. Bedford Row London,* the card of England and Wales has statistical information in a second small panel and a slightly different Allen imprint (see below). The rules booklet has the imprint *A Geographical Game – Allen's English Atlas ... being a set of county maps on cards published ... directs June 4th 1811.*

The Devon card in a second set of these cards recently found[2] has the amended Allen imprint: *by J ALLEN, 3 Hampden Str. Sommers Town.* In addition, at the bottom of the map, in place of Robert Rowe's imprint there are two lines with information from the 1811 census. The two maps are practically identical, eg Holoworthy (sic) has not been corrected, there are no new roads and neighbouring counties have not been named, but mileages have been added on some roads. The implication is that if Allen originally planned to market these cards together with Rowe, who possibly engraved them, the partnership broke up early and Allen began to delete the Rowe imprint. Allen is known to have cooperated with Rowe on other projects: he engraved a map of London for Rowe in 1811. Rowe had already prepared one set of playing cards for Fairburn (compare **61**) and went on to produce a folio county atlas, *The English Atlas*, which appeared in 1816 (**81**).

Size 85 x 60 mm.

Scale of Miles (10=8 mm).
Scale 1M=0.8 mm.

DEVONSHIRE. Imprint: **Pub. by J. ALLEN, 3 Hampden Str. Sommers Town. 1811.** just below the county title. Second imprint: **Also by R. ROWE, N⁰. 19 Bedford Str. Bedford Row, London.** embedded in the lower border.

1. 1811   *A Geographical Game – Allen's English Atlas.*
London. J Allen & R Rowe. 1811.   CB[3].

2. 1811   First imprint reduced: **by J ALLEN, 3 Hampden Str. Sommers Town** (Ca). Panel of topographical information in lower border replaces lower imprint.
Mileages from London added.

Geographical Game – Allen's English Atlas.
London. J Allen. (1811).   CB.

3. 1823   Allen's imprint is deleted, neighbouring counties named.
       (E), (DEI).

The New English Atlas
London. J Thomson. 1823.   B.

Pocket Tourist and English Atlas
London. O Hodgson. (1827).   **CCCLXXI**, BL, B.

1. Yasha Beresiner; in *Map Collector*, Issue 30; March 1985; pp 40-41.
2. Kit Batten; Second Edition of Allen Cards; in *IMCoS JOURNAL*; Issue 58; Autumn 1994.
3. Illustration courtesy of Clive Burden and Philip Burden.

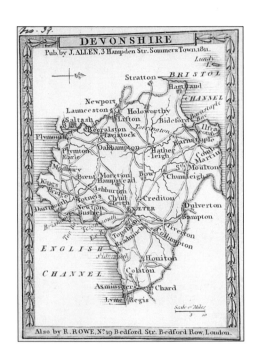

75.1 Rowe/Allen *A Geographical Game - Allen's English Atlas...*

76

WILLIAM EBDEN
1811

Robert Laurie (1755-1836) and James Whittle(1757-1818) formed a publishing partnership in 1790 and bought Robert Sayer's business after his death in 1794. Robert Laurie was an established engraver who invented a process for mezzotint engraving in colour. He won an award from the Royal Society of Arts in 1776. He was highly regarded for his engravings of biblical scenes and portraits. The firm of Laurie and Whittle was a leader in the publication of maps and worked extensively with well-known cartographers of the day, but also including many revisions of earlier works by Kitchin, Jefferys, Faden, Sayer and Bennett, and others. They reprinted much of Sayer's stock: Benjamin Baker's work for the *Universal Magazine* (57); Bickham's views as *A Birds-Eye View of the Counties* in 1796 (36); and coastal charts, including Sayer's own charts of the Devon coast. In 1806 they published their road-book *Laurie and Whittle's New Traveller's Companion*.

In 1812 Robert Laurie retired from the business and was replaced by his son, Richard Holmes Laurie (*fl.*1814-*d.*1858), the company then trading as Whittle and Laurie until R H Laurie took the firm over in 1818, trading under his own name from then until 1903. The famous nautical chart firm Imray, Laurie, Norie and Wilson Ltd is the continuation of the same family business.

The map was engraved by William Ebden who engraved a second Devon county map on a smaller scale in 1825 which was reissued a number of times (95).

Size 558 x 730 mm.

Scale of Statute Miles (11=79 mm).
Scale 1M=7.2 mm.

LAURIE & WHITTLE'S New Map of DEVONSHIRE, DIVIDED INTO HUNDREDS Exhibiting The Whole of THE MAIL, DIRECT AND PRINCIPAL CROSS ROADS, Gentlemen's Seats, Rivers, &c. &c. By WILL^M EBDEN. Imprint: **Published 12 Aug^st. 1811 by Robt. Laurie and Ja^s. Whittle, N°. 53 Fleet Street, London.** (CeOS). Signature: **Engraved by W. Pearcy.** (EeOS).

1. 1811   As described as a separate sheet, cut, mounted, folded and cased.   (C), (E¹).

2. 1826   Title changed to **A New Map of DEVONSHIRE ... By WILL^M. EBDEN**. Imprint altered to read **Published April 21st. 1826 by RICH^D. HOLMES LAURIE, N°. 53, Fleet Street, London.**

            Only seen as a separate sheet, cut, mounted and cased.   (E).

---

¹· Illustration courtesy of the Exeter Westcountry Studies Library.

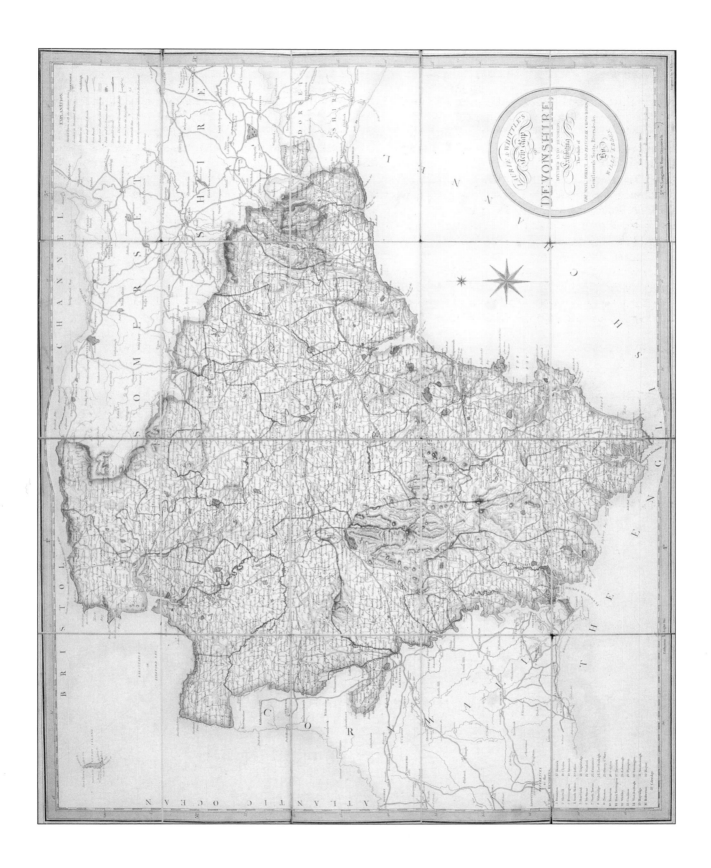

76.1 Ebden *Laurie & Whittle's New Map of Devonshire*

77

JAMES WALLIS
1812

Although the name James Wallis in the context of county mapping only appears for a brief span of ten years (1810-20) he worked on three separate county atlases in this time (see also **78** and **88**). The first of these, *Wallis's Travellers Companion,* appeared *c.*1812. This was a miniature atlas with maps similar to those in *Cary's Traveller's Companion* (**69**), similar atlas title and even the unusual orientation: although the names are to be read with the map held with the title to the top, the map is oriented with north to the right. Copies of the atlas were available from Davies and Eldridge of Exeter; their name was added below Wallis's address on the title page.

The maps were used by P Martin and W Lewis. William Lewis (*fl.*1819-36) had premises at 21 Finch Lane London.

Size 132 x 93 mm.   **Scale of Miles** (12=16 mm).
Map panel 110 x 85 mm.   Scale 1M=1.33 mm.

DEVONSHIRE. Imprint: **London. Publish'd by J Wallis, Engraver, 77 Berwick Str^t. Soho.** (CeOS).

1. 1812	*Wallis's New Pocket Edition of the English Counties or Travellers Companion* London. J Wallis. (1812).		**CCCXLIV**, RGS, W, (NDL).
2. 1814	Plate number **11** added (EaOS).		
	Wallis's New Pocket Edition ... or Travellers Companion London. J Wallis. (1814).		RGS, B, (E).
3. 1816	New imprint: **London. Publish'd by P Martin N° 198 Oxford Street.** Hill hachuring removed.		
	Martin's New Traveller's Guide London. P Martin. (1816).		CB.
	Martin's Sportsman's Almanack for 1818 (and *1819*) London. Simpkin and Marshall. 1818, 1819.		CB, (KB); C.
	Lewis's New Traveller's Guide London. W Lewis. (1819).		W.
4. 1819	Imprint removed.		
	Lewis's New Traveller's Guide London. W Lewis. (1819).		CB.
5. 1819	New imprint: **London. Publish'd by W. Lewis Finch Lane.** (CeOS).		
	Lewis's New Traveller's Guide London. W Lewis. 1819¹ (1821), (1824), (1825), (1827).		W; **CCCLXIV**, BL, W; B; B.
	Lewis's New Traveller's Guide and Panorama of England and Wales London. W Lewis. 1835, 1836.		**CCCLXV**, BL, B; **CCCLXVI**, BL, W.

---

^{1.} The Preface is dated 1819 in each issue. Watermarks are a guide to the earliest issue dates.

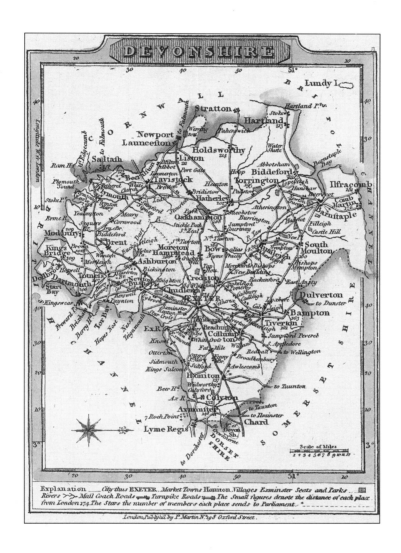

77.3 Wallis *Martin's Sportsman's Almanack for 1818*

78

JAMES WALLIS
1812

James Wallis produced two county atlases at the same time (see preceding entry). *Wallis's New British Atlas* (folio 23 plates, some containing 2/3 maps per plate) appeared in 1813: although the title page is dated 1812 the maps are dated either 1812 or 1813. When it was reissued, possibly the same year, it had the title *A New and Improved County Atlas*, which was the second title of the original work.

The map of Devon is interesting as it has longitude reading from the left as though the zero meridian was at Land's End and full degrees (3 to 5) reading left to right: this mistake was compounded by Hebert who added a note *Longit. West from Green*[h]. for the second edition without changing the degrees. The BL atlas with Devonshire in state 2 is a composite atlas with maps of mixed date and imprint. Besides the west country maps of Cornwall, Devon and Somerset only the maps of Cheshire, Hunts., Northants., Sussex, Westmoreland and South Wales have Hebert's imprint. (North Wales is dated 1816.)

The maps were reissued by Ellis in 1819 without imprints. G Ellis was a publisher with premises in Smith's Square, Westminster.

Later issues: The British Library holds a number of Wallis's maps with the imprint of Wyld, but not that of Devon. However there is the possibility that a much amended lithograph may have been sold as a loose map. This would have been prepared for a Wyld atlas (*Wyld's Atlas of the English Counties* of 1842 – Chubb DV) which was probably planned but never published. Only a few loose sheets with the imprint *Published by Jas Wyld, Charing Cross East* have been found.

Size 180 x 265 mm.	**Scale of Miles** (14=31 mm).
	Scale 1M=2.2 mm.

DEVONSHIRE with signature **Engraved by J. Wallis.** Imprint: **London Published by S.A.Oddy, 1812.** (CeOS).

1. 1812
    A New and Improved County Atlas. Wallis's New British Atlas
London. J Wallis. 1812 (post-1813 on watermark).   **CCCXLIX**, C.

    Wallis's New British Atlas
London. S A Oddy. 1812 (1813).   **CCCL**, RGS, W, C.

    Wallis's Second and Superior British Atlas
London. James Wallis. (1814).   BL.

2. 1816
    Imprint amended: **London. Published by J Wallis. 1814.** New imprint: **Second Edition, with Considerable Improvements & Additions. by L Hebert, Geographer** (CaOS). Numerous changes including addition of **Longit. West from Green**[h]. (CeOS in border), mileages corrected and **Bigbury Bay** added.

     (NDL).

    Wallis's Second and Superior British Atlas
London. James Wallis. (1816).   BL, W.

3. 1819
    Imprint erased.

    Ellis's New and Correct Atlas of England and Wales
London. G Ellis. 1819.   **CCCLXVII**, BL, RGS, W.

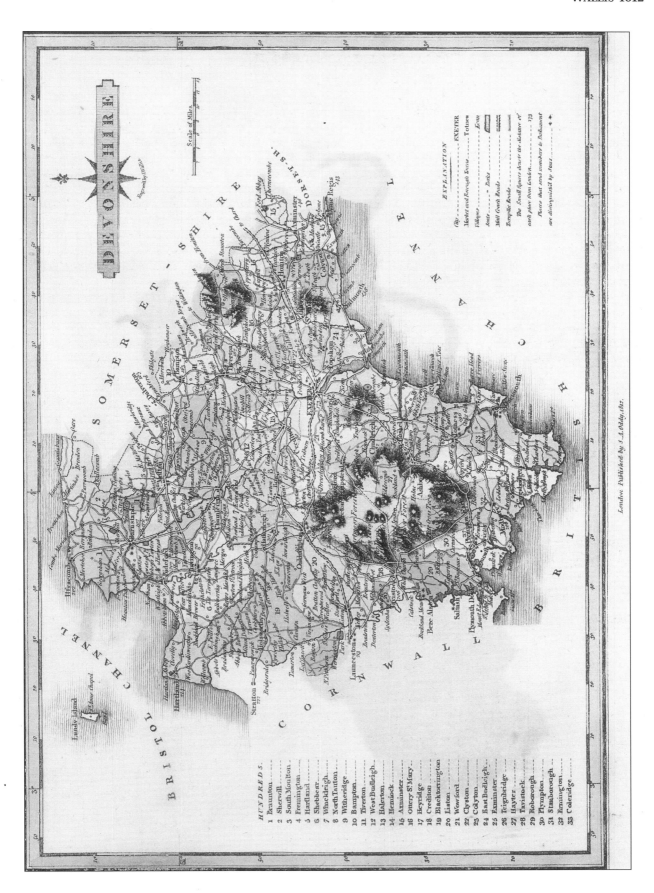

78.1 Wallis *Wallis's New British Atlas*

NEELE/CUNDEE
1812

Samuel John Neele (1758-1824) and his son Josiah (*d*.1845) were well-known engravers in the Strand who produced work for many publishers. Working sometimes with George and James Neele the family were responsible for many maps in county atlases including maps for Wilkes (see **64**), the *Traveller's Pocket Atlas* of Capper (as Neele & Son), Pinnock's *County Histories* (Neele & Son, see **86**), Cadell & Davies's *Magna Britannia* (Neele & Son), Greenwood's *Atlas of the Counties of England* (as J & J Neele, see **97**), Bell's *Comprehensive Gazetteer* (as J Neele & Son, see **107**) as well as Thomson's *Guide through Scotland* (Neele & Son).

From *c*.1812 they engraved the maps for James Dugdale's *The New British Traveller* (4to, 45 maps). This was produced in four volumes with the imprint of James Cundee the publisher. These maps reappeared dated 1818 with a new imprint of James Robins, an author, bookseller and publisher who traded under the name of J Robins & Co. He also compiled a number of works unrelated to cartography under the pseudonym of Robert Scott. His only important cartographic works were the reissue of *The New British Traveller* and the *Robin's Atlas of England and Wales;* both published in 1819. The imprint in Robin's Atlas refers to the Albion Press, London, which was also Cundee's address. Some atlases were collections of stock items with differing map imprints and dates. Many atlases were tightly bound so that the imprint, which was almost a centimetre below the map, was lost, ripped or cut off when the maps were removed.

E W Brayley issued sections of *The Beauties of England and Wales* with special titles *A topographical and historical description of the county of* ... illustrated with engravings. A copy of Hertford is known which includes Neele's map.

Size 198 x 250 mm.

British Miles (10=27 mm).
Scale 1M=2.7 mm.

DEVON. Imprint: **Published by James Cundee Albion Press London January 1st. 1815.** (CeOS).
Signature: **Neele Sculpt Strand** (EeOS).

1. 1812	Loose sheet. Probably from a part-set.		(K.B)

2. 1815 New imprint: **Published by J & J Cundee, Albion Press London, January 1, 1815** (CeOS).

The New British Traveller by James Dugdale Vol II
London J & J Cundee (1815)   C.

The New British Traveller by James Dugdale Vol.II
Issued with three title pages: one engraved titlepage each for Cundee and Robins (dated 1819) plus either a Cundee type-set titlepage (1), or a Robins type-set titlepage (2)
(1)RGS, (2)W.

3. 1818 New imprint: **Published by J Robins and Co, Albion Press London. January 1st. 1818.** (CeOS).
(E), (NDL).

Robin's Atlas of England and Wales
London. J Robins & Co. 1819.   CCCLXII, BL, B.C

The New British Traveller   Vol 1
London. J Robins & Co. 1819.   CCCLXIII, BL, C, W, BCL.

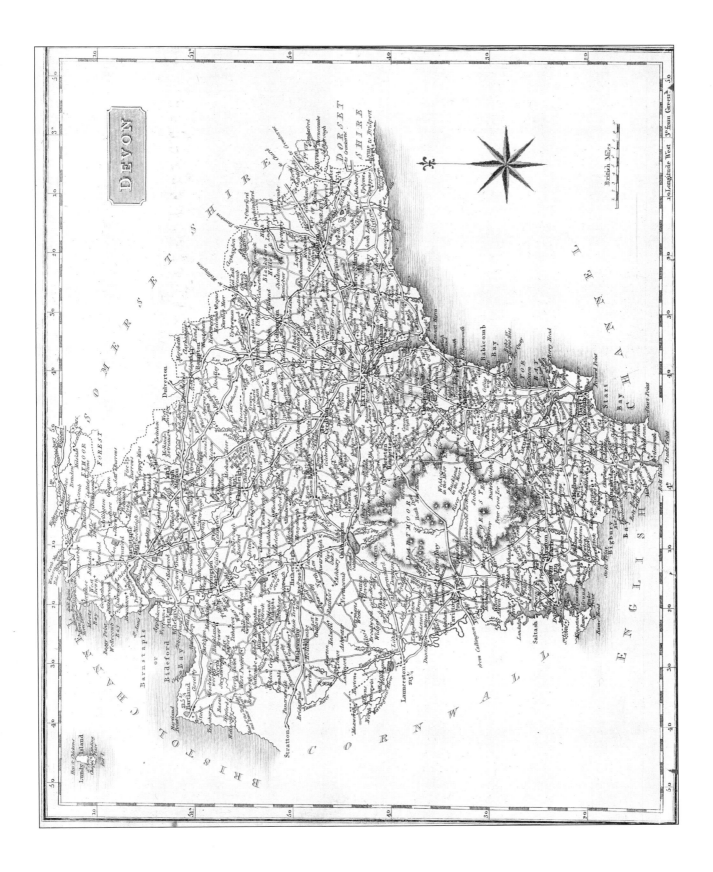

79.3 Neele/Cundee *Robin's Atlas of England and Wales*

80

PALMER/CARY
1813

The first Ordnance Survey of Devonshire was published in 1809 (**74**) and soon it was being used by map publishers as the basis for all large-scale maps. Even John Cary, who is credited with carrying out his own surveys on behalf of the Postmaster General, exploited the Ordnance Survey work and produced a large-scale map of Devon clearly labelling his work as *Reduced from a Survey made by Order of the Board of Ordnance.* The area covered is that of the original survey. (G F Cruchley, who took over Cary's business, also produced a large-scale folding map of Devon in the 1860s, *Cruchley's Reduced Ordnance Map of Devonshire.* Measuring 1200 x 925 mm it was a close copy of the Ordnance Survey map.)

The Board of Ordnance objected to its work being copied and the Master General banned sales of the ordnance maps. However, the map sellers were able to argue successfully that as the work was carried out at public expense they had a duty and a right to reproduce the work at reduced sizes and at scales of their choosing.

Cary's map was produced on four plates initially printed in unlettered form. These were probably issued for approval and for others to add local information. The only known part (North Devon) was sent to Lord Clifford of Ugbrooke House. Robert Edward Clifford was chairman of the committee for the internal defence of Devon at that time.[1] The map showed rivers and roads but was otherwise without any topographical features.

Hartland Point is shown but nothing west of Stoke and only half of Ford to the east. The map is heavily hachured and the sea coast shaded. Exeter Canal is shown but not the Grand Western. The signature is that of J Palmer about whom nothing is known.

Size 1218 x 931 mm.

SCALE OF MILES (12=150 mm).
Scale 1M=12.5 mm.

A Topographical Map OF DEVONSHIRE, Including parts of the adjacent Counties REDUCED from a Survey made by Order of the Board of Ordnance Under the direction of Col. Mudge. LONDON: Published by JOHN CARY, June 4ᵗʰ. 1813. Imprint: Etched by J. Palmer (CeOS).

1.	**1813**	Blank plate. Only North Devon is known in this state.	(P).
2.	**1813**	As described.	(E²).

---

[1] W. Ravenhill; The South West in the Eighteenth-Century Re-mapping of England; in *Maps and History in South-West England*; Ed. Barker, K and Kain, R; University of Exeter Press; 1991.

[2] Illustration courtesy of the Exeter Westcountry Studies Library.

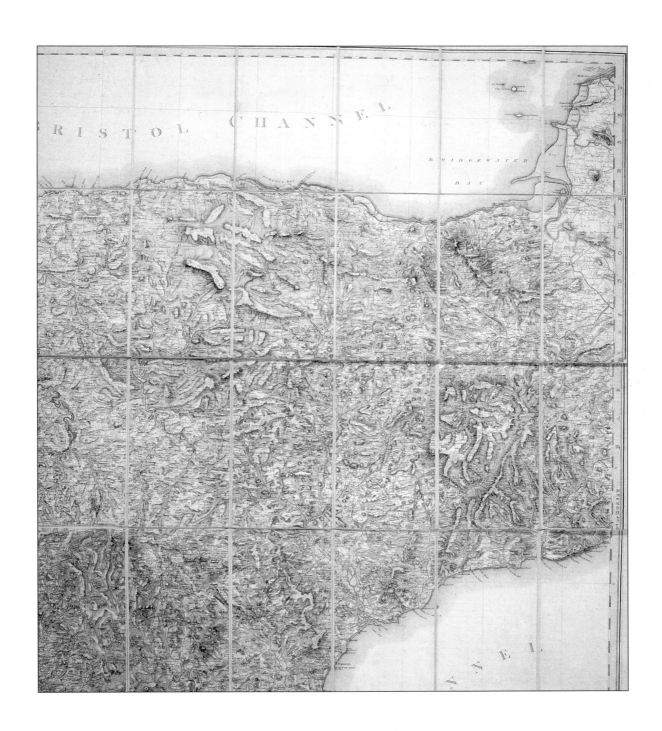

80.2 Palmer/Cary *A Topographical Map of Devonshire* (detail)

81

ROBERT ROWE
1816

Robert Rowe (1775-1843) was an engraver and publisher of a great number of maps including two sets of cards (**61**, **75**) and one atlas, *The English Atlas,* which was published in 1816 (folio, 46 maps) with some maps dated as early as 1813. Although Rowe produced the original atlas it was not long before it was taken over by the company of Henry Teesdale, publishers at 302 High Holborn (this address was deleted between 1830-40) and 2 Brunswick Row Queen Square (1842).

Watermarks reveal some anomalies concerning dating: the RGS 1830 copy has a watermark *J Whatman 1830* although the map of Middlesex has an 1831 watermark. In addition the Signet library has dated its copy 1833 and Whitaker also lists an 1833 issue.

Later issues: Teesdale's *Improved Edition* was only printed once more, in 1842, although Chubb notes an 1840 edition.

The plates then changed hands often; from 1848 they were in the possession of H G Collins who published lithographs from them in his part-work *New British Atlas* as well as producing a series of folding maps. When published by Collins in his *British Gazetteer* an attractive foliate decoration was added to the outer frame as well as a *Gazetteer* title panel. This was also issued as a folding map labelled *Collins' Devonshire with its Railways.* Some changes were made including the addition of a label stuck over the gazetteer title. The map was folded to 250 x 155 mm. Shortly afterwards the plates passed into the hands of W S Orr. He produced folding maps in covers *c.*1855. The maps were finally taken over and issued between 1855 and 1864 as folding maps by George Philip in his *Popular Series of County Maps* as well as an atlas, *Philips' County Atlas* (*c.*1857).

This pattern of early ownership was repeated with the *New Travelling Atlas* of Teesdale (**99**).

In addition to these issues a note in *The Romance of the Road* by Cecil Aldin (London. Eyre & Spottiswoode. 1928.) referred to an *English Atlas* by Teesdale 1828.[1]

Size 340 x 415 mm.   **Scale** (1+14=65 mm) **Miles**.
Plate 8   Scale 1M=4.3 mm.

A NEW MAP of the COUNTY of DEVONSHIRE Divided into Hundreds. By R. Rowe. in oval frame (Ea). Imprint within title oval: **London: Printed for R Rowe, Nº 19, Bedford Street, Bedford Row, Jany 1. 1816.**

1. 1816	*The English Atlas by R. Rowe* London. R Rowe. 1816.		**CCCLIVa**, B.
2. 1819	Year in imprint amended: **1819**.		
	The English Atlas by R. Rowe London. R Rowe. 1816 (1821).		CB.
	A single sheet, cut, mounted and cased.		(C).
3. 1829	Title oval removed, and title re-engraved **DEVONSHIRE**. (Da). Imprint: **London, Published by Henry Teesdale & Cº. 302, Holborn** (CeOS). Plymouth Breakwater added.		
	New British Atlas corrected to the year 1829 London. Henry Teesdale & Co. 1829.		**CCCCIX**, BL, W, C.
	New British Atlas corrected to the year 1830 London. Henry Teesdale & Co. 1830.		**CCCCX**, RGS, C.

---

[1]. Eugene Burden; *County Maps of Berkshire 1574-1900*, (1988) 1991.

4. 1831 **Rail Roads** added to Explanation. Upgrading of roads and inclusion of new roads, eg Plymouth to Totnes, Newton Abbot and Chudleigh as Mail Coach Road. Dartmoor Railway, Exeter and Tavistock Canals with Grand Western Branch to Tiverton. Proposed extension to Trent Tree and Shebbear of Tamar Navigation north of Tamerton and Canal Axmouth-Dorset.

New British Atlas corrected to the year 1831
London. Henry Teesdale & Co. 1831.   **CCCCXI**, BL, C, W, (E).

5. 1832 Completely amended to include Parliamentary notes: the **NORTHERN** and **SOUTHERN DIVISIONS** are depicted and Maltese Crosses show polling places.
Note on population and taxes added. Note added below the title regarding parliamentary representation.

Improved Edition of the New British Atlas corrected to the year 1832
London. Henry Teesdale & Co. 1832.   **CCCCXII**, BL, C, W, B, (NDL).

6. 1835 With plate number **14** added (EaOS). Without Great Western Railway added.

Improved Edition of the New British Atlas corrected to the year 1835
London. Henry Teesdale & Co. 1835.   W, (E).

7. 1835 With Great Western Railway added.

Improved Edition of the New British Atlas corrected to the year 1835
London. Henry Teesdale & Co. 1835.   **CCCCXIV**, B, C.

DIX/DARTON
1816

Thomas Dix was a surveyor and schoolmaster of North Walsham who produced a *Juvenile Atlas* (1811) and maps of Bedfordshire (1818), York (1820, 1835) and Chester (1830).

William Darton Senior (and successors) were engravers and publishers with a map, print and chart warehouse at 40 Holborn Hill until 1806 and then at 58 Holborn Hill. In 1822 they published the *Complete Atlas of the Counties of England* (folio, 42 maps). This contained a number of maps by Thomas Dix, who had started the project. He died before it was completed and the remaining maps were completed by William Darton. Although the atlas appeared in 1822 some maps have much earlier dates: Devon is dated 1816. The maps were issued separately either as single sheets or cut, mounted and cased. The atlas was reissued as *The Counties of England* about 1835. The Dartons also produced a *Miniature Atlas of England and Wales,* 1821 (**85**) and republished Wilkinson's *General Atlas,* 1826.

An attractive vignette of Dartmouth Castle appears on the map. This is the only Devon map with this scene and was the first map of Devon since Bowen's *Royal English Atlas* (1763) to have a vignette view.

Later issues: Dix and Darton's maps were reissued: Hereford, Lancs, Lincs and Surrey have been noted in red covers as *The Post Office Map of* .... *Dedicated to Rowland Hill* (*c.*1850); a loose, folding copy of Devon in state 3 but with date deleted and inclusion of the railway may have belonged to this series; Melville and Co used them as a source; a *Directory of Berkshire, Oxfordshire, Cambridgeshire, Bedfordshire and Northamptonshire* appeared in 1867. Lithographs were also issued; *Berkshire. The Official, County Map and Guide* had the appropriate Dix and Darton map[1] and Smith[2] has reported an interesting set of folding maps produced in the early 1860s: *Darton and Hodge's Railway, Commercial and Tourist's Map.*

Size 355 x 445 mm.

Scale of Miles (15=66 mm).
Scale 1M=4.4 mm.

A NEW MAP of the County of DEVON Divided into Hundreds by M[R]. THO[S] DIX. in circular frame (Ae). Vignette of **Dartmouth Castle.** Imprint: **Published 23rd July 1816 by W. Darton Jun[r] 58 Holborn Hill, London** (CeOS). Table: **Explanation** (Da).

1. 1816	Single sheet unfolded 410 x 540 mm (watermark *Whatman 1818*).		(KB).

A Complete Atlas of the English Counties commenced by the late Thomas Dix ... carried on and completed by William Darton, London.
London. William Darton. 1822. **CCCLXXXVII**, W, C, BCL.

2. 1830	Year in imprint amended: **Published 23rd July 1830.**	
	As folding map, dissected and mounted.	(BL), (KB).

3. 1833 Title altered and moved: **DEVONSHIRE, Divided into Hundreds AND THE Parliamentary Divisions.** with no frame (Da). List of Market Towns and Days added (Eb). **Explanation.** (Ad). Thorncomb area omitted. New imprint: **LONDON: WILLIAM DARTON & SON, HOLBORN HILL, 1833.**

The Counties of England   (E).
London. William Darton and Son. (1835), (1838).   B; BL.

[1.] Eugene Burden; *County Maps of Berkshire 1574-1900,* (1988) 1991; p.111.
[2.] David Smith; An Unrecorded Edition; in *IMCoS JOURNAL*; Vol. 1 No. 3; February 1981.

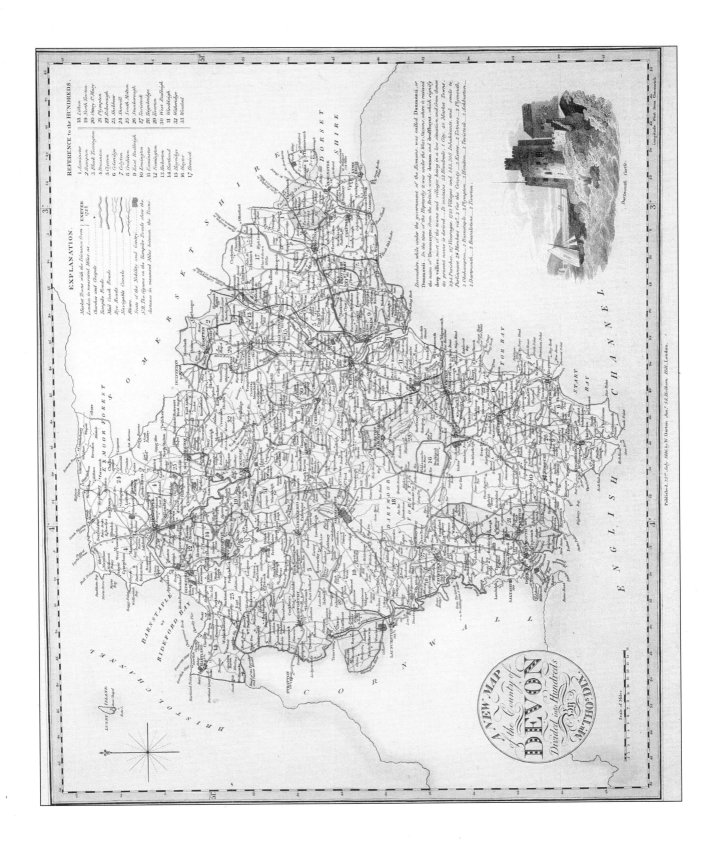

82.1 Dix/Darton *A New Map of the County of Devon*

83

E A EZEKIEL
1816

The *Exeter Pocket Journal* was first published in the eighteenth century and copies for 1788 (by E Thorn), 1791 and 1796 are known but these did not include maps. In an 1816 edition a map of Devon and Cornwall was included. This was one of the few maps to have been executed by a local person: E A Ezekiel, an optician and goldsmith in Exeter. The journal for 1827 lists him on the page of *Persons of Eminence, Genius and Public Notoriety* as *eminent engraver, miniature painter and optician*. According to the journal he was born about 1757 in Exeter and died in 1806. If the latter date is correct it leads one to the conclusion that the map is in fact older, and that earlier copies of the *Pocket Book* may yet be found. G and A Ezekiel were still trading as engravers and opticians in Fore Street in the late 1820s.

Trewman and Son had already printed Polwhele's *History of Devonshire* for Cadell, Johnson and Dilly in 1797. In a trade directory for 1827 they were registered as Trewman and Co. *printers, booksellers, bookbinders and stationers* in the High Street, Exeter.

The map shows Devon and Cornwall together and was in fact part of a larger regional map: it extends as far as Bridgewater and Lyme Regis and the wording relating to the neighbouring counties has been cut (ie only PART OF SOMEI and DOR remain). Mail coach roads are shown and, although graticuled, there are no references. The map was folded twice to fit the journal.

This map was replaced in the 1822 edition by a new map of Devon engraved by Smith and Davies (**93**).

Size 138 x 215 mm.   Scale bar (16=29 mm) **Scale of Statute Miles**.
                                                          Scale 1M=1.8 mm.

MAP of DEVON and CORNWALL Abridged & Engraved by E A EZEKIEL Optician & Goldsmith, EXETER. Imprints: **Engraved for the EXETER Pocket Journal** (CaOS) and **Exeter, Published by Trewman & Son, Printers Book-sellers and Stationers** (CeOS)

1. 1816   *The Exeter Pocket Journal Or, West-Country Gentleman's and Tradesman's Memorandum Book,*
                    For the Year of our Lord 1816
                    Exeter. Trewman & Son. 1816.   E[1].

[1.]   Illustration courtesy of the Exeter Westcountry Studies Library.

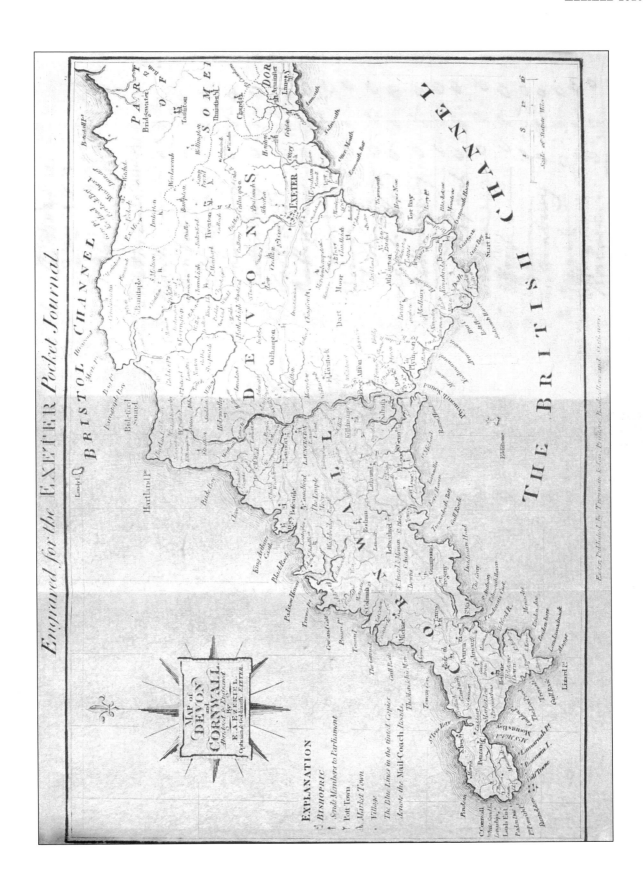

83.1 Ezekiel *The Exeter Pocket Journal*

84

LANGLEY/BELCH
1817

Edward Langley (*fl.*1800-35) was a well-established bookseller and publisher as well as an engraver with premises at 173 High Street, Borough. He is known for his maps of London, Bedford and Essex. Early in his career he formed a partnership with William Belch (*fl.*1802-20) and until 1820 they published together including the *New County Atlas.*

The 52 maps in this (4to) atlas are variously dated between 1816 and 1818 and have attractive vignettes of town views or buildings relating to the appropriate county. It is interesting that vignettes as part of the map are commonly associated with the Victorian age. However, vignettes were popular only over a period of twenty years, namely from 1816 (Dix and Darton's view of Dartmouth Castle) to 1836 (Schmollinger's views of Tavistock Abbey and Exeter County Sessions) and few, if any, Victorian county maps included such views. During this period some nine maps had vignettes. The most popular view was Exeter Cathedral as illustrated in this map. Other vignettes only appear once: those mentioned above, Babicombe Bay (Babbacombe near Torquay by Walker/Fisher) and Exeter Guildhall (Dower/Moule). This does not include the Crabb cards which had views added around the sides of the original map by Reuben Ramble (**85**).

There was possibly an earlier version as a now broken and lost atlas included other counties without the Mail and Turnpike roads symbols (or where these had been added by hand), but a Devon copy has not been seen.

The Langley and Belch partnership ended in 1820 with Langley publishing under his own imprint and Belch publishing on his own from 1 Staverton Row, Newington Butts. After the break-up of the partnership another edition of the atlas was issued by Joseph Phelps with amended imprint. A dissected map of Berkshire is known with Joseph Phelps' imprint on the cover of the slip case. A later version of Sussex with imprints removed and a new separate panel added has also been reported.

Early states were issued singly, folding into a slipcase. Rather strangely the maps were used by William Cobbett in 1832 in an early edition of his *Geographical Dictionary.* A copy has been reported which included Langley and Belch maps trimmed at the edges. These were replaced in the same year by a new map (**106**).

Size 170 x 257 mm.

Scale (10=22 mm).
Scale 1M=2.2 mm.

LANGLEY'S new MAP of DEVONSHIRE. Vignette of **Exeter Cathedral.** Imprint: **Printed and Published by Langley & Belch, Nº 173, High Street, Borough, London, August 12th. 1817.** (CeOS).

(E), (NDL), (DEI).

1. 1817   *Langley's New County Atlas of England and Wales*
London. Langley & Belch. (1818).   **CCCLIX**, BL, W, B, C.

Langley's New County Atlas of England and Wales
London. Joseph Phelps. (1820).   B.

A Geographical Dictionary ... by William Cobbett
London. William Cobbett. 1832.   [P].

2. 1820   New imprint: **Printed & Published by J Phelps, Nº 27, Paternoster Row, London.** 1820. (CeOS).

Langley's New County Atlas of England and Wales
London. Joseph Phelps. (1820).   **CCCLX**, CB.

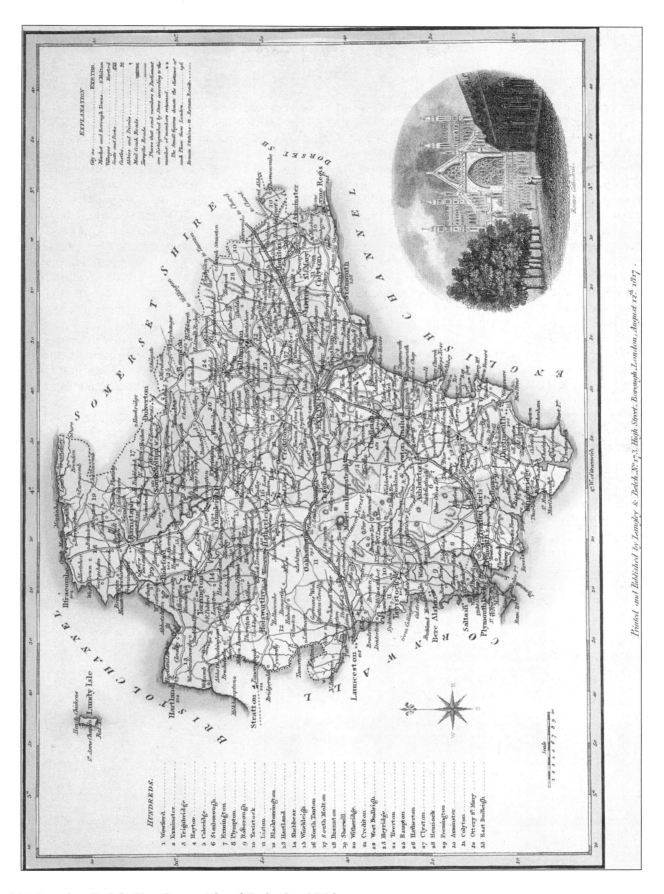

84.1 Langley/Belch *New County Atlas of England and Wales*

85

CRABB/(Ramble)
1819

Thomas Crabb, a London publisher, engraved a set of maps on cards about 1819 (the date on the card of Scotland) which were closely similar to the maps published the following year in Reid and Wallis's *The Panorama; or, Traveller's Instructive Guide* (**88**). As the address on the Crabb cards of both Scotland and Cheshire is 1 Ivy Lane, Paternoster Row is also the address of C Hinton, whose name appears on the imprint of the Reid and Wallis maps, it would seem clear that co-operation took place (Crabb moved to John Street in 1820). A card of Devon has not been found but may be assumed, as others in the set were reissued by Robert Miller in his *Miniature Atlas*. Miller was a bookseller and publisher who often worked closely with William Darton: it was Darton who subsequently reissued the maps about 1822 (and 1825 according to Chubb – CCCXLII – but no copy is known).

Later issues: In 1845 a lithographed series of 40 maps (4to) with decorative views surrounding the original maps was produced by Reuben Ramble although some counties are found in this state as early as 1839. The atlas, *Reuben Ramble's Travels,* was clearly designed to appeal to children (Chubb DXVII – see illustration). The map of Devon is now surrounded by typical Devon scenes including cider making and Plymouth Breakwater which was shown from an impossible angle. On the map itself the title was erased and replaced without frame or hatching; a symbol for Railways was added below and the railway to Exeter is shown. The size of the whole is now 216 x 165 mm. There may have been two issues of *Reuben Ramble's Travels Through the Counties of England* in 1845 (London. Darton and Clark) as well as an edition of 1850 (London. Darton and Co.). Additionally the maps appeared in *Reuben Ramble's Travels in the Western Counties of England.* This work was also published in parts. One of these lithographs probably appeared in an edition of *The Child's Treasury of Amusement and Knowledge; or, Reuben Ramble's Picture Lessons* (London. Darton and Clark. *c.*1846).

Reuben Ramble was a pseudonym for the Rev. Samuel Clark, Rector of Eaton-Bishop who published under the name Sam Clark.

Size 68 x 105 mm.   **Scale of Miles** (10=9.5 mm).
                                                              Scale 1M=1 mm.

DEVONSHIRE. Imprint: **London. Published by T Crabb 15, John Street, Blackfriars Road** (CeOS).

1. 1819   One of a set of cards (this state is supposed – see text)
              London. T Crabb. 1819.

2. 1821   **Long. W. from Lon^n.** in border (BeOS). New imprint: **London. Published by Robert Miller, 24, Old Fish Street.** (CeOS). Plate number **42** added vertically (EeOS).

              Miller's New Miniature Atlas
              London. R Miller. (1821).   **CCCXL**, BL, C, W.

              One of a set of playing cards; the other cards were based mainly on Reid's *Panorama* but not Devon or Somerset

                                                                            BL.

3. 1822   New imprint: **London. William Darton; 58, Holborn Hill.** (CeOS).

              Darton's New Miniature Atlas
              London. William Darton. (1822).   **CCCXLI**, BL, W.

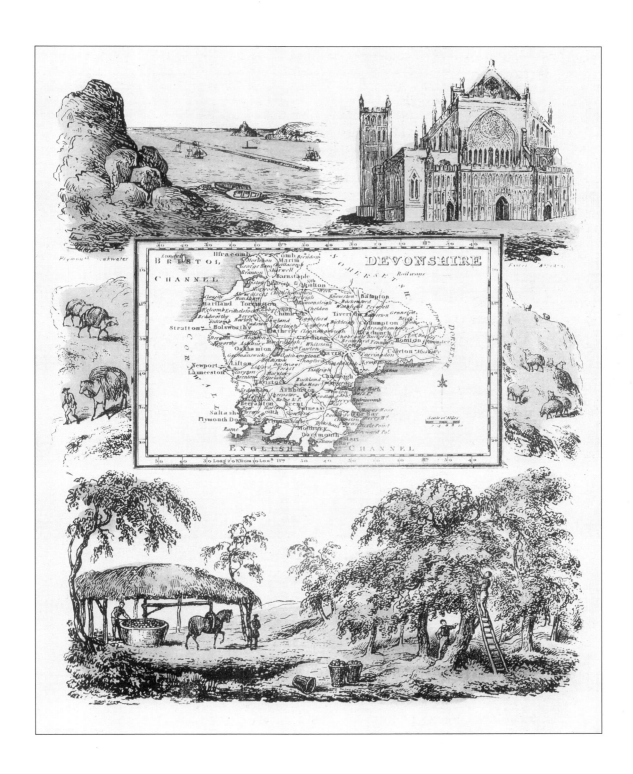

85.4 Crabb/(Ramble) *Travels Through the Counties of England*

NEELE/PINNOCK
1819

William Pinnock (1782-1843) of Alton, at first a schoolmaster then a bank teller, was also a historian and topographer. He joined Samuel Maunder in 1817, marrying his sister. They published educational books including Catechisms and Geographies and the *History and Topography*. Pinnock edited *The Guide to Knowledge* (**108**) with the interesting white on black maps by Joshua Archer. Maunder (1785-1849), a Devonian, was mainly a compiler of dictionaries. His *little gazetteer* was published in 1845.

Pinnock's *History and Topography of Devonshire* was one volume in a series of eighty-three County Catechisms published by Pinnock and Maunder. The series was published in parts, each county being published separately, with Bedfordshire and Berkshire appearing first. The text of the histories was set out in question and answer format consisting of some seventy pages, and included such information as the sites of fairs. From this we learn that Upottery had a toyfair in October, Denbury a cheese and soap fair on September 8th and many towns held wool markets in the autumn. The page size was only 130 mm so that the Neele imprint from the *Histories* is often missing, the map being cut along the bottom border and folded twice. Later editions have Whittaker's imprint; he possibly bought the plates when Pinnock got into financial difficulties. Whittaker also published editions of *A Topographical Dictionary* with maps by Cooper (**72**).

Size 128 x 160 mm.   **Scale of Statute Miles** (10=17 mm).
                                                                          Scale 1M=1.7 mm.

DEVONSHIRE. Signature: **Neele & Son, fe, 352, Strand.** (EeOS). No Explanation key.

1. 1819	*Pinnock's History and Topography of England and Wales Vol I.* London. Geo. B Whittaker. 1825.		**CCCXCVI**, BL.
2. 1820	**Explanation** key added above title.		
	The Traveller's Pocket Atlas London. Pinnock & Maunder. (1820).		C.
	Pinnock's County Histories. The History and Topography of Devonshire London. G & W B Whittaker. (1820).		C, E.
3. 1821	Imprint: **Published by G. & W. B. Whittaker, Ave-Maria Lane, 1821.** (CeOS).		
	The Traveller's Pocket Atlas London. G & W B Whittaker. 1823[1].		**CCCXC**, BL, W, B, C, RGS.
	Pinnock's History and Topography of England and Wales Vol I. London. Geo. B Whittaker. 1825.		[P].
	Pinnock's County Histories London. G Whittaker & Co. (1835).		FB.

---

[1] Harold Whitaker records a 1821 edition by the same publishers – entry 375; in *Maps of Northumberland*; Society of Antiquaries and Public Libraries Committee; 1949.

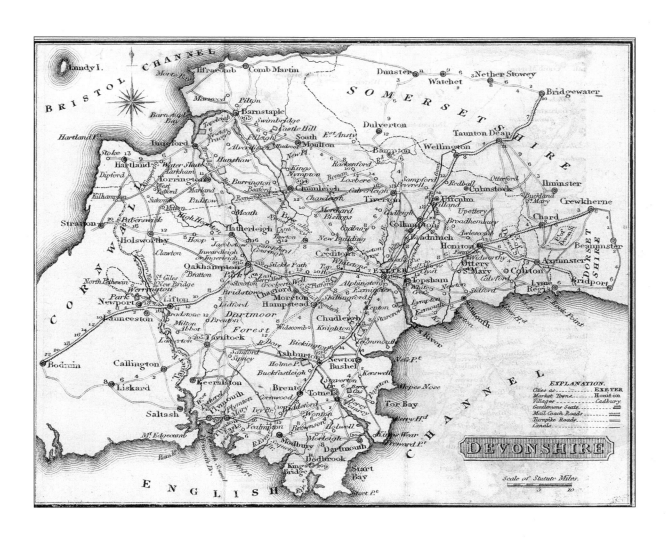

86.2 Neele/Pinnock *The History and Topography of Devonshire*

87

HALL/LEIGH
1820

A publisher in the Strand, Samuel Leigh published only one cartographic work, with simple miniature maps by Sidney Hall, largely notable for the number of times it was reprinted. *Leigh's New Pocket Atlas* was published first in 1820[1] with 56 maps (12mo). In subsequent editions, after 1825, this was usually bound together with *Leigh's New Pocket Road-book of England and Wales*. The book could be bought with or without maps and cost 12s or 8s. From *c.*1834 Leigh's business was run by his widow, Mary Anne Leigh and later by his son.

Later issues: The *Atlas* was reissued four more times, each issue accompanying an edition of the road-book which had the imprints: Leigh & Son. 1839; Leigh and Co. 1840; G Biggs. 1842; G Biggs and Orlando Hodgson. 1842, 1843. The final series had the planned railway to Exeter added.

Sidney Hall produced one further popular series of maps (**101**).

Size 120 x 68 mm including title. | **English Miles** (30=30 mm).
Scale 1M=1 mm.

DEVONSHIRE. Plate number **9** (EeOS). Imprints: **Pub. by S. Leigh, 18. Strand.** (AaOS) and **Sid**^y. **Hall Sculp**^t. (AeOS).

(E).

1. 1820   *Leigh's New Pocket Atlas of England and Wales*   CCCLXXIII, W, B.
London. Samuel Leigh. 1820.

Leigh's New Atlas of England and Wales
Bound together with *Leigh's New Pocket Road Book* (1st & 2nd Editions).
London. Samuel Leigh. 1825, 1826.
    CCCLXXIV, BL, RGS; **CCCLXXV**, C.

Leigh's New Atlas of England and Wales (bound with 3rd edition of roadbook).
London. Samuel Leigh. 1831.
    CCCLXXVI, W, B.

2. 1834   Imprint: **Pub. by M. A. Leigh 421 Strand.** (AeOS). Additions, eg **Devonport**.

Leigh's New Atlas of England and Wales (bound with 4th edition of roadbook).
London. M A Leigh. 1834.   **CCCLXXVII**, BL, RGS.

Leigh's New Pocket Atlas ... corrected since the passing of the Reform Bill.
London. M A Leigh. 1834.   B.

Leigh's New Atlas of England and Wales (bound with 5th edition of roadbook).
London. Leigh & Son. 1835.   **CCCLXXVIII**, C.

3. 1837   Hall's signature erased.

Leigh's New Atlas of England and Wales (bound with 6th edition of the road-book which has the imprint: London. Leigh & Son. 1837.).
London. M A Leigh. (1837).   **CCCLXXIX**, BL, W.

---

[1] Harold Whitaker records a 1820 edition of *Leigh's New Picture of England and Wales* by the same publishers – entry 367a; in *Maps of Northumberland*; Society of Antiquaries and Public Libraries Committee; 1949.

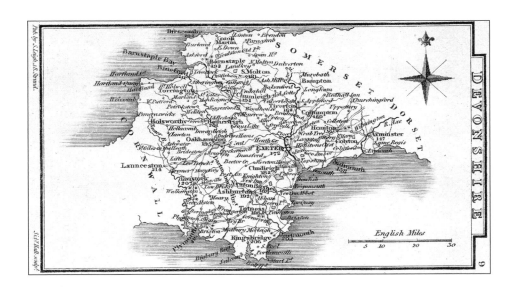

87.1 Hall/Leigh *Leigh's New Atlas of England and Wales*

88

WALLIS/REID
1820

James Wallis who had already produced two county atlases (**77**, **78**) only produced one more notable cartographic work some eight years later. His third atlas was published by W H Reid, whose name appears on the frontispiece, hence the maps are often referred to as Wallis and Reid maps. The maps are similar to the Crabb maps of 1819 (**85**) and one may be a copy of the other. C Hinton was also involved in the publication of these maps and his address was the same as one of Crabb's addresses. In 1825 the maps were produced as playing cards but two cards (Devonshire and Somersetshire) did not come from the *Panorama*. They were Crabb's maps as reissued by Miller in 1821.

The atlas was published in 8vo format and consisted of 53 maps. Devon faced page 29 in the atlas and the map was followed by four pages of information such as principal towns, principal fairs, principal seats and parks, members of parliament and even a list of county bankers.

Size 68 x 103 mm.   **Scale of Miles** (10=10 mm).
                                            Scale 1M=1 mm.

DEVONSHIRE. Imprint: **Published by J Wallis, 77 Berwick Str. Soho; & C Hinton, Ivy La. Paternoster Row.** (CeOS).

1. 1820   *The Panorama: or Traveller's Instructive Guide Through England and Wales*
                London. W H Reid. (1820).
                                            CCCLXXII, BL, RGS, W, C, (E).

2. 1820   Imprint erased.

                The Panorama: or Traveller's Instructive Guide
                London. W H Reid. (1820).   B.

3. 1825   Imprint added: **Published by Hodgson & C⁰. 10, Newgate Street.** (CeOS).

                The Panorama: or Traveller's Instructive Guide
                London. Hodgson & Co. (1825).   B.

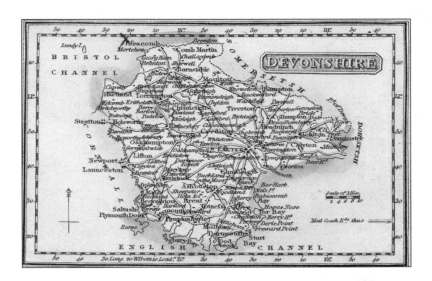

88.2 Wallis/Reid *The Panorama: or Traveller's Instructive Guide*

89

MUTLOW/LYSONS
1822

Thomas Cadell (*b*.1742) is best known for the work which he produced together with William Davies. Cadell established his publishing business in the Strand in London and was joined by the engraver, Davies, shortly after. Individually they were both successful in their respective works. Cadell established his reputation by publishing *Cooks Voyages* in 1773, whilst Davies engraved work for Arrowsmith and Kelly. Together Cadell and Davies published several works, including maps that had been engraved by Lowry for Arrowsmith, and published them jointly with Longman and Rees.

H Mutlow engraved maps for Cadell and Davies including the map of Devon for *Magna Britannia* by the Reverend Daniel Lysons and Samuel Lysons. This was planned as an updated improvement on William Camden's *Britannia* and was produced in parts beginning with Beds, Berks and Bucks in the first volume dated 1806 with a reprint dated 1813.[1]

Mutlow also engraved many town plans; including a very attractive map of Exeter copied from Braun and Hogenberg (and thus Hooker) in *c*.1780. He also engraved some maps, including one of Devon for Marshall (**60**). Apart from this not much is known about him. One source notes that the firm of T Woodman and H Mutlow took over the business of John Spilsbury, the inventor of jigsaw puzzles, about 1771. Spilsbury's address was Russell Court which was Mutlow's address as found on the imprint of his map for Marshall. Tooley[2] only lists I Mutlow, engraver, active from 1794 to 1816.

The earlier maps from *Magna Britannia* have an imprint naming both Cadell and Davies but Devonshire names Cadell alone (Davies died in 1819): the earlier maps also have Volume and Page references in the corners, not present on Devon. The volumes on Devon and Cornwall contain birds-eye views of harbours – Devon has views of Dartmouth, Plymouth and Exmouth.

The map is graticuled at full degrees.

The *Magna Britannia* proved harder work than the historians planned and, with the death of Samuel in 1819, Daniel was only persuaded to complete Devon before the project was abandoned. In all only six volumes, including ten county maps, were produced.

Size 345 x 235 mm.

British Statute Miles (18=56 mm).
Scale 1M=3.1 mm.

DEVONSHIRE. Inset map of **Lundy Isle.** Imprint: **Published Feb**Y. **1**st. **1822, by T. Cadell, Strand, London.** (CeOS). Signature: **Mutlow, sculp.** (EeOS).

1. 1822   *Magna Britannia being a concise topographical account of the several counties of Great Britain by the Rev.*
          Daniel Lysons ... and Samuel Lysons ... Volume the Sixth containing Devonshire
          London. T Cadell. 1822.

BL, C, E, (NDL).

[1]   David Smith; The Demise of the Nineteenth Century Cartographic Project; in *IMCoS JOURNAL*; Issue 53; 1993.
[2]   R V Tooley; *Dictionary of Mapmakers*; Map Collector Publications; 1979.

89.1 Mutlow/Lysons *Magna Britannia*

90

J WALKER
1822

Benjamin Crosby (1768-1815), a Yorkshireman, first produced his gazetteer in 1807, with only two general maps. After Crosby's death his assistants Simpkin and Marshall retained their share when the business passed to Baldwin, Cradock and Joy. They were joined by J Bumpus, a member of a well-known booksellers founded in 1816. The gazetteer was then reissued in 1815 and 1818. The 1822 edition, in which county maps were first issued, reused the 1818 title page — but the date on many of the maps is 1822.

The small county maps for *Crosby's Complete Pocket Gazetteer*[1] were engraved by J Walker. Shirley[2] writes about the confusing number of J Walkers but his John Walker of Wakefield who produced a map of that area and a large folding map of Great Britain is unlikely as the engraver of these small-scale maps. The maps are certainly different to those produced by J and C Walker (**102**, **103**, **113** and **116**), although a few years later the firm of J and C Walker would become famous. It has been suggested that the cartographer for these miniature maps may have been James Walker of Littlehampton[3]. Nothing is known about J Cox the engraver.

The original maps had information on the size of county, inhabitants and parliamentary information which was erased when the maps were used by Samuel Tymms. The *Scale of Miles* was also erased: the scale as drawn gave a distance Exeter-Plymouth of fifteen miles!

The maps appeared again some ten years later when *The Family Topographer* was published in seven volumes from 1832 to 1843. *A Compendious Account of the Western Circuit*, which appeared in 1834, was also a topographical work with maps, the *Circuit* referring to the judicial area of the Courts of Assize.

Later issues: In 1842 *Camden's Britannia Epitomized and Continued* by Samuel Tymms appeared with the same maps. This was published in London by H G Bohn. This work in six volumes, again presenting the individual judicial circuits together with copious notes based on Camden, was the last work to be based on Camden.

Size 120 x 75 mm.   **Scale of Miles** (10=25 mm).
                                                          (Scale 1M=2.5 mm.)

DEVONSHIRE. Imprint: **London. Publish'd May 1st. 1822, by I Bumpus, No 6 Holborn Bars.** under map frame (CeOS). Signatures: **J. Walker del.** (AeOS) and **J. Cox sculp.** (EeOS). **Scale of Miles** (Ee). Panel along lower border with statistical notes.

1. 1822   *Crosby's Complete Pocket Gazetteer of England and Wales*
               London. Baldwin, Cradock & Joy, Simpkin & Marshall and J Bumpus. 1818 (1822).   TB.

2. 1832   Signatures, imprint, scale-bar and panel containing statistical notes removed. Note added: **The figures affixed to the Towns show the distances from London & Exeter** (CaOS). New imprint: **London. Published Jany. 1st. 1832, by Nichols & Son, 25 Parliament Street.** (CeOS). Towns added, eg **Painton**, **Brixham** and **Comb Martin.**
                                                          (DEI).

               The Family Topographer By Samuel Tymms Vol. I
               London. J B Nichols & Son. 1832.   CCCCXLI, BL, E.

               A Compendious Account of the Western Circuit
               London. J B Nichols & Son. 1834.   [RRL].

1. For an account of this gazetteer see David Smith; A Previously Unknown Pocket Gazetter Found; in *The Map Collector*, Issue 29; December 1984; pp. 34-35.
2. R J Shirley; Mapping Great Britain's Industrial Revolution; in *IMCoS JOURNAL*; Vol. 7 No. 1; Spring 1987.
3. David Kingsley; *Printed Maps of Sussex*; Sussex Record Society; 1982.

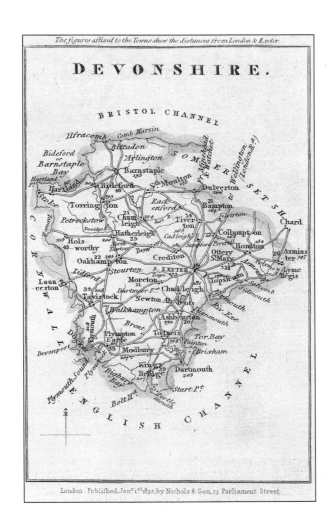

90.2 **Walker** *The Family Topographer*

91

GARDNER/SMITH
1822

Publisher, engraver, map and globe seller, Charles Smith was highly successful, eventually becoming Map Seller Extraordinary to HRH the Prince of Wales. From premises at No 172 Corner of Surrey Street in the Strand (1803-1862), and from 1864 at 63 Charing Cross, the firm produced a number of notable cartographic works including the *New English Atlas* (**63**).

In 1822 a reduced version of this atlas (4to, 44 maps), the title remaining the same, was published with the map of Devon engraved by W R Gardner (with other maps by John Pickett). It is very similar to John Cary's *New and Correct English Atlas* (**73**) map of the county but Plymouth Breakwater is shown for the first time (it was begun in 1812 but not finally completed until 1844) and various mileages not included by Cary. A close copy of Gardner's map was executed for Trewman's *The Exeter Pocket Journal* of the same year (**93**).

A copy of *Smith's New English Atlas* with title-page dated 1825 but published in 1827 (based on the map of Yorkshire) has been reported.[1] There is a possibility that the date in the imprint of the Devon map was erased earlier: Kingsley[2] recorded two states of Sussex in 1825 editions.

In 1826 Smith compiled a road book with Gardner's name appearing once again as engraver. Charles Smith was also responsible for several additional works including maps of London (1803) and Bristol (1829), and plans of rivers and canals.

Later issues: The railways were first added for the final issue of the atlas published in 1844. The maps may also have been available folded with a cover from *c*.1845 as *Smith's ... (County)*.

Size 195 x 230 mm.

Scale of Miles (20=52 mm).
Scale 1M=2.6 mm.

DEVONSHIRE. Distances from London to Exeter via 5 different routes, and from London to Plymouth via 3 different routes. Imprint: **Printed for C. SMITH, Nº. 172 Strand 1822.** (CeOS). Signature: **Gardner sculp**[t] (EeOS).

(E[3]).

1. 1822   *Smith's New English Atlas being a reduction of his large folio atlas*
London. C Smith. 1822, 1825.   **CCCLXXXVIII**, BL, W, C; C.

2. 1828   Date in imprint erased. New link road just north of Chudleigh added.
(Yorkshire maps are dated 1827, 1829, 1830 and 1834 respectively.)

Smith's New English Atlas
London. C Smith. 1828, 1828 (1829), 1828 (1830), 1833 (1834).

CB; B; C; [P].

One undated map exists cut, mounted and booked.   (C).

[1]. Eugene Burden; *County Maps of Berkshire*; (1988) 1991; p.117 – atlas now broken.
[2]. David Kingsley; *Printed Maps of Sussex*; Sussex Record Society; 1982.
[3]. Illustration courtesy of the Exeter Westcountry Studies Library.

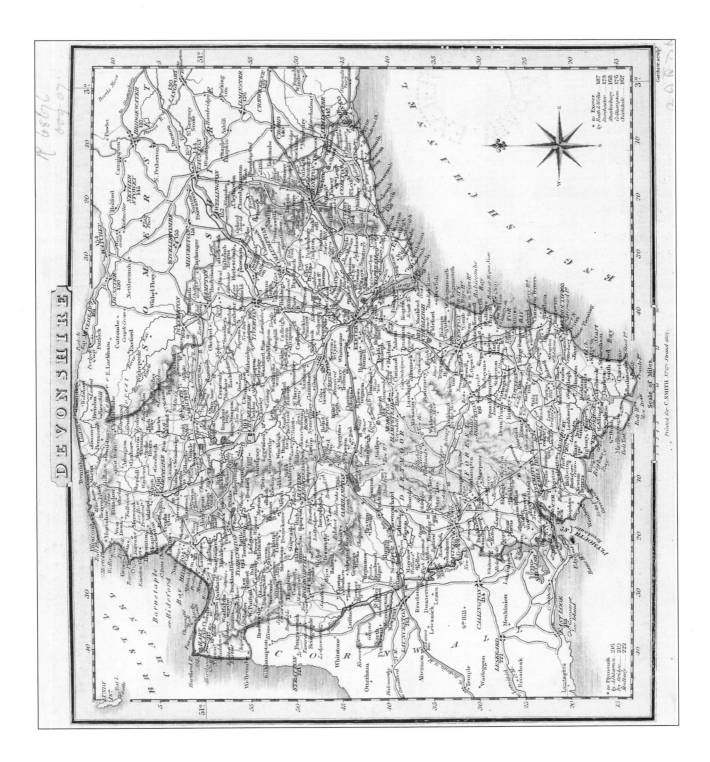

91.1 Gardner/Smith *Smith's New English Atlas*

92

GEORGE & JOHN CARY
1822

Cary's Traveller's Companion had first appeared in 1790 with Devon dated 1789 (**55**). After 1791 the atlas did not reappear until 1806 by which time a new plate had been engraved (**69**). There were a number of reissues with the last dated 1821 which could have been printed and bound the year before. In 1820 there was a fire at the Cary premises and it is possible that the plates were destroyed. Whether or not this was the cause, when the atlas was issued in 1822 the maps were again from new plates.

The plates for this third version are quite different to those of the first two although the orientation is still with north to the right. Now the engraving is such that in order to read the map, one must turn it 90 degrees anti-clockwise. The scale is now vertical to the map title and the imprint is that of John Cary's sons, George and John Cary, with address at 86 St James's Street. This map is more accurate than its predecessors: some roads have been updated; the coasts have been redrawn and extended into Somerset; new roads appear (Ashburton-Two Bridges) and some are omitted (S Molton-E Ansty); new places are shown (Plymouth Dock). The distance notes at the foot of the map remain though some mileages are revised (Exeter now 166 miles from London).

Later issues: The last 'engraved' atlases known were published *c*.1838 but a single map of Surrey is known with revisions dating it *c*.1842.[1] When Cruchley took over the Cary business in *c*.1844 he also acquired these plates and used lithographic copies of the maps in his *Railroad Companion to England and Wales* (*c*.1862): with title, compass, list of towns and imprint erased and borders redrawn. The title was written in simple but heavy lettering along the side. Gall and Inglis acquired the plates in 1877 and there is evidence that they at least contemplated a reissue.[2]

Size 130 x 93 mm including title.

Statute Miles (10=13 mm).
Scale 1M=1.3 mm.

DEVONSHIRE. Imprint: **London. Published by G. & J. Cary, Nº. 86 Sᵗ. James's Str.** (CeOS).

1. 1822 *Cary's Traveller's Companion*
London. G and J Cary. 1822, 1824.

CCLXXXIII, BL, RGS; **CCLXXXIV**, W.

Cary's Traveller's Companion
London. G and J Cary. 1826, 1828.

CCLXXXIVa, RGS; **CCLXXXV**, BL, W.

Cary's Traveller's Companion
Both title pages have a label: **Sold by J Wyld Geographer to his Majesty CHARING CROSS EAST, nearly opposite Northumberland House, LONDON.**
London. G and J Cary. 1828.

RGS, B.

2. 1828 Roads added, eg Moreton Hampstead-Knighton. Dock changed to **Devonport**.

Cary's Traveller's Companion
London. G and J Cary. 1828 (1838).

RGS, C.

---

[1] See Eugene Burden's Letter to the Editor: An unusual atlas; in *The Map Collector*, Issue 72; Autumn 1995; p.54.
[2] *Ibid.*

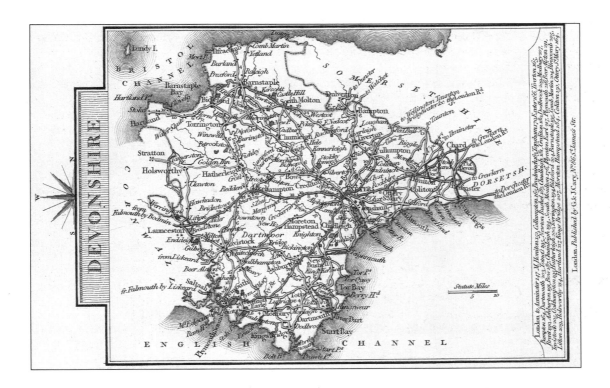

92.1 Cary *Traveller's Companion* the third engraving

93

SMITH /DAVIES
1822

The *Exeter Pocket Journal,* later *Exeter Journal,* was first published in the eighteenth century but did not include maps. In the 1816 edition a map of Devon and Cornwall was included (**83**). This was replaced in the 1822 edition by a close copy of the Gardner map produced for Charles Smith the same year (**91**) which may explain the unusual imprint *re-sculpsit.* The map contains some new information: Plymouth Breakwater is shown and part of the Bude Canal is drawn together with the anticipated line of the Grand Western Canal. The inner border is graduated and broken by Lundy, the north coast and Prawle Point. Various differences to the Gardner map include: the Dartmoor prisoner of war camp is shown, distances are given to Devonport (not Plymouth), the hundreds are listed and the scale bar is now drawn separately.

The map was probably included every year but only the journals for the years listed below are known to have maps. The discrepancies regarding signatures and imprint may be a result of old stock being used for later editions. The 1827 Journal was printed on paper watermarked SC 1825: probably from the company of paper manufacturers Street and Coopers who had premises in South Street, Exeter.

Later issues: The Journal was produced annually and copies for the years 1830, 1831, 1833, 1835-1837, 1853 and 1854 are known (E) but without the map. An 1839 edition has a new signature *Lewis, Exeter, Re-sculpsit.* An 1849 journal exists with a loose map with imprint *Published for R J Trewman & C^{os}. Pocket Book.* In the 1850 Journal (DEI) the map has been up-dated and shows the railway to Plymouth and the imprint raised nearer to the border. In the 1853 edition (BL) the Reference to the Hundreds has been raised with Exeter mileages below and includes distances from London to Plymouth instead of Devonport. The imprint is *Exeter Journal and Almanack. Exeter. R J Trewman.* (1853). In 1856 the map is dated appropriately. In 1858 Henry Besley acquired the Journal and introduced a new map.

Size 190 x 225 mm.   **Scale of Miles** (20=50 mm).
                                                     Scale 1M=2.5 mm.

DEVONSHIRE. Imprint: **Published by Trewman & Co. expressly for the Exeter Pocket Journal** (CeOS). Signatures: **Smith. Exeter. re-sculpsit.** (AeOS) and **Davies fe. 31 Compton Str. Bruns^K. Squ. London.** (EeOS). Distances to both Exeter and Devonport.

1. 1822   *The Exeter Pocket Journal Or, West-Country Gentleman's and Tradesman's Memorandum-Book*
              For the Year of Our Lord 1822.
              Exeter. Trewman & Son. 1822.   E.

              The Exeter Journal
              Exeter. Trewman & Co. 1832.   E.

2. 1827   Smith signature is erased.

              The Exeter Journal Or, Gentleman's, Merchant's and Tradesman's Complete Annual Accompt Book
              For the Year 1827 (and *1828*) .
              Exeter. Trewman & Co. 1827, 1828.   KB; E.

3. 1834   Davies signature is erased.

              The Exeter Journal and Annual Companion
              Exeter. R J Trewman. 1834.   E¹.

---

1. Illustration courtesy of the Exeter Westcountry Studies Library.

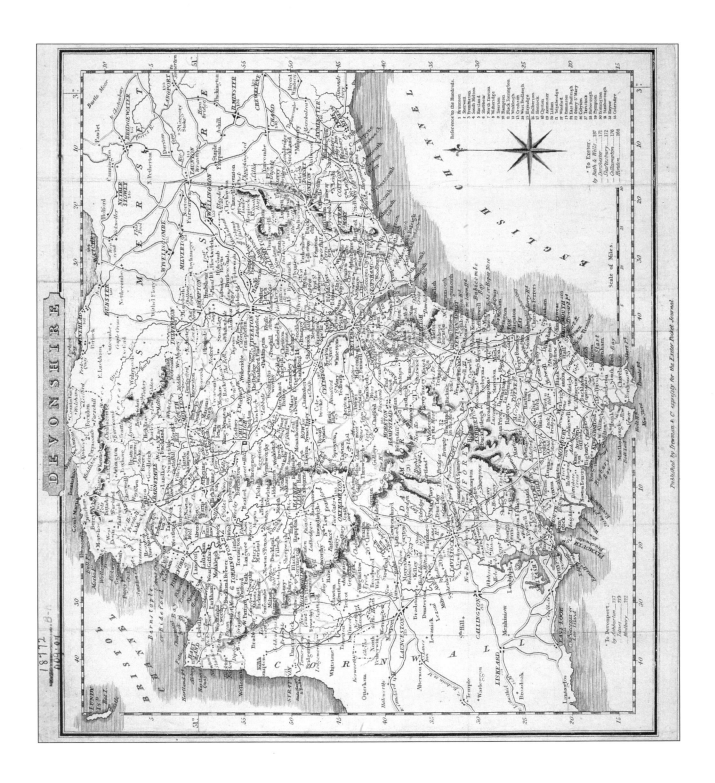

93.3 Smith/Davies *The Exeter Pocket Journal*

94

ARISTIDE MICHEL PERROT
1823

Few county maps are available from foreign atlases. One of the most curious, but also most attractive, maps of Devon is that by the French geographer, Aristide Perrot (1793-1879) and published in *L'Angleterre ou Description Historique et Topographique*, a geographical work by G B Depping. The maps are very small and with little detail; only about thirty towns and the larger rivers are named but hills are hachured, although these are shown as a single, continuous range from Plymouth to Combe Martin. The whole of the sea is shaded and Bristol Channel is named; Lyme Bay is shown as *B. D'EXETER*. The map is approximately one-third of the engraving. The rest shows produce of the area above the map, and possible features of the county below. However the products, eg wheat, hare and slates lead one to believe the engraver was using a little bit of poetic licence!

L'Angleterre was a miniature (12mo) atlas in six volumes with a total of 75 maps and views. There were three editions; only the first edition has been seen with page numbers. George Depping, the writer, was born in Munster in 1784, moved to Paris and took French citizenship. The engraver was probably Adrien Migneret (1786-1840) of Paris[1].

Although the map is as described below, with both page number (eg P.59) and volume number (with T for *Tôme* followed by a Roman numeral), these are seldom present on loose maps. The page was often cut at the point where these were engraved, which was approximately 122 mm above the signatures. It is also possible that these were in fact erased from the plate. The BL example has page numbers and volume numbers only in Vol. I and Clive Burden's copy only has volume numbers.

Size 105 x 65 mm.   Scale 1M=0.7 mm.
Map area 50 x 50 mm.

DEVON. No borders. Imprint: **A.M.Perrot 1823** (Ae) and signature: **M^e. Migneret Sc**. (Ee). Volume number (Aa) and page number (Ea) where visible (see text).

1. 1823	*L'Angleterre ou Description Historique et Topographique du Royaume Uni de la Grand Bretagne par G. B. Depping* Paris. Etienne Ledoux. 1824.		BL.
	L'Angleterre ou Description Historique. Seconde Edition. Paris. Etienne Ledoux. 1828.		W.
	L'Angleterre ou Description Historique. Troisieme Edition. Bruxelles. L J Brohez. 1828.		C, CB.

---

[1] David Kingsley; *Printed Maps of Sussex*; Sussex Record Society; 1982.

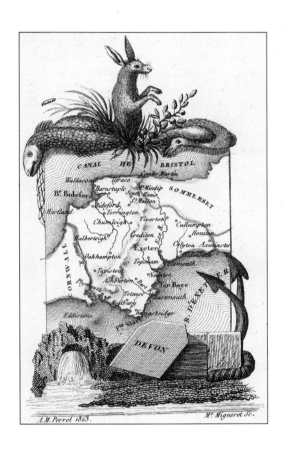

94.1 Perrot *L'Angleterre ou Description ... de la Grand Bretagne*

EBDEN/(Duncan)
1825

James Duncan was a publisher of Paternoster Row, London. It is thought that he might have issued *The Scotch Itinerary* of 1805. *A New Atlas of England and Wales* (folio, 44 maps) appeared in 1833. However, the map of Devon contained in the atlas had already been issued under different titles and imprints. The map was prepared in 1825 by William Ebden who had already produced a large map of Devon for Laurie and Whittle (**76**). The maps were engraved by Edward Hoare and J Reeves whose imprint appears on the Berkshire map .

Later issues: There may have been one more issue of *A New Atlas*: the British Library has a copy with 1840 added to the cover as well as a collection of maps without title page of approximately the same date.

Henry George Collins (*fl.*1850-9) was a London publisher who issued editions of *Teesdale's Atlas* (see **99**) and in 1859 a *Junior Classic Atlas*. Collins acquired Duncan's plates *c.*1850 and reissued them in *The New British Atlas c.*1853. Simultaneously they were issued as single maps with a new title *COLLINS' RAILWAY AND TELEGRAPH MAP OF DEVONSHIRE* and new imprint *London. Pub. by Henry George Collins, Paternoster Row*. It was issued dissected and mounted on linen, folding into a cloth cover with the title *England Depicted* (it was No. 9 in the series). The folding maps were finally issued by Edward Stanford *c.*1866 with the earlier title, *New Map of the County*, and Stanford's imprint.

Size 227 x 381 mm.

SCALE (20=86 mm) **Miles**.
Scale 1M=4.3 mm.

EBDEN'S New Map of the County of DEVONSHIRE; Divided into Hundreds laid down from Trigonometrical Observations by W EBDEN. Imprint: **London. Published Feby 22. 1825, by WILLIAM COLE, late HODGSON & Co. 10, Newgate Street.** (CeOS).

1. 1825   Published as loose sheets sold separately by a succession of publishers between 1825 & 1828.

(TB[1]).

An incomplete set with no title page probably published by S Maunder, No. 10 Newgate Street, London.

W.

2. 1833   Title now: **New Map of the County of DEVONSHIRE Divided into Hundreds Containing the District Divisions and other Local Arrangements effected by the REFORM BILL** (Ea). Sign for Polling places added vertically alongside Explanation key. Imprint changed: **London. Published by J Duncan. Paternoster Row.** (CeOS).

(E), (NDL).

A New Atlas of England and Wales
London. James Duncan. 1833.

BCL.

A Complete County Atlas of England and Wales
London. James Duncan. (1835), 1827 (in error for 1837), 1837, (1838).

CCCCLV, BL; P; W; CB.

[1.] Illustration courtesy of Tony Burgess.

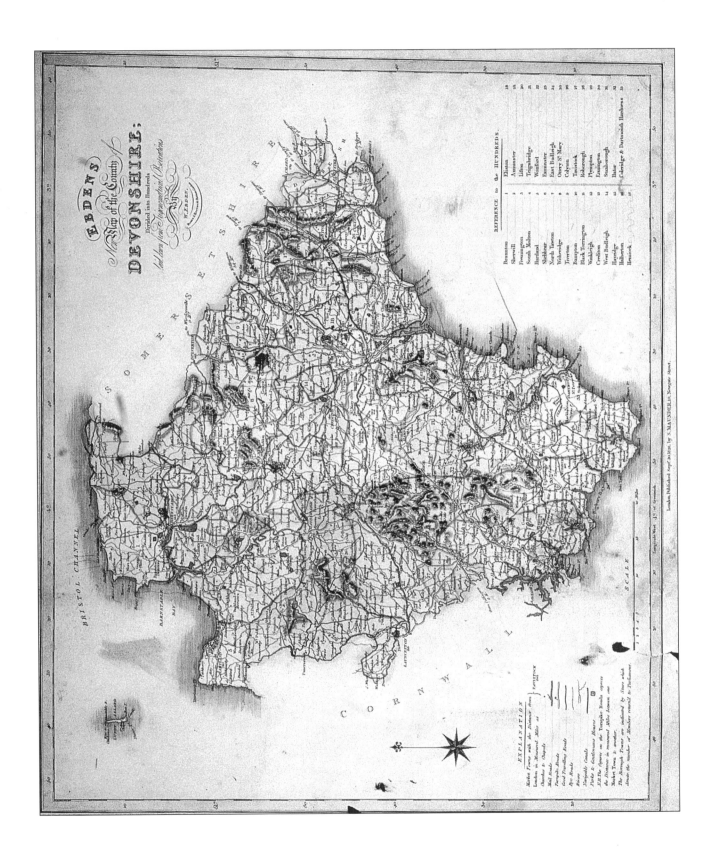

95.1 Ebden *New Map of the County* a loose sheet

CHRISTOPHER & JAMES GREENWOOD
1827

A surveyor of Wakefield, Christopher Greenwood (1786-1855) moved to London in 1818. He compiled and published large-scale maps of the counties of England during the years 1817-31 (the first one to be completed - Yorks – was surveyed 1815-17). From 1821 he was in partnership with his brother, James, who was also a surveyor and publisher (*fl.*1821-40) and they traded together as C & J Greenwood.

The Greenwoods had many other partners and many addresses but both the maps of Devon were published from Regent Street and their complete *Atlas* (**98**) from Burleigh Street in the Strand.

They carried out entirely new surveys in opposition to the Ordnance Survey. Their accurate and detailed maps of the country took only 17 years to complete compared to the nearly 100 years by the Ordnance. The County maps sold for 3 Guineas and the whole set was available for £125. Devon was surveyed in 1825-26, and the map appeared in 1827.

The map contained a vignette of the North West View of Exeter Cathedral, which has the signatures of *W Woolnoth sculpt* and *R Creighton delt*; the latter may have been the same Creighton who produced maps for Lewis (**103** and **113**). The map also showed County and Hundred boundaries, market and parish towns, villages, Parliamentary Seats, turnpike and cross roads, tolls, churches, chapels, houses, castles, canals, mills, parks, pleasure grounds and railways such as the Heytor granite railway and the Plymouth Railway to Dartmoor together with the Prison. A reduced version appeared in their *Atlas of the Counties of England*, published in parts from 1829 (**97**).

Although printed originally on nine sheets the final sheet with the vignette of Exeter Cathedral is sometimes missing: probably the vignette was framed and is hanging in a number of hallways! In later states the map was generally issued in one of three forms:

1) the separate sheets were bound into a book – in this state each sheet had an imprint either top or bottom: *London. Published by Greenwood & Co. Febr*^{y} *20*th *1827*;

2) the sheets were trimmed (losing the imprints) and pasted into two or three vertical pieces, then cut up, linen backed and cased;

3) the sheets were trimmed (losing the imprints) and pasted as one sheet then cut up, linen backed and cased.

Size 1900 x 1865 mm.   **SCALE OF STATUTE MILES** (1+7=200 mm).

Scale 1 inch = 1 mile.

MAP of the County of DEVON From an Actual Survey MADE IN THE YEARS 1825 & 1826. BY C. & J. GREENWOOD, Most Respectfully Dedicated to the Nobility, Clergy and Gentry OF THE COUNTY BY THE PROPRIETORS GREENWOOD, PRINGLE & Co.*see* Greenwood, Pringle & Co **Regent Street Pall Mall LONDON. PUBLISHED FEBR**^{Y} **2 1827**. (Ea). Map on 9 sheets. Large vignette of **NORTH WEST VIEW OF EXETER CATHEDRAL** (Ee). Piano key border with **West Longitude from Greenwich** (DeOS). Inset map of **LUNDY ISLAND** with separate border (Aa). Scale and **EXPLANATION** (Ae).

1. 1827   As described: the title date is **Febr**^{y} **2 1827**.   BL, C (bound).

2. 1827   Title is corrected to **20**th. Note outside boundary **To Wiveliscombe**.

       BL, TQ, FB (cased).

3. 1827   Further notes outside boundary: **From Launceston** and **From Liskeard**.

       BL, C, BCL, E (cased).

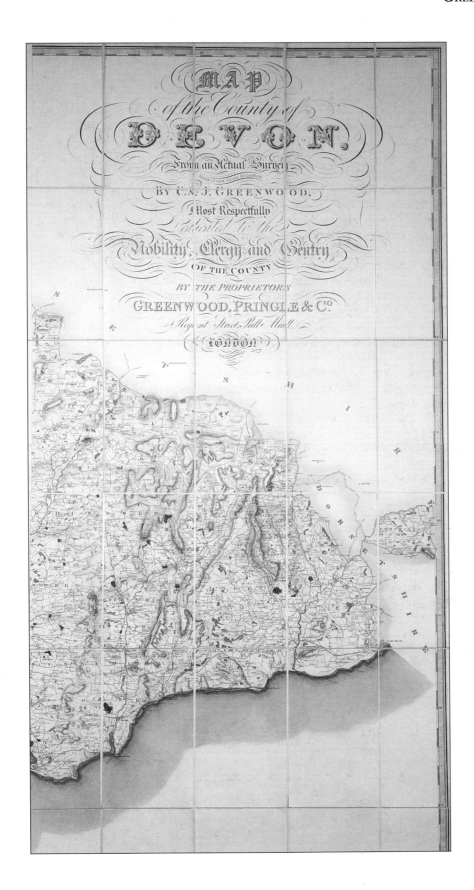

96.2 Greenwood *Map of the County of Devon From an Actual Survey* (detail)

97

CHRISTOPHER & JAMES GREENWOOD
1829

Christopher and James Greenwood had already produced a large-scale map of Devon in 1827 – *Map of the County of Devon* – a map on 9 sheets (**96**). Subsequently a reduced version of this was issued and appeared in *Greenwood & Compy's Atlas of England and Wales* first published in parts in 1829, 1830, 1831 and 1834 (folio, 46 maps). Only the fourth part included parliamentary representation but in the second state all the previously published maps were so modified. Various states of these maps might have also been available as loose maps at this time. Although the *Atlas* title page only refers to J & C Walker as engravers, Dower (see **111**) engraved the map of Berkshire, and Devon was possibly engraved by J & J Neele of 352 Strand, London.

The atlas was printed with the maps coloured or uncoloured and was available in a boxed set of dissected maps in four volumes entitled *Greenwood's Atlas of England and Wales*.

Although *Lundy* in Norse means *puffin island,* and therefore the word *island* is superfluous, both Greenwood maps have inset maps of *Lundy Island* (sic). This was a mistake made by the vast majority of map producers: interestingly Jansson has simply Lunday.

Size 615 x 695 mm.   **Scale of Miles** (8 Furlongs and 10 miles=90 mm).
Scale 1M=8.2 mm.

Map of the County of DEVON From an Actual Survey MADE IN THE YEARS 1825 & 1826, by C. & J. GREENWOOD Published by the Proprietors GREENWOOD & Co. 13, Regent Street, Pall Mall, London. July 4th. 1829 CORRECTED TO THE PRESENT PERIOD. Inset map of **LUNDY ISLAND** and vignette of **EXETER CATHEDRAL**.[1]

1. 1829	*Greenwood & Compy's Atlas of England and Wales* – Part First.		
	London. Greenwood & Co. (1829).		BL.
	A number of loose sheets, issued separately or from broken up atlas		(E).
	Atlas of the Counties of England from Actual Surveys made from the Years 1817 to 1833 by C. & J. Greenwood. Published by the proprietors Greenwood & Co Burleigh Street, Strand, London. Engraved by J & C Walker. Published April 1st 1834.		
	London. Greenwood & Co. 1834.	**CCCCLVIIIa/b**, BL, B, W, C, RGS.	
2. 1834	Parliamentary borough boundaries are added with tables of Polling Places etc. according to the Reform Act of 1832.		
	Atlas of the Counties of England		
	London. Greenwood & Co. 1834.		B, W.

---

[1] Illustration courtesy of Malcolm Woodward.

97.1 Greenwood *Atlas of the Counties of England*

98

JAMES PIGOT
1829

James Pigot (*fl.*1794-1842) started as an engraver for Dean's *Manchester Directory*, but later set up his own business publishing the *London and Provincial New Commercial Directory*, at first with Dean and then alone from 1822-3. For the third edition in 1827, a number of maps were added and in 1830 the maps were separately published in *Pigot & Co's British Atlas* (folio, 41 maps).

In 1828 the Pigots moved from 24 to 17 Basing Lane. In 1832 they briefly moved to No. 1. In 1838 they moved to 59 Fleet Street.

The maps themselves were printed from steel plates, the first county maps known, and are finely engraved and decorated with equally fine vignette views of an abbey, church or cathedral. Devon has a vignette of Exeter Cathedral. When reduced versions of these maps were produced (**114**) the vignette was removed but engraved on the facing page.

Later issues: Only the atlas was issued by Pigot and Co., again before James' death in 1843. *Pigot and Co's British Atlas* appeared *c.*1839, c.1840 (Pigot & Co.) and c.1843 (Pigot & Slater). The directories were issued until c.1857. In 1844 Isaac Slater joined the younger Pigot, soon acquiring the business and using the imprint *I Slater (late Pigot & Slater)* on title pages. In 1846 map imprints and signatures changed to *I Slater*. He issued the atlas again *c.*1846, 1847 and 1857, as *I Slater's New British Atlas*.

Size 220 x 350 mm.   **Scale** (10=30 mm) **Miles**.
                                                                            Scale 1M=3 mm.

DEVONSHIRE. Imprint: **Published by Pigot & Co. 24 Basing Lane London & Fountain St Manchester** (CeOS). Signature: **Engraved on Steel by Pigot & Son Manchester** (EeOS).

1. 1829	*Pigot & Co's British Atlas of the Counties of England* 4th Edition London & Manchester. J Pigot & Co. 1829.		GL.
	Pigot & Co's British Atlas of the Counties of England 5th Edition London & Manchester. J Pigot & Co. 1832.		GL.
2. 1830	Imprint address changed: **17 Basing Lane London & 18 Fountain S^t. Manchester.** Addition of **Long West from Green^h** between borders (BeOS).		(E), (NDL).
	Pigot & Co's British Atlas of the Counties of England London & Manchester. J Pigot & Co. 1830, 1831.		GL, W^1, B; **CCCCXXV**, C, W.
	Pigot & Co's National Commercial Directory London & Manchester. J Pigot & Co. 1830.		GL, WM.
3. 1831	Polling places added. **North Division** and **South Division** added.		(NDL).
4. 1832	Imprint address amended: **1 Basing Lane London & Fountain S^t. Manchester.** Roads upgraded and added.		
	Pigot & Co's British Atlas of the Counties of England London & Manchester. J Pigot & Co. 1831 (1832).		C.

[1.] *Pigot & Co's British Atlas* – In 3 parts. No title page (1829/30).

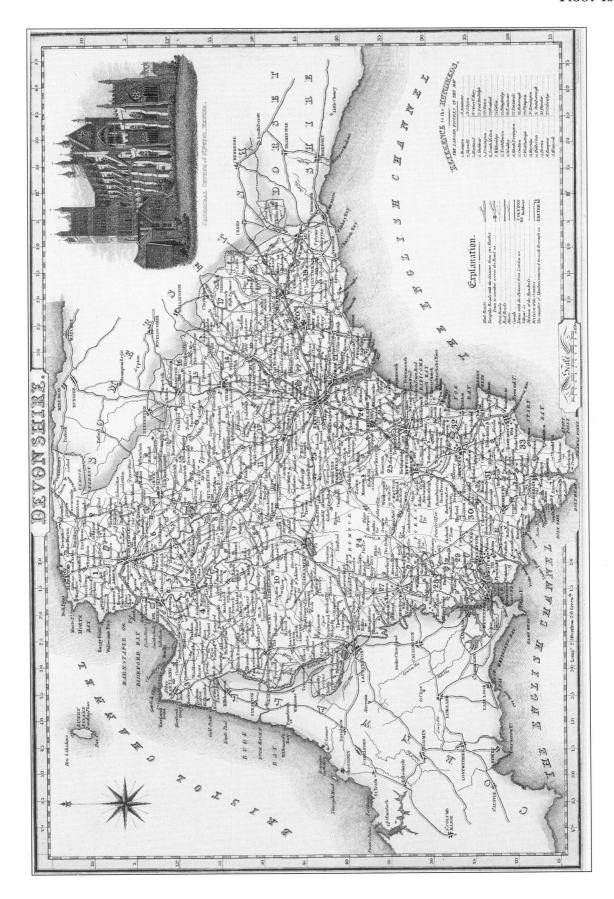

98.2 Pigot *British Atlas of the Counties of England*

99

HENRY TEESDALE
1830

Henry Teesdale (*fl.*1828-43), a London map publisher, produced a number of large-scale maps, world charts, a world atlas and published two county atlases. He acquired Robert Rowe's *English Atlas* in the 1820s and reissued it as his own with much altered plates as *New British Atlas* (**81**). His *New Travelling Atlas* appeared with 45 maps all dated 1830.

When the map of Devon was originally published in 1830 it had a piano-key border and the title had a hatched frame surrounding it.

Later issues: Although the maps were not reprinted again until 1843 the maps had a long life, being used for over fifty years in updated states. The imprint was erased and a plate number added (AaOS) when *A New Travelling Atlas Revised and corrected to the year 1843* was issued by Henry Teesdale & Co. in 1843 and by Henry Teesdale & Co. and D W Martin in the same year. All later issues were lithographs.

The piano-key border and hatched title frame were removed when Henry George Collins issued lithograph versions of the map in 1848 and 1850 with his imprint. Thereafter W S Orr acquired the plates but only published them once (with amended imprint) in a similar state, *c.*1852. Between 1852 and 1858 John Heywood took over the plates and reintroduced the piano-key border and the frame around the title for his *Travelling Atlas of England & Wales* of 1858 (address *170 Deansgate, Manchester*) and 1860 (address *143 Deansgate & Brazenose St., Manchester*); but the map itself remained essentially the same. The plates were used by Heywood until *c.*1882 with continual updating.

In 1864 and *c.*1865 the atlas had a new title: *The Tourist's Atlas of England and Wales.* However, after these two editions the previous title, *Travelling Atlas,* was again used, often together with a new title *John Heywood's County Atlas of England and Wales.* In *c.*1875 Heywood's address was *141 & 143 Deansgate, & Excelsior Works, Manchester.* The reference to *Excelsior Works* disappeared *c.*1879 but reappeared as *Excelsior Buildings* in *c.*1880. The final address as used in the *c.*1882 atlas was *Deansgate & Ridgefield, Manchester*, although a loose map is known with imprint *JOHN HEYWOOD, LITHO. MANCHESTER & LONDON* which might be from an even later edition of the atlas.

The illustration opposite shows Heywood's Devonshire as it appeared *c.*1864 in *The Tourist's Atlas of England and Wales.* This was published in Manchester by John Heywood and in London by Simpkin, Marshall, and Co.; Hamilton, Adams and Co.; and W Tegg. There are very few differences to the original map: Dawlish has been added; Devonport replaces Dock; and railways and planned railways have been added including the first projected rail link with France!

Size 150 x 195 mm.

Scale of Miles (10=18 mm).
Scale 1M=1.8 mm.

DEVONSHIRE. Imprint: **London, Published Septr 1830 by Henry Teesdale & Co. 302 Holborn.** (CeOS).

1. 1830 *A New Travelling Atlas Revised and corrected to the year 1830*
London. Henry Teesdale & Co. 1830. CCCCXVIII, C.

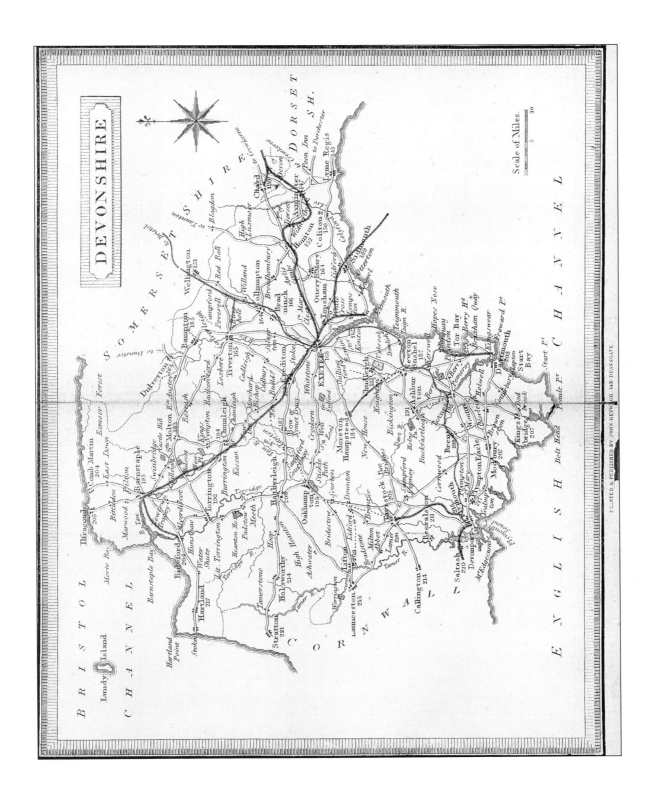

99 Teesdale as used by Heywood in his *Tourist's Atlas.*

100

T LAURIE MURRAY
1830

The only atlas to appear under T L Murray's name was the *Atlas of the English Counties*, issued in 1830 (folio, 44 maps). Murray was a publisher and surveyor who used the maps of the Ordnance Survey on which to base his own. The large maps are without any decoration at all and are similar in many ways to Cary's larger maps. The hundreds are shown and distances from London for the larger towns.

The atlas was reissued in 1831 and 1832 and these issues are readily identified as the date in the imprint was changed each time, although the NDL have a loose 1831 variation.

Later issues: There was only one further reprint: an *Index of Reference to Parochial Unions* was first introduced when the map was used by William Robson & Co in their *Commercial Directory of London and the Western Counties* in 1840. The imprint was also changed to: *William Robson & C⁰ Directory Office London*.

Size 355 x 455 mm.   **SCALE** (15=63 mm) **miles**.
                                                             Scale 1M=4.2 mm.

DEVONSHIRE. Imprint: **London. Published May, 1ˢᵗ. 1830, by T. L. Murray. 19 Adam Street, Adelphi.** (CeOS) and signatures: **Drawn under the Superintendence of T. L. Murray.** (AeOS) and **Hoare & Reeves fe** (EeOS).

1. 1830 *An Atlas of the English Counties ... Exhibiting the whole of the Inland Navigat'n Rail Roads, &c. Projected on the basis of the Trigonometrical Survey By Order of the Honᵇˡᵉ. The Board of Ordnance. Under the Superintendance of T L Murray*
London. T L Murray. (1830).   **CCCCXIX**, BL, W, C, BCL, (E).

2. 1831 Imprint amended to **1831**.

An Atlas of the English Counties ...
London. T L Murray. (1831).   **CCCCXX**, BL, W, C, (E).

3. 1831 A faint pecked line shows the proposed North & South Divisions.   (NDL).

4. 1832 Imprint amended to **May, 1ˢᵗ. 1832**. A further Explanation is added below title. A supplement is added to the Explanation for the parliamentary boroughs and polling stations and these are shown on the map together with strengthened division line.

An Atlas of the English Counties ...
London. T L Murray. (1832).   C, (E).

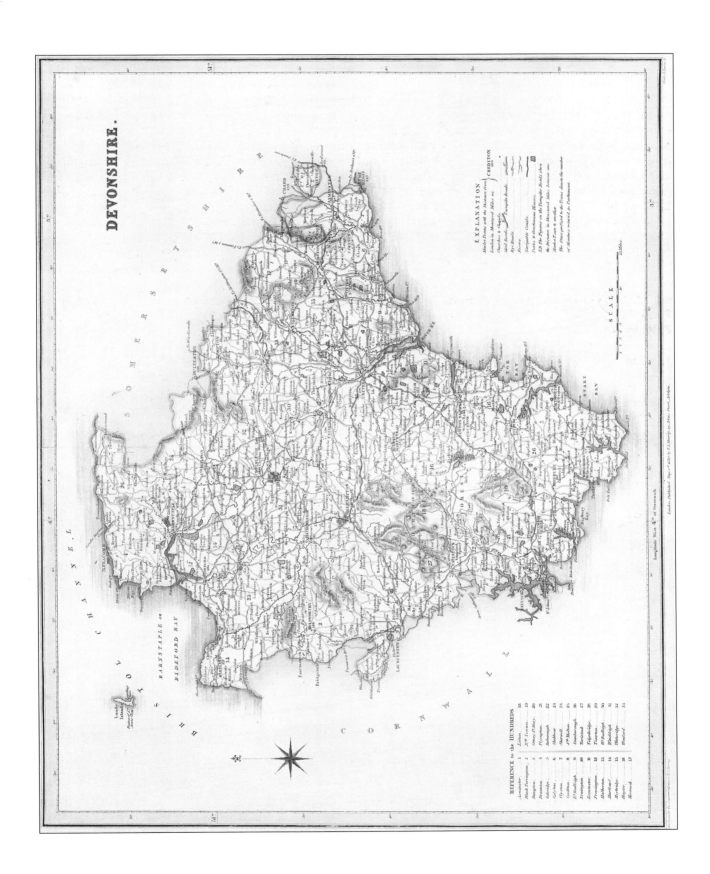

100.1 Murray *An Atlas of the English Counties*

101

SYDNEY HALL
1830

An engraver and publisher, Sidney Hall (*fl.*1817-60) was a prolific cartographer. His first work was for the Arrowsmith Company in 1817, when he was best known for his map engravings. Later he had his own premises in Bloomsbury, 18 Strand, London. He later produced a World Atlas for the Society for the Diffusion of Useful Knowledge published between 1844-76.

Hall contributed to two British county atlases; Samuel Leigh's *New Picture* (**87**); and, in 1831, *A Topographical Dictionary of Great Britain and Ireland* by John Gorton (*d.*1835). This appeared with 54 maps engraved by Hall. Gorton also produced a biographical dictionary.

Later issues: The maps reappeared from 1842 in *A Travelling County Atlas,* which was reprinted almost annually until 1858, and in *A New County Atlas* issued in 1847. Plate number *10* and a new imprint, *London. Published by Chapman & Hall, 193 Picadilly,* were added *c.*1852. From 1857 lithographic reproductions were issued in editions of *A Travelling County Atlas* until *c.*1885 at roughly two-yearly intervals.

Size 185 x 242 mm.	**English Miles** (20=50 mm).
	Scale 1M=2.5 mm.

DEVONSHIRE. with signature **ENGRAVED BY SID^Y. HALL.** Imprint: **London, Published by Chapman & Hall N°. 168 Strand, Augt. 1830.** (CeOS).

(DEI).

1. 1830   *A Topographical Dictionary of Great Britain and Ireland by John Gorton with Fifty-two Quarto maps drawn and engraved by Sidney Hall Vol I.*
London. Chapman and Hall. (Vol I) 1831. (Vol II – 1832.)   W, B.

A Topographical Dictionary of Gt Britain and Ireland with 54 Quarto maps
London. Chapman and Hall. 1833.   **CCCCXLVI**, BL, B.

Pocket County Maps (Atlas with no title page).   BL.

Issued cut, linen-backed and fitted into a case (93 x 108 mm) at a price of 1s. 6d by Chapman and Hall   (E).

Sidney Hall's British Atlas (Atlas with no title page).   C.

2. 1833   Imprint amended: **London, Published by Chapman & Hall N°. 186 Strand, 1833. NORTH DIVISION** and **SOUTH DIVISION** added to the map.

(NDL).

A New British Atlas
London. Chapman and Hall. 1833, 1834.
    CCCCLI, RGS, W, BCL; **CCCCLII**, BL, W, C.

3. 1835   Year in imprint removed.

Sidney Hall's British Atlas
London. Chapman and Hall. 1835.   CB.

A New British Atlas
London. Chapman and Hall. 1836.   **CCCCLIV**, BL, B, W.

Sidney Hall's British Atlas (Title on cover).   W.

Dissected, mounted and hard-backed to form a small book of the county.   RGS.

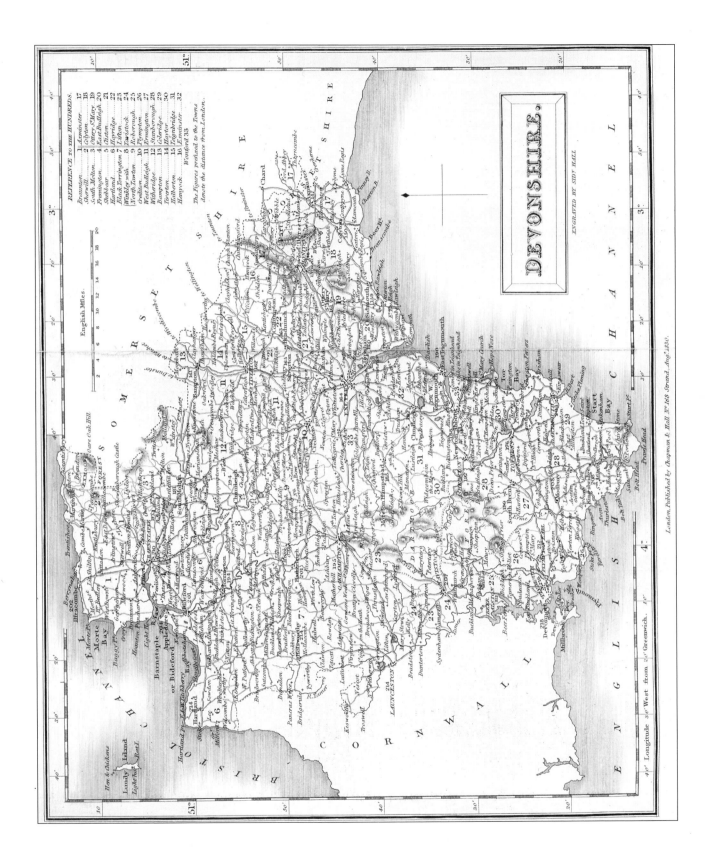

101.1 Hall *A Topographical Dictionary of Great Britain*

102

WALKER/FISHER
1831

Henry Fisher (*fl*.1816-37*d*) and his son were publishers at the Caxton Press in St Martin-le-Grand, London. They published two maps, one each of Devon and Cornwall, which they included in the topographical west-country works *Devonshire Illustrated* and *Cornwall Illustrated*. The maps were both engraved by J and C Walker, well-known engravers of a large number of county maps (see also **116** and Creighton **103** and **113**).

Devonshire Illustrated and *Cornwall Illustrated* were combined into one volume with each county having a separate engraved title page: eg *Devonshire Illustrated in a series of views of Cities, Towns, Public Buildings, Streets, Docks, Churches, Antiquities, Abbeys, Picturesque Scenery, Castles, Seats of the Nobility etc etc.* above a vignette view of Lydford Cascade. According to the subscription Thomas Allom and W H Bartlett were mainly responsible for the original drawings which were engraved on steel by Heath, Miller, LePefit, Wallis and others. The historical and descriptive accounts were supplied by J Britton and E W Brayley who had provided the text to *Beauties of Britain* for which the maps of Cole and Roper were prepared (see **67**). The title page to the combined work has the imprint *Fisher, Son and Co. London 1829*. The Cornwall title page is similarly styled but omits Bartlett, changes the order of the engravers and is dated 1831.

The two maps, Devon dated 1831 – which had an attractive vignette view of Babbacombe Bay (*Babicombe Bay* signed by Allom and Floyd) not found on any other county map – and Cornwall dated 1832, were introduced as frontispieces when the two parts were brought together in *Devon & Cornwall Illustrated* of 1832.

In 1842 the company completed *Fisher's County Atlas of England and Wales*, an atlas originally started by Gilbert. They also traded under the name, Fisher Son & Co.

Size 185 x 235 mm.

English Miles (20=46 mm).
Scale 1M=2.3 mm.

DEVONSHIRE. (CaOS). Vignette view of **BABICOMBE BAY**. Imprint: **FISHER, SON & C⁰. LONDON, 1831.** (CeOS) and signature: **Drawn & Engraved by J & C. Walker.** (EeOS).

(C), (E), (NDL), (DEI).

1. 1831   *Devonshire Illustrated*
London. Fisher Son & Co. 1832.   E.

Devon & Cornwall Illustrated
London. H Fisher, R Fisher and P Jackson. 1832.   FB.

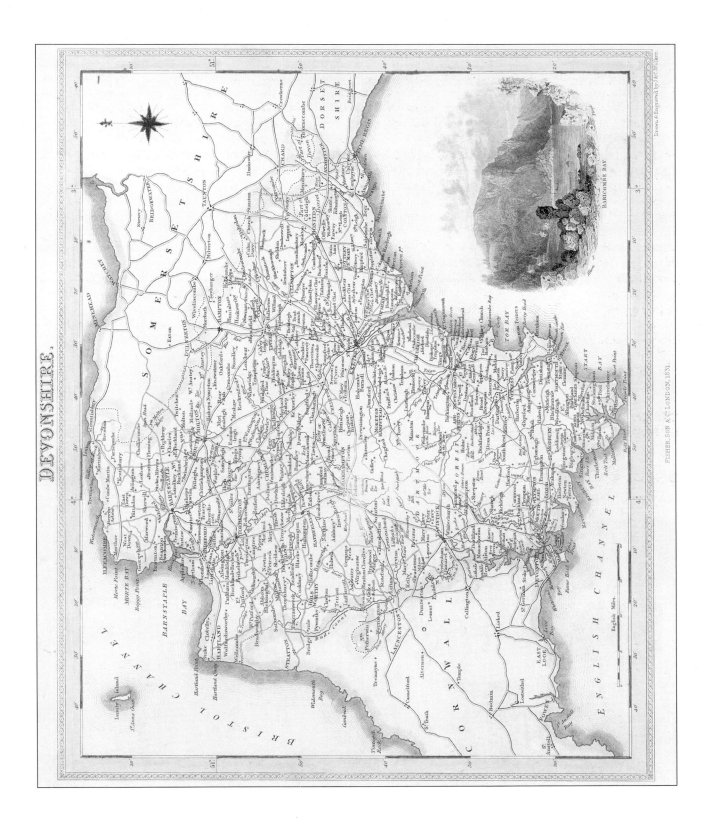

102.1 Walker/Fisher *Devon & Cornwall Illustrated*

103

CREIGHTON/LEWIS
1831

Samuel Lewis (*fl.*1830-48), trading under the name S Lewis & Co., was draughtsman, cartographer and publisher operating from 87, Aldersgate Street, and 13, Finsbury Place South, London. He is best known for his topographical dictionaries of all parts of the UK with specially produced maps.

The first dictionary was published in four volumes (quarto) in 1831 and comprised forty-three maps including one of England and Wales and a plan of London and environs. The maps were all drawn by R Creighton and engraved by either Thomas Starling or J and C Walker. The former's maps can be differentiated as Starling used upper case letters on his *Scale of Miles*. When the third edition appeared in 1835 it contained a parliamentary map as well, again drawn by Creighton (**113**) and engraved by J and C Walker (**102, 116**).

Later issues: In 1840 the maps appeared in the fourth edition with a *Reference to the Unions* added to the map area (Ad), and the poor-law unions were keyed and shown.

The topographical dictionary went into many editions: early editions contained the maps usually bound in with the county reference. After 1840 the maps were contained in an atlas published separately to accompany the *Dictionary* with the title *Atlas to the Topographical Dictionary(-ies) of England (and Wales)* or as *An atlas comprising maps of the several counties divided into unions*. There were reissues until *c.*1849 with the addition of railway information.

Size 235 x 298 mm.   **Scale of Miles** (20=59 mm).
                                                       Scale 1M=3 mm.

DEVONSHIRE. No Reference to Places of Election or to the Unions. Imprint: **ENGRAVED FOR LEWIS' TOPOGRAPHICAL DICTIONARY** (CeOS). Signatures: **Drawn by R. Creighton.** (AeOS) and **J. & C. Walker. Sculp^t.** (EeOS).

1. 1831   *A Topographical Dictionary of England Vol. II.*
London. S Lewis & Co. 1831.   **CCCCXXX**, BL, W, RGS, (E), (NDL).

2. 1833   Parliamentary map with **NORTHERN DIVISION** & **SOUTHERN DIVISION** added and **Places of Election** added above top border.
Two roads and **To Taunton** added at Bampton.

(E).

A Topographical Dictionary of England 2nd Edition
London. S Lewis & Co. 1833.   **CCCCXXXI**, BL.

A Topographical Dictionary of England 3rd Edition
London. S Lewis & Co. 1835.   **CCCCXXXII**, BL, W.

3. 1837   The top imprint with notes on Polling Places and Places of Election removed. Devon was now the first map in Volume II.

A Topographical Dictionary of England 3rd Edition
London. S Lewis & Co. 1837, 1838[1].   C.

The maps were also available in a separate volume without a title page to accompany late impressions of the text to the third edition.   W.

[1]. An atlas seen by Eugene Burden and since broken up.

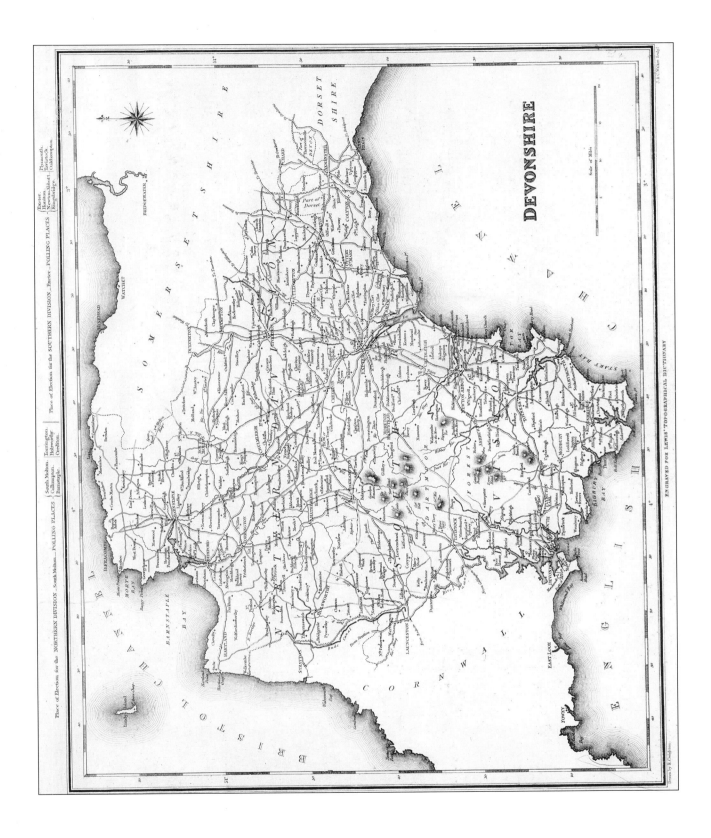

103.2 Creighton/Lewis *A Topographical Dictionary of England*

104

DAWSON/NETHERCLIST
1832

Lieutenant, later Lieutenant-Colonel, Robert Kearsley RE (1798-1861) was the son of Robert Dawson, a Devonian, who had been active during the first Ordnance Survey of Devon of 1809 (**74**). R K Dawson entered the Royal Engineers in 1818 and worked in Scotland under Thomas Colby, Superintendent of the Ordnance Survey. Dawson prepared the boundary surveys for 277 county maps and city plans of England and Wales which were printed as a result of the Reform Bill of 1831 and related to the Boundaries Act passed in July 1832. The maps and plans were subsequently published in two volumes in 1832 in *Plans of the Cities and Boroughs of England and Wales.* Most volumes have maps in various states.

The whole work was produced by lithography by James and Luke Hansard in London and is an early example of the use of this process. Luke Hansard (1752-1828) took over the business of Hughes, printers to the House of Commons, in 1798. In 1806 he also took over William Cobbett's reports of the debates of the House (see also **106**). His sons continued printing for the House, especially the reports on proceedings now known as *Hansard.*

There are two distinct variations of the Devon map not including the individual states. One variation is signed *Robt. K. Dawson* (**105**) and this earlier one signed *R. K: Dawson.* The earlier map described below also has Newton Bushel (later changed to Newton Abbot) and the title is in attractive script. The untidy engraving and the clumsy addition of the polling places in the second state below may have convinced Dawson to have the map re-engraved.

Size 300 x 300 mm.

Scale of Miles (10=47 mm).
Scale 1M=4.7 mm.

Devonshire in attractive script (Da). Imprint: **J. Netherclist Lithog: 54 Leicester Sq^r** below scale bar (Ee). Script signature: **R.K:Dawson Lieut.R.E.** just below **Explanations:**.

1. 1832　　　*Parliamentary Representation. Further Return to an Address to His Majesty, dated 12 December, 1831.*
　　　　　　London. House of Commons. 1832.　　　　　　　　　　　　BL (Off. Pub.).

2. 1832　　　Symbol, Maltese cross, for polling places added rather amateurishly immediately to left of Dawson's signature. Polling places such as Plymouth and Exeter shown.
　　　　　　Loose sheets probably from:

　　　　　　Plans of the Cities and Boroughs of England and Wales ...
　　　　　　London. James & Luke G Hansard & Sons. 1832.　　　　　　　　(BL).

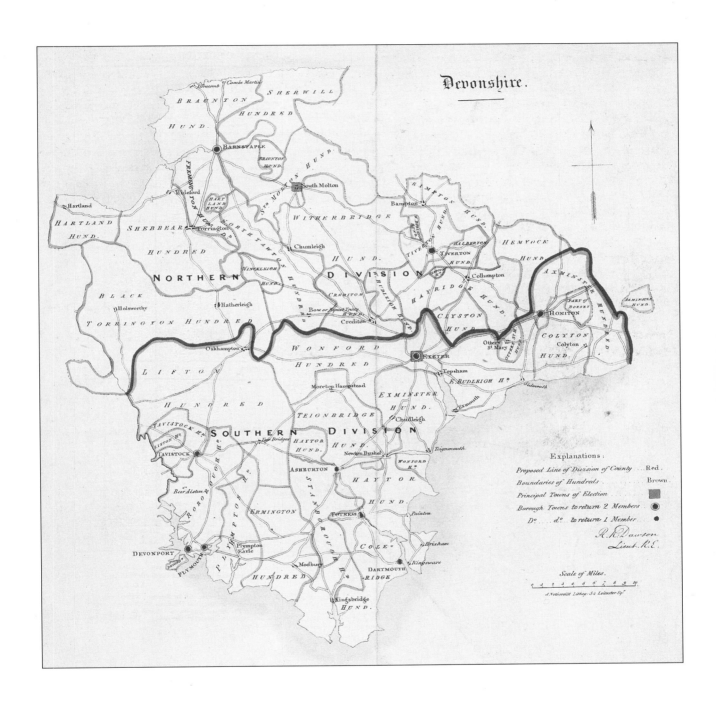

104.1 Dawson/Netherclist *Parliamentary Representation ...*

DAWSON/GARDNER
1832

Robert Kearsley Dawson prepared the boundary surveys as a result of the Reform Bill of 1831 and related to the Boundaries Act passed in July 1832. The original maps were prepared for government reports and were subsequently published in two volumes in 1832 in *Plans of the Cities and Boroughs of England and Wales*. Most volumes have maps in various states.

There are two distinct variations of the map of Devon. The earlier map is signed *R. K: Dawson* (**104**) and this later one is signed *Robt.K.Dawson*. The later map also has a new engraver's signature *J Gardner Regent Street*. Both maps have the same outline and are the same size but the placing of town names clearly shows the two maps are distinct. This later map has a legend *Explanation* which properly includes the Maltese Cross; this had been clumsily added to the first version. Other changes which identify this state are the plain style of lettering in the title and Newton Abbot (not Newton Bushel).

The earlier map is clearly of inferior quality and was updated with the polling places information. The lettering and outline engraving of this later map are much superior. Either the first plate was very worn or Dawson or the publishers were unhappy with the quality of the previous map, and had a new map engraved using the same outline as the first.

James Gardner's father, also James, was an official Agent for the Sale of Ordnance Maps. James junior took over the business in Regent Street but moved to Brewer Street during the early 1840s and returned to Regent Street (**129**) in 1846. He probably ceased trading before 1850.[1]

Size 300 x 300 mm.

Scale of Miles (10=47 mm).
Scale 1M=4.7 mm.

DEVONSHIRE in plain script (Da). Imprint: **Engraved by J. Gardner, Regent Street.** below scale bar (Ee). Script signature: **Robt. K. Dawson Lieut. R. E.** just below **Explanation** which includes Polling Places shown by Maltese Cross.

(E), (DEI).

1. 1832   *Instructions given by the Secretary of State for the Home Department with reference to Parliamentary Representation. Reports from Commissioners on Proposed Division of Counties and Boundaries of Boroughs. Part 1. 1832.*

W.

Plans of the Cities and Boroughs of England and Wales; showing their boundaries and divisions into wards.
London. James & Luke G Hansard & Sons. 1832.

CCCCXXXIX, BL, B.

Boroughs Of England
A volume without title page but title on the spine.

CB.

[1]   J B Harley and Yolande O'Donoghue in the introduction to; *The Old Series Ordnance Survey Maps of England and Wales* – Vol II; H Margary; Lympne Castle; 1977; p.xxxviii.

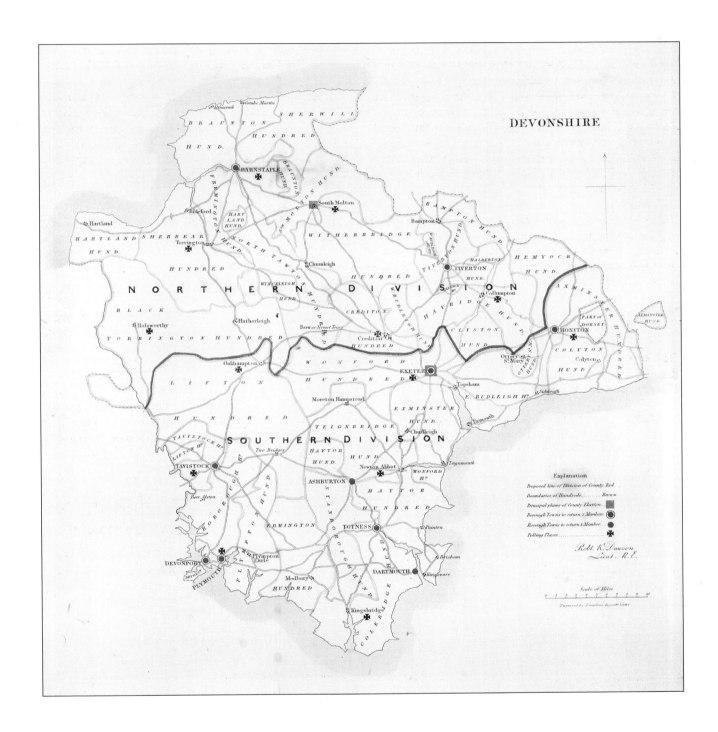

105.1 Dawson/Gardner *Plans of the Cities and Boroughs ...*

WILLIAM COBBETT
1832

William Cobbett (1763-1835) was a publisher and author with premises at 11 Bolt Court, Fleet Street. Cobbett served in the army but bought his discharge in 1791 and went to the United States. On his return he at first attacked the radicals Tom Paine and Priestly, but slowly changed his outlook and became the champion of Radicalism. He initiated the publication of the Parliamentary debates which were later taken over by James and Luke Hansard (see also **104**). He became a well-known author and among other books published his *Political Register* and *Rural Rides*.

Cobbett, hopeful of winning Honiton for the radicals, persuaded his friend Thomas Cochrane to stand for the seat in 1806. After initial defeat and a little bribery Cochrane was successful at his second attempt. Although Honiton had a very large electorate of about 500 (while Tiverton at one time had only 24 votes) it was not uncommon in those days for votes to be bought and Cobbett claimed that Honiton lived by its votes[1]. After the Reform Bill in 1832 Cobbett himself entered parliament as member for Durham.

In 1832 he published an atlas with very simplified maps. Although an edition of this atlas, *A Geographical Dictionary,* was published with Langley's maps (**84**) it could be that Cobbett intended to insert his own maps and used the Langley maps until his own were finished. Alternatively he may have used them without permission and hurriedly had to produce his own for a second printing; this, at least, would explain the poor quality of the maps. His own maps then appeared in a second issue of 1832 (8vo, 52 maps).

This map of Devon is extraordinary being a very basic somewhat kidney-shaped map of the county with 32 towns named and no rivers or hills depicted. The north-west/south-east dimension is halved. This gives the anomaly that although Plymouth to Exeter and Exeter to Bideford are roughly equal at 36 miles, the former distance is 75 mm and the latter only 40 mm. To complete the triangle, Plymouth to Bideford (45 miles) measures 87 mm.

Later issues: A second edition appeared in 1854 (Chubb CCCCXLa – but no atlas has been recorded) and these maps are recorded as being larger than the originals[2].

Size 172 x 100 mm.   Scale is irrelevant.

DEVONSHIRE. Imprint: **Drawn & Engraved for Cobbett's Geographical Dictionary of England & Wales** (CeOS).

1. 1832   *A Geographical Dictionary of England and Wales ... by William Cobbett*
               London. William Cobbett. 1832.
                                                              CCCCXL, BL, RGS, W, C, BCL.

1. R R Sellman; *Aspects of Devon History*; Devon Books; (1962) 1985; p. 104.
2. Yasha Beresiner; *British County Maps*; Antique Collectors' Club; 1983.

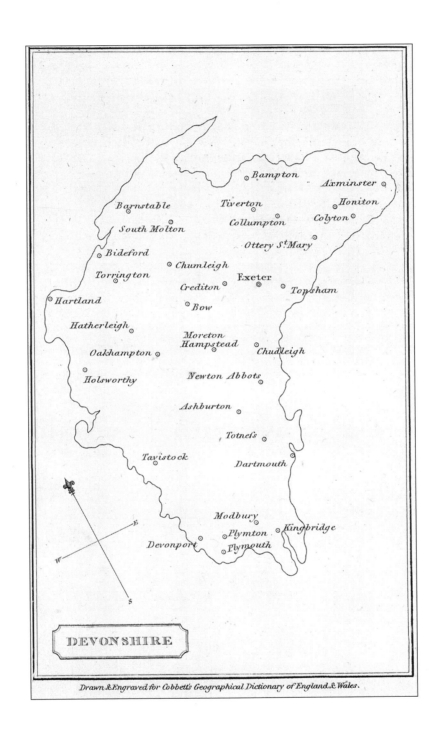

Drawn & Engraved for Cobbett's Geographical Dictionary of England & Wales.

106.1 Cobbett *A Geographical Dictionary of England and Wales*

SCOTT/FULLARTON
1833

James Bell (1769-1836) issued a *New and Comprehensive Gazetteer of England and Wales* in 1833-4 in 4 vols (8vo, 44 maps). Bell was a geographical author who edited Rollin's *Ancient History* (1828) and wrote a *System of Geography* (1830). The maps in his gazetteer all bear the imprint of the publisher and were engraved by Gray & Son, Josiah Neele & Co or Robert Scott (1771-1841), an engraver from Edinburgh who engraved the map of Devon. The map of Devon is a very close copy of Sidney Hall's map of 1830 (**101**).

As Smith writes: *Pilferage of ... any source, was a simple matter in an age when copyright protection was rarely enforced with any strength.* Archibald Fullarton reprinted both the maps and the text of Bell's *New and Comprehensive Gazetteer of England and Wales* in his *Parliamentary Gazetteer.* Admitting that the material *still possessed of value* had been *digested into and incorporated into the present Work,* he was more than angry at what he perceived to be an *extremely disingenuous attempt to underrate the value and importance of their laborious and accurate Compilation* on the grounds that *these materials do not constitute one-third part of the present Publication.* Fullarton obviously did not believe this was a large enough proportion to warrant accusations of plagiarism.[1]

Ironically enough, it was James Bell who had pirated many articles from Samuel Lewis' *Topographical Dictionary* (**103**). Consequently, in 1839, Lewis obtained an injunction and Bell's *Gazetteer* was withdrawn.[2] Fullarton, Bell's publisher, acquired the plates and issued the maps in his own *Parliamentary Gazetteer of England and Wales.*

Archibald Fullarton (*fl.*1834-70) founded the firm A Fullarton and Co, publishers and engravers of Glasgow 1833-40, of London, Edinburgh and Glasgow 1840-43, and of London, Edinburgh and Dublin, from 1845. Fullarton was also responsible for other works including Rev. J M Wilson's *Imperial Gazetteer of Scotland* and Bartholomew's *Imperial Map.*

Later issues: Fullarton's first edition of his *Parliamentary Gazetteer of England and Wales* appeared in 1840. Reprints followed in 1842, 1843 and 1844 with *Edin*[r] added under Scott's signature and with the planned railway just short of Exeter (Glasgow, Edinburgh and London. A Fullarton and Co. – Chubb DX); in 1845 and 1846 with Glasgow erased from the imprint and with new railway information (London, Edinburgh and Dublin – DXI); finally in 1848 and 1849 with the imprint shortened to *Archd Fullarton & Co.*

Size 185 x 235 mm.

English Miles (14=34 mm).
Scale 1M=2.4 mm.

DEVONSHIRE. with vignette of **EAST VIEW OF EXETER CATHEDRAL &c.** Imprint: **Published by Arch**[d]**. Fullarton & Co. Glasgow.** (CeOS). Signature: **Eng**[d]**. by R. Scott** (EeOS).

(DEI).

1. 1833   *A New and Comprehensive Gazetteer of England and Wales by James Bell*
Glasgow and Edinburgh. A Fullarton and Co. 1833, 1834, 1836, 1837.

CCCCXLV, B; C; **CCCCXLVa**, BL, B; RGS.

[1] David Smith; *Victorian Maps of the British Isles*; Batsford; 1985; p.32.
[2] David Kingsley; *Printed Maps of Sussex*; Sussex Record Society; 1982.

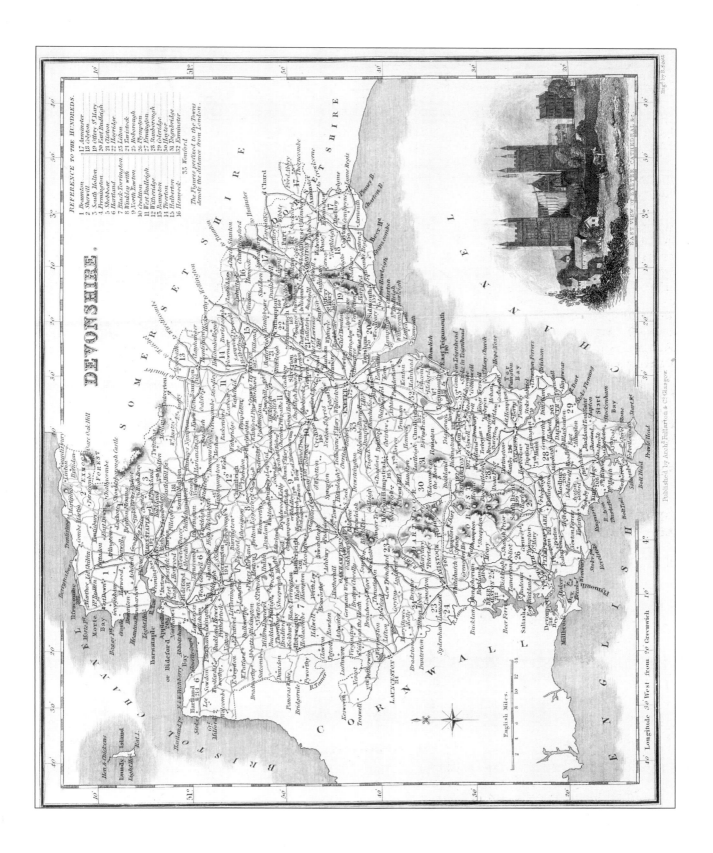

107.1 Scott/Fullarton *A New and Comprehensive Gazetteer of England and Wales*

108

ARCHER/PINNOCK
1833

William Pinnock was responsible for two cartographic works concerning British counties. The first was his *History and Topography* with maps engraved by Neele (**86**). His second work, *The Guide to Knowledge*, is unique in the history of county mapping: the maps, engraved by Joshua Archer and Sidney Hall, were cut into a wood block and printed directly so that they appeared white on black. The maps were issued weekly, the early ones by James Gilbert, and some maps have *R Clay, Printer, 7, Bread-Street-Hill, Cheapside* on the reverse. *The Guide to Knowledge* appeared in 1833 and with altered maps in 1838 when it was probably published by Orlando Hodgson. All later issues were lithographs.

The map of Devon, engraved by Archer, appeared on 11th May, 1833 on pages 417/418 followed by the description of the county on pages 419/420. It has the plate number, title and price to right of map frame, ie across top of page as the map was bound in sideways. Many copies apparently have a crack through Barnstaple, possibly caused by uneven paper during printing (see illustration).

Later issues: Signatures were removed and new panels (CeOS) added when *SHEPHERD & SUTTON'S New Series OF DESCRIPTIVE COUNTY MAPS* was issued in parts. These lithographic versions of the maps appeared in *Descriptive County Atlas of England and Wales* edited by William Bayne (the incomplete set of parts has this title page, published by Shepherd & Sutton and dated 1844). The maps were printed in relief in pale brown ink and then coloured by hand in red (railway), green (parks), orange (turnpikes) and blue (boundary). The map appeared at the same time in black relief and hand coloured as folding maps in cases (London. Shepherd & Sutton, and Richard Groombridge. 1844.).[1]

In 1844 *The Guide to Knowledge by the late W Pinnock Esq Illustrated by ... maps &c.* edited by William Bayne in six volumes was promised but only the first volume is known (London. Shepherd & Sutton. 1844).

The maps reappeared (without signatures and without the added title panels) in 1847, this time published by Thomas Johnson, again lithographically but without the relief process. They were last reissued in a second Johnson edition of 1863.

Joshua Archer also engraved maps for Thomas Dugdale's *Curiosities of Great Britain* (which replaced those of Cole and Roper from *c.*1842, see **67**).

Size 165 x 225 mm.

English Miles (15=33 mm).
Scale 1M=2.2 mm.

DEVONSHIRE with imprint: **London. W Edwards, 12 Ave Maria Lane.** The arms of Devonshire with motto **Semper Fidelis** (Ae). Signature: **J. Archer sc. 100 Drummond Str Euston Sq.** (Ee). **Longitude W. from Greenwich** (EeOS) embedded with latitude and longitude in plain double line frame. No roads in surrounding counties.

1. 1833 *The Guide to Knowledge. Edited by W Pinnock ... Vol 1*
London. W Edwards. 1833.   BL, C.

2. 1838 Arms removed. New, simpler arms added (Ed). Grecian Key frame. Many new roads especially in neighbouring counties. Sea and hill shading. Title, price etc has been reset but is almost identical to first printing.

The Guide to Knowledge. Edited by W Pinnock ... Vol 1
London. The Proprietors. 1838.   EB, (KB).

---

[1] Burden, Webb and Burgess; Pinnock's Guide to Knowledge Maps; in *IMCoS JOURNAL*; Issue 36; Spring 1989.

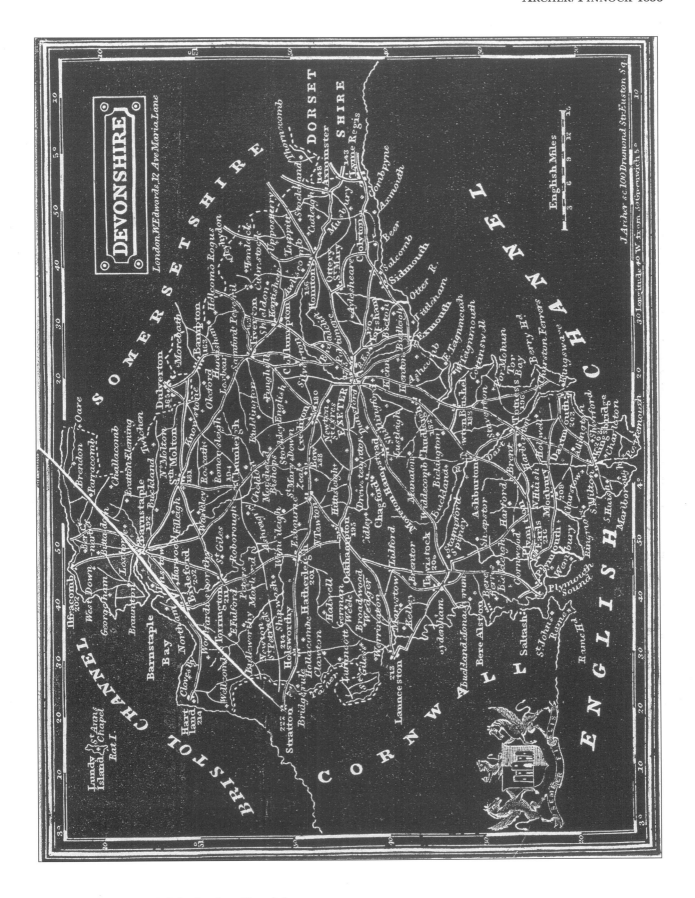

108.1 Archer/Pinnock *The Guide to Knowledge.*

109

JAMES WYLD
1833

The Wyld family were very influential in the world of cartography throughout the 19th century. James Wyld the Elder (1790-1836) founded the firm becoming Geographer to His Majesty and HRH Duke of York and was a founder member of the Royal Geographical Society in 1830. He is credited with introducing lithography into map printing in his plans of the Peninsula Campaign in 1812. The company acquired William Faden's business in 1823 including his shop at 457 West Strand. In 1830 Wyld senior was joined by his son, James Wyld the Younger (1812-1887), a Master of the Clothworkers Company and subsequently MP for Bodmin 1847-52 and 1857-68. A prolific publisher, the elder Wyld is reputed to have died of overwork.

The Wylds reissued the works of many others. Maps from Smith's *New English Atlas* (**63**) and copies of *Cary's Traveller's Companion* (**92**) are known with a label over the imprint *Sold by J Wyld. Geographer to His Majesty* (1832 edition). Lithograph copies of Wallis's *New British Atlas* have been found with the imprint: *London. Published by Jas Wyld Charing Cross East.* It is believed that James Wyld the Younger planned a County Atlas in 1842 but the venture never succeeded – loose maps with Wyld's imprint are possibly from this atlas. Wyld also reprinted the large map of Devon – Baker's reduction of Donn (**62**) – which he must have obtained when he took over Faden's business. Among the firm's most curious works was a globe which was 60 feet high and stood in Leicester Square 1853-61.

The Ordnance Survey of Devonshire was completed in 1809 (**74**). Many companies used it as the basis for their maps, arguing successfully that the Ordnance was providing a service for the public and that they, the publishers, were doing their duty in making the results known like Wyld in 1833.

Size 1188 x 915 mm.
Scale (10=126 mm) **Miles**.
Scale 1M=12.6 mm.

MAP OF THE COUNTY OF DEVON, Drawn from the Topographical Survey taken by Order of the HONOURABLE BOARD OF ORDNANCE, under the Direction of Lt. Colonel W. Mudge Roy:Art:F.R.S. and with Permission Reduced from the large Map in eight Sheets by a Scale of One Inch to Two Statute Miles. London Published by Ja^s. Wyld, Geographer to His. Majesty. Charing Cross, East, 1833. Inset map of **Lundy** (122 x 91 mm) (Aa). Inset map of the **ENVIRONS of PLYMOUTH** (Ee).

1. 1833   Only known as a single map; cut, mounted, folded and cased.   (E¹).

---

¹· Illustration courtesy of the Exeter Westcountry Studies Library.

109.1 Wyld *Map of the County of Devon* (detail)

HOUSE OF COMMONS
1833

As a result of the various parliamentary reforms and rapid industrialisation, increased awareness was being taken of population and statistical information of the regions of Britain. In 1833 a report was issued in the Government Accounts and Papers outlining the population statistics and the Parish Register Limits: *Abstract of the Answers and Returns made pursuant to an Act, passed in the Eleventh Year of the Reign of His Majesty King George IV, Intituled An Act for taking Account of the Population of Great Britain and of the Increase or Diminution thereof. Parish Register Abstract. MDCCCXXXI.* This was accompanied by maps of the counties. The account of Devon began on page 63 with the Baptismal, Burial and Marriage statistics of Axminster and ended with the Mortality figures for Plymouth, Stoke Damarel (later Devonport) and Stonehouse *deduced from the foregoing Account of Ages* on page 78. The map of Devon and Somerset was included here. The Accounts and Papers are all contained in 17 volumes covering the Session 29th January to 29th August 1833.

The map itself is very plain with hundreds being grouped together with up to three others depending on size. The Devon statistics were then listed on the left hand side of the map and included the population statistics for the years 1801, 1811, 1821 and 1831, together with the figures for baptisms, burials and marriages in the previous years. Devon was coloured pink and Somerset green.

Only the county of Cornwall is a single county map. All other English counties are grouped together with up to four other counties. As well as sixteen maps covering the counties, which includes north and south Wales on two maps, there is a map of the *Metropolis* and a map of *England and Wales.* Only the latter map is signed: *S Arrowsmith Lithog.* and it would seem likely that he engraved all the maps.

Samuel Arrowsmith also engraved a map of Devon and Cornwall for the House of Commons and published in the *Third Report from His Majesty's Commissioners* in 1836 (**117**).

Size 288 x 363 mm.   **Scale of English Statute Miles Nine=One Inch** (10+40=135 mm).
                                                          Scale 1M=2.7 mm.

COUNTIES OF DEVON AND SOMERSET. Scale bar (CeOS).   (E¹).

1. 1833   *Population of Great Britain – 1831; Accounts and Papers, 1833, XXXVIII, 1. Abstract of the Answers and Returns. Ordered by the House of Commons to be printed 2 April 1833.*
                   London. House of Commons. 1833.   BL, B.

                   Abstract of the Answers and Returns; Parish Register Abstract Vol III
                   Ordered to be printed 14th February 1834.
                   (London. House of Commons 1834).   KB.

---

¹· Illustration courtesy of the Exeter Westcountry Studies Library.

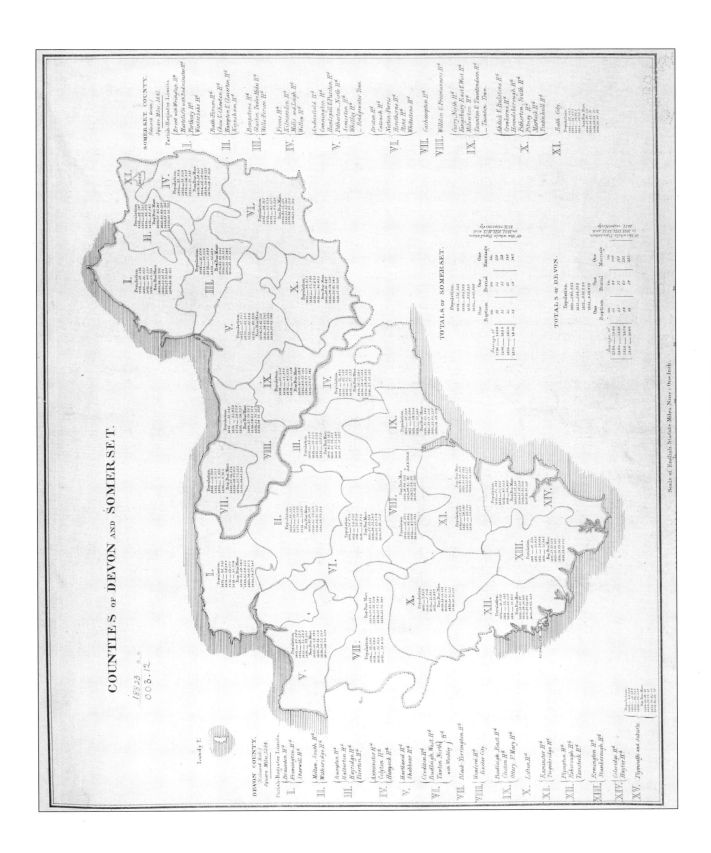

110.1 House of Commons *Abstract of the Answers and Returns ...*

111

DOWER/MOULE
1834

Thomas Moule published books and papers on topography, history, genealogy, heraldry and architecture. Born in 1794 at St Marylebone he was a bookseller in Duke Street, Grosvenor Square, from about 1816 until 1823, when he became Inspector of blind letters. He was also Chamber-keeper in the Lord Chamberlain's Department with official residence in the Stable Yard of St James' Palace, where he died on 14th January 1851.

Moule's English Counties was issued as a part-work[1], including maps of each English county and town plans, including Plymouth and Devonport, between 1830 and 1836 before being combined from 1837. The maps, engraved on steel, were also sold individually as *Moule's Pocket County Maps*. Although some early issues of these maps may be found in contemporary colour-wash most have recent colour. At least eight states of Berks were published 1837-1839; it is likely that different states of Devon remain to be discovered.

The three engravers employed by Moule were Schmollinger, who engraved perhaps the most decorative county maps (see **115**), John Bingley and John Dower, who engraved most of the west country maps. Early examples of Devon have the engraver's name: John Crane Dower (*fl.*1820-47), a specialist map engraver who worked from premises at 6, Cumming Place, Pentonville throughout his career. He engraved a large-scale map of Great Britain in 1839 for Samuel Lewis[2]. It showed roads, rivers, canals and railways at a scale of five miles to the inch. He died in 1847. His son and successor was John James Dower (*b.*1825) who was very active in the second half of the nineteenth century producing work for the *Weekly Despatch* and *Hobson's Fox-hunting Atlas* (see **116**). Another son, Frederick James (*b.*1829), was also a map engraver, serving an apprenticeship with Alexander Findlay in the 1840s.

Later issues: Moule's *English Counties* was reprinted in 1839. After this the Rev. James Barclay reissued the maps in his *A Complete and Universal English Dictionary, ... revised by Henry W Dewhurst* and *A Complete and Universal Dictionary* (London. Geo. Virtue.) from 1842: the imprint was removed, plate number *23* added (EeOS) and the Exeter and Bristol Railway was shown. The contents varied from copy to copy. Plate numbers were added and erased at random and the plates were under constant revision especially regarding railway and parliamentary information. The *Dictionaries* were reprinted frequently until *c.*1858 and, being slightly smaller than Moule's original, maps were often trimmed. After 1852 some of the counties can be found in sets of *The History of England* by Hume and Smollett (later extended by Edward Farr).

Size 185 x 245 mm.   Scale 1M=2.1 mm.

DEVONSHIRE. Vignette of the **GUILDHALL EXETER.** Two coats of arms including that of the Bishop of Exeter. Imprint: **Engraved for MOULES' ENGLISH COUNTIES by I. Dower.** (CeOS).

1. 1834   *Moule's English Counties* issued as a monthly series
             London. G Virtue, Simpkin & Marshall, Jennings & Chaplin. 1834.   BL.

             The English Counties Delineated by Thomas Moule
             London. G Virtue. 1837.   **CCCCLXXI**, C, (E), (NDL).

2. 1837   Parliamentary stars added. Note added below the list of hundreds:
             County returns 4 members.

             The English Counties Delineated by Thomas Moule
             London. G Virtue. 1837, 1838.   **CCCCLXXII**, BL, W; BCL.

[1.] Tony Campbell; The Original ... Numbers of Moule's English Counties; *The Map Collector*; Issue 31; June 1985.

[2.] R J Shirley; Mapping Great Britain's Industrial Revolution; in *IMCoS JOURNAL*; Vol. 7 No. 1; Spring 1987.

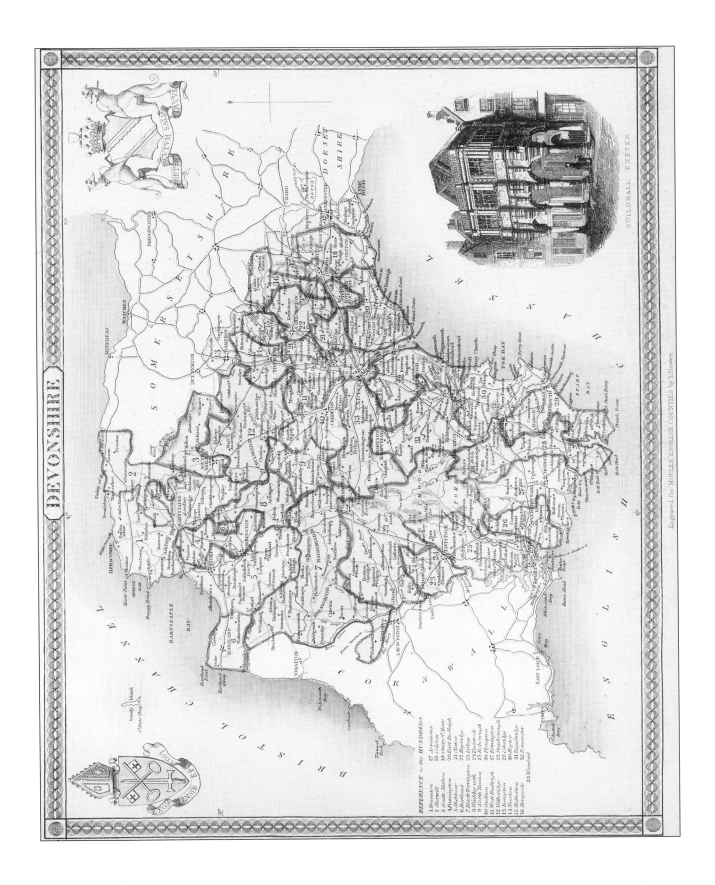

REFERENCE to the HUNDREDS

1 Braunton
2 Sherwill
3 South Molton
4 Fremington
5 Shebbear
6 Hartland
7 Black Torrington
8 Winkley with
9 North Tawton
10 Crediton
11 West Budleigh
12 Witheridge
13 Bampton
14 Tiverton
15 Halberton
16 Hayridge

17 Axminster
18 Colyton
19 Ottery St Mary
20 East Budleigh
21 Cliston
22 Haytridge
23 Wonford
24 Exminster
25 Teignbridge
26 Plympton
27 Roborough
28 Stanborough
29 Coleridge
30 Ermington
31 Haytor
32 Exminster
33 Hemiford

111.1 Dower/Moule *The English Counties Delineated*

112

MARY MARTHA RODWELL
1834

Mary Martha Rodwell has the distinction of being the only woman cartographer or publisher to offer a county atlas under her own name (as opposed to those who carried on their husband's business[1]). She prepared a geography containing 118 maps on 59 plates of the counties of Great Britain and Ireland, *The Geography of the British Isles* (8vo), in 1834.

These were miniature maps, each one accompanied by explanatory text. They formed part of a children's instructional work and were printed two to a page; Devon was printed below Dorset. The maps are without scale, compass or other wording. The rivers, towns and geographical features are marked by letters or numerals which are identified by a key at the beginning of the relevant text: numbers **1-26** for towns, rivers **a-k**, bays and capes **A-I** with Lundy **H**. The names of surrounding counties are replaced by lines of dashes (not apparent on the illustration). The text itself is set out as a dialogue between Mrs Rowe (ostensibly the teacher) and two children, Anna and George, who seem to have a great deal of knowledge concerning geography, history and personages of the county.

Devon and Dorset appeared on page 104 with the appropriate text for Devon beginning on page 111 and continuing until page 117.

Size 75 x 90 mm.   Scale 1M=1 mm.

DEVONSHIRE.

1. 1834   *The Geography of the British Isles, interspersed with many historical facts and biographical sketches; selected from the best authors, and illustrated with separate blank maps and explanatory keys; showing the relative situations, boundaries, principal towns, rivers &c of each county. For the use of young persons and schools. By Mary Martha Rodwell. Vol 1*
London. Longman, Rees, Orme, Brown, Green and Longman. 1834.
                                                                                        CCCCLVIIIc, BL[2].

[1.] Interestingly R V Tooley does not list Rodwell in his list of Women in the Map World in *The Map Collector* (Issue 4 September 1978). Of the many women listed most, such as Anne Lea and Elizabeth Bakewell, took over their husband's or father's business and were quite successful. A few women are reported as publishing maps and atlases for others including Mary Cooper, who was well-known in the book trade in the 1750s, and Joyce Gold who published Rowe's *English Atlas* (1816).

[2.] Illustration courtesy of the British Library.

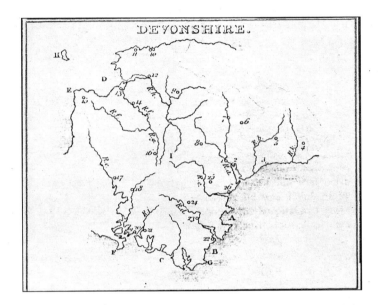

112.1 Rodwell *The Geography of the British Isles*

113

CREIGHTON/LEWIS
1835

Samuel Lewis issued his *Topographical Dictionary* in 1831 (**103**). He subsequently produced a new parliamentary atlas in 1835 to accompany it, *View of the Representative History of England*. This contained county maps showing the electoral boundaries and changes following the 1832 reform act. He also included these in the third edition of *A Topographical Dictionary of England* which then contained two maps of the county.

The plate from which the second map was taken was apparently never used for direct intaglio printing. It was intended to give parliamentary information, and, apart from this, shows only the hundred boundaries, main roads and chief towns. Both of the maps used by Samuel Lewis were engraved by J and C Walker who produced a number of county maps including two maps of Devonshire (**102, 116**).

Lewis published town plans of the boundary changes, also drawn by R Creighton, in the *View of the Representative History of England*. While Plate XIX was the county map, Plate XX has Exeter and Tavistock together; Plate XXI – Barnstaple, Tiverton, Ashburton and Dartmouth; Plate XXII – Devonport, Plymouth, Honiton and Totnes.

Later issues: The third edition of the *Dictionary* was reprinted in 1837 and 1838[1]. Changes were made to the polling stations on other counties but this has not been verified for Devon. The only copy of 1837 known is in a private collection and the 1838 dictionary has been broken up. The last edition of *View of the Representative History of England* was issued by S Lewis & Co. in 1840.

Size 182 x 233 mm.

Scale of Miles (30=69 mm).
Scale 1M=2.3 mm.

DEVONSHIRE. Plate number **XIX** (EeOS) vertically. Imprint: **Engraved by J. & C. Walker.** (EeOS). Signature: **Drawn by R. Creighton.** (AeOS).

(E).

1. 1835   *A Topographical Dictionary of England   3rd Edition, Vol V*
London. S Lewis & Co. 1835.

CCCCXXXII, BL, W.

View of the Representative History of England
London. S Lewis & Co. 1835.

RGS.

[1.] Eugene Burden; *County Maps of Berkshire*; (1988) 1991; p.153 – atlas now broken.

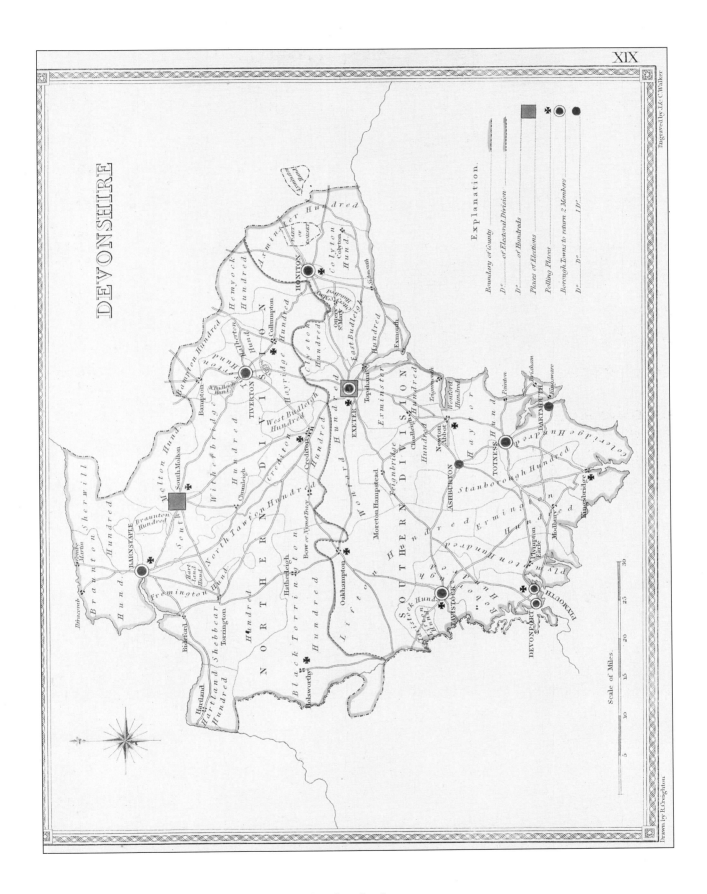

113.1 Creighton/Lewis *A Topographical Dictionary of England*

114

JAMES PIGOT
1835

In 1826/7 James Pigot & Co. issued their *London and Provincial New Directory* which became *Pigot & Co's British Atlas of the Counties of England* (**98**). This was very successful running to many reprints before being taken over by Isaac Slater. In 1835 they brought out *Pigot and Co's Pocket Atlas, Pocket Topography and Gazetteer* with reduced versions of these maps, without the vignettes, as lithographs. These were first published fortnightly or monthly in separate parts. The vignette of Exeter Cathedral, removed from the old plate, was printed on the page facing the map together with a distance table of Devonshire.

Later issues: Pigot and Co. issued the atlas again as *A Pocket Topography and Gazetteer of England* in *c*.1841 and *c*.1850 (see illustration). The publishers were Pigot & Co. in London together with Longman and Co., Sherwood and Co., and Simpkin and Marshall, while in Manchester Pigot and Slater were the distributors (Chubb CCCCLXII; CCCCLXIII: the British Library holds copies of both issues).

Size 100 x 165 mm.   **Scale of Miles** (10=14 mm). Scale 1M=1.4 mm.

DEVONSHIRE. Imprint: **PUBLISHED BY PIGOT & C^O. LONDON. AND MANCHESTER.** (CeOS). Signature: **Pigot & Son, Engravers Manch^r.** (EeOS).

1. **1835**   First issued fortnightly in separate parts.   (E).

Pigot & Co's Pocket Atlas, Topography and Gazetteer of England
London and Manchester. J Pigot & Co. 1835.   B, E.

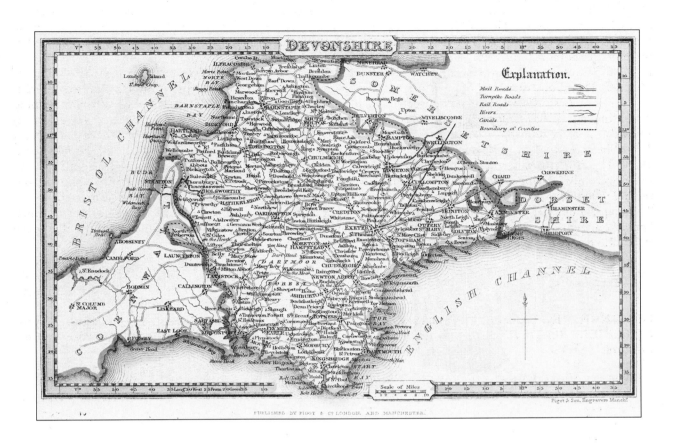

114 Pigot *Pocket Atlas, Topography and Gazetteer of England*

231

115

W SCHMOLLINGER
1836

W Schmollinger (*fl.*1831-37) engraved a number of maps for Thomas Moule's *English Counties* (**111**); for example, he engraved the map of Sussex and the town plan of Boston. Little is known of Schmollinger outside his work on the Moule maps. He seems to have been a specialist map engraver; at least he is so advertised in an 1837 trade directory. He had premises at 27 Goswell Terrace, Goswell Road, and later in Aldine Chambers, Paternoster Row. He may well have been the son of the Joseph Schmollinger and Mary Drew who married at St Leonard Shoreditch in 1799[1].

In 1836 Schmollinger engraved an attractive map of Devon in a similar style to those in Moule's *English Counties*. The frame, typical of Moule's maps (although not Devon) has columns right and left with two different and very ornate stonework patterns between. The map was published by R Colliver of Exeter of whom nothing is yet known. It has Colliver's imprint, is dated 1836 and has been inserted into editions of *The History of Devonshire from the earliest period to the present by Rev. Thomas Moore. Illustrated by a series of views drawn and engraved by and under the direction of William Deeble.* London: Published by Robert Jennings, 62 Cheapside, September 1, 1829. The *History* was issued as a part-work[2] which probably explains the conflicting dates and suggests that the maps were always tipped in when the volumes were bound. The book was published in two volumes; the second volume has a town plan of Exeter by Schmollinger, published by Colliver, and similarly inserted.

The map is unusual in having vignette views of Tavistock Abbey and County Sessions House, neither of which appear on any other maps of Devon. The former view looks a little bit out of place, almost as if the Reference to Hundreds might have been moved to create space for it.

Size 205 x 270 mm.

English Miles (20=45 mm).
Scale 1M=2.25 mm.

DEVONSHIRE. Vignettes of **Tavistock Abbey** and **County Sessions House**. Imprint: **Pub. by R. COLLIVER. *EXETER*. 1836**. (CeOS) and signature: **Engraved by W. Schmollinger Paternoster Row London.** (AeOS).

1. 1836   *The History of Devonshire ... by Rev. Thomas Moore.*
London. Robert Jennings. 1829 (1836).   E, NDL, FB.

---

1. Laurence Worms; Some British Mapmakers; *Ash Rare Books Catalogue and Price List*; 1992.
2. Part XXXIX of *Moule's English Counties* (**111**) contained an advertisement for the various parts of Vol. I of Moore's work. See Tony Campbell; The Original Monthly Numbers of Moule's 'English Counties'; *The Map Collector*, Issue 31; June 1985; p. 31.

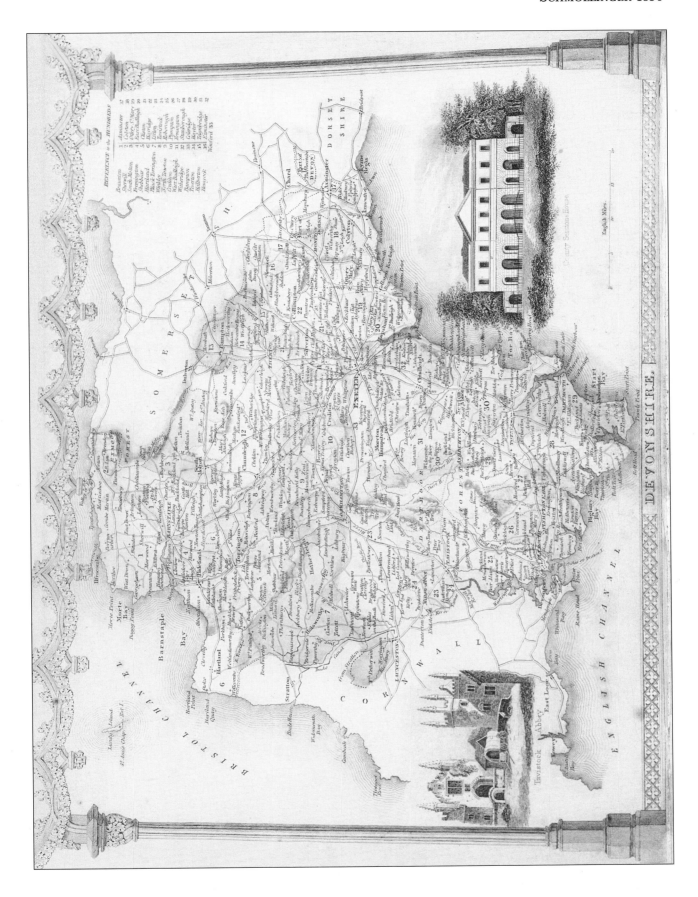

115.1 Schmollinger *The History of Devonshire*

116

JOHN & CHARLES WALKER
1836

John and Charles Walker were sons of John Walker who worked for Alexander Dalrymple, Hydrographer to the East India Company in 1779 and for the Admiralty in 1795. John took over as hydrographer in 1808 and when he died Sir Francis Beaufort (of the wind force scale) was appointed. The younger John also became hydrographer to the East India Co. in 1836. He and Charles continued the family firm until 1890.

They were prolific engravers for other cartographers (**102**, **103** and **113**) as well as for themselves and they published maps of India, the provinces, the Americas and the world, working from a number of London addresses.

In 1837 their most important county cartographic work appeared, the folio *British Atlas* (47 maps), jointly published with Longman, Rees and Co. The maps were extremely popular and many editions of the Atlas were produced, often with a confusing inclusion of old stock so that maps with different addresses in imprints can be found together in one atlas. The earliest maps had lists of the hundreds according to *the Quarter Sessions 1830* (Ed) but this was replaced in later editions by those of *1839*. Most of the maps were offered singly in folding covers, eg *WALKER'S DEVONSHIRE*. The maps were also issued as boxed sets from 1837 as *Walker's County Atlas* (as well as being offered from 1842 by G F Cruchley).

Later issues: Walker's *British Atlas* was reprinted frequently until 1879. From 1849 many place names were added or revised to allow lithographic transfers to be taken, especially for *Hobson's Fox-Hunting Atlas* showing the meeting places of hounds. This was very popular and was reprinted until *c.*1882. *Walker's Fox-Hunting Atlas* appeared *c.*1882 and *c.*1895.

The maps of Devon and Cornwall also appeared in John Murray's *Handbook of Devon and Cornwall* from the 1850s before being replaced by a map of the two counties together by W A K Johnston (*c.*1872). When Devon was later printed separately a map by John Bartholomew was used.

William White wrote a *History, Gazetteer and Directory of the County* which also appeared with Walker's Devon map (first edition 1850, second edition 1878/9).

In the 1880s the maps were further reissued and appeared in *Lett's Popular County Atlas* (1884-*c.*1889). These were extensively revised and overprinted with information, eg lifeboat and coastguard stations.

Size 320 x 385 mm.   **English Miles 69.1 to 1 Degree** (8 **Furlongs** + 20=91 mm).

Scale 1M=4.3 mm.

DEVONSHIRE with signature: **BY J. & C. Walker**. Imprint: **Published by Longman, Orme, Rees & Co. Paternoster Row, London, May 1ˢᵗ. 1836.** (CeOS).

(NDL).

1. 1836   *To their Royal Highnesses the Duchess of Kent & the Princess Victoria, this British Atlas ...*
            London. Longman, Rees and Co. and J & C Walker. 1837.

CCCCLXXVI, BL, C, W.

To her most excellent Majesty Queen Victoria, and to Her Royal Highness the Duchess of Kent, this British Atlas ...
London. Longman, Rees and Co. and J & C Walker. 1837.   BL.

Also in boxed sets of dissected maps labelled *Walker's County Atlas*.   C.

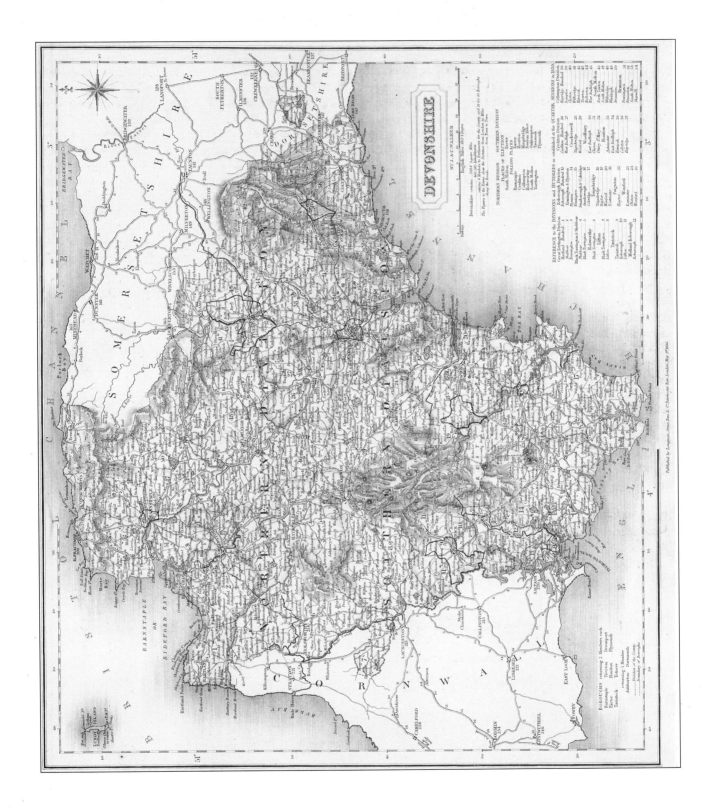

116.1 Walker ... *this British Atlas*

117

SAMUEL ARROWSMITH
1836

Aaron Arrowsmith (1750-1823), originally from Durham, carried out some of the surveys for Cary when the latter was preparing his *Traveller's Companion* published in 1790. Aaron set up his own business about this time and built himself a reputation for maps of the Americas and various parts of the world, especially the South Seas. He was succeeded by his two sons, Samuel and Aaron (*fl.*1820-30). However, it was left to a nephew, John Arrowsmith (1790-1873), to take over the firm on Samuel's death in 1839.

During the 1830s the Government set up a Commission *to consider the state of the Established Church*; also to consider the finances and report on the pay structure of the clergy. These reports were accompanied by maps. In common with most of the maps there are two counties together; in this case Devon and Cornwall as these two counties contained the four arch-deaconries in the Southwest peninsula which made up the bishopric of Exeter. The four are labelled A-D and constituted three in Devon: Barnstaple, Exeter and Totnes; with Cornwall as the fourth. Each Archdeaconry is subdivided into up to nine Deaneries.

The Devon and Cornwall map is signed *S Arrowsmith lithg* and was the seventh in this report coming at the end of the appropriate section on page 14. Only Exeter is shown (with the Cathedral church and Bishop's residence).

Considering the finances of the county a number of suggestions were made including one that fees were to be apportioned so that the Bishop of Exeter, as head of one of the smaller Diocese, should receive more than £4000 but less than £5000 per annum. Proposition eight concerned area and suggested that the Scilly Isles come under the jurisdiction of the Bishop of Exeter and the Arch-Deaconry of Cornwall.

Samuel Arrowsmith also engraved a map of *England and Wales* for the House of Commons and published in the *Accounts and Papers* in 1833. It is possible that he engraved the map of Devon and Somerset (**110**).

Size 312 x 320 mm.   No scale.

EXETER (unaltered). Signature: **S Arrowsmith lithg** (EeOS). Page number **7** (AeOS).

1. 1836   *Third Report from His Majesty's Commissioners appointed to consider the state of the Established Church*
               with reference to Ecclesiastical Duties and Revenues. 20. May 1836. Appendix.
               Reports from Commissioners. 1836. Vol 36 (280); XXXVI;p.7.
               London. S Arrowsmith. 1836.   **CCCCLXXa**, BL (Off. Pub.)[1].

---

[1] Illustration courtesy of the British Library.

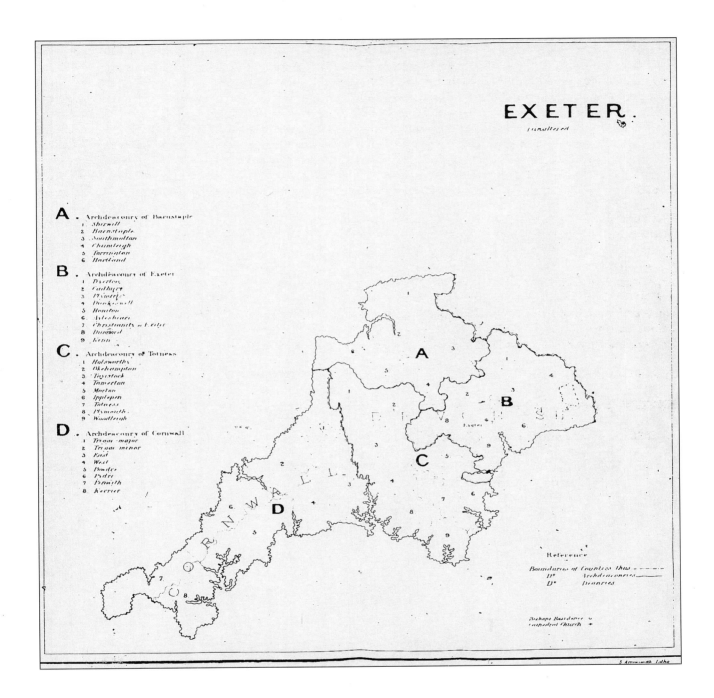

EXETER.
(unaltered)

A. Archdeaconry of Barnstaple
  1 Shirwell
  2 Barnstaple
  3 Southmolton
  4 Chumleigh
  5 Torrinton
  6 Hartland

B. Archdeaconry of Exeter
  1 Tiverton
  2 Cadbury
  3 Plimtre
  4 Dunkeswell
  5 Honiton
  6 Aylesbeare
  7 Christianity in Exeter
  8 Dunsford
  9 Kenn

C. Archdeaconry of Totness
  1 Holsworthy
  2 Okehampton
  3 Tavistock
  4 Tamerton
  5 Morton
  6 Ipplepen
  7 Totness
  8 Plymouth
  9 Woodleigh

D. Archdeaconry of Cornwall
  1 Trigg major
  2 Trigg minor
  3 East
  4 West
  5 Powder
  6 Pydar
  7 Penwith
  8 Kerrier

Reference
Boundaries of Counties thus
D° Archdeaconries
D° Deanries
Bishops Residence
Cathedral Church +

117.1 Arrowsmith *Third Report from His Majesty's Commissioners*

BIBLIOGRAPHY

Barker, K & Kain, R (Eds)   *Maps and History in S.-W. England*; Univ. Exeter Press; 1991.

R Baynton-Williams   *Investing in Maps*; London; 1969.

Yasha Beresiner   *British County Maps*; Antique Collectors' Club; 1983.

Eugene Burden   *County Maps of Berkshire 1574-1900*; (1988) 1991.

Sir H G Fordham   *Studies in Carto-bibliography*; Dawson's; 1969.

Sir H G Fordham   *John Cary, Engraver and Map Seller*; Cambridge; 1910.

A G Hodgkiss   *Discovering Antique Maps*; Shire Publications Ltd; 1988.

Donald Hodson   *The Printed Maps of Hertfordshire*; 1974.

Donald Hodson   *County Atlases of the British Isles*; Vol 1; Bracken Press; 1984.

Donald Hodson   *County Atlases of the British Isles*; Vol 2; Bracken Press; 1989.

IMCoS JOURNAL   Magazine of the International Map Collectors' Society. Quarterly.

David Kingsley   *Printed Maps of Sussex*; Sussex Record Society; 1982.

C Koeman   *Atlas Neerlandici*; Amsterdam; 1967.

Mann, S & Kingsley, D   Playing Cards; in Vol. 87 of *Map Collector's Circle*; 1972.

The Map Collector   Published Quarterly; Issues 1978-1995.

Moreland, C & Bannister, D   *Antique Maps*; Phaidon; 1986.

R R Sellman   *Aspects of Devon History*; Devon Books; (1962) 1985.

R A Skelton   *County Atlases of the British Isles; 1575-1701*; Carta; 1970.

David Smith   *Victorian Maps of the British Isles*; Batsford Books; 1985.

R V Tooley   *Maps and Mapmakers*; Batsford Books; 1987.

Tooley, R V & Bricker, C   *Landmarks of Mapmaking*; Wordsworth; 1989.

Laurence Worms   *Some British Mapmakers*; Ash Rare Books Cat. and Price List; 1992.

INDEX

In order to keep the index as simple as possible all entries refer simply to page numbers. An attempt has been made to include all relevant entries and atlas names are often repeated with or without the author's name(s) where this will help in finding the correct atlas.

Authors are only included here in the index where their details are not to be found in the bibliography on page 238. Place names have been provided only when there is some relevant information in the text. Selected subjects have been included, eg longitude, coats of arms etc, where these may help the collector to identify a map or where there is some discussion of the topic.

–A–

Aa, Peter van der 28
abridgement of Camden's Britania 18
Abstract of the Answers and Returns 222
Acart, Giulleme 6
Accounts and Papers 222
acid etching ix
Adams (Hamilton, Adams & Co.) 200
Adams, Robert xii
Adlard & Browne (printers) 70
Agreeable Historian 60
agriculture 6; 120; 122; 142; 144
Aikin, John 114; 142
Aldin, Cecil 164
Algemeene Oefenschoole 80
All the Shires of England and Wales xiv; 2; 40
Allard, Carol (Karel) 25
Allen's English Atlas 152
Allen (Lackington, Allen & Co.) 134
Allen, Joseph 124; 152
Allom, Thomas 206
Alphabetical Chronology of Remarkable Events 136
An Atlas of England & Wales 3
Andrews, John xiv
andromache 52
Anglia Contracta 42
Annual Register 62
antiquities 42; 52; 70; 116; 206
Antiquities of England and Wales 70
Archer, Joshua 136; 218
Arrowsmith, Aaron junior 236
Arrowsmith, Aaron senior 180; 236
Arrowsmith, John 236
Arrowsmith, Samuel 222; 236
Aspley, William 10
Atlas Anglicanus (Bowen) 98
Atlas Anglicanus (Seller) 15; 42
Atlas Anglois (Lea) 40
Atlas Anglois (Mortier) 25
Atlas Britannique 94
Atlas Major 25; 26
Atlas Minor 24
Atlas minor Gerardi Mercatoris 28
Atlas Novus 26
Atlas of England (Butters) 132
Atlas of England and Wales (Greenwood) 196
Atlas of England and Wales, Robin's 162
Atlas of Great Britain and Ireland 106
Atlas of the British Islands 146
Atlas of the Counties of England (Luffman) 134
Atlas of the English Counties (T L Murray) 202
Azores xiv

–B–

Babbacombe Bay 206
Badeslade, Thomas xi; 56
Baker, Benjamin xiv; 66; 116; 126; 150; 154
Baker, Robert 18
Bakewell, Elizabeth 86; 226
Bakewell, Thomas 36; 86
Baldwin, Cradock & Joy 136; 182
Baldwin, Robert 70; 72; 90
Ball, Sarah 18
Barfort, Peter 130
Baring, John 90
Bartholomew, John 216
Bartlett, W H 206
Bassett, Thomas & Chiswell, Richard 9; 12; 15
Batten, Kit 90; 102; 152
Bayne, William 218
Beauties of England and Wales 136; 160
Beche, Henry de la 150
Bedford on reverse 94
Belch, William 170
Bell, Andrew 46
Bell, James 216
Bennett, John 54; 68; 94
Bennett, Richard 84
Bent, William 116
Beresiner, Yasha 152
Berry, William 32
Bertius, Petrus 9
Besley, Henry 188
Bickham, George Senior and Junior 74; 154
Bideford Bay (crack) 9
Biggs, G 176
Bill, John xiv; 18
Billingsley, B 34
Billingsley, John 120
Bingley, John 224
Birds-Eye Views of the Counties 74; 154
Birr, Mary 88
Birt, Samuel 64
Bishop Nicholson 30
Bishop, George 10
Bladon, Samuel 70
Blaeu, Cornelis 26
Blaeu, Joan (Jan) xi; xiii; xiv; 14; 24; 26; 38
Blaeu, Willem Janszoon 8; 26
Blome, Richard x; xiii; xiv; 30; 36
Blythe, F 70
Board of Agriculture 120; 122; 142
Boazio, Baptist 8
Bodleian Library 14; 18; 52; 58
Bodley, Sir Thomas 18

Book of the Names of all Parishes 22
Booke of the Names of all Hundreds 22
Borlase, William 90
Borough Island 90
Boroughs Of England 212
Boswell, Henry 70
Boundaries Act 212
Bourne, Ebeneser 150
Bowen, Emanuel x; xi; xiv; 50; 66; 76; 78; 80; 86; 88; 98; 100
Bowen, Owen 78
Bowen, Sarah 88
Bowen, Thomas 70; 78; 98
Bowes, W 4; 6; 20; 34
Bowles's New Medium English Atlas 98
Bowles's Pocket Atlas 100
Bowles & Carver 76; 98
Bowles & Son 100
Bowles, Carington 50; 68; 76; 77; 86; 94; 100
Bowles, John 50; 52; 68; 76; 77; 86; 100
Bowles, John & Son 77
Bowles, Thomas 50; 52; 77; 86; 100
Bowles, Thomas & John 40
Bowles, Thomas (father) 100
Bowyer, William 44
Brahe, Tycho 26
Braun, Georg & Hogenberg, Frans 4; 12; 180
Brayley, Edward Wedlake 136; 160; 206
Brief Description of England and Wales 32
Brine see Rattle & Brine's library
Britain Or A Chorographical Description 10
Britannia (Blome) 30; 36
Britannia (Camden) 10
Britannia (Cary) 110
Britannia (Morden) 44; 46; 76
Britannia (Ogilby) xiv
Britannia (Oldys) 36
Britannia Depicta Or Ogilby Improv'd 50
Britannia, ... Regnorum Angliae, Scotiae, Hibernia 10
Britannia: Or A Chorographical Description 44
Britannia: or, A Geographical Description 30
British Atlas (Cole & Roper) 136
British Atlas (Cooke) 138
British Atlas (Walker) 234
British Atlas, Hall's 204
British Atlas, Sidney Hall's 204
British Gazetteer 164
British Monarchy, 74
Britton, John 136; 206
Brixham Key 40
Brohez, L J 190
Brown see Longman etc
Browne (Adlard & Browne) 70
Browne, Christopher 10; 15; 38
Browne, Daniel 64
Browne, I 16
Bumpus, John 182
Bur(r) Island 90
Burden, Eugene 84; 186; 218
Burgess, Tony 218
Burghley, Lord 2
Burroughs, Jane 88
Burroughs, Joseph 88
Burroughs, S 46
Busbie, I 16
Butters, R 132
Byrne, P 122

–C–

Cadell, Johnson & Dilly 44; 104; 168
Cadell, Thomas 180

Camden's Britania, The abridgement (Bill) 18
Camden's Britannia (Cary) 110
Camden's Britannia (Morden) 44
Camden's Britannia Abridg'd 42
Camden's Britannia Epitomized and Continued 182
Camden Society 10
Camden, William xiv; 4; 6; 8; 9; 10; 12; 16; 18; 24; 26; 28; 30; 36; 42; 44; 46; 110; 180; 182
Campbell, Tony 224; 232
Capper, Benjamin Pitts 146
Capper, William see Capper, Benjamin Pitts
Carnan, Thomas 82
Cary's New and Correct English Atlas 44; 104; 148
Cary's New English Atlas 144
Cary's Traveller's Companion ix; 84; 112; 140; 156; 186; 220; 236
Cary, G & J 145; 186
Cary, George 186
Cary, George the elder 110
Cary, George the younger 110
Cary, John ix; x; xi; xiv; xv; 10; 84; 104; 110; 112; 116; 120; 140; 144; 148; 156; 162; 184; 186; 220; 236
Cary, John (son) 110; 186
Cary, Mary 110
Cary, William 110
Catherine of Braganza 32
Cavendish, William 15; 50
Cecil, William xii
Chandler, Richard 46
Chaplin (Jennings & Chaplin) 224
Chapman & Hall 204
Child's Treasury of Amusement and Knowledge 172
Chiswell, Richard see Bassett & Chiswell
Chorographia Britanniae 56
Chubb, Thomas 10; 100; 134; 148; 158
Churchill, John 44
cider making 86; 172
circular map 134
Clark (Darton & Clark) 172
Clark, J 56
Clark, Rev. Samuel 172
Clark, Sam see Clark, Rev. Samuel
Clay, R 218
Cleave, Isaac 42
Clifford, Lord Robert Edward 162
cloth industry 134
Coasting Pilot xiv
coats of arms
    Bishop of Exeter 224
    Devonshire 60; 218
    Exeter 12; 66; 72; 96; 102
    John Greville, Earl of Bath 30
    outside border 54
    Royal Arms 2; 3; 12
    shields 12; 24; 26; 38; 40
    Thomas Seckford 3
    William Cavendish 15; 40; 50
Cobbett's Geographical Dictionary 170; 214
Cobbett, William 170; 210; 214
Cobley & Co. 142
Cochrane, Thomas 214
Cockerill, Thomas 46
Colby, Thomas 150; 210
Cole & Roper 136
Cole, George 136
Cole, William 192
Collection of Maps of the Counties 8
Collins' Devonshire with its Railways 164
Collins' Railway and Pedestrian Atlas of England 136
Collins' Railway and Telegraph Map of Devonshire 192
Collins England 136
Collins, B C 118

Collins, Greenville xv; 52
Collins, Henry George 136; 164; 192; 200
Colliver, R 232
colouring x
compass 2; 8; 46; 60; 132; 138
Compendious Account of the Western Circuit 182
Compleat English Traveller 60
Compleat Geographer, 52
Complete and Universal English Dictionary 224
Complete Atlas of the Counties of England 166
Complete County Atlas of England and Wales 192
Complete Historical Descriptions 70
Complete Pocket Gazetteer 182
Complete Set of... All the Counties 52
Concise View of England And Wales 68
Conder, Thomas 102
condition of the plate xii
Cooke's Modern British Traveller 138
Cooke, Charles 138
Cooke, George Alexander 138
Cooper, H 146
Cooper, Mary 62; 64; 68; 226
Cooper, Thomas 62
Coopers (Street & Coopers) 188
Coote, J 70
copper plate engraving ix
Corbett, C 84
Cornish Mountains, The 122
Cornwall
    agricultural review 120
    directions 52; 54; 60; 78; 80
    Gascoyne's map xiv; 70; 76
    incomplete county series 62
    map above Devon map 102
    map of Devon with Cornwall 16; 168; 234; 236
    Norden's map xiv; 58
    part of on Devon map 122
    published in volume with Devon 36; 138; 206; 222; 234
    text on reverse of Devon map 10
    title page 206
    towns 8; 12; 72
Cosmography and Geography 36
Cotton, Sir Robert 12
Counties of England 166
County Atlas of England and Wales 200
County of Devon reduced 126
County Sessions House 232
Covens & Mortier 25; 28
Covens, Johannes 25
Cowl, Richard 90
Cowley, John 62
Cox, H 34
Cox, J 182
Cox, Thomas 46; 58; 60
Crabb, Thomas 172; 178
crack through plate 218
cracks and dating xii
Cradock *see* Baldwin, Cradock & Joy
Creighton, R 194; 208; 228
Crockern Torr 120
Crooke, Andrew 10
Crosby's Complete Pocket Gazetteer 182
Crosby, Benjamin 182
Crowder, S 118
Cruchley's County Map 144
Cruchley's New Pocket Companion 148
Cruchley's Railway and Station map 144
Cruchley's Railway Map 144
Cruchley's Reduced Ordnance Map of Devonshire 162
Cruchley's Travelling County Atlas 148
Cruchley, George Frederick x; 144; 148; 162; 186; 234

Cundee, J & J 160
Cundee, James 160
Curiosities of Great Britain 136
Curious Antique Collection of Birds-Eye Views 74; 154
Cyder Tax 86

–D–

Dalton, William Hugh 102
Dartmoor Prison 188; 194
Dartmouth Castle 166
Darton's New Miniature Atlas 172
Darton & Clark 172
Darton & Co 136; 172
Darton & Harvey 116
Darton & Hodge 166
Darton, William 166; 172
dating xi; xii
Davey, P 64
Davies (engraver) 188
Davies and Eldridge (Exeter mapsellers) 156
Davies, William 180
Dawson, John 9; 14
Dawson, Robert 150
Dawson, Robert Kearsley 210; 212
Dean (*Manchester Directory*) 198
Debrett, J 122
Dee, John xii
Deeble, William 232
Defoe, Daniel 64
Depping, George Bernard 190
Des Nieuwen Atlantis Aenhang 24
Description of the several Counties of South Britain 74
Descriptive County Atlas of England and Wales 218
Devon
    blank plate 162
    harbour views 180
    printed below Cornwall 102
    printed below Dorset 226
    printed upside-down 18
    with Cornwall 16; 168; 234; 236
    with Somerset 222
Devon & Cornwall Illustrated 206
Devon & Cornwall Notes & Queries 40
Devon and Cornwall Record Society 90
Devonshire Illustrated 206
Devonshiring or Denshiring 122
Devonstire 22
Dewe, Thomas 16
Dewhurst, Henry W 224
Dicey, Cluer & Co 15; 38; 40
Dilly (Cadell, Johnson & Dilly) 44; 104; 168
Direction for the English Traviller 4; 20; 22
distance table xiv; 20; 22; 230
Dix, Thomas 166
Dodsley, James 62
Dodsley, R & J 88
Dodsley, Robert 62
Domville, W 70
Donn, Benjamin xi; xiv; xv; 90; 92; 126
Dorset
    border 44; 62
    detached part of Devon 68; 150
    imprint 104
    map of Isaac Taylors 90
    misspelt Dersetshire 38
    now written in full 130
    on reverse 94; 112
    part of on Devon map 122
    printed above Devon 226
    published in volume with Devon 138
    towns 8

Dower, John Crane 196; 224
Dower, John James 224
Drake, Daphne 40
Drayton, Michael xii; 16
Drew, Mary 232
Dugdale, James 160
Duke of Bedford, John 76
Duncan, James 192
Dury, Andrew 94; 98
Dyer, G 142

—E—

Earl of Bath 30
Earl of Orford 74
Ebden's New Map of the County of Devon 192
Ebden, William x; 154; 192
Eddystone lighthouse 42; 52; 58; 60; 74
Edwards, William 218
Eldridge (Davies & Eldridge) 156
Ellis's New and Correct Atlas of England and Wales 158
Ellis, G 158
Ellis, Joseph 88; 94; 102; 106
Elstrack, Renold 14
embroidery 108
Encyclopaedia Londinensis 130
England and Wales Delineated 136
England Delineated 114
England Depicted 192
England Displayed 70
England Exactly Described 36
England Fully Described – Overton Atlas VI 38
England Fully Described – Speed (Overton) I–IV 15
England Illustrated 62; 88
England, Wales and Ireland. Their Severall Counties 9
England, Wales, Scotland and Ireland Described 9
English Atlas (Bowen) 86
English atlas (Dicey) 15
English Atlas (Ellis) 94
English Atlas (Rowe) 164
English Atlas Or A Concise View of England And Wales 68
English Atlas, Allen's 152
English Counties Delineated 224
English Geography, the Game of 124
English Pilot 42
English Topography 136
English traveller 58; 60
Evans, T 70
Exeter
    Bay of 190
    Bishop's arms 224
    bishopric 236
    Cathedral 86; 170; 194; 196; 198; 216; 230
    coat of arms 12; 66; 72; 96; 102
    County of 118
    County Sessions House 170; 232
    Guildhall 224
    longitude 116
    mileages 188
    plan xiii; 12; 25; 40; 90; 180; 232
    text page 50
Exeter Journal 188
Exeter Journal and Almanack 188
Exeter Pocket Journal 168; 184; 188
Exshaw's Magazine 72
Exshaw, Edward 72
Exshaw, John 72
Exshaw, Sarah 72
Eyre & Spottiswoode 164
Ezekiel, E A 168

—F—

Faden, William 90; 92; 126; 150; 220
Fairburn, John 124; 152
Family Topographer 182
Farr, Edward 224
Fifty New and Correct Maps 52
Fifty Six New and Accurate Maps of Great Britain 46
Fifty two Counties of England and Wales 32
Fisher's County Atlas of England and Wales 206
Fisher Son & Co. 206
Fisher, Henry 206
Fisher, R 206
Fletcher, Miles 9
Flyn, J 84
Fowler, W 94; 96
Frankfurt Book Fair 18
Fraser, Robert 120; 142
Frostick, Raymond 28
Fullarton, Archibald 216

—G—

Gall, James & Inglis, Robert 110; 144; 186
Game of English Geography 124
Gapper, J 100
Gardner, James 150; 212
Gardner, James junior 212
Gardner, W R 184; 188
Garrett, John 20; 22
Garrett, William 12
Gascoyne, Joel xiii; 70; 76; 90
General and County Atlas 108
General Magazine Of Arts and Sciences 78; 80
General View of the Agriculture of ... Devon 120; 142
General View of the County of Devon 120
Gentleman's Magazine 106
Gentleman's, Merchant's and Tradesman's Complete Annual Accompt Book 188
Geographia Generalis 30
Geographia Magnae Britanniae 64
Geographia Scotiae 64
Geographiae Blavianae 27
Geographical Description ... Four Parts ... World 30
Geographical Dictionary 170; 214
Geographical Game, A 152
Geographical, Chronological and Historiograph. Cards 34
Geography Of England (Dodsley/Cowley) 62
Geography of England and Wales (Moll) 52
Geography of the British Isles 226
geology 120; 122; 142; 144
Gibson, Edmund 44
Gibson, John 82; 96
Gilbert, James 206; 218
Goadby & Son 84
Gold, Joyce 226
Goldsmith, Rev. J 142
Goodwin, James 136
Goos, Abraham 28
Gorton, John 204
Gough, Richard xiii; 110
Grand Western Canal 128; 144
graticule xiv; 25; 42; 76; 86; 88; 90; 94; 98; 100; 106; 108; 168; 180
Gray's New Book of Roads 138
Gray & Son 216
Gray, George Carrington 138
Great Consols mine 106
Green *see* Longman etc
Green, Robert 32
Green, William 132

Greenwich 116; 128
Greenwood's Atlas of England and Wales 196
Greenwood, C & J x; xv; 100; 194; 196
Greenwood, Christopher 194; 196
Greenwood, James 194; 196
Greenwood, Pringle & Co 194
Greville, John 30
Greville, Sir Fulke 12
Grismand, John 16
Groenewegen & Prevost 25
Groombridge, Richard 218
Grose, Francis 42; 70
Guide to Knowledge ix; 174; 218
Guilielmi Cambdeni Brittannia Magna Illustrata 25
Guilielmi Camdeni, Viri clarissimi Britannia 9
Gwillim, John 42

–H–

hachuring x; 156; 160; 190
Hall *see* Chapman & Hall
Hall, Rev. Anthony 46
Hall, Sidney 176; 204; 218
Halley, Edmund xiv
Hamilton, Adams, and Co 200
Hamilton, Robert 70
Handbook of Devon and Cornwall 234
Hansard 210
Hansard, James & Luke 210; 214
Harley, J B 2; 150; 212
Harrison, John 108
Harrison, John (chronometer) xiv
Harvey (Darton & Harvey) 116
Hatchard, John 132
Hatchett 88; 102; 106
Haywood, James xiv; 108
Heath 206
Heb, Andrew 10
Hebert, L 158
Hedgeland, P 142
Helme, I 16
Heytor granite railway 194
Heywood, John 200
Hill, Rowland 166
Hinton, Charles 172; 178
Hinton, John 66; 76; 116
Historical Descriptions of New and Elegant Views 70
Historiographical Cards 34
History and Topography of Devonshire 174
History of Devonshire (Moore) 232
History of Devonshire (Polwhele) 44; 104; 144; 168
History of England (Hume and Smollett) 224
History of England (Rapin de Thoyras) 108
History of England (Seller) 42
History, Gazetteer and Directory of the County 234
Hitch, C 56
Hoare, Edward & Reeves, J 192; 202
Hobson's Fox–Hunting Atlas 234
Hodge (Darton & Hodge) 166
Hodges, Sir James 64
Hodgson & Co 178; 192
Hodgson, Orlando 152; 176; 218
Hogenberg, Frans *see* Braun & Hogenberg
Hogenberg, Remigius ix; 2
Hogg, Alexander xv; 70; 102
Hole, William 10; 16
Holland, Philemon 10
Hollar, Wenceslas ix; 30; 36
Homann, Ebernezer 114
Hondius, Jodocus 8; 12; 24; 28

Hondius, Jodocus II 26
Hood *see* Vernor etc
Hooghe, Cornelis de 2
Hooker, John xiii; 12; 180
Hoole, John 54
Hooper & Wigstead 42
Hooper, S 42; 84
House of Commons 210; 222; 236
Humble, George 8; 9; 12; 14
Humble, William 9; 14
Hume and Smollett 224
hundreds xiii; 2
Hurst *see* Longman etc
Hutchinson, Thomas 64

–I–

Ich Dien 126
Imperial Gazetteer of Scotland 216
Imperial Map (Bartholomew) 216
Imray, Laurie, Norie & Wilson Ltd 154
Inglis *see* Gall & Inglis
inset map
    Exeter 12; 40; 90
    Lundy 90; 126; 194; 196; 220
    Plymouth 76; 90; 220
    Plymouth Dock 90
    Scilly Isles 102
    Stoke Town 90
Instructions given by the Secretary of State 212
Intended Guyde for English Travailers xiv; 20

–J–

Jackson, Peter 206
Jansson, Jan ix; x; xi; xiv; xvi; 8; 24; 26; 28; 38
Jansson, Jan the Elder 24
Janssonius, Guilielmus *see* Blaue, Willem Janzsoon
Jefferys, Thomas xiv; xv; 40; 68; 76; 78; 90; 92; 94; 126
Jenner, Thomas xiv; 20; 22
Jennings & Chaplin 224
Jennings, Robert 232
Johnson (Cadell, Johnson & Dilly) 44; 104; 168
Johnson, Dr Samuel 110
Johnson, Joseph 114
Johnson, Thomas 218
Johnston (bookseller) 90
Johnston, William 56; 64
Jones (engraver) *see* Smith & Jones
Jones (publisher) *see* Sherwood, Neely & Jones
Joy *see* Baldwin, Cradock & Joy
Junction of the Counties in England and Wales 124

–K–

Kaerius, Petrus *see* Keere, Pieter van den
Keere, Pieter van den xi; xii; xiv; 8; 12; 18; 28
King Charles II 32
King of spades 6
Kingsley, David 6
Kingston, Felix 10
Kip, William x; 10; 16; 20
Kitchen's English Atlas 88
Kitchin's Pocket Atlas 100
Kitchin, Thomas ix; x; xiii; 64; 66; 68; 70; 72; 76; 78; 86; 88; 96; 100; 102; 106
Kitchin, Thomas (father) 88
Knapton, James and John 44
Knapton, John 52

–L–

L'Angleterre ou Description Hist. et Topographique 190
L'Atlas Soulagé de son gros et pesant fardeau 28
La Galérie Agréable Du Monde 28
Lackington, Allen & Co 134
Lamb, Francis xiv; 2; 30; 40
Land's End, prime meridian 158
Langeren, Jacob van 20
Langley's New County Atlas 170; 214
Langley, Edward 170; 214
Large English Atlas 54; 76
Latham, George 10
latitude xiv; 98
Laurie & Whittle 54; 68; 74; 76; 94; 116; 154
Laurie & Whittle's New and Improved English Atlas 116
Laurie & Whittle's New Map of Devonshire 154
Laurie, Richard Holmes 116; 154
Laurie, Robert 154
Law, Bedwell 64
Lawrence, Heather xv
Lazius, Wolfgang xv
Le Grand Atlas Anglois 77
Le Petit Atlas Britannique 58
Lea, Anne 226
Lea, Philip xiv; 2; 40; 42
Ledoux, Etienne 190
Lee, Mathew 90
Leggatt, John 10; 14
Leigh's New Atlas of England and Wales 176
Leigh's New Pocket Atlas 176
Leigh's New Pocket Road-book 176
Leigh, Mary Anne 176
Leigh, Samuel 176
Leland xii
Lenthall, John 32; 34; 48
LePefit 206
Lett's Popular County Atlas 234
Lewis's Topographical Dictionary 216
Lewis (Exeter engraver) 188
Lewis, S & Co 208; 228
Lewis, Samuel 208; 216; 228
Lewis, William 156
Lhuyd, Humphrey 2
Lieut.-Col. R K Dawson *see* Dawson, Robert Kearsley
Lily, George xii; 2
lithography x; 220
Lodge, John xv; 88; 102; 106; 116; 132
London Magazine 70; 72; 88; 96
London Magazine And Monthly Chronologer 72
longitude xiv; 18; 44; 98; 128; 158
Longman & Co 230
Longman, Hurst, Rees, Orme & Brown 146
Longman, Orme, Rees, & Co. 234
Longman, Rees & Co 180; 234
Longman, Rees, Orme, Brown, Green and Longman 226
Lost Landscapes of Plymouth 76
Lownes, M 16
Lownes, Sam 36
Luffman, John x; 134
Lunday, (Lundy) 25
Lundy xiv; xv; 90; 92; 126; 194; 196; 220
Lydford Cascade 206
Lysons, Rev. Daniel 180
Lysons, Samuel 180

–M–

MacRae, C 120
Magna Britannia (Cox) 46; 58; 60; 70

Magna Britannia (Lysons) 180
Magna Britannia Antiqua et Nova 46
Magna Britannia et Hibernia 46
Maltese cross 210; 212
Manchester Directory 198
manuscript maps 114
Map of Devon and Cornwall 168
Map of the County of Devon 92
Map of the County of Devon (Donn) 90
Map of the County of Devon (Greenwood) 194
Map of the County of Devon (Wyld) 220
map on card 112; 172
Maps of all the Shires in England and Wales 3
Maps of Northumberland 174; 176
Maps of the English Counties 108
Maps of the Several Counties and Shires of England 116
Marcombe, David 2
Margary, Harry 8; 32; 150; 212
Mariner's Mirror xiv
market days 96; 166
Marriott, John 16
Marshall *see* Simpkin & Marshall
Marshall, J (publisher) 42
Marshall, William 122; 142
Martin's New Traveller's Guide 156
Martin's Sportsman's Almanack 156
Martin, Benjamin 78
Martin, D W 200
Martin, P 156
Martin, R 86
Martyn, Thomas 90
Mathewes, Augustine 16
Matthews, Mary 44
Maunder, Samuel 174; 192
McLean, Thomas 136
McMillan, B 142
Meijer, Pieter 78; 80
memory cards 6
Mercator, Gerard xii; 2; 10; 24; 26; 28
Migneret, Adrien 190
Millar, Andrew (Miller) 64
Miller 206
Miller's New Miniature Atlas 172
Miller, Robert 172
Milton, John 20
mines 52; 54; 88; 102; 106
Miniature Speeds xi
Minikin, George 32
Modern British Traveller 138
Moll's British Atlas 52
Moll, Herman ix; xiii; xiv; xv; 46; 52; 54; 58; 60; 106
Monthly Magazine 142
Moore, J 122
Moore, Rev. Thomas 232
Morden, Robert xiii; xiv; 10; 32; 34; 38; 44; 46; 48; 52; 62; 64; 70; 76; 104
Morning Herald 108
Morphew, John 46
Mortier, Cornelius 25
Mortier, David 25
Mortlock, Henry 34
Moule's English Counties 224; 232
Moule's Pocket County Maps 224
Moule, Thomas 224; 232
Mount Edgcombe 12
Mudge, William 150; 162; 220
Münster, Sebastian ix; xii
Murray, J 106; 132
Murray, John 234
Murray, T Laurie 202
Mutlow, H 122; 180

–N–

Natural History of England 78; 80
Needell, Keith xv; 120
Neele, George 160
Neele, J & J 196
Neele, James 160
Neele, Josiah 160; 216
Neele, Samuel John 84; 120; 130; 142; 160
Neely *see* Sherwood etc
Netherclist, J 210
New and Accurate Maps of the Counties 82
New and Complete Abridgement 70
New and Complete English Traveller 102
New and Comprehensive Gazetteer 216
New and Correct Atlas of England and Wales (Ellis) 158
New and Correct English Atlas ix; xi; 44; 104; 120; 148; 184
New and Improved County Atlas 158
New and Improved English Atlas 116
New Atlas of England and Wales (Duncan) 192
New Atlas of England and Wales (Leigh) 176
New Book of Roads 84
New British Atlas (H G Collins) 192
New British Atlas (Hall) 204
New British Atlas (Stockdale) 110
New British Atlas (Teesdale) 165
New British Traveller (Dugdale) 160
New British Traveller (Walpoole) 102
New County Atlas (Hall) 204
New County Atlas (Langley & Belch) 170
New Description and State of England 46
New Description of England and Wales 52
New English Atlas (Bennett) 84
New English Atlas (Ellis) 94
New English Atlas (Smith – 1801) 128
New English Atlas (Smith – 1822) 184
New English Atlas (Thomson) 152
New English Atlas, Cary's 144
New Geological Atlas 144
New Medium English Atlas 98
New Miniature Atlas 172
New Picture of England and Wales, Leigh's 176
New Pocket Atlas and Geography 134
New Pocket Atlas of England and Wales 176
New Pocket Road-book of England and Wales 176
New Present State of England 84
New Sett of Pocket Mapps Of all the Counties 62
New Travelling Atlas 164
Newbery, John 82
Newman, H 42
Nicholls, Sutton 38; 44
Nichols, J B & Son 182
Nicholson, John 46
Nicol, G 122
Nieuwen Atlas 25
Nine New & Accurate Maps *54*
Noble, E 110
Norden, John xiii; 4; 8; 10; 12; 20; 22
Norie *see* Imray, Laurie, Norie & Wilson Ltd
North, Braham 18
Norton, John 10; 18
Norton, Joyce 10
Nouveau Petit Atlas 28
Nouvel Atlas ou Theatre du Monde 24
Nova Totius Geographica Telluris Projecto 25
Novus Atlas Absolutissimus 25
Novus Atlas Oder Welt-Beschreibung 24
Novus Atlas Sive Theatrum Orbis Terrarum 24; 25
Novus Atlas, Das ist Welt-beschreibung 27
Nowell, Laurence xii; 2

Nuevo Atlas del Reyno de Ingalaterra 27
Nutt, E & R (printers) 46
Nutt, M 46

–O–

O'Donoghue, Yolande 150; 212
Oakhampton 148
Oddy, S A 158
Ogilby, John xiii; xiv; 32; 40; 50; 66
Old Series Ordnance Survey Maps of England and Wales 150; 212
Oldys, William 36
Ordnance Survey xiii; xiv; xv; 116; 126; 150; 162; 194; 202; 210; 220
Orme *see* Longman etc
Orr, W S 164; 200
Ortelius, Abraham 2; 8; 12; 18
Osborne, John 64
Osborne, Thomas 64
Outlines of British Geography 112
Overton Atlas I 26; 27
Overton Atlas II 25
Overton Atlas III - VI 38
Overton Atlas VII & VIII 12; 15
Overton Atlases xi
Overton, Henry 12; 15; 38; 54; 86
Overton, Henry (nephew) 38
Overton, John 24; 25; 26; 27; 38
Owen's New Book of Roads 84
Owen, George 10
Owen, John 50
Owen, William 78

–P–

Paine, Thomas 142
Palk, Sir Lawrence 142
Palmer, J 162
Palmer, Richard 30; 36
Palmer, William 94; 116
Panorama or Traveller's Instructive Guide 172; 178
paper x
Parker, Henry 86
Parliamentary Representation. Further Return 210
Pask, Joseph 32
Pass, J 130
Payne, J 96
Payne, M 68
Payne, T & Son 110
Pearcy, W 154
Penny, R 36
Perrot, Aristide x; 190
Pestis Patriae Pigrities 2
Phelps, Joseph 170
Philip, George 164
Phillips, Richard 142; 146
Pickett, John 184
Picture of England 132
Pigot & Co 230
Pigot & Co's British Atlas of the Counties of England 198
Pigot & Co's National Commercial Directory 198
Pigot & Co's Pocket Atlas 230
Pigot & Slater 198; 230
Pigot, James ix; 198; 230
Pinnock's County Histories 174
Pinnock, William ix; 174; 218
plagiarism 216
Plans of the Cities and Boroughs 210; 212

playing card xii; xiv; 4; 6; 32; 34; 48; 124; 152; 178
Plymouth
    Breakwater 129; 164; 172; 184; 188
    Dock 112; 145; 148; 186
    fair at Plymouth Dock 56
    mileages 184
    plan 76; 90; 220; 224; 228
    plan of Plymouth Dock 90
    Sound 112
    spy maps 76
Pocket Atlas, Bowles's 100
Pocket Atlas, Pigot & Co's 230
Pocket Atlass, Kitchin's 100
Pocket Book of all the Counties of England and Wales 32
Pocket County Maps 204
Pocket Topography and Gazetteer of England 230
Pocket Tourist and English Atlas 152
Political Magazine 106; 132
Polwhele, Rev. Richard 44; 104; 144; 168
Poly-Olbion or A Chorographicall Description xiii; 16
Post Office Map 166
Pottinger, J 84
Prevost *see* Groenewegen & Prevost
Price, Charles 78
Price, Owen 70
Priestley, Joseph 114
prime meridian xiv; 18; 44; 116; 128; 158
Prince of Orange 40; 42
Pringle *see* Greenwood, Pringle & Co
Printed Maps of Somersetshire 120
Prospect of the most famous parts of the World xi; 9; 14
Ptolemy xii
Publick Register\: or Weekly Magazine 62

–Q–

Quantoc Hills 122
Quartermaster's Map ix; xiv; 22

–R–

Railroad Companion to England and Wales 186
Ramble, Reuben 172
Ramshaw 150
Rattle & Brine's library 145
Ravenhill, W 90; 162
Rea, Roger the Elder and younger 9; 15
Read, Thomas 58; 60; 70
Recreative pastimes by Card play 34
Redmayne, William 34; 48
Rees *see* Longman etc
Rees & Co. (of Plymouth) 142
Reeves *see* Hoare & Reeves
Reform Bill 212
Reid & Wallis 172; 178
Reid, W H 178
Reports from Commissioners 212; 236
Reuben Ramble's Picture Lessons 172
Reynolds, Nicholas 2
Rice, J 122
Rivington, C 52
roads xiv
Robin's Atlas of England and Wales 160
Robins & Co. 160
Robins, James 160
Robinson, G G & J 122
Robinson, G G J & J 110
Robinson, Jacob 64
Robson's Commercial Directory 202

Rochette, Louis de la 94
Rocque, John ix; 58
Rocque, Mary Ann 58
Rodwell, Mary Martha 226
Rollos, George 70; 84
Romance of the Road 164
Roper, John 136
Rowe, Robert 116; 124; 152; 164
Royal English Atlas 86
Royal Geographical Society 220
Royal Observatory xiv
Royal Society of Arts 90; 126; 154
Roycroft, Thomas 30
Rudd, John xii; 2
Rural Economy of the Southern Counties 122
Rural Economy of the West of England 122; 142
Russell, John 116
Russell, P 70
Russell, Percy xv
Rutlinger, Johannes 2
Ryall, John 86
Ryther, Augustine (Anglus) ix; 2; 4

–S–

Saxton, Christopher ix; x; xi; xii; xiii; xiv; 2; 4; 8; 10; 12; 18; 40;
    44
Sayer, Robert 40; 54; 58; 68; 74; 76; 77; 86; 92; 94; 154
scale-bar added 80; 150
Scatter, Francis 2
Schenk, L 80
Schenk, Peter xiv; 24; 26
Schmollinger, Joseph 232
Schmollinger, W 224; 232
Scilly Isles 102; 236
Scott, Robert (engraver) 216
Scott, Robert (pseudonym) 160
sea charts xv
Seale, Richard William 54; 66
Seckford, Thomas xii; 2
Seller, John xv; 15; 24; 30; 42; 52
Senex, John xiv
Set of Fifty New and Correct Maps 52
Seyffert, C G 84
Sharp *see* Vernor, Hood & Sharp
sheepdogs 122
Shepherd & Sutton 218
Sherwood & Co 230
Sherwood, Jones & Co 138
Sherwood, Neely & Jones 138
Shires of England and Wales (Lea) 40
Shirley, R J 182; 224
shotsilk x; 8; 14; 18
Signet library 164
Simmons, Mary 9; 20
Simmons, Matthew x; xiv; 4; 20; 22; 100
Simpkin & Marshall 156; 182; 224; 230
Simpkin, Marshall, and Co 200
Simpson, Samuel 60
Sir Richard Phillips *see* Phillips, Richard
Slater, Isaac 198; 230
Small British Atlas, 58
Small English Atlas 68
Smith's New English Atlas 220
Smith's New English Atlas (1801) 128
Smith's New English Atlas (1822) 184
Smith's New Series of County Maps 128
Smith & Jones (London engravers) 128
Smith (Exeter engraver) 188
Smith, Charles x; xiv; 128; 184

Smith, David 84; 118; 166; 180; 182
Smith, Joseph 25
Smith, Ralph 46
Smith, William 144
Smith, William (Speed) 12
Smollett 224
Snodham, Thomas 14
Society for the Encouragement of Arts, Manufactures and
    Commerce 90
Society of Gentlemen 102
Somerset
    agricultural report 120
    Ashbrittel 2
    coast 70
    identified as Devonshire 108
    issued with Devon 104
    issued with Devon and Cornwall 98
    Lundy 16
    map of Devon with Somerset 222
    new plate 38
    pagination mark 8
    part of on Devon map 122
    playing card 178
    printed on same plate as Devon 68
Soon, J 80
South Molton 86
South Wales 56; 146; 150
Speed's Maps Epitomiz'd 30; 36
Speed (Overton) I - IV 15
Speed, John xi; xiii; xiv; 8; 12; 24; 26; 28; 30; 38; 42
Spenser Society 16
Spenser, Edmund 16
Spottiswoode (Eyre & Spottiswoode) 164
Sprint, S & John 46
spy maps of Plymouth 76
St Michael's (Rock) 90
St Michael's, prime meridian 18
St Nicholas Island x
St Paul's Cathedral, prime meridian 44
Stamp Act 62
Stanford, Edward 192
Starling, Thomas 208
statute mile xiii
steel engraving ix
Stent, Peter 38
stippled sea x
Stockdale, John 110; 114
Stoke Town 90
Street & Coopers 188
Stuart, Elisabeth 76
Stumpf, Johann xv
Sturt, John 44; 48
Sudbury, John 12; 14
Sudlow, E 108
Sutton (Shepherd & Sutton) 218
Swale, Abel 44
Symonds, H D 70

–T–

Tallis, John 136
Tallis, Lucinda 136
Tamar Navigation 128
Tavistock Abbey 232
tax stamp on playing cards 34; 48
Taylor, Thomas 36
Taylors, Isaac 90
Teesdale & Co. 200
Teesdale, Henry x; 164; 165; 200
Teesdale, Henry & Co 165

Tegg, W 200
Terwoort, Leonard 2
Theatre du Monde ou Nouvel Atlas 27
Theatre of the Empire of Great Britaine xi; 14
Theatrum Imperii Magnae Britanniae 14
Theatrum Orbis Terrarum, sive Atlas Novus 26; 27
Third Report from His Majesty's Commissioners 236
Thomson, J 152
Thorn, E 168
Thoyras, Paul Rapin de 108
Tielenberg, Gerrit 28
Tindal, Nicholas 108
Tinney, John 76
Toms, William Henry 56
Tooley, R V 94; 180; 226
Toonneel des Aerdrycks, oft Nieuwe Atlas 27
Topographical and Statistical Description of ... Devon 138
Topographical Dictionary (Cooper) 146
Topographical Dictionary of England 208; 228
Topographical Dictionary of Great Britain and Ireland 204
Topographical Dictionary of the United Kingdom 146
Topographical Dictionary, Lewis's 216
Topographical Ecclesiastical & Natural History 46
Topographical Map of Devonshire 162
Topographical Survey ... of Devon 138
Topographical Survey of the Counties 118
topography x
Topography of Great Britain 138
Tor Bay 42
Torquay 142
Totnes 86
Tour Through the Whole Island of Great Britain 64
Tourist's Atlas of England and Wales 200
Tourist's Pocket Directory 138
town symbols x
Townsend, Leonard 136
Tozer, Charles 120
Traveller's Companion (Moll) 52
Traveller's Companion, Cary's 112; 140; 186
Traveller's Companion, New 154
Traveller's Companion, Wallis's 156
Traveller's Pocket Atlas 174
Travelling County Atlas 204
Travels in the Western Counties of England 172
Travels Through the Counties of England 172
Treacher & Arnott 146
Trewman & Co 168; 188
Trewman, R J 188
Trueman & Son 118
Tunnicliff, William 118
Turner, Robert 34
Turpin, Homan 32
Tymms, Samuel 10; 182

–U–

Ugbrooke House 162
Universal Magazine of Knowledge and Pleasure 66; 116; 154
Upcott, William 44; 144
Upham, E 142
upside-down directions 46; 52; 54; 58; 60

–V–

Valk, (Valck) Gerard xiv; 24; 25; 26
Vancouver, Charles 120; 142; 146
Varenius, Bernhard 30
vellum, maps on 90; 92
verdigris x

Vernor & Hood 136
Vernor, Hood & Sharp 136
Vierde Stuck der Aerdrycks-beschryving .. Engelandt 27
View of the Representative History of England 228
vignette 170
    Babicombe Bay 206
    cider making 86
    County Sessions House 232
    Dartmouth Castle 166
    Exeter Cathedral 86; 170; 194; 196; 198; 216; 230
    Exeter Guildhall 224
    Lydford Cascade 206
    Tavistock Abbey 232
Virtue, George 224
Vittelius, Regner 9
von Engelandt 28

–W–

Waesberghe, Johannes van 24
Wagenhaer, Lucas Janszoon xiv
Wakefield, Gilbert 114
Waldseemüller, Martin ix
Walker's County Atlas 234
Walker, James 182
Walker, John & Charles 182; 196; 206; 208; 228; 234
Walker, Robert 58; 60
Wallis 206
Wallis's New British Atlas 158; 220
Wallis's Second and Superior British Atlas 158
Wallis, Helen 8
Wallis, James 156; 158; 178
Walpoole, George Augustus 102; 106
Ward, Caesar 46
Ware, R 44
Warter, William 48
watermarks x; xi; 3; 44; 94; 104; 106; 156; 158; 164; 166
Web, William 2; 3; 40
Webb, David 218
Weekly Magazine 62

West-Country Gentleman's Memorandum-Book 188
Whatman 114; 164; 166
Whitaker, Harold 40; 52; 174; 176
Whitaker, Richard 10
white on black maps 218
white satin, map on 108
White, W 234
White, William 120
Whittaker, G & W B 174
Whittaker, George Byrom 146; 174
Whittaker, Treacher & Co. 146
Whittle & Laurie 154
Whittle, James *see* Laurie & Whittle
Wigstead *see* Hooper & Wigstead
Wild, Joseph 42
Wilford, J 52
Wilkes, John 130
Wilkinson, Robert 76; 77; 86
Willdey, George 40
Wilson *see* Imray, Laurie, Norie & Wilson Ltd
Wilson, Rev. J M 216
Wit, Frederic de 26
Wogan, P 122
wood-cut ix
Woodgate, Henry 84
Woolcot, Simon 150
Woolmer, S 142
Woolnoth, W 194
Worms, Laurence 88
Woutneel, Hans 20
Wright, John 30
Wyld's Atlas of the English Counties 158
Wyld, James 126; 128; 158; 220
Wyld, James the younger 126; 220

–Y–

Young, 120
Young, Richard 10